W9-CJF-151

The Singing Voice

Robert Rushmore
The Singing Voice

*Why is life different when
the singing stops?*
—James Reeves

Illustrated with photographs and drawings

DEMBNER BOOKS
NEW YORK

Dembner Books
Published by Red Dembner Enterprises Corp., 1841 Broadway, N.Y., NY 10023
Distributed by W. W. Norton & Company, Inc., 500 Fifth Avenue, N.Y., NY 10110

Library of Congress Cataloging in Publication Data

Rushmore, Robert.
   The singing voice.

   Bibliography: p.
   Includes index.
   1. Singing—History and criticism.   2. Singers.
I. Title.
ML1460.R88   1984   784.9   84-7102
ISBN 0-934878-50-1

Second Edition

Grateful acknowledgement is made to the following for permission to reprint the material indicated:

C. M. Bowra for quotation from *Primitive Song,* published by Weidenfeld & Nicholson, 1962. Copyright © 1962 by C. M. Bowra.

Friedrich S. Brodnitz for quotation from *Keep Your Voice Healthy,* published by Harper & Row, Copyright © 1953 by Friedrich S. Brodnitz.

E. P. Dutton & Co., Inc. for two drawings by Gluyas Williams from *People of Note* by Laurence McKinney, Copyright © 1939, 1940 by Laurence McKinney. Renewal Copyright © 1967 by Laurence McKinney. Reprinted by permission of E. P. Dutton & Co., Inc.

Harper & Row for quotation from two books by L. de Hegermann-Lindencrone, *In the Courts of Memory,* Copyright © 1912 by Harper & Brothers and *The Sunny Side of Diplomatic Life,* Copyright © 1914, by Harper & Brothers.

Houghton Mifflin Company for quotation from *Men, Women and Tenors* by Frances Alda, Copyright © 1937 by Frances Alda.

The Macmillan Company for quotation from *How to Sing* by Lilli Lehmann, Copyright © 1924 by The Macmillan Company.

Methuen & Co., Ltd., for quotation from *The Teaching of Elisabeth Schumann* by Elizabeth Puritz, published © 1956.

The New York Historical Society for quotation from *Life of Emma Thursby* by Richard Gipson, Copyright © 1940 by the New York Historical Society and Richard McCandless Gipson.

Opera for quotation from book review by Rupert Bruce Lockhart of *Anatomy of a Voice,* April, 1966.

Oxford University Press for quotation from *A Natural Approach to Singing* by Judith Litante, Copyright © 1959 by Judith Litante.

Punch for quotation of "Schmaltztenor" by M. W. Branch, Copyright © by *Punch,* London.

G. Schirmer, Inc. for quotation from *Singing* by Herbert Witherspoon, Copyright © 1925 by G. Schirmer, Inc.

Continued on page 336

To the memory of
three who deeply loved
the singing voice

Sidney Dietch
Mary Ellis Peltz
and
Fanny Rogers

Contents

Acknowledgments

It was Frank Merkling who, during his splendid years as editor of *Opera News*, published the series of articles that became the basis of the first edition of *The Singing Voice*. Now, thirteen years later, it is Frank Merkling, semi-retired but filled with wisdom and editorial assurance, who has gone over this greatly enlarged second edition of *The Singing Voice*, querying, correcting and generally putting things straight when they were definitely bent. I'm deeply grateful to him for his help and encouragement over the years, not to speak of the friendship that I cherish with him and his wife, Erica.

William Cole gave me the initial push to write the first edition of this book more than a decade ago and others in those years who lent their backing and interest were John Richardson and the late Alfreda Huntington Rushmore.

When Andrew McLaren, headmaster of the Tuxedo Park School, suggested that I give a series of lectures on the singing voice, it presaged a return to the fascinating vocal world. I am grateful to him for what proved to be his catalytic act as well as to him and his wife, Elinor, for their friendship. Other supportive friends and neighbors have been Joan Melhado, Webb and Jocelyn Turner, and Jackie Kornfeld. Nor should I fail to mention the residents of the house next to mine, Charles and Norma Gorovoy, she with the lovely soprano voice that the world at large has been denied hearing. Renate Nash in all her abundant enthusiasm has introduced me to many vocal experiences that I would not have found out on my own.

I could not possibly have produced this book through the malevolent winter of 1984 without the faithful maintenance of

Dean and Susan Abbott. I give them deepest thanks and as well to Ann McCormick for looking after me with such care.

The staff of *Opera News*, Robert Jacobson, Gerald Fitzgerald, John Freeman, and Rhonda Neu, have been most helpful in supplying photographs for this book, not to speak of the charming drawings by Susan Perl. The bulk of the photographs have come from the extraordinary collection of my friends Vivian Liff and George Stuart to whom I express affectionate gratitude.

I have worked in the Library for the Performing Arts at Lincoln Center, also the New York Society Library. I am grateful to the staffs of these institutions for their help, as well as to those who work at the fine library in Tuxedo Park, New York.

Finally to those who comprise the organization known as Red Dembner Enterprises, all three of them, my deepest thanks: to Red and Ann for their enthusiasm and encouragement and to Therese Eiben, who must be every writer's ideal of a conscientious, thoughtful editor.

A Note to the Reader

After reading the manuscript of the first edition of this book my wife put it down and said in an outraged tone, "But you haven't mentioned Tito Gobbi!" A good friend riding a couple of pre-dinner drinks began excitedly to make *lists* of his favorite vocalists to whom I had not referred. An outside reader for a publishing house snuffled and snorted his way through the manuscript and gracefully mixing his metaphors complained that I had not fashioned a work "with the ring of authority and the hallmark of sterling."

This book, however, was only conceived as a loose, informal survey of some of the varying aspects of the subject of the singing voice. The author has no degree in music of any kind, has never sung professionally and can make no scholastic nor academic claims to authority over his subject other than those bestowed by extensive vocal training plus a pair of ears. Though I have struggled for objectivity in commenting on some of the battles that so fiercely rage over the fields of vocalism, the book by its very nature is a subjective one. When, for instance, the need to mention a singer with a certain type of voice has come up, naturally I have chosen my favorite to the possible exclusion of a reader's beloved. The discussions of pop singers are limited because it seems to me that they belong more properly in a book about stage personalities rather than one dealing with the singing voice per se. Finally the reader will note that artists heard mainly in New York and London are mentioned—for the simple reason that these cities have been home bases for the author during his lifetime.

For all sins of omission or favoritism, I humbly ask the reader's indulgence. Volume after volume could be written about the singing voice and the subject not exhausted nor the treatment ever be wholly authoritative. This book is offered as a highly personal review of the singing voice by one voice-lover to the thousands and thousands who share this love—in the hope that it will interest, perhaps stir, but not outrage.

H. Toulouse-Lautrec: A Concert at the Opera.

The Vocal Spell

THE FAIR SINGER

To make a final conquest of all me,
  Love did compose so sweet an enemy,
In whom both beauties to my death agree,
  Joining themselves in fatal harmony:
That while she with her eyes my heart doth bind,
She with her voice might captivate my mind.

I could have fled from one but singly fair:
  My disentangled soul itself might save,
Breaking the curléd trammels of her hair:
  But how should I avoid to be her slave,
Whose subtle art invisibly can wreathe
My fetters of the very air I breathe?

It had been easy fighting in some plain
  Where victory might hang in equal choice;
But all resistance against her is vain,
  Who has the advantage both of eyes and voice:
And all my forces needs must be undone,
She having gainéd both the wind and sun.
                              —*Andrew Marvell*

"Would you like to hear my Pearly Gates recording?"

"Pearly Gates?"

"The record I'd want to hear when I go through the Pearly Gates."

"Are you sure you're *going* to go through the Pearly Gates?"

"Oh yes." Jocelyn Kress Turner, in diaphanous white like a

Wili, floated into the house in the direction of the record player. A full mid-summer moon had risen over the ridge and shimmered in the little lake by which her guests sat on a patio after dinner. A moment later a beatified soprano voice arcing over a rich orchestra sang in the night. At once we were caught, held, transported as though to the altitude of the moon by the spell of the creamy, extending tones.

"It's Kiri Te Kanawa," said our hostess worshipfully. "The last of Strauss's 'Four Last Songs.'"

When it was done a discussion of "What's *your* Pearly Gates recording?" instantly arose among the guests, many of whom were ardent music lovers.

A handsome German-born woman and passionate lover of opera said excitedly, "The last trio from *Rosenkavalier*: Schwarz-kopf, Ludwig, Stich-Randall."

"Leontyne Price singing that aria from *La Rondine*. Doesn't *rondine* mean *swallow*?" a devilishly handsome lady-killer asked ingenuously of that bird whose habit is to fly away.

An amusing woman, American by nationality but born and raised in Europe, said in her cautious British accent, "I'm not certain about going through those Pearly Gates, but if I should go the *other* way I'd want Edith Piaf singing '*Non, je ne regrette rien.*'"

A little night breeze sprang up with the laughter.

And so on and on they came, the names of the great practitioners of the vocal art: Caruso, Melba, Ruffo, (unexpected-ly) Richard Tauber, Frank Sinatra, Maria Callas, Judy Garland, Marilyn Horne. . . .

To our amazement we found a traitor in our midst. The fine headmaster of the local school proclaimed in a dour Scots manner that he really didn't care for the singing voice at all. A moment later he broke the aghast silence by saying, "Well, perhaps one. The voice of Paul Robeson always gets to me in some visceral way."

When it came to me I smiled and said, "One above all the others—and I never heard her in the opera house or a concert hall. Once when she was in her late fifties she sang in her own house. But her voice is supreme." I gazed over the night scene as the others waited. I could hear the tubby sound of the orchestra in the record made in 1928 and then the voice stealing in:

Casta diva, Casta diva . . .

As the wind striated the surface of the pond I remembered how Willa Cather, the great American novelist, had said of the aria that "it begins so like the quivering of moonbeams on the water."

Out loud I said, "Rosa Ponselle. There was never anyone like her." And my voice trembled a bit at the mention of the name of the diva—which after all means goddess.

Let it not be forgotten that the term *fan* is a shortening of *fanatic*. And that is how some of our little group that evening by the lake could be described—fanatic admirers of certain singers and on behalf of them, excitable, argumentative, jealous and adoring. Fanatics about the singing voice in the mid-1980's, we were part of a long never-ending line of fans stretching back through history to the misty time of mythology and legend.

Orpheus was the first great singer, perhaps the greatest one of all. Legend describes that "there was every kind of bird brought under the spell of the singing, and all beasts of the mountains and whatever feeds in the recesses of the sea, and a horse stood entranced, held in control, not by a bridle, but by the music . . . You could see . . . the rivers flowing from their sources toward the singing and a wave of the sea raising itself aloft for love of the song . . ."

Orpheus, son of Apollo and grandson of Zeus, also knew the secrets of magic and astrology, thus confirming the association of the supernatural with singing. In what must have been one of the most thrilling song contests of all times, Orpheus protected the Argonauts from the deadly dangerous singing of the Sirens by the greater enchantment of his own vocal art. With the vanity characteristic to vocalists, the Sirens could not bear being outsung by a rival and threw themselves into the sea and became rocks.

Ironically, an end was put to the singing of this demigod by none other than his fans. These were the wild Bacchic women known as the Maenads who, furious at being rejected by Orpheus out of his faithfulness to the memory of Eurydice, tore him to pieces.*

The antiquarian Alexander S. Murray relates that the "head and lyre" of Orpheus "floated down the Hebrus, and were carried

---

*Frank Sinatra was almost strangled to death after a concert when two over-excited fans clutched at either end of his bow tie.

by the sea, the lyre sounding sweetly with the swell and fall of the waves, to the island of Lesbos, celebrated in after times for its poets and musicians. There the head was buried, and nightingales sang sweeter beside it than elsewhere in Greece."

Though the ancient Greeks and Romans had favorite singers it was not until the seventeenth century that the singing voice began to emerge in the compass and range that is familiar today. When the great solo singers came on the scene so did the fans in all their passionate partisanship. Take, for example, the period in English history when in late winter, 1727, riots began to break out in and around the King's Theatre, London. Demonstrations occurred frequently among the common mobs of that hurly-burly era but in this case it was the aristocrats—the Countess of Burlington, Sir Robert Walpole—who were proving themselves to be every bit as animal as the members of the lower orders. And what was the issue that had aroused such violence? Not as might be supposed, differences over religion, or politics, or affairs of state. Far simpler, it was whether one opera singer called Francesca Cuzzoni was preferable to another named Faustina Bordoni. The controversy which at one moment seemed almost to threaten England with civil war raged over the merits of a pair of sopranos. In the end revolution was averted by the management offering the proud, stingy Cuzzoni one less guinea for her next season's appearances than Faustina, an arrangement that vanity would not permit. Ambrose Phillips, a poet of the time, wrote Cuzzoni's exit lines:

> Tuneful mischief, vocal spell,
> To this island bid farewell;
> Leave us as we ought to be
> Leave the Britons rough and free.

A hundred years earlier, because of the interdiction against women singing in the Catholic Church, there also emerged a strange band of male singers known as the *castrati*. (See also the next section.) Mutilated just before the voice change, they possessed the treble range of a boy emitted from the often outsize, barrel-chested frame of a man. After he had made a "name," as Angus Heriot writes in *The Castrati in Opera*, fans would collect around the *castrato*, "going *en masse* to the theaters every time he sang and hanging on every note as if it were pure gold, barracking the other singers and refusing to admit that, beside their idol, these miserable braying donkeys could be said to sing at all." How familiar this sounds of the behavior of today's fans! Mr. Heriot also adds: "There would be an exchange of sonnets, satires and pasquinades between the new star's devotees and the rival cliques; artistocratic ladies and gentlemen would imagine themselves in love with him and engineer a piquant interview. . . ."

One of the strangest cases of the devotion of a fan for a singer is the often cited story of King Philip the Fifth of Spain, who suffered from melancholia, and the *castrato* Carlo Broschi, known as Farinelli. In the hope of assuaging her husband's sadness (and avoiding becoming a dowager regent), the Queen invited Farinelli to sing for Philip, who immediately fell under the spell of the eunuch's song. For nine years, as the story is told, the *castrato* sang for the monarch a program that included one or more of four songs that were absolute requisites. During that time, and for another nine years after Philip died and Ferdinand VI ruled, the singer had enormous influence at the court of Spain. Extraordinarily, such was his kindness and generosity that he made few if any enemies, and only stepped down from his days of glory when Charles II came to the throne in 1759. Farinelli retired to Bologna where the noted musicologist Charles Burney visited him and published an account of their meetings in his famous *Present State of Music in France and Italy*.

With the nineteenth century and the growing repertory of operas as well as the song literature, the worship of singers by their devotees gathered in force and intensity. Madame Catalani, Maria Malibran, Giuditta Pasta and the romantic and beautiful couple Grisi and Mario all attracted their respective hordes of fervid admirers. During this period we read increasingly of what came to be a cliche gesture of the fans' admiration. After a performance they would unharness the horses of the star's carriage waiting to convey her (usually) back to her hotel and, turning themselves into animals, drag the vehicle triumphantly through the streets from the opera house. A passionate fan of the opera stars Grisi and Lablache was Princess Victoria. The painter Eugène Delacroix, who adored the singing voice, found Maria Malibran wanting in artistry because of her impulsive interpretations. But of all the singers of the nineteenth century, perhaps because of the moral, almost pious quality of her character that

matched the spirit of the Victorian era, none was more greatly
worshipped than the Swedish soprano Jenny Lind.

Although she achieved tremendous success in her native
country and on the continent in France and Germany, it was not
until Jenny Lind made her debut in London on May 4, 1847, in
Meyerbeer's *Robert le Diable* that the epidemic as invasive as
cholera, which came to be known as "Jenny Lind fever," swept
the country. Such was the sensation that this modest, deeply
religious prima donna made in England, that her likeness soon
appeared on chocolate boxes, scented soaps and toilet waters. At
Jenny Lind's debut Victoria, then queen, became so excited that
she hurled the royal bouquet at this vocal monarch. At subsequent performances the newspapers reported "scenes of crashing
and crowding and squeezing; of torn dresses and evening coats
reduced to rags; of ladies fainting in the pressure and even of
gentlemen carried out senseless." At the House of Commons
which met in the evenings a measure could not be voted upon for
lack of a quorum. The members were off attending a Jenny Lind
night at the opera. A song with many verses became popular.
Here is one:

> Now everything is Jenny Lind
> That comes out each new day,
> There's Jenny Lind shawls and bonnets too,
> For those who cash can pay.
> Jenny Lind coats and waistcoats,
> Shirts, whiskers too and stocks,
> Jenny Lind gowns and petticoats,
> And bustles such a lot.

When the great Phineas T. Barnum signed the soprano,
unheard, on the strength of her reputation, for an American tour
she had to be smuggled on the steamer at Liverpool in disguise
lest she be mobbed by the thousands waiting to see her off. On
the other side of the Atlantic a crowd of ten thousand greeted her
arrival though none had heard her utter a note. It is said that
Jenny Lind invented the scalper. Tickets for her first appearance
in the immense Castle Garden Theater at the Battery overlooking
New York Harbor sold for up to two hundred dollars. After she
had sung (nervously) the first serpentine phrase of the *Norma*
"Casta diva" the New World was swept by the same "Jenny Lind
fever" that had infected Great Britain. Soon a similar variety of

Magnus: Portrait of Jenny Lind.

products were offered to the American public: Jenny Lind bonnets, Jenny Lind sofas, Jenny Lind sausages, even Jenny Lind cigars. A whistling kettle could be had that when it boiled sang like Jenny Lind.

"She had not swum across the English Channel; she had never crossed the Atlantic Ocean in a flying machine; nor had she done anything else that was sensational and spectacular and useless," writes one of her many biographers, Edward Wagenknecht. "She was simply a singer. The fact remains that this woman captivated the imagination of her century as no other artist has done."

"She was simply a singer"—a modest description of one who had the powers of a goddess, enchantress, priestess, lover.

Looking over the history of the fans of singers, oddly we find that staid, reserved Great Britain frequently comes up with the most flagrant exhibitions of worshipful adoration, perhaps because these occasions have released emotions ordinarily repressed. When the handsome, towering (she was well over six feet) contralto Clara Butt married the equally good looking baritone Kennerly Rumford (he just made it to her forehead) in Bristol in 1900, "factories, ships and offices were given a half-holiday, all the church bells were set ringing, streets blocked, a cathedral crammed with duchesses . . . special trains to London," etc. About the same time in New York two thousand people jammed into the standing room space (there were no fire regulations limiting the numbers) of the old Metropolitan Opera House to hear the last appearance of Jean de Reszke. So many in the mob fainted that the ushers used six bottles of ammonia, so goes the report. At other performances of the great tenor, women climbed under the orchestra rail at the final curtain to touch de Reszke's knees and feet when he bowed. And that was still the Victorian era!

Nellie Melba records in her memoirs that following a final performance in Russia while signing programs her pencil was seized then "bitten to pieces with a single crunch of strong, white teeth and distributed by a young man to his close friends" who received the relics with reverence.

To have something that the divinity has worn or touched, or simply to touch the god or goddess supplies a feeling of oneness.

If we examine the traits of singing fans on a national basis, it can be safely declared that the most passionate, vehement—and dangerous—are the Italians. Take for instance performances in the strange, checkered career of Maria Callas. At a *Lucia di Lammermoor* in La Scala on January 18, 1954, the audience was in a "delirium" and cheered and clapped for four minutes after the soprano's "Mad Scene." Only a year later, however, the audience went into a different sort of delirium and heckled and booed during her "Sempre libera" from the first act of *La Traviata*. (She was also booed about this time at a performance of *Andrea Chénier*, but that demonstration was said to have been arranged by a faction of Renata Tebaldi's fans who thought that *their* favorite should be singing the heroine, Madeleine de Coigny.)

As the career of Callas lurched on to its tragic end, the Italian audiences responded not only with cruel jeers and catcalls but also one night with a bouquet of radishes. Acutely short-sighted, the wretched diva picked up the "floral" tribute and pressed it to her bosom in gratitude. By 1958, when she seemed to prefer parties of *le monde* to singing in opera, she had to cancel in Rome a gala performance of *Norma* after singing one shrill and strident act before an audience of notables including the president of Italy. In their rage the fans blocked all exits from the opera house and the diva had to be smuggled out through an underground passage that fortunately connected with her hotel. For the rest of the night a crowd stood beneath her windows shouting up epithets and foul abuse. The next day *Il Giorno*, the newspaper, commented in a fury that Callas was "a second-rate artist" who "for several years has followed a path of melodramatic debauchery. . . . A disagreeable performer who lacks the most elementary sense of discipline and propriety."

In most cases the relationship of fan to singer is symbiotic. Though fan worship can on occasion be a nuisance or even a danger to an artist, on the whole it answers the ever-present questions in the performer's mind, "Did I sing well?" "Am I still on top?" An eager crowd besieging a star's dressing room after a performance, waving programs to be signed, is a singer's reward and reassurance.

A fabled prima donna, the soprano Mary Garden, however, disliked receiving admirers backstage. At a matinee in Philadelphia in 1912, when she sang Marguerite in *Faust*, Garden gave instructions that no one was to be admitted to her dressing room as she wished to catch the first train back to New York where her mother was ill. A day or so later she picked up the newspaper to read with horror the headline "Girl Kills Self Over Mary Garden." The story recounted how an admiring fan, a young woman, having been denied entrance to Miss Garden's dressing room following the performance, went out and shot herself. Later, the paper published a letter from the girl's mother saying that her daughter had not even met Mary Garden but "had developed a mad infatuation for her. . . . This was not the first time my daughter had become infatuated with a celebrity. . . ."

Equally fans' lives have been affected by *being* fans, mainly by becoming friends with the artists they have revered. A devotee of the handsome tenor Franco Corelli became familiar with his apartment by helping to decorate it. The refrigerator of the mezzo-soprano Giulietta Simionato was filled by a fan who stocked it with Italian goodies.

It works both ways: The singer needs the admirer. Zinka Milanov used fans as escorts. When the husband of Renata Scotto is unable to travel with her, she is known to invite a fan in his place.

Perhaps the most unusual case of zealous fan worship is that of two hearty British sisters, Louise and Ida Cook. Earning secretaries' salaries of perhaps two pounds a week in the 1920's, the older sibling, Louise, saved up her half-pennies for a gramophone with enough to include the purchase of ten records besides. When the attendant in the music shop recommended the latest release by the reigning coloratura soprano of the day, Amelita Galli-Curci, the Misses Cook had no idea who she was. Once the needle was lowered on the disc there commenced the first of a number of passionate love affairs carried on by this pair of maidenly sisters. Galli-Curci appeared in London for a series of recitals, but to their dismay they learned that she only sang opera in New York City. There was nothing for it then but to save up again for a trip to America. To the prima donna just before her last London concert they wrote of their intention. "If you ever succeed in coming to America," came the unexpected reply, "you shall have tickets for everything I sing. Come and see me at the Albert Hall on Sunday to say goodbye," added the diva known for her warm-heartedness.

"To go round backstage at the Albert Hall," wrote Ida Cook in her memoir *We Followed Our Stars* "was . . . like receiving a summons to Buckingham Palace. To *speak* to one of the greatest exponents of singing . . . was, and still remains, our favorite form of intoxication. . . ."

Amelita Galli-Curci as Gilda in *Rigoletto*.

In two years Louise and Ida Cook managed to save the money for their passage to the United States. Galli-Curci made good on her promise of tickets to all her performances and wined and dined them at her apartment as well. The newspapers got hold of the story and wrote it up and when they returned in the hold of the old S.S. *Aquitania* to England, Ida Cook set down the details of the adventure in her own words, which subsequently lauched her on a career of journalism and novel writing.

From then on the Cook sisters never looked back. Rosa Ponselle, Ezio Pinza, Elisabeth Rethberg were transformed from idols worshipped from afar to close friends. These intrepid fans made return visits to America and also to the continent, to the Salzburg Festival and to Germany, where by 1938 Clemens Krauss the conductor and his soprano wife, Viorica Ursuleac, held positions at the Munich Opera. In the course of their travels the Cook sisters did not fail to observe what atrocities were being perpetrated against the Jews. Now their positions as super-fans of various opera singers gave a strange twist to their lives.

By the end of the 1930's, before Hitler had totally overrun Europe, the only way for Jews to escape Nazi persecution and eventual extermination was for someone to put up a sum of money in England and guarantee them shelter. The pair of singer-mad fans found themselves in the strange position of go-betweens. As Ida Cook writes, "Our visits to Germany and Austria began to mean cases, cases and yet more cases, where we knew we were the last (often the only) hope of people who were in deadly danger and hourly terror."

The brisk, ever-smiling British sisters founded a refugee committee, soliciting funds and above all guarantors for those seeking asylum in England. Louise Cook learned German in order to negotiate the rescues more fluently, while shy Ida Cook steeled herself to giving lectures around England for the cause. Back and forth across the perilous borders, the sister-fans made their way, ostensibly seeking out the singing stars that they admired in the German-speaking countries, but actually arranging the salvation of hundreds of otherwise doomed Jews. Sometimes they even smuggled jewelry and other valuables that the refugees were forbidden to take out and which would guarantee their refuge in England.

When the Nazis captured all of Western Europe the rescue

efforts had perforce to cease, but after enduring the Battle of Britain and all the bombing, the Misses Cook resumed their fan-like ways. These included "call Rosa" parties on the twenty-eighth of May every year, which was the anniversary of Rosa Ponselle's first appearance in London in 1929. Collecting a group of fans around an amplified telephone, a call would take place for twenty minutes to the retired diva on the other side of the Atlantic in Maryland. The admirers in England would give worshipful greeting while the extraordinary soprano would respond with a song or an aria in a voice undiminished by time.

In more recent times the radio and television broadcasts of opera and concerts sung by great artists have swelled the number of fans into the millions. Generations have now grown up on the Saturday matinee opera broadcasts, producing fans with varying idiosyncrasies. An elderly lady wrote in to say that she always got out her long black velvet evening gown for a broadcast since she would be listening in "the company of dukes and duchesses." Another reported that as he also had a passion for football he watched the game on the television with the sound muted while he also listened to the opera. Following the telecast of the tenor Luciano Pavarotti on "Live From Lincoln Center," the network received a hundred thousand letters. The phenomenon of the rock concerts at which thousands of screeching, jungle-like fans gather to worship their idol, reaches into the realm of mass hysteria influenced by drugs and alcohol. The secret desire of a true devotee of a great star is to connect with the beloved in a close, not to say intimate, manner without sharing this benefi-cence with a horde of rivals.

Here is a tale of a fan: She is German, married, a non-professional musician but a devoted lover of opera. In the late 1970's she was cleaning her New York apartment between flights when over a classical music station came the sound of a tenor voice. The mop stilled in her hand. She was caught, enraptured. Six months later she heard the voice of the wonderful tenor again over the radio. This time she bought tickets to one of his performances at the Metropolitan Opera House. Once she had found him, she'd never let him go, to paraphrase the lines from the lovely Rodgers and Hammerstein song "Some Enchanted Evening." Utterly enchanted, the fan followed this rule. She went every time her idol sang, arranging her airline schedule to suit his singing one. She sent him letters and even gifts: a gold clip in the shape of a clef sign, German sausages.

One day back in her apartment where the affair had begun the telephone rang and there he was! She froze, stammered, lost her use of English. (His wasn't very good either.) Thereafter he continued to call but they still did not meet—as though the reality might crush the fantasy. After a time, he offered her tickets to a performance, and during an intermission with watery knees and feeling faint she made her way backstage and introduced herself.

Now the affair has turned into a fine friendship. Whenever he is in New York she plays tennis with him or he comes out to visit in the country. They speak frequently on the telephone even when he is overseas. In short, she has achieved the dream of every fan.

The Vocal Spell. "She was only a singer," writes the biographer of plain, unassuming Jenny Lind, who by her singing voice and without the aid of records, radio or television captured the imagination and hearts of hundreds of thousands in the nineteenth century. How can we explain this extraordinary spell that the singing voice is capable of casting over mankind? What is it about the vocal art that can transform apparently rational human beings into near maniacs, causing them to suffer hardships, go without sleep, practice extremes of economy, risk bodily injury (and inflict it) and offer their lives in the service and worship of a deified singer?

Little about the vocal spell can be discussed in a truly scientific way. The singing voice is so closely linked with inconsistent human behavior that much has to be adduced or hypothesized with no actually provable conclusion. Nonetheless the fact seems inescapable that the spell the voice casts is very much a sexual one.

As a rule fans are usually attracted to a singer of the opposite sex. From Orpheus to Ezio Pinza, from Jean de Reszke to Elvis Presley, the male singing voice has stirred a frenzied desire in their female admirers. The squeals of feminine teenagers hearing the tones of a beloved male singer could pass for mating calls. In the younger days of Frank Sinatra when he was appearing at New York's Paramount Theater, the staff reported that the seats and carpets of the enormous auditorium ran with the urine of the almost entirely young female audience that had packed it.

Among older women it is noticeable that the manly tones of a baritone or bass, particularly when they issue from the big, strapping frames of a baritone such as Sherrill Milnes or bass James Morris, stir up fluttery sighs of response.

Reversing the genders, there is this comment from a masculine reviewer about the breathy, intimate-sounding voice of Peggy Lee, "For a male listener it could be and still can be stupefyingly sexual." In the opera house over the years Mary Garden, Geraldine Farrar and Maria Jeritza dispersed waves of sex appeal across the footlights along with exciting soprano voices. In later times followed Grace Moore, Risë Stevens and the extraordinary orange-red-headed Ljuba Welitsch who bared a confection of alabaster colored flesh on her debut as Salome at the old Metropolitan Opera House in February 1949. The voices of Lena Horne, Maria Callas, Marlene Dietrich, Shirley Verrett, and Dinah Shore, to name just a few, have emitted a message to their captivated male listeners as strong as the scent of a lady dog in season.

Further corroboration of the sexual response to the singing voice can be found among those people who *only* prefer the male or the female voice. A sensitive woman and excellent writer in the author's acquaintance can't *stand* the sound of a woman singing. "I'm not prepared to take in all those women's animal passions," is the way she explains her prejudice. Some people shy away particularly from the "vapid," "foolish" sounds made by a coloratura soprano. Others are put off by the reticent tones of the average English oratorio tenor. One in this category was the British conductor Sir Thomas Beecham who compared the sound to "the sort of noise one would expect a giraffe to make were it so to forget itself as to yawn during the obsequies of a president of the Royal Zoological Society."

Let it not be thought, however, that the vocal spell is exclusively sexual. Another kind of fascination that singers hold over mankind is the ability to banish cares and allay melancholy. The mercurial Saul was calmed by the beautiful playing and singing of David "the sweet singer of Israel." The soothing powers of Carlo Broschi, called Farinelli, over the depressions of King Philip V of Spain have been mentioned. How understand this comforting, soothing spell that the singing voice can exert? The explanation may well be a very simple one. Along with our sexual drives, one of our strongest urges is to be taken care of, to go back to the sheltered, irresponsible condition we knew as infants. What accomplishes this return more swiftly than the sound of a singing voice returning us to a time when a lullaby close to our ears meant safety . . . warmth . . . contentment?

For this reason we respond to singers because their voices give us a childhood feeling of the parents, of being surrounded by a pair of arms and looked after. Not for nothing did Sophie Tucker, with her girth and her warm, all-embracing, almost baritonal voice call herself "the last of the Red Hot Mamas." Equally rotund Kate Smith was like a kind of mother to all the nation when she launched into "God Bless America" in her steady rock-like tones. Pearl Bailey also emanates that protective, making-everything-all-right feeling to which she adds a sly innuendo that she is a "naughty" Mama as well.

That same calm, easy assurance was conveyed by the singing of Bing Crosby from whose mellifluous tones the tragic or earthier passions were absent. On a more omnipotent level the rumbling voice of the *basso profundo* conveys a sense of noble authority, particularly when singing the music of Handel or the arias that Mozart wrote for Sarastro in *Die Zauberflöte*. The amazing depths of the basses heard in the Russian liturgy fill us with awe and a sense of being in the presence of the Almighty.

In reverse, there are voices that transform their hearers into quasi parents—caring, custodial. The fragile, vulnerable tones of Lucrezia Bori or Bidu Sayão, the poignant quality of Victoria de los Angeles; the "little girl" timbre often heard in the late 1920's and early thirties from singers like Ruth Etting and Helen Morgan evoked from their "Daddy" fans responses of wanting to cuddle and protect. This same reaction arises in the legions of female admirers of the great tenor Luciano Pavarotti, a response that despite his massive size, he is really a little boy, tender, vulnerable and in need of a pair of maternal arms around him to make him safe.

Not only are there fanatic worshippers of singers and great singing, there is another group who have quite different reactions to the sounds emanating from a human throat, varying from diffidence through discomfort to downright desperation. "I have sat through an Italian opera," complained Charles Lamb, "till for sheer pain and inexplicable anguish, I have rushed out into the noisiest places of the crowded streets to solace myself."

A violent dislike of singing—particularly the operatic kind—has always been a fecund source for humorists. In the old cartoon strip of *Jiggs and Maggie* Jiggs is forever trying to get out of going to the opera with Maggie who believes it confers social status upon herself. She also sings as well—excruciatingly. In top form, Mark Twain describes going to a performance of *Lohengrin* in *A Tramp Abroad*. "There were circumstances that made it necessary for me to stay through the four hours to the end . . . yet at times the pain was so exquisite I could hardly keep the tears back. At those times, as the howlings and wailings and shriekings of the singers and the ragings and roarings and explosions of the vast orchestra rose higher and higher and wilder and wilder and fiercer and fiercer, I could have cried . . ."

Again we have to ask why should there be some so indifferent or even hostile to the beauties of the singing voice? And again we can only turn to speculation for an answer. Perhaps it lies in the nature of music itself, which divides up roughly into the kind that is sung and the kind that is played. In the great masterworks of symphonic and chamber music only the distillations of human emotions—impersonal joy, sadness, exultation—are heard. The *specific* as adumbrated by words set to music and sung, the expressions of petty man—"I love, I hate, I envy, I yearn"—are left out.

Voices then are characterizations and very strong responses to them are as subjective and often inexplicable as in ordinary human intercourse. We have types: gentlemen prefer blondes; a female wants a man with hair on his chest. Meeting somebody for the first time we react because they remind us of someone. This is true of the singing voice: from one listener it will evoke tears, from a second one indifference. No two singing voices are alike. Science has proved this to be so by perfecting a system of "voice prints" which reveals that each voice has a pattern as unique to its possessor as a fingerprint.

In addition the scientists tell us that one pair of ears does not hear a voice the same as another. We have a greater and lesser response to frequencies of sound, as well as to vibrato—the swings of pitch present in every sung note.

So, an in-depth investigation of the singing voice makes the subject murkier and less factual. This is true of the history and development of man's song. The Emperor Nero was a singer, but what did he really sound like? Was the *castrato* Farinelli really such a marvellous vocalist? Or Jenny Lind? Until the invention of the phonograph just over a century ago we have to rely on descriptions or recollections of legendary singers, many of which, because of the loyalties and prejudices of fans, may well be over-stated.

In a very abbreviated review of the history of song, let us consider these vocalists of the past as possessing "hearsay voices."

H. Gissey: Design for a grotesque male costume representing music

The Hearsay Voices

First Songs. Our information as to how singers sounded before the invention of the phonograph is entirely dependent on hearsay—the highly subjective reactions and observations of people who committed them to paper and left us a written, not an aural, record of the great singers of the past. Some idea of the range and flexibility of these voices of legendary vocalists is provided by the music that they performed. But previous to the twelfth century only the scantiest fragments survive; before the Age of Pericles, virtually nothing. Once more then, we are forced into the realm of speculation, a place, however, in which any true lover of singing is delighted to find himself.

How and when man first evolved his remarkable ability to speak and to sing is of course not known. The usual stereotype of the caveman is an ape-like creature who makes only grunting sounds. Darwin believed that the voice evolved from man's need to attract a mate, thus eliminating the task, so often depicted, of having to go out and drag one back to the cave. Darwin's theory is made more believable because of the direct connection that exists between man's voice and his sexual development. Other anthropologists, however, decry the idea that man first lifted his voice in imitation of the mating calls of animals and birds, pointing out that of the very earliest songs known to us, the themes are not erotic, but relate to religion, battle or domestic matters.

Some scholars believe that when man first discovered he possessed the power to make a variety of sounds differing in pitch and duration, the result was neither speech nor song, but a combination of the two—a kind of intoning. When this marriage broke up is of course again not known. "It is indeed tempting to

21

surmise," writes C. M. Bowra in his *Primitive Song* "that in the late Paleolithic Age, c. 30,000-15,000 B.C., when men delighted in painting and carving and modeling, they delighted also in the melodious arrangement of words and that the hunters of mammoth, bison and rhinoceros who recorded their hopes or their achievements so splendidly on the walls of caves celebrated them in song. But just as we know nothing of their speech . . . so we know nothing of any specialized purposes to which it may have been put. Certainty of any kind is out of the question . . ."

If we have no knowledge of how our primitive ancestors actually sang there are at least some indications of the subject matter of their songs. This hasn't varied, with the exception of perhaps a greater preponderance of love songs, from what we feel the need to sing about today. There were religious songs—the church hymns of twenty millenniums ago; there were songs that described heroic deeds of war. Not long ago the country's favorite hit was "The Battle of New Orleans." There were songs describing the evil and tragedy in fighting, atavistic counterparts of the "protest" songs heard all over the world in our time. There were songs of animal life and nature:

> Glittering stars of the white night,
> Moon shining on high,
> Piercing the forest with your pale beams,
> Stars, friends of white ghosts,
> Moon, their protectress.

A feeling towards the moon in this song handed down among the Gabon pygmy tribe quickly brings to mind Norma's apostrophe to the moon, "Casta diva," or the thousand and one popular songs of which the moon is the subject. And then there were songs of death and resurrection such as this invocation to an ancestor:

> My departed one, my departed one, my God!
> Where art thou wandering?

If none of the music of these songs is known to us, though presumably it was as primitive and limited as the people who sang them, scholars nonetheless believe that they were very often sung accompanied by some kind of rhythmic body action—the waving of an arm, the stamping of a foot. This sounds totally contemporary when one thinks of today's pop singers wracked, it seems, by rhythmic spasms as they give their all to their numbers. Many of the songs of earliest man were antiphonal, that is, a question and answer pattern between two groups, the answer returned in a kind of refrain. This too seems entirely familiar when we remember the arrangements of many pop groups today with one singer delivering the line of a song and the others immediately echoing it.

The feminist writer, Sophie Drinker, suggests that among the singers of ancient times women were superior to men, who couldn't sing as readily while out chasing and killing the day's rations. A woman's more routinized domestic duties allowed for a greater cultivation of the art and Mrs. Drinker believes that the peculiarly rapt expression often seen on the faces of women choristers even today is simply a continuance of how females many thousands of years ago looked as they went about their daily domestic routines singing. The birth of a baby in many tribes was also an important occasion for which women would sing in order to ward off evil spirits and ease the labor of the mother. Once delivered, women have of course sung to their babies from time immemorial. (The syllables "lu lu" seem to have had a peculiar fascination for primordial women for purposes of singing: hence the word "lullaby," also "alleluia," and "ululate" which means "to wail.")

Other anthropologists agree with Mrs. Drinker that our female ancestors may have sung better and certainly more frequently than the males. If then modern man has evolved by making new and increased demands on his intelligence and physical equipment, this would explain why over the aeons, women, in asking more of their voices, now generally have a range of at least three more notes (and sometimes up to an octave) than the finest male singers.

Anthropologists also tell us that with the exception of a few tribes in which women were forbidden to sing, the female maintained a complete equality with the male. Allowing a thousand years out for the time when the Christian Church restrained the singing of women on the grounds that it was lascivious, the female has continued to maintain her rare equality with the other sex. Singing is at least one field in which a woman can and does compete successfully with the male, enjoying the fullest possible recognition of her status.

At first the songs of our ancient antecedents seem to have been mainly communal. But as the singing voice began to develop it was natural that certain individuals among the group should be discovered to have superior voices and musical talent. Solo singing on a very limited scale therefore slowly developed and the soloist in a tribe by skillful use of his voice—sometimes by mere mimicry of animal noises—was often expected to drive away evil spirits. These solo singers were powerful and held in awe, but also feared and even disliked. In the minds of a superstitious, primitive people the magical effect of the singing voice seemed to be linked in some way with the terrifying spirits themselves. Something of this superstitious awe would seem to carry over in our worshipful attitude towards singers of today. They are creatures not as we, but in touch with supernatural forces capable of evoking from us frightening and mysterious responses to their vocal art.

Voices of Antiquity. Let us now move on to comparatively recent times, that is to say the seventh century B.C. Then for the first time we have a visual documentation of an attempt at a vocal "method" among the Mesopotamians, as shown in a bas-relief in the British Museum. Together with a group playing various instruments, we see a choir of six women and nine children. One of the women has her hand on her larynx and is squeezing it so as to produce the thin, whiny high notes favored in the East to this day.

By this time the epics of Homer, his *Odyssey* and *Iliad*, had come into being. Though the hexameters of these poems are believed to have been sung, no one is certain what kind of singing was involved. Evidence points to an extremely limited type of vocalization, with an occasional chord plucked from the lyre or *kithara* to mark a change of mood. We know of course that the Greeks of Homer's time and in the later years of the Golden Age revered music, so much so that as Paul Henry Lang points out in his monumental *Music in Western Civilization:* "an educated and distinguished man was called a musical man (ἀνὴρ μουσικός), whereas an inferior and uncouth person was simply 'unmusical' or a man without music (ἀνὴρ ἄμουσος) . . . They [the

Greeks]," he goes on to say, "had two souls in their breasts, one striving for clarity, temperance and moderation (σωφροσύνη), the other driving them towards the fantastic and orgiastic, the cult of Dionysus. For this very reason they preached the idea of σωφροσύνη with great fervor."

It seems probable that in ancient Greece the singing voice and its art—the attractions of which, it has to be admitted, come down fully on the side of Dionysus—never approached the range and power of the other performing arts of acting and dancing. Singing there certainly must have been both religious and secular. Plato disapproved of the latter, the professional singers who could be hired to entertain during dinner parties, but then Plato, like most of the high-minded Greeks, conceived of music as a moral force, controlled, subservient to the word, the idea. Of the various modes or primitive scales that had come into being Plato held disapproving views. The Ionic and the Lydian he considered "effeminate and gossiping harmonies," and in general saw no need for "a great many strings, nor a variety of harmony in our songs and melodies." Music was conceived of by men such as Plato in intellectual terms, and regarded as a placator of passions not a stimulant to them, as an unrestrained voice lifted in song can so easily be. Music was meant to ennoble the character and perfect the soul. In such a moral climate the art of singing was not likely to develop and at least one authority has concluded that Greek vocal music "was not music in our sense of the term at all, but a special way of reciting poetry, determined by nuances of expression which had been steadily and continuously refined by the most artistic people on earth but throughout their history more akin to the method of speaking than of the singing voice."

With the rise of the Roman Empire history definitely instructs that the ascendancy of music and singing as an art is linked with the moral spirit of the people—a fact that the newly founded Christian Church began to recognize about the same time. The Romans took much from the earlier Greek civilization but not its moral spirit of control and restraint. Quite the opposite: the Roman ideal came to be pleasure, surrender to the senses. In this spiritual atmosphere, Greek music speedily changed, quickened, gained rhythm, became more animalistic and sexy. Oriental music full of elaboration was brought to Rome from the campaigns in Egypt.

By the third century A.D. music seems to have become an integral part of Roman life. Rather the way music follows us about today in elevators and restaurants and airport lounges, a wealthy Roman would have his slaves make music for him at home while he dressed or ate, or when he made journeys by land and sea. At banquets it was customary for the warlike Romans to sing songs accompanied by flutes in praise of famous heroes. They also attended concerts of massed vocal choirs or instruments at which, according to Cicero, "the audience would give vent to its disapproval if the singer or player made mistakes"—a custom that sounds similar to the behavior of Italian audiences today.

With such a national enthusiasm for music, virtuosi naturally emerged, among them great singers together with the usual jealousies, rivalries and claques that swirl about great vocal stars. One of the renowned singers of his day was Tigellius who sang and composed at the court of Augustus. As capricious and temperamental as the most explosive prima donna, he was quite capable of refusing to sing even when commanded by the emperor, if the mood was not upon him; equally he might perform throughout an entire banquet whether bidden or not. A number of the emperors themselves, most notably Hadrian, were amateur singers of talent, though some condemned the practice of music as unmanly. All Roman society was shocked by the Emperor Nero, not because he was obsessed by music but for appearing as a professional singer and actually competing in contests, in which, not oddly, there was little suspense as to who would be the winner. Suetonius tells us that Nero had a "thin, husky voice" and in an effort to improve it would lie with a metal weight on his chest to strengthen his breathing. This vain, decadent emperor also kept close watch over his diet in case certain foods injured his voice, and refused to command his soldiers in person lest he strain his vocal cords—all practices that might be prescribed in the vocal studio of today. Nero made his first public appearance in Rome in 59 A.D., sang in the contests at Naples in 64 and reappeared at the Theatre of Pompey in Rome the following year. Towards the end of 66 he made a professional tour of Greece, singing and accompanying himself on the *kithara,* as he had been instructed by his Greek master, Terpnus. Nero's performances usually consisted of personal interpretations of a tragic role or theme, such as Orestes killing his mother, or

Oedipus blinded. His success in these roles cannot be doubted given the fact that he possessed a claque numbering five thousand, which had been carefully instructed in the three ways of making applause gratifying to the Emperor's ears: *bombi*, a sound like the buzzing of bees; *imbrices*, resembling the noise of rain or hail falling on a roof; and *testae*, the crashing of pots together. Suetonius found one of Nero's performances "interminable." This, an early instance of the rich and powerful buying public appearances as a singer, is certainly not the last.

No account exists of the range and general quality of the voice of a celebrated singer such as Tigellius, nor do we know what vocal feats, if any, he may have performed. Contemporary reports do tell us that a number of singing teachers existed, that singers practiced scales and were expected to lead the healthy temperate life necessary to the maintenance of their art. "Quintilian relates how they protected their throats by holding handkerchiefs before their mouths when speaking," writes Dr. Lang, "and how they avoided the sun, fog and wind. On the other hand Martial reports that some of the singers overexerted themselves to such a degree that they suffered ruptured blood vessels. This was due, no doubt," he adds, "to the large proportions of the theaters and rooms, which demanded loud singing."

To what extent vocal art at this period might have developed is entirely a matter of conjecture, for by about the third century A.D. a force had come into the world that was to have the greatest possible effect on the singer and his song. This was the Christian Church.

The Devil's Songs. That singing was godly there could be no doubt. The disciples themselves sang after the Last Supper before going up onto the Mount of Olives. And did not Paul exhort the Ephesians to "be filled with the Spirit, speaking to yourselves in psalms and hymns and spiritual songs, singing and making melody in your heart to the Lord"? Earlier religions had employed chanting and song in the performance of their rites; it was natural for the founding fathers of the Church to adopt the same practice. Chants, mainly Jewish, using one or at the most two notes to a syllable and having melodic sequences but no rhythm or measures were intoned by the congregations of the first Christian churches. As Christianity spread, Greek and Byzantine influences were brought to bear on the music of the service and it became enriched. Certain men of the early Church recognized that music could be a powerful stimulus to belief and a means of attracting converts. They composed new psalms and hymns and encouraged enthusiastic singing among their flocks. By the third century it had become customary to hear at a service the men of the congregation singing out a verse of the psalm, the women and children replying with another, and both joining together in the refrain—a pattern of song already thousands of years old.

Though singing was capable of raising religious exaltation, the Church fathers soon became aware that it also brought out other emotions and impulses of a kind distinctly in contradiction to the teachings of Christianity. Within an orthodoxy of obedience and self-denial, the free, exhilarating expression of singing sat most uncomfortably. Above all, the Church preached the sinfulness of sex and the desirability of celibacy. But the warm, sensuous tones of the singing voice, particularly of a woman, evoked all too powerfully the earthiness of man's nature. "So often as I call to mind the tears I shed at the hearing of the church songs . . . whenas I am moved not with the singing but the thing sung," wrote St. Augustine. "And yet so often it befalls me to be moved with the voice rather than the ditty, I confess myself to have grievously offended, at which time I wish rather not to have heard the music." In 318 A.D. the Church fathers moved against the disturbing power of the singing voice by forbidding the voluptuous song of women to be heard in church. By 367 neither men nor women of the congregation were permitted to lift their singing voices in praise of God, only specially trained members of the clergy.

These men were called canons—"singing men"—and at their ordination, as W. J. Henderson writes in his interesting *Early History of Singing*, they were charged as follows: "See that thou believe in thy heart what thou singest with thy mouth, and approve in thy works what thou believest in thy heart." Specially instructed in vocal technique and musicianship, able to embellish their solos with *appoggiaturas, portamenti* and ornaments of various kinds, these canons soon developed into the singing stars of their time. The world does not change and we learn from Henderson that "they speedily acquired the self glory which has clung to singers ever since . . . and began to swell with vanity."

This was expressed in terms of personal adornment, particularly by the length of their hair, the luxuriance of which these Beatle-like canons doubtless believed added to the effect of their singing as they stood before their congregations.

Again we have no actual description of how these men sounded nor what the range and power of their voices were like. We do know something about their training at the Schola Cantorum, which is usually thought to have been founded by Gregory when he became Pope in 590, but which was probably started at a somewhat earlier date. The course, for example, lasted nine years, much of this time evidently consumed in memorizing the chants. What we know of this music suggests that the voices of these canons may have possessed some of the power and flexibility which have long been associated with the best Italian singing, or "bel canto" as it has come to be called. Technical problems such as breathing, the placing of the voice, learning to sing a controlled legato line must have all been studied at the Schola Cantorum and presumably mastered. An ability to sing florid passages was also a necessity, for coloratura-like phrases were common in the liturgies of the Eastern Church, and later, in that of Spain, the latter's being derived from the much turned, highly ornamented music of the Moors.

For the next seven or eight hundred years the Church held the curious position of building and maintaining a technical and aesthetic standard of singing by presenting to the public, so to speak, fine professional vocalists, while at the same time trying to prevent the public from singing themselves. All secular music, love songs, work songs, the folk songs that are as natural to people as breathing itself were denounced as sinful and lascivious. Particularly suspect was the woman's singing voice. In the fifth century Bishop Hippolytus declared an edict: "A woman who attracts people with her beautiful but deluding sweetness of voice (which is full of seduction and sin) must give up her trade and wait forty days if she is to receive communion." Another bishop, a hundred years later, complained with horror, "How many peasants and how many women know by heart and recite out loud the Devil's songs, erotic and obscene." The only female singing condoned was that of nuns, and their tones were trained to sound sexless and devoid of human expression. It is odd to realize that the present designation of women's voices, "alto" and

"soprano," have in fact masculine endings and refer to boys'
voices, "higher" and "highest" above the normal range of men's
voices. No terms existed to describe the type and range of sound
that women made while singing.

Forbidding men and women so natural a means of expression
as lifting their voices in song proved, of course, as unrealistic as
trying to prohibit the birds their notes. Secular singing, though
much suppressed, continued to give vent to man's feeling about
his life and the life of others. Singing also became associated with
magic and incantations. "If we have a headache," remarks St.
Augustine, "we run to the singer of incantations; I see this occur
every day." Since Church music was all that people were exposed
to, often parts of the liturgy were simply borrowed and given
different words. By the eleventh century when men were
beginning to feel the first stirring of their own individual worth,
secular singing, far from being blotted out, had increased, and it
was then that the first solo singers of note came into being. These
were the troubadours.

Singers of Grace. For centuries the Church had suppressed the
singing voices of women, had condemned their sound as lewd
and a device for sexual ensnarement. Now curiously—and then
again perhaps not so curiously—when the solo secular voice was
raised again in Western Europe it gave extravagant praise to
women. Of the various kinds of wandering musicians and singers
during the eleventh century the first was the *jongleur,* the tough,
bawdy, traveling entertainer of his day, a one-man vaudeville
show with his songs, dances, funny stories and tricks. Like all
such troupers of any age he was a sound and experienced
musician. At the opposite end of the social scale were the
troubadours of noble, sometimes royal birth who appeared in the
twelfth and thirteenth centuries. Perhaps the most celebrated
among these was Richard Coeur de Lion, skilled in the art of
composing and singing verses in praise of chivalric love, as was
his friend, Blondel de Nesle. Legend has it that when Richard was
imprisoned secretly in a castle high on a hill overlooking the
Danube, his friend found his way to this rocky retreat and
climbing up under one of the windows of the castle began to sing
a lay which he and the monarch are thought to have composed
together. To Blondel's joy and delight he heard the familiar voice

of Richard take up the song along with him. Thus the singing voice proved its power to effect the rescue of one of Europe's most important rulers.

Passing the tedious months in prison, Richard is also said to have composed and sung in the customary Provençal these sad, rather bitter lines:

> No prisoner can tell his honest thought,
> Unless he speaks as one who suffers wrong;
> But for his custom he may make a song . . .
> My friends are many, but their gifts are nought.

Brothers to the Gallic troubadours were the German Minnesingers who with Teutonic thoroughness constructed an elaborate set of rules and regulations on the composing of songs—those strictures which Wagner mocks so thoroughly in *Die Meistersinger.*

What kind of voices did they possess, these the first solo secular singers to emerge in comparatively recent times? From all that can be adduced their sounds seem to have been very limited. Most of the troubadours' music that has survived reveals that the singer was required to have a compass of no more than an octave; frequently the range of a song is a sixth. Here again emphasis was on the word and there was no ideal of either vocal beauty or display for display's sake. Professor Donald Jay Grout, a noted musicologist, believes that the quality of tone of the troubadours—light, thin, clear and without vibrato—was quite different from that of singing voices we are used to today.

Around 1900, about the time that Henry Adams wrote his masterly study of medieval architecture and life, *Mount-Saint-Michel and Chartres*, there occurred a revival of interest in the *chansons*, the music of the troubadours that evolved in the twelfth century. Paradoxically, a chief promoter of this restoration of a song literature that celebrated romantic love and grace and beauty was a *chanteuse* who began her career by singing often pornographic selections that dealt with alcoholics, syphillitics and the generally down-and-out. This was the flat-bosomed, tiny-waisted Yvette Guilbert, with her plain, expressive face beneath coils of dyed orange hair. Perhaps because he found a measure of his crippled self in the songs of this dynamic performer, Henri Toulouse-Lautrec turned out sketch after sketch of Yvette Guilbert singing in "the middle and lower registers of her voice"—a fact noted by another admirer, George Bernard Shaw.

At the height of her career Yvette Guilbert underwent the painful and at that time dangerous removal of a kidney (said to have been caused by the tight lacing of her corsets) and after a long recovery she was changed into a plump middle-aged woman of a bourgeoise appearance. Nothing daunted, Guilbert, with her innate theatrical sense, researched the literature with the patience and perseverance of a true scholar and transformed herself into a lecturer-singer on the *chansonniers*. In this guise she gave programs entitled "The Great Songs of France Reconstructed by Madame Yvette Guilbert from the Literary Monuments of the Poets: Trouvères, Jongleurs and Clerks" all over the United States in such staid academic outposts as Smith and Bryn Mawr. This was the same Yvette Guilbert who two decades earlier had to bribe the Paris police to allow her to sing her scandalous repertory.

While the troubadours sang of chivalric love in the secular world, inside the Church singers celebrated God. Some evidently made attempts at vocal display but the practice was discouraged. "These people break up their melodies with hockets, debase them with discants, and load them with moteti and tripla in the vulgar style," thundered Pope John XXII in 1324, who ordered the vocalists to desist or undergo penalties. Church music until the seventeenth century was highly polyphonic, a musical style which does not aid in the evolution of the singing voice nor in the highly individual art of solo singing.

To bring out all the brilliance, power and expressiveness inherent in the workings of the human lungs and larynx, a new kind of musical form was needed. Not until the start of the seventeenth century did it finally emerge and the first age of bel canto was born, product of the hybrid art form known as opera.

The Counterfeit Voices. The development of the singing voice as we know it today very much parallels the development of man as we know him today. With the coming of the Renaissance and the so-called Age of Humanism, men really began to emerge as individuals. Until then they had mainly been as members of a unit, as were their voices, since vocal music was almost entirely polyphonic. When individual man began to assert his uniqueness, the singing voice responded with its special claim to uniqueness too.

In 1600 Jacopo Peri, himself a singer, wrote what is generally conceded to be the first opera, *Euridice*, and there commenced in Italy a golden age of singing, which some look back upon and rue will never come again. Peri took his example from the Greeks, as did many artists of that period, and composed a declamatory kind of music in which the sense of the word was all-important. The greatest master of this kind of vocal writing was Claudio Monteverdi. His full-length opera, *L'Incoronazione di Poppea*, which has been produced and recorded in recent times, is a work that seems strangely modern to us today, telling a story of very real, passionate people wonderfully characterized by the music. No display of the voice of any kind is introduced; if there are repeated notes or embellishments it is purely for emphasis. The voice is the complete servant of the word and never has it been used in a more human way.

But as a taste for the baroque gathered this almost austere vocal music gave way to display, ostentation and artificiality; to lines that were long, serpentine and highly ornamented. The singing voice, as it was uniquely capable of doing, led the way in creating this style of music and so emerged the first great operatic voices.

Some of these belonged to the "prima donnas," a term that in its original usage had no pejorative overtones. It meant simply the leading lady of an opera company. But as Kurt Pahlen points out in *Great Singers*, these historical divas such as Vittoria Archilei or Leonora Baroni "soon became all-powerful; they not only dictated terms to the operatic impresario, they told the composer and librettist just what kind of role they wanted to sing and the vocal embellishments they required. In time they formed round them such an aura of scandal and selfishness, pride and caprice, extravagant displays of temperament and demands for fees, that the term *prima donna* took on a new and derogatory meaning."

Such a rush of power to their heads seems understandable if one considers that this was practically the first time in history that, thanks to her singing voice, a woman could achieve equality with the male. What must have been the dismay of these early female prima donnas to soon discover that they had to compete against so-called men possessing a strange, powerful facsimile of their own womanly vocal quality? These were the vain, strutting singers who invaded the opera house via the Church called the *castrati*.

"Viva il coltello"—"Hooray for the knife"—audiences some-times shouted after a particularly remarkable performance by one of these tall, full-chested male singers who produced the sound of a woman's voice. For the development of this curious vocal taste the Church, ever a force over the destinies of the singing voice, must take the perhaps not so unwitting blame. Having banished the sexually arousing sound of the female voice from services it now had to rely on the capabilities of boys to cope with the higher ranges that rightfully belong to women. When by the end of the fifteenth century a number of polyphonists began to emerge— particularly in the Netherlands—who composed highly complex and glorious music that required voices of power and stamina, it soon became evident that the voices of boys were inadequate. At best, boys had never been totally satisfactory; after years of careful musical training and practice their voices, maddeningly, might break overnight, and all their valuable instruction and experience be instantly lost. Unless . . .

Tampering artificially with the sex of a male and his ability to procreate was definitely interfering with one of the basic works of God, and the Church promised excommunication to anyone participating in such a crime against nature. Nevertheless the Church also took the attitude that if a husky male well-trained musically and in vocal production, from whom emanated a voice with a female range, appeared on the doorstep, so to speak, this was the will of God. Accordingly the singer would be promptly accepted into the choir to gain honor, wealth and, above all, security in this most insecure of times. As a result, all over Italy, mainly among desperate peasant families, boys displaying any kind of singing voice and musical talent were put to the knife. Most of them never made careers and were left to finish their lives as eunuchs—the targets of mockery and derision.

Shame, indignation, revulsion have generally been the reac-tions of people towards the unsexing of a man by surgery for the sake of retaining his boy's range and quality of tone. "Can British matrons take their daughters to hear the portentous yells of this disenfranchised of nature, and will they explain the cause to the youthful and untutored mind?" demanded the London *Times* when one of the last celebrated *castrati*, Giovanni Velluti, ap-peared in the English capital in 1825. Here, however, is a modern view on the castrating of boys to preserve their singing voices in a letter to *Stereo Review*, November 1966, from a lady in California:

"I do not believe the practice of producing *castrati* for their special musical purpose 'ghastly' or 'shameful' when the operation is performed on the initiative of the individual, as was often the case, nor do I regard the *castrati* themselves as being 'mutilated' . . . I have many friends, some of them quite prominent in musical circles, who agree with me that if there is to be a serious and widespread revival of Baroque and bel canto opera, there must necessarily be a return of the *castrati* to sing the roles they alone can handle with dramatic and vocal legitimacy. . . . I definitely do not advocate force, but if a young singer should possess a fine voice which he wishes to preserve, I can sympathize with no reason for discouraging him. Children in general are far more reasonable, intelligent beings than most adults want to believe, and a gifted child is a thorough pragmatist to whom nothing is more important than his talent."

From appearances in church the next obvious step for the *castrati* was to invade the more glamorous and exciting theaters and opera houses where they were at greater liberty to indulge themselves in what they were most adept at—embellishments and interpolations of highly elaborate cadenzas into their music. Certainly from a vocal point of view the knife created a unique physical situation. During puberty a man's vocal cords or folds lengthen to an average of seven-twelfths of an inch and also thicken; so do a woman's, only less so. For this reason a woman's voice is more flexible. The vocal folds of a boy are proportionately smaller and thinner still, and these by one stroke of the knife were placed in a male body with male strength, stamina and above all lung power. An examination of the music in which *castrati* excelled usually shows that they were able to execute tremendously long, elaborate phrases in one breath.

The vocal feats of the *castrati* are legendary and with all such tales perhaps subject to some disbelief. Johann Quantz, the flutist, who heard many of the great singers of this first golden age of bel canto, tells us that Farinelli had a range the same as today's lyric or dramatic sopranos—that is, slightly more than two octaves ranging from A, below middle C to the high C" or even D". Yet when one examines excerpts of the music that he is supposed to have sung, replete with an infinite number of trills, runs and other complicated embellishments, it appears that he

J. Amigoni: Carlo Broschi, called Farinelli.

lacked comfort and ease above the G' below high C", nor does the music go lower than the D just above middle C—a range in fact of eleven notes. Difficult as these fast-moving, scale-like figures, runs, jumps and rapidly repeated notes are to execute, would they hold any terrors for Joan Sutherland?

Contemporary accounts of the *castrati* also sometimes proudly point out that the intonation of such and such a singer was good and that he always sang in tune. This mention of the ability (or lack of it) to sing on pitch also frequently occurs in descriptions of the great vocalists of the pre-recording days in the nineteenth century, suggesting that audiences in both eras seemed to have been far more tolerant of out-of-tune singing than we are today.

Would we have admired the vocal art of these strapping, often gawky men who appeared in female parts, lavishly gowned and adorned with jewels? Certainly sexual inconsistency does not worry audiences in opera houses of today when a well-busted woman puts on the breeches of amorous youths like Octavian and Cherubino. But would we have reacted with the same adoring adulation that English and Italian audiences gave to these artificially created vocal anomalies? (The practical French, incidentally, never had a taste for the singing of the *castrati*.) Naturally it is almost impossible to judge. Certainly we would have been impressed by their remarkable vocal technique just as we are amazed and delighted by the coloratura abilities of a Sutherland or Berganza today. On the other hand how would we react to the actual quality of the voice of a *castrato*? Contemporary accounts often speak of its sweetness and the pathetic quality that it possessed, but into more than one description creeps the word "shrill."

One castrated singer from Rome's Sistine Chapel continued into the age of the phonograph when there is evidence, other than hearsay, of how such a vocalist sounded. Alessandro Moreschi, aged thirty-two, committed his male soprano voice to wax in 1902 and again two years later, making a total of nine records. G. B. Steane writes in *The Grand Tradition*: "I have heard only one, Tosti's 'Ideale,' where the voice is direly afflicted, the style gusty and the total effect sadly comical."

The Bel Canto Mystique. By now there have been several references to the term "bel canto" or "bel canto singing." What is

A. Chalon: Caricature of Giuditta Pasta as Medea.

meant by bel canto and do we have bel canto singers today?

As with so much concerning the singing voice, utter confusion reigns over the meaning of the term which in English is literally "beautiful singing." Some people regard bel canto as a technique

Nellie Melba as Juliette.

of wonderful singing, the secrets of which are lost forever. If this is so, at what period in history did it exist? Already by 1723, when highly developed solo singing had been known for about a century, the *castrato*, Pier Francesco Tosi, is wailing over a *decline*

The young basso, Luigi Lablache, singing teacher of Princess Victoria.

in vocal standards. "The fault is in the Singers," he complains in his *Observations on the Florid Song*, the first of countless volumes that have poured forth ever since purporting to teach the reader a singing technique. "They praise the Pathetick, sing the Allegro," he continues. "They know the first to be most Excellent, but they lay it aside, knowing it to be the most difficult." From this we may infer that the singers at this period—which some declare to be the golden age of singing—lacked the ability to sing a long, sustained line, the flowing legato that those who claim to understand what bel canto is would say was its essence. Well then, perhaps true bel canto singing came later . . .

Angelica Catalani, renowned soprano of the early nineteenth century.

"In Italy music is decadent, there are no more schools, nor great singers . . . I do not know to what may be attributed the real cause, since the ancient systems have fallen into disuse, and the good customs of ancient schools no longer regulate our Profession." It is now fifty years later, the time of another supposedly golden age of song. The writer is the celebrated singing teacher Giambattista Mancini. While offering some faint recognition to the great vocalists of his era—the celebrated *castrato* Pacchierotti, for example, or the extraordinary soprano Lucrezia Agujari, with her range up to C''' above high C'', whom Mozart heard—he bewails the demise of true bel canto singing and the methods that produced it . . .

On to the next golden age, the one in which singers such as Maria Malibran, Giuditta Pasta, Giulia Grisi, Henrietta Sontag, Angelica Catalani, Giovanni-Battista Rubini and Luigi Lablache starred, and which many people take to have been the truly great age of bel canto. "Today one hardly ever hears a really beautiful and technically correct trill; very rarely a perfect mordent; very rarely a rounded coloratura, a genuine unaffected soul-moving portamento, a complete equalization of the registers, a steady intonation through all the varying nuances of crescendo and di-minuendo. Most of our singers, as soon as they attempt the noble art of portamento, go out of tune; and the public, accustomed to faulty execution, overlooks the defects of the singer, if only he is a skilled actor and knows the routine of the stage."

This was published in 1834 at the very height of a supposedly great era of bel canto singing, and the writer is none other than Richard Wagner, who, though he is supposed to have destroyed bel canto as it was once known, appears to be familiar with its concepts . . .

Let us move on still later in our search for the true period of great singing. "Singing is becoming as much a lost art as the manufacture of Mandarin China or the varnish used by the old masters." Here the writer is the immensely knowledgeable singing teacher, Manuel Garcia II, lamenting "the disappearance of the race of great singers, who, besides originating that art, carried it to the highest point of excellence." The year is 1894 when the celebrated nonagenarian pedagogue could have heard Adelina Patti, Nellie Melba, Lillian Nordica, Emma Eames and the two de Reszkes, to choose a random selection from the luminaries of that reputedly golden age.

"It is plain to every careful observer that the race of beautiful singers is diminishing with every year, and that in its place there is growing up a generation of harsh, unrefined, tuneless shout-ers." By now we've reached 1938 and the eminent music critic, W. J. Henderson, an expert on voices, who wrote those words, could have heard in New York that year Kirsten Flagstad, Lauritz Melchior, Kerstin Thorborg, Helen Traubel, Lawrence Tibbett, Lily Pons, Bidu Sayão and, making his debut, Jussi Bjoerling.

Every earlier age, so it seems, was the golden one when bel

canto reigned supreme. It resembles old men sighing for the bright days of their youth when everything seemed fresh and beautiful and wonderful. But was it? Did an age of singing ever exist more glorious than at any other time in history? As one observer shrewdly sums it up:

"From the beginning [vocal reformers] have insisted that the art of bel canto is lost . . . Three of the greatest teachers of the old Italian school all lamented the decadence of the art of singing. Others before and since have done the same thing . . . From this we draw some interesting conclusions: first, that the real art of singing was lost immediately after it was found. Second, the only time it was perfect was when it began. Third, that ever since it began we have been searching for it without success."

Nonetheless the quest for bel canto as a method of singing continues. Many people believe that the old Italian singers, including the celebrated *castrati*, practiced some secret vocal technique, perhaps a way of holding the tongue or taking breath, which is now lost, and if it could but be recaptured true bel canto singing would be restored to the world. Hopes high, they turn to an early work on singing technique but are rebuffed by its generalities: "Learn to breathe so that you can sing through the phrases." "Do not sing too loudly." "Do not sing too softly." If there were specific technicalities in the so-called "Italian" method, Tosi was not prepared to divulge them. Nevertheless to some bel canto will continue to mean a method of singing, lost forever, a kind of fantasy vocalism the like of which they have never heard.

Others conceive of bel canto as a tremendous agility of voice. A male or female to be a true bel canto vocalist must possess the ability to trill, to sing runs quickly, execute turns, big jumps and so forth—in other words bel canto means to them all the *batterie de la voix* that the human larynx possesses. The only trouble with this concept of bel canto is that not all voices possess innate flexibility. To quote from what some regard as one of the great manuals on bel canto, Mancini's *Practical Reflections on Figured Singing* (1774): "The agility of the voice cannot be perfect if it is not natural; and if it is not perfect, instead of bringing pleasure and delight to the listener, it will bring annoyance and boredom.

"Then," goes on the author, "he who does not have it from nature should never lose time vainly in trying to acquire it . . . thus the prudent master, finding the scholar to lack a natural disposition for singing agility, should cease to conduct him by this route, but lead him to another, since in this profession the ways are many, the styles are varied, as are the dispositions by which one may arrive at the desired honor of being a good and admired virtuoso."

For still others, bel canto is simply a concept: round, beautiful tones melting one into the next, forming a line to the singing that is an essence of the art. Of the bel canto voice, one observer has conceived the tones as having a "rock-like steadiness" which are "shot through with an astonishing vibrance, or to use the Italian term, *vibrazione* . . . This extreme intensity of tone, this emotional-tone, is the main character of the bel canto singer."

To return to our original question, do we have bel canto singers today? If we accept the last definition of the bel canto voice as having astonishing vibrance and rock-like steadiness of tone, then such artists as Leontyne Price, Birgit Nilsson, Sherrill Milnes and Nicolai Ghiaurov triumphantly affirm that we certainly do have bel canto singers. Though it may shock purists I would go so far as to say that vocalists such as Ella Fitzgerald and Dinah Shore with their creamy, supple voices and round tones, not to speak of Sarah Vaughan, the possessor of a near three-octave range and astonishing flexibility besides, are all exponents of bel canto singing.

If, however, we take a practitioner of bel canto singing to mean one who can toss off roulades, staccati, trills and other amazing vocal feats, we can look to Joan Sutherland, Beverly Sills and Marilyn Horne. It is hard to believe that any golden age of singing, including the one over which the *castrati* ruled, was graced by any more remarkable singing than from this triumvirate nicknamed in order, "La Stupenda," "Bubbles" and "Jackie." On the foundation stones of supreme breath control, perfectly equalized registers and accuracy of pitch the three divas—two sopranos with big voices and one mezzo-soprano—have built their astonishing careers. All of them however, declare that they were much influenced by the singing of a soprano whose voice broke into three disparate registers, whose top was often wobbly and strident, whose bottom buzzed unpleasantly, and who, when emitting notes in the middle of her range sometimes sounded as though she was shifting a wad of cotton around in her mouth.

This was the controversial, maniacally intense and ultimately tragic Maria Callas whom some called "La Divina."

Until the comet-like appearance of Callas, devotees of the vocal art had to look back to the legendary Rosa Ponselle to find a soprano with a big voice full of dramatic chiaroscuro yet capable of the flights of coloratura required in the operas of Donizetti, Rossini and Bellini. Ponselle sang Spontini's largely forgotten *La Vestale* and the tremendously demanding name part in *Norma*. Callas, with a big soprano voice, sang these roles but also Lucia di Lammermoor and Amina in *La Sonnambula*, heroines usually associated with the bird-like tones of Tetrazzini, Galli-Curci or Lily Pons. Moreover, Callas found in these parts hitherto unheard accents of pathos and tragedy that were a revelation to her listeners. Single-handedly, it seemed, she had brought back true bel canto singing.

But had she? If bel canto was taken to mean singing of great vocal beauty then she made a mockery of the definition. Even at the outset of her career when she was freshest (and heaviest) her first recordings of the "Liebestod" and "Qui la voce" from Bellini's *I Puritani* reveal that she lacked the intrinsically beautiful tone quality of say, Renata Tebaldi or later, Kiri Te Kanawa. (And here it may be stated that all singers are born with a fundamental vocal quality that can be molded, colored, and enriched but that will always retain the basic endowment as received from nature.) As the career of Maria Callas progressed critics were soon pointing out the "strange quality" of her voice, its "harsh, nasal tones," its "ugly" timbre. When urged to coach with the great Ponselle, then retired, Callas refused, saying bitterly, "She started with more than I did."

"In singing I would like my voice to always *obey* me," she wrote to her husband, Giovanni Battista Meneghini, in November 1948, "and do what I *want*. But it seems that I demand too much from it. The vocal organ is ungrateful, and doesn't do as I wish. You could even say that it's rebellious and doesn't wish to be commanded." Later she wrote, "I'm unhappy with my voice. It will not do what I want." Less and less would it obey her as the years passed.

Yet again if bel canto is taken to mean intense dramatic power combined with the shaping of a musical phrase, then Maria Callas sang in company with the great bel canto vocalists of the nineteenth century: the Garcia sisters, Maria (Malibran) who was really a mezzo with a stretched top; Pauline (Viardot) whose voice was compared to bitter oranges, and above all the wonderful Giuditta Pasta whose voice was unequalized and veiled and who frequently sang off pitch, but of whom the English actress and acute observer of opera stars Fanny Kemble wrote that having heard all the great nineteenth century singers from Angelica Catalani to "little Adelina Patti," she thought that unquestionably Pasta "was the greatest of them all."

So in the career of Maria Callas, "La Divina," are to be found all the contradictory elements of what constitutes bel canto singing, an argument that will continue as long as the contentious lover of the singing voice exists.

As to the various golden ages of singing, George Bernard Shaw who liked to have the last word summed up all the disputation when he wrote in 1950, "Let us hear no more of a golden age of bel canto. We sing much better than our grandparents."

A scene from *Lucia di Lammermoor* starring Joan Sutherland at the Metropolitan.

The Operatic Voices
of Today

Today's voices are supposed to sound the same as those heard around 1700 (with the exception of the tones emitted by the *castrati*). Man, however, constantly evolves. Judging from clothing and furniture that has survived, today's human beings are of much larger average proportions. It is reasonable to suppose then that many of today's singing voices are bigger and more powerful than those heard two hundred years ago. What would the *castrati* with their celebrated lung power have thought of our Wagnerian singers and their ability to make themselves heard over an immense orchestra of more than a hundred players? Surely this strength and size of voice evolved too when there was a demand for it.

Today, too, we have another comparatively new kind of voice in the husky, almost masculine sounding tones produced by most female pop singers. Before about 1925 this kind of singing was scarcely ever heard except among folk singers in Spain who have always had a taste for that particular vocal quality.

Then there are the ranges of the modern voice to consider, which in turn raises the question of pitch. As with everything concerning the singing voice, nothing seems to be certain. What is an A? Today's knowledgeable musician would swiftly answer: "An A is a sound of 440 vibrations per second in the United States, 439 vibrations in England." But this was not always so. In the past three hundred years since the time of the *castrati*, pitch has steadily risen, urged on by instrumentalists for whom higher pitch gives greater brilliance. A tuning fork handed down from the time of Handel (1685–1759) sounds an A of 422.5 vibrations per second. In general eighteenth century pitch varied between A 415 and A 430. Thus the famous F″ above high C″ that Mozart wrote for his sister-in-law, the first Queen of the Night in *Die Zauberflöte*, was nearly a half tone lower than what contemporary high-ranging sopranos must emit.

Halfway through the nineteenth century the sensible French formed a commission of composers which included Auber, Berlioz, Halévy, Rossini and Ambroise Thomas, who in 1858 established a standard pitch of A 435. The contrary British (who drive on the left side of the road) set their Philharmonic pitch at A 452.5. Consequently the diva Adelina Patti refused to sing in England unless the pitch was lowered, which, because of her importance, it was.

By the turn of the century English orchestras acceded to an international pitch of A 440, though not British bands. Thus the poor horn or trumpet band player who wanted to perform with an orchestra had to own two differently tuned instruments. To add to the confusion pipe organs were also tuned differently: A 441–445 for church; A 451–453 for concerts. Even to this day when the organ should peal forth thrillingly on to the prelude of *Die Meistersinger* sensitive ears may hear that the instrument sounds slightly out of tune with the orchestra.

In addition musicianly singers do not render the same pitch for say, F sharp and G flat as a well-tempered piano gives forth. Vocalists make a differentiation, the G flat being infinitesimally lower than the F sharp. The choral conductor Margaret Hillis recalls how as a student listening with a score to Kirsten Flagstad (who had absolute pitch) singing Isolde, she was amazed when the soprano, sustaining a long note over orchestra chords that changed enharmonically, tuned her tone up from D flat to C sharp.

A Catalogue of Voices. When it comes actually to cataloguing today's voices it is essential that we enter the opera house. Only there can be heard in the greatest variety the capabilities of man's singing voice. However beautiful the voices of concert singers may be, or especially those of pop singers, they are no more than diminished versions of the operatic voices. By examining what type of voice sings what roles in the standard operatic repertory we ought to be able to cover the amazing variety of today's singers.

Unfortunately there is a great deal of overlapping among the various kinds of voices and before making a catalogue of them (however imprecise) we should perhaps bear in mind that every voice is a broad characterization. A high, light, woman's voice, for example, suggests girlishness, innocence and fragility. With an increase in the size of the female voice, it assumes greater pathos, while the largest take on dramatic force and qualities either tragic or heroic. The same is more or less true with the various high male voices. In both sexes the lower ranges have a darker quality sometimes associated with sexiness, but more often with evil. Frequently a parental or authoritarian connection is made with these lower tones.

Each operatic composer, therefore, writes for the particular kind of voice that will best suit the character whom he is bringing to musical life. How carefully Giuseppe Verdi considered this aspect of his art we know from a letter to his librettist when Eugenia Tadolini had been suggested to take the part of Lady Macbeth. "Madame Tadolini sings to perfection and I should prefer Lady Macbeth not to sing. Madame Tadolini has a splendid voice, clear, pure and powerful; and I should like in Lady Macbeth a hard, hoarse, gloomy voice." Rossini as a creator of operatic character has been done an injustice by the high coloratura sopranos who steal the role of Rosina in *Il Barbiere di Siviglia* from the darker voiced coloratura mezzo-soprano for whom it was written. These high, light, twittering voices have the effect of turning Rosina into an arch, kittenish creature. When the role is sung by the lower voice as the composer intended, warmth and womanliness come into the character.

While the range and tessitura of an operatic role largely determine what kind of voice will sing it, the personal tastes of the manager of an opera company may influence its casting, also singers themselves anxious to extend their repertories and appear in new roles. Let us now try to break down the different kinds of singing voices into their varied categories.

Highest of all. Generally the soprano voices are loosely classified as coloratura, lyric and dramatic. In addition we hear of the lyric-coloratura, also the *spinto*. And what is the soprano *leggiero?*

Of the coloraturas there are several kinds. Highest of all is the soprano *acuto sfogato* with a range:

Soprano Acuto Sfogato

Voices with these dizzying top registers are extremely rare, but it is interesting to note that at least two occurred during the lifetime of Mozart. One belonged to his sister-in-law Josefa Hofer, born Weber, for whom he wrote the high-lying arias of the Queen of the Night. The other, Lucrezia Agujari (whom the Italians graciously nicknamed *La Bastardella*), Mozart heard sing at Parma when he was fourteen years old. We know that she sang the following phrases because he copied them out in a letter to his sister:

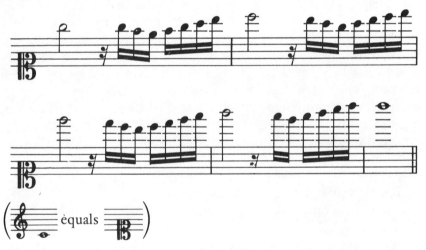

Agujari's Range

The quality of tone of the acutely high coloratura soprano is almost always thin and childlike in the upper register. Indeed, by some physical accident, this singer seems to have retained the range of her childhood pre-pubescent voice (often little girls can make a sort of squeak up to the C''' above high C'') coupling it with fuller but still very light tones in the middle of the range. The lowest notes in these voices are usually unsubstantial and almost lacking in tone, a fact which introduces an almost implacable rule that applies to all singing voices: one extreme has always to be sacrificed for the other. Voices most brilliant at the top almost invariably lack the same power and fullness at the bottom. Examples among today's great singers are Leontyne Price, whose tones are weakest in the lowest part of her range, glorious and soaring at the top, and Joan Sutherland, whose bottom notes are also thin. If a full, round lower register is developed and what are known as the chest tones (to be discussed later) emphasized, the extreme top notes will go flat, have to be screamed or be lost altogether. Birgit Nilsson with both brilliant top and bottom notes has paid for it in a weakening of her middle range. This payment is inexorable in the vocal technique of all singers, even the greatest: power for flexibility, size for subtlety, high notes for low. As has been remarked over and over, "There has never been a perfect voice."

Small and girlish is the voice of the soprano *acuto sfogato*, and so often is its possessor. (This explains why the ragings of the tempestuous Queen of the Night which must be sung by this type of coloratura rarely come over effectively in the opera house.) Some notable high coloratura sopranos of recent times have included Frieda Hempel, Selma Kurz, Maria Ivogün, Lily Pons, Mado Robin, Erna Berger, Kathleen Battle and Editha Gruberova.

There have been several sopranos with freak ranges extending to the C''' above High C'' whose extreme top notes suggest the quality of a peanut vendor's whistle. One of these was Erna Sack, who curiously enough began her career singing contralto roles and then went on to appear very successfully in the high coloratura parts all over Europe during the 1930's, though the middle range of her voice was weak. Even more bizarre to the ears was the voice of the Incan princess, born in Peru and named Emperatriz Chavarri, but known to her fans as Yma Sumac. Her range covered almost four octaves from a masculine, "torch" sounding lower register, to piccolo-like twitterings at its top. Though she never sang in opera and began her career in the United States on the Catskills "borscht" circuit, the beautiful princess built up a tremendous following giving concerts all over the world to audiences awed by the capabilities of the human larynx.

Soubrettes. A second type of light high woman's voice, having some kinship with the soprano *acuto sfogato* because it often has a similar girlish, delicate quality, is sometimes called the soubrette soprano. This voice is as small, light and flexible as the high coloratura but simply lacks her extraordinary top range. (It will, in consequence, have more fullness in the middle and lower part of the compass.) The soubrette soprano sings roles such as Susanna in *Le Nozze di Figaro,* Zerlina in *Don Giovanni,* Despina in *Così fan Tutte* and Sophie in *Der Rosenkavalier,* and not surprisingly the very high coloraturas—Roberta Peters is one—looking for new opportunities will climb down from their heights to sing these juicy, non-coloratura roles.

Possibly because this bright, pretty voice often emanates from young ladies with bright, pretty faces and figures to match, the composers of light operas, operettas and musicals have demanded it of their heroines. As far back as the eighteenth century when John Gay put together *The Beggar's Opera,* he cast Polly Peachum as a soubrette soprano. The heroines of the Gilbert and Sullivan operettas such as Patience, Phyllis in *Iolanthe,* Yum-Yum in *The Mikado* (with her charming "The Moon and I") all call for this type of voice sometimes with a slight coloratura technique as in the staccato passages of Mabel's "Poor Wandering One" in *The Pirates of Penzance.* Offenbach's naughty heroines are light soubrette sopranos as are Victor Herbert's virtuous ones. Lehar, Friml and Romberg all wrote some of their most attractive melodies for this most attractive, if small kind of voice. So did Jerome Kern for his heroine, Magnolia, in what might be described as the first significant American musical, *Showboat,* which he composed a year or so after the new technique of amplifying and recording the voice electrically had been introduced.

This invention of course has had a staggering effect on singing and the singing voice. As far as the soubrette or operetta kind of soprano was concerned it enabled pretty singers to make a career in the theater with a voice of small carrying power. The introduction of the sound movie allowed a number of smiling soubrette sopranos to sing their way into the hearts of millions of people. Jeanette MacDonald, the girlish Deanna Durbin, whose pretty soprano matured when she was in her early teens (as this kind of voice often does), Jane Powell, equally girlish in looks and positively infantile and tiny in sound, were but a few of the stars that people crowded into the movie houses to see and hear. Irene Dunne, though only secondarily a singer, could often be expected to break into a song with her attractive soubrette soprano voice during a quieter moment of one of the madcap comedies in which she frequently played. It is true that in this era various opera stars such as the sopranos Lily Pons and Grace Moore, and the mezzo-sopranos Gladys Swarthout and Risë Stevens also appeared in movies, but they of course never actually needed the amplification that, say, Jane Powell or Kathryn Grayson required.

These last two sopranos remained entirely in the realm of electric enhancement of their voices. In 1942, however, Jeanette MacDonald chose a different path, embarking on a concert career at the height of her fame when she was thirty-nine. Touring the country she gave recitals (unamplified, of course) that included songs by Mozart, Schumann, Hageman and Samuel Barber. In May 1943 she made her debut at Montreal in Gounod's *Roméo et Juliette* with Ezio Pinza as Frère Laurent and Wilfrid Pelletier conducting. Her first live operatic appearance was pronounced a triumph and she went on tour in the opera throughout Canada and in American cities as well, though she did not risk an appearance in New York. She herself was critical of the thinness of her voice and went to study with Lotte Lehmann who was teaching in Santa Barbara. Though they worked on Marguerite in *Faust*, the famous German soprano thought it was too late for her to make an operatic career. They also studied *lieder* and French art songs and in this repertory her teacher was astounded at Jeanette MacDonald's gifts. As late as November 1944 the lovely movie star was still continuing her operatic career in Chicago alternating in *Faust* with Pinza as the Devil and the fine tenor Raoul Jobin as her seducer, and again in *Roméo et Juliette*.

In the thirties there also emerged a star who in a chesty, insinuating voice declared, "My Heart Belongs to Daddy." Less well remembered is that in her early years Texas-born Mary Martin aspired to be a pretty soubrette soprano like Jeanette MacDonald and would audition a MacDonald favorite such as Delibes's "Les Filles de Cadiz." When the great popular composer Jerome Kern heard this rendition he advised Miss Martin to find her own metier and style. Nevertheless as a straight operetta soprano she went out to Hollywood and made a fairly disastrous film called *The Great Victor Herbert*, which comes back occasionally in the lateness of the television night. As everyone knows the utterly charming Miss Martin did find her own metier and style though many years later on a television show with Noel Coward she lapsed back into her old territory by singing in English Madama Butterfly's aria, "Un bel dì."

On the American radio of the 1930's and forties before the onset of television, light sopranos such as Jessica Dragonette, Vivian Della Chiesa and Margaret Speaks had their innings and even sang fairly heavy operatic selections secure in the fact that their voices were riding a boosting system of electronic impulses. One who had the volume to fill the largest of opera houses was strangely enough created by radio. In the 1940's CBS put on an interesting program called "Invitation to Music" which, lacking a sponsor, could be heard late in the evening after the "prime time" hours. On it appeared a young soprano with an extraordinarily beautiful voice who had the opportunity to sing all kinds of music—arias, lieder, French songs and folk songs to the delight and wonder of, I suppose, a limited radio audience. This was Eileen Farrell, the short, chubby wife of a policeman in Staten Island, not committed to the exigencies of a concert and opera career until her children were raised. No one, hearing her only over the radio, could be absolutely certain of the size of her voice because of the power of the microphone to deceive, so that when she finally appeared in person, unamplified, in a stunning recital at Carnegie Hall the audience was left gasping.

The vogue for light operetta sopranos carried into the "golden age" of musicals during the late forties and fifties. The heroines of *Carousel, Most Happy Fella* and *Kiss Me Kate* all call for this appealing, feminine sounding voice, and though today the electronic clangs and bangs of the pop singers and their groups would appear to be drowning it out in popularity let us not forget the mighty drawing power of pert, winsome Julie Andrews—and her pert, winsome sounding soubrette soprano voice.

A Variety of Sopranos. Most of the fine so-called lyric-coloratura sopranos of past and present such as Patti, Melba, Tetrazzini, Galli-Curci, Bidu Sayão, Anna Moffo and Judith Blegen are most properly classified by the Italian term, soprano *leggiero*. Their range usually does not exceed E″ flat or E″ natural and looks like this:

Soprano Leggiero (usual coloratura soprano range)

In the main the soprano *leggiero* usually has the same light, sparkling, ingenue quality of her acutely high-ranging sister, combined with an agile coloratura technique. In recent years their favorite parts—Lucia di Lammermoor, Gilda in *Rigoletto*, Amina in *La Sonnambula*—have been plundered by heavier-voiced sopranos with the requisite agility to sing them. The trail-blazer was Maria Callas, quickly followed by Joan Sutherland and Renata Scotto. Sutherland by transposing the second act aria even attempted the Queen of the Night, but it was not one of her great successes.

The soprano *leggiero* also sings more lyric parts such as Marguerite in *Faust* and the Massenet Manon in which there is an occasional opportunity to display her ability to sing *fioritura*. And there is the poignant role of Mimi in *La Bohème*. Equally these roles can be sung by the slightly larger-voiced lyric soprano who usually has a limited (if any at all) coloratura technique. This kind of soprano, which is the most common of the female voices, cultivates the following range:

Lyric (also Soubrette) Soprano

The lyric soprano has a generous and appealing repertory from which to choose. She may sing Puccini's much put-upon Madama Butterfly or Liù in *Turandot*. She can get stabbed as Nedda in *Pagliacci* or strangled as Desdemona. If she prefers a more cheerful evening's work she can always move in on the soubrette soprano territory and sing the charming roles of Susanna and Zerlina. Classic examples of the lyric soprano at the Metropolitan Opera House have been Dorothy Kirsten and Licia Albanese.

The Massenet Manon Lescaut is sung by a lyric soprano. The Puccini Manon, a heavier role, is sung by lyric and *spinto* sopranos.

Their repertory included Mimi, Manon Lescaut, Violetta in *La Traviata*, Micaela and Marguerite. Both these singers, however, eventually went in the other direction and pushed on to the part of Tosca, a role usually undertaken by the next-size larger soprano, the *spinto*, or even the largest, the dramatic.

"*Spinto*" is the Italian for "pushed, urged on" which exactly defines this type of voice—a lyric soprano "urged on." The *spinto* has the same range as the lyric, but her low notes must have more power and emphasis to do justice to such roles as the Leonoras in *Trovatore* and *La Forza del Destino*, Tosca, Aida and the Countess in *Le Nozze di Figaro*. At the same time the possessor of this voice must be able to shade it down to a fine pianissimo, right up to the high C″ called for in Aida's Nile Scene aria, and to move it in passages where flexibility is demanded, as in the fast-moving sections of Leonora's arias in *Il Trovatore*. The voice of Leontyne Price is a perfect example of a *spinto* and Verdi might almost have had her in mind when he wrote the operas of his middle years, *La Forza del Destino, Don Carlo, Un Ballo in Maschera* and *Aida*, as well as the soprano part of the *Requiem*. It would probably be correct to describe Renata Tebaldi as a *spinto* also, though with great versatility she essayed an essentially lyric part such as Mimi as well as taking on the heavy roles of Madeleine in *Andrea Chénier* and La Gioconda. In passing, it is interesting to note that Joan Sutherland originally possessed a voice capable of being trained as a *spinto*, but instead lightened it to gain the wonderful agility it now possesses—another example of the inevitable bargain that has to be struck in the vocal process. Nevertheless Miss Sutherland has an unusually large voice for the soprano *leggiero* roles that she most often sings.

Currently we have examples of two Italian artists who have pushed on to become *spinto* sopranos. When Maria Callas sang with the La Scala company at the Edinburgh Festival in 1957 she cancelled the last of her performances of Amina in *La Sonnambula* for reasons of poor health, though she then flew off to Venice for a party at which was present Aristotle Onassis. Back in Scotland a twenty-two-year-old soprano *leggiero* named Renata Scotto was rushed in to replace Callas and won a huge success. Scotto had a lovely fluid voice and great dramatic talent. (She has always said she was greatly influenced by Callas.) Continuing her career, she sang the *leggiero* roles—Lucia, Gilda—continued into the lyric parts—Mimi, Manon Lescaut—and then embarked on, to her cost, the *spinto* requirements of Tosca, Adriana Lecouvreur and, most disastrously of all, Norma. Today, while her voice in the middle range still retains something of its erstwhile sheen, the high notes are wobbly and strident and the emphasized low notes husky and guttural.

A second Italian soprano who has pushed on is the charming Mirella Freni, a winning Mimi (she appeared opposite Luciano Pavarotti in the first in the series of "Live from the Met" broadcasts in 1977), a vulnerable Marguerite and Liù. Lately however, Freni has forced her voice into parts such as Aida or Elisabetta in *Don Carlo* and again the cost is apparent. The quality has suffered a loss of bloom and there is now a more evident break between the registers of her voice.

With the *spinto* we reach the first kind of soprano heavy enough to perform a Wagnerian heroine—Eva in *Die Meistersinger* (the lightest); Elsa in *Lohengrin;* Elisabeth in *Tannhäuser;* Senta in *Der Fliegende Holländer* and Sieglinde in *Die Walküre*. This is a repertory that the incomparable Leonie Rysanek has explored with such success for twenty-five years and into which, currently, Anna

Eva, in *Die Meistersinger*, is sung by the *spinto* and (occasionally) dramatic soprano.

Tomowa-Sintow and Eva Marton are feeling their way. The rest of the Wagnerian soprano roles, Isolde, the *Ring's* three Brünnhildes and Kundry in *Parsifal*, together with Richard Strauss's frenzied Elektra, require the services of the heaviest of high women's voices, the dramatic soprano.

"The dramatic soprano is the rarest voice produced by nature," writes Blanche Marchesi, one of the less manic and more intelligent authorities on the subject of the singing voice. "It is like a new-born Newfoundland dog, clumsy, heavy, shapeless . . . The heavier and bigger the voice the more carefully must it be trained."

The dramatic soprano has about the same range as the *spinto:*

Dramatic Soprano

This voice must be able to soar over great Verdian ensembles or the heavy Wagnerian orchestra as well as to sustain literally hours of singing in one evening. The three Brünnhildes, Isolde, Elektra, Leonore in *Fidelio*, Donna Anna in *Don Giovanni* and Norma are all usually sung by a dramatic soprano, though the last three are also undertaken by singers with slightly lighter and smaller voices. In our own time Zinka Milanov was described as a dramatic soprano but eschewed Wagnerian roles; Rosa Ponselle never did either (though there is a ravishing early recording of her singing Elsa's "Traum" in Italian). Both, on the other hand, sang Norma, which Lilli Lehmann, the extraordinary dramatic soprano at the turn of this century who sang practically everything, declared to be much more demanding and exhausting than the *Götterdämmerung* Brünnhilde.

The whole classifying of voices is made still more troublesome by the fact that singers change and that as they grow older their voices become bigger, darker and less flexible. Eleanor Steber, for example, began her career at the Metropolitan singing a light, lyric part such as Sophie, and ended up portraying the Marschallin and Elsa and Donna Anna as well. Tebaldi ranged from Mimi through the *spinto* Tosca and two Verdi Leonoras, *Il Trovatore* and *La Forza del Destino*, to the dramatic La Gioconda. In days of yore these progressions from light parts to heavy were more extreme. The hard working American, Lillian Nordica, made her way from Gilda to Isolde, while the most amazing of all, Lilli Lehmann, sang everything from the Queen of the Night to the three Brünnhildes. Age appears to be an important factor in the maturing of the dramatic soprano voice. Flagstad, for example, working her way through the lighter parts—Mimi, Nedda and eventually Aida—never sang a Wagnerian role until she approached thirty-five. She did not possess a coloratura technique like Lilli Lehmann but her voice, while lacking flexibility was definitely larger and more opulent.

In our own day we have had the extraordinarily versatile Birgit Nilsson who switched from the *spinto* parts of Aida and Amelia in

The Marschallin in *Der Rosenkavalier* has been sung by almost every kind
of soprano voice.

Un Ballo in Maschera to Elektra, Isolde and the three Brünnhildes.
Nilsson never sang Norma because it required too much of a
coloratura technique; nevertheless Winthrop Sargeant writes, in a
profile of the soprano, that she could sing the second act Queen of
the Night aria from *Die Zauberflöte* with its repeated F"s above
high C" but only after her voice had warmed up for several hours.
When the conductor, Karl Böhm, impugned her claim she bade
him come to her dressing room after conducting a performance of
Götterdämmerung in which she was the Brünnhilde. Böhm com-
plied and Nilsson delivered the aria just as she had said she
could.
    When she was not yet twenty-six years old, Maria Callas,
whose voice was properly classified as a *spinto* soprano, performed the astonishing feat of alternating the dramatic soprano
role of Brünnhilde in *Die Walküre* with the *leggiero* one of Elvira in *I
Puritani*. It is one more example of the reckless self-destructive-
ness that brought down her career, as she was far too young to be
attempting the heavy Wagnerian part. Later, when Callas was a
superstar she refused to alternate Violetta in *La Traviata* and the

slightly heavier Lady Macbeth at the Metropolitan Opera whereupon General Manager Rudolf Bing shocked the operatic world by firing her.

Throughout this discussion the reader may have noticed that I have scarcely mentioned one of the most celebrated of all operatic roles—Violetta in *La Traviata*. What kind of soprano sings this rich, starring part? So wonderfully complex and complete is the musical characterization that almost every kind of soprano voice suits it. Violetta's gaiety, her shallowness, her frailness could be well expressed by the tones of the soprano *leggiero* and so such artists as Melba, Tetrazzini, Galli-Curci and Bidu Sayão have taken the part with great effect. Because Violetta is still a young woman, warm, feminine and lovely, lyric sopranos such as Lucrezi Bori, Licia Albanese, and Mirella Freni have also sung the role. Violetta is also a woman with a certain grandness of character, noble in her sacrifice of Alfredo and her struggle against affliction, so that the larger-voiced *spinto* sopranos such as Claudia Muzio, Rosa Ponselle and Renata Tebaldi proved equally effective in the part.

All sopranos, of course, long to sing Violetta and since only the very heavy dramatic voices are unsuited to it, most great singers have attempted the role over the years. Some, not already mentioned, include Christine Nilsson, Sembrich, Nordica, Melba, Geraldine Farrar, Mary Garden and Maria Callas. The tremendously self-disciplined Lilli Lehmann sang, in all, 170 different roles in 119 operas. Towards the end of her career when she was close to sixty, she gave an interview to the music critic W. J. Henderson, at her home just outside of Berlin. Among the questions raised was whether Frau Lehmann would retire as usual to the Tyrol for the summer. Not before she first sang three engagements at Ischl, was the reply. And what part would she be singing, inquired Henderson.

"A beautiful and yet somewhat roguish smile broke across her noble face," he writes, "as she said in a half whisper: 'Violetta.'"

The Mystical High C″. Before climbing down from the altitudes of the soprano voice let us linger a little longer to consider that famous note around which whirls such excitement and glamor—the high C″. In giving the *spinto* and dramatic soprano ranges I have indicated what notes *ideally* these kind of voices should possess. Many of us recall the effortless high C″ of Flagstad in her prime. More recently we heard the amazing Birgit Nilsson who approached this note from the top and sometimes sang it a tiny bit sharp. But for every Nilsson and Flagstad there are dozens of *spinto* and dramatic sopranos for whom the high C″ is just out of reach or else is achieved by what must in all honesty be called a scream. Is it any wonder? To utter a high C″ absolutely on pitch the tiny edges of a soprano's vocal cords must flutter over a thousand vibrations per second.

Usually high C″ comes easily enough to a lyric soprano. The natural extent of some beautiful *spinto* and dramatic soprano voices, however, seems often to be only to a high A′ or B′ flat; after that extreme difficulty is encountered in reaching the B′ natural and top C″. This appears to be another example of the inexorable rule of sacrifice in vocalization: since these larger-voiced sopranos have very full middle and lower registers they must pay the price for it with their high tones.

"When you wish to discuss great singers," soprano Geraldine Farrar is supposed to have said, "there are two you must put aside. One is Caruso, the other is Rosa Ponselle." Yet the wonderful Ponselle with her "seamless" scale and fascinating quality of tone never seems to have had secure top notes. She transposed the "Casta diva" in *Norma* down a whole tone and after she cracked on a high C″ in *Aida* one evening never sang the role again. Helen Traubel during a radio broadcast of *Tannhäuser* broke on the high note in Elisabeth's joyous greeting to the Hall of Song. Cruel and inhuman it would seem for a great artist to be remembered for one blot on an otherwise sensitive and beautiful performance, but it is often the case.

In more recent times Renata Tebaldi at the end of her career, having a large middle and lower voice had to scream her B′ naturals and high C″s, which the listener almost dreaded to hear. Victoria de los Angeles, who possessed unusually luscious middle and lower sections to her voice, came more or less to do the same. Time and age have something to do, of course, with the destruction of a singer's high C″, but in their younger days neither of these artists ever had an easy top.

Is it possible for a soprano with a fine *spinto* or dramatic voice but lacking a proper top C″ to make a career? Let us examine a random sampling of roles. All the heavier Mozart parts, with the exception of Constanze in *Die Entführung aus dem Serail*, are available to her—that is, Donna Anna, Donna Elvira, the Countess and Fiordiligi. Though Richard Strauss often wrote cruelly for the singing voice, she can also do the Marschallin. Wagner has a reputation for having made impossible demands on the voice, but in fact it is possible to sing almost all his heroines without a high C″. Elsa, for example, goes no higher than a hysterical high B′ natural when the nobles rush in to kill Lohengrin. In fact Ortrud's music, peppered with A′ sharps, would appear to have a higher tessitura than Elsa's, though Ortrud is not required to sing beyond A′ sharp or B′ flat. In *Die Walküre* Brünnhilde only touches high C″ in her opening shout, but must sustain a high B′ natural at the conclusion of it—a cruel test for a singer on making her entrance. Thereafter she has no more of these extreme top tones to perform. Nor does Sieglinde, ever. The *Siegfried* Brünnhilde however, full of B′ flats and naturals, also has two high C″s (the second optional) and for this reason must be accounted the most arduous of the three Brünnhildes even though it is the shortest.

It is when we examine the Italian repertory that still more difficulties arise for our high C″-less soprano. Some of the fascinating heroines of Verdi's middle and late operas she can manage such as Leonora in *La Forza del Destino*, in which she must sustain a B′ natural, but nothing higher. Verdi, however, gives the high B′ flat a tremendous workout as he does also in *Il Trovatore*. Here, there are high C″s and even D″ flats in the runs and cadenzas of the other Leonora's music, but these can be either lightly touched—far easier than sustaining the note—or the D″ flat in the cadenza of the last act aria changed to B′ flat.

What if a soprano lacking a high C″ wishes to sing the role of the hapless Aida? Lurking in the second part of her aria "O patria mia" is a top C″ within the following slow phrase:

From "O patria mia"

There is no escaping it. It cannot be transposed nor glossed over. Mercilessly it demands that the soprano reveal the state of her high C" to the audience, a revelation which unfortunately may not be altogether pleasing. Sometimes we are treated to a scream. At others it will be a musical note of a sort but sagging below the pitch. When Leontyne Price sings this passage she soars up to the C" with total assurance, diminishes the note as Verdi demands, and glides back down the phrase in one breath, triumphantly asserting that the art of great singing has not been lost.

S O P R A N O S
Some acuto sfogato *and* leggiero *soprano roles*

Amina (*La Sonnambula*)	A part sung by Callas and Sutherland with *spinto* voices.
Fiakermilli (*Arabella*)	
Gilda (*Rigoletto*)	Toscanini chose Zinka Milanov, a dramatic soprano, to sing Gilda's third act music, but it is usually done by a girlish, innocent-sounding voice.
Lakmé	
Lucia di Lammermoor	
Olympia (*Les Contes d'Hoffmann*)	"The one role properly suited to the coloratura soprano since it calls for a negation of human intelligence," wrote record administrator Walter Legge of this mechanical part.
Philine (*Mignon*)	
Queen of Shemakha (*Le Coq d'Or*)	
Queen of the Night (*Die Zauberflöte*)	A part that has to be sung by the high soprano *acuto sfogato* with a F" above high C".
Rosina (*Il Barbiere di Siviglia*)	Written for the mezzo *leggiero* but grabbed by coloratura sopranos who transpose the music upwards.
Zerbinetta (*Ariadne auf Naxos*)	The most difficult and demanding of the *acuto sfogato* roles.

S O P R A N O S
Some Soubrette Soprano Roles

Adele (*Die Fledermaus*)
Adina (*L'Elisir d'Amore*)

Blonde (*Die Entführung aus dem Serail*)
Despina (*Così fan Tutte*)
Gretel (*Hänsel und Gretel*)
Lauretta (*Gianni Schicchi*)

Florence Easton created the part at the Metropolitan the same season she sang Isolde.

Marzelline (*Fidelio*)
Nanetta (*Falstaff*)
Norina (*Don Pasquale*)
Sophie (*Der Rosenkavalier*)
Susanna (*Le Nozze di Figaro*)
Zerlina (*Don Giovanni*)

A mezzo-soprano, Maria Ewing, currently sings this role at the Metropolitan as recently did Rosalind Elias, but it is not customary.

SOPRANOS
Some Lyric Roles

Antonia (*Les Contes d'Hoffmann*)
Cio-Cio-San (*Madama Butterfly*)
Desdemona (*Otello*)
Euridice (*Orfeo ed Euridice*)
Juliette (*Roméo et Juliette*)
Louise
Liù (*Turandot*)
Manon (Massenet version)
Manon Lescaut (Puccini version)
Micaela (*Carmen*)
Mimi (*La Bohème*)
Musetta (*La Bohème*)
Nedda (*I Pagliacci*)
Pamina (*Die Zauberflöte*)
Rosalinda (*Die Fledermaus*)
Violetta (*La Traviata*)

A heavy lyric part which might also be classified as light *spinto*.

See discussion in text (p. 63).

SOPRANOS

Some Spinto *and Lighter Dramatic Roles*

Adriana Lecouvreur
Aida
Amelia (*Un Ballo in Maschera*)
Amelia (*Simon Boccanegra*)
Arabella
Ariadne (*Ariadne auf Naxos*)
Chrysothemis (*Elektra*)

Constanze (*Die Entführung aus dem Serail*)	A role requiring a *spinto*-sized voice having the technique of a soprano *leggiero*. Difficult to cast.
Countess (*Le Nozze di Figaro*)	The versatile Marguerite Matzenauer, a mezzo-soprano was cast—or perhaps miscast—in the 1917 revival at the Metropolitan.
Donna Anna (*Don Giovanni*)	Requires considerable agility.
Donna Elvira (*Don Giovanni*)	Slightly lighter voice than Donna Anna, but also demands some agility.
Elisabetta (*Don Carlo*)	
Elisabeth (*Tannhäuser*)	Also sung by heavy dramatic sopranos such as Flagstad or Nilsson.
Elsa (*Lohengrin*)	As Elisabeth.
Elvira (*Ernani*)	
Fiordiligi (*Così fan Tutte*)	
Gioconda	A heavy part, taxing to the light *spinto* voice.
Giulietta (*Les Contes d'Hoffmann*)	Also sung by the mezzo-soprano.
Gutrune (*Götterdämmerung*)	
Lady Macbeth	Sometimes sung by mezzo-sopranos, with their darker, more evil sounding tone quality.
Leonora (*La Forza del Destino*)	
Leonora (*Il Trovatore*)	
Marie (*Wozzeck*)	
Marschallin (*Der Rosenkavalier*)	The first Marschallin at the Metropolitan was Frieda Hempel, who the same season sang the Queen of the Night. Another was the heavy dramatic soprano, Helen Traubel.

Mistress Ford (*Falstaff*)

Norma   A tremendously taxing role, requiring great stamina, extreme flexibility and a voice of noble proportions. Joan Sutherland was the sixth soprano to attempt the part in the history of the Metropolitan. Lately a number of singers have performed it, often with lamentable results.

Salome   Occasionally sung by a heavy dramatic soprano like Nilsson. The lyric soprano Teresa Stratas has also performed it.

Santuzza (*Cavalleria Rusticana*)   A mettlesome role that is sung by either a *spinto* or a mezzo-soprano and gives trouble to both ranges of voices.

Senta (*Der Fliegende Holländer*)

Sieglinde (*Die Walküre*)   Also sung by heavy dramatic sopranos.

Tatiana (*Eugen Onegin*)

Tosca

Turandot   The versatile Birgit Nilsson, a heavy dramatic soprano, sang this role. It requires a brilliant top to the voice.

SOPRANOS

The Heaviest Dramatic Roles

3 Brünnhildes (*Die Walküre, Siegfried, Götterdämmerung*)   Melba, a soprano *leggiero*, sang one disastrous *Siegfried* Brünnhilde. The mezzo-sopranos, Marguerite Matzenauer and Karin Branzell sang the *Die Walküre* Brünnhilde at the Metropolitan.

Elektra

Isolde   Matzenauer sang this role at the Metropolitan also.

Kundry (*Parsifal*)   Frequently sung by mezzo-sopranos such as Tatiana Troyanos and Mignon Dunn.

Leonore (*Fidelio*)   Sung also by the lighter-voiced sopranos like Lotte Lehmann and presently Hildegard Behrens.

THE LOWER WOMEN'S VOICES

Some people use the word "alto" to describe all women's voices
that are not sopranos, but the term is a loose one to say the least,
if one considers that there are at least four categories of lower
women's voices (which, needless to say, overlap) and indeed a
fifth if we include that large band of lady pop singers who belt out
their songs entirely in what is known as the chest register. Let us
begin with the most unusual of these five.

The Coloratura Mezzo. In the mid-1930's, when I was ten years
old and commencing a life-long passion for the singing voice,
coloratura singing meant one thing: the agile, running tones of a
high soprano such as Marcella Sembrich (heard on a one-sided
Red Seal record on my grandfather's cabinet, wind-up "Talking
Machine"). Contemporary coloratura singers were the incomparable Lily Pons and at the second Student performance presented
at the Metropolitan Opera in 1938, charming Bidu Sayão as
Rosina in *Il Barbiere di Siviglia*.

Not until a few more years had passed did a record of Ernestine
Schumann-Heink reveal that the darker, heavier sounding mez-
zo-soprano could also move her voice with the flexibility of her
higher ranging sisters. *Il segreto per esser felice . . .* trumpeted
forth the extraordinary Schumann-Heink in the "Brindisi" from
Donizetti's *Lucrezia Borgia*. Her voice had last been heard at the
Metropolitan in 1932 when, aged seventy-one, she sang the
Siegfried Erda. But here she was on a record made many years
before uttering trills, *gruppetti* and great skips with effortless ease.
Further recordings revealed another huge-voiced singer with a
coloratura technique: Sigrid Onegin, born in Sweden of German
parents, had a sumptuous yet fluid voice replete with an
astonishing trill. Further research turned up the charmingly
florid, if vibrato-ridden technique of the Spanish mezzo-soprano
Conchita Supervia. But at the time of which I am writing, the late
1930's, there were no mezzo-sopranos who performed coloratura
music, not Risë Stevens, not Bruna Castagna, not Kerstin
Thorborg.

Only in 1945 did American audiences hear a *live* coloratura
mezzo-soprano when the French-trained Jennie Tourel sang
Rosina in *Il Barbiere di Siviglia* at the Metropolitan in the original

Rosina in *Il Barbiere di Siviglia,* written for the coloratura mezzo but grabbed by the coloratura soprano.

key that Rossini wrote. Nor was this novelty rapturously received. The critic of the New York *Sun,* Oscar Thompson, thought that though she sang the notes "as they were written" the composer must have had "a brighter voice in mind irrespective of the compass of the role."

Once again the fortunes of the coloratura mezzo foundered until the appearance of one of the most extraordinary virtuoso singers in the history of singing. I speak of the peerless Marilyn Horne. Strangely, Marilyn Horne's American debut at San Francisco in 1960 was as Marie in *Wozzeck,* a highly difficult soprano part. Not until several years later did she create a furore as a large-voiced mezzo-soprano with an astonishing coloratura technique when with Joan Sutherland she sang a concert performance of Rossini's *Semiramide* in Carnegie Hall. Since then she has sung everything from Carmen to Eboli in *Don Carlo* and, in recital, the "Immolation Scene" from Götterdämmerung to "I Dream of Jeannie with the Light Brown Hair" accompanied by a harp. During the Metropolitan Opera's centennial season the company mounted their first production of a Handel opera *Rinaldo,*

especially for Marilyn Horne. With her bravura feats she scored
another in a long succession of triumphs.

Since Miss Horne's first brilliant assumption of mezzo *leggiero*
roles there has been a resurgence of this kind of voice, particularly
among lighter-voiced mezzo-sopranos such as Patricia Johnson,
Huguette Tourangeau and at the Metropolitan the winsome
Frederica von Stade and the beguiling Maria Ewing.

Heavier-voiced mezzo-sopranos of our time with what is
known as a *voce d'agilità* have included Shirley Verrett, Agnes
Baltsa and Christa Ludwig. The latter can be heard singing in a
recording a remarkable "Una voce poco fa" from *Il Barbiere di
Siviglia*—in German, however, so that it comes out: "Frag ich
mein beklomm'nes Herz."

The coloratura mezzo and the lyric mezzo share the same
range:

Light and Lyric. With the same range as their coloratura counterparts but lacking their proficiency in florid song, lyric mezzo-
sopranos are heard in such roles as the poignant Mignon in
Thomas's opera or the seductive Maddalena in *Rigoletto*. Sometimes they venture into bigger, more dramatic territory, as
traversed by Charlotte in Massenet's *Werther*. Risë Stevens, a
much admired lyric mezzo-soprano of her time, undertook the
big part of Dalila but she never attempted Verdi's heavy dramatic
parts of Eboli or Amneris in *Aida*.

Lyric mezzo-sopranos are also likely to turn up as amorous
youths, Cherubino in *Le Nozze di Figaro*, Octavian in *Der Rosenkavalier*, cynical youths such as Nicklausse in *Les Contes d'Hoffmann*
or just plain boys like Hänsel in *Hänsel und Gretel*. Sopranos
however, sometimes steal Cherubino and Hänsel from the
mezzos, particularly in Germany. It has happened in New York as
well: Geraldine Farrar sang Cherubino at the Metropolitan as has
another charming soprano, Teresa Stratas. *Spinto* sopranos such
as Maria Jeritza or more recently Gwyneth Jones are more likely to
make off with Octavian.

Another part that the lyric mezzo-soprano claims on the basis of tradition but has a dreadful time holding on to is Carmen. Georges Bizet originally offered the title role of his opera to a beautiful Frenchwoman with a light soprano voice named Marie Roze. Fortunately she recognized that she was not suited to "the very scabrous side of this character," as she put it, and turned down the offer. Bizet's next choice was a mezzo-soprano, Célestine Galli-Marié, and she became the first Carmen. Thus we are not really enlightened as to what kind of voice the composer intended for his wonderful operatic creation.

Carmen is like Violetta, a varied role full of every kind of opportunity in which to shine. Not only do the various kinds of mezzos battle among themselves to sing it, but the sopranos have also moved in to wrest the role—with variable results however—from their darker voiced sisters. The kittenish Adelina Patti, for example, sang Carmen and it was pronounced one of her few failures. The majestic Lilli Lehmann sang Carmen and it was pronounced one of *her* few failures. The much admired singing actress Olive Fremstad, though popular in the part in Germany, gathered little enthusiasm for her Carmen in the United States. The beautiful sopranos Geraldine Farrar and Maria Jeritza did not wholly please with their interpretations of the role, and even the fabulous Rosa Ponselle was scathingly reviewed when she sang the gypsy; though some of these criticisms were later retracted. This would seem to prove that Carmen was perhaps intended for the darker, more voluptuous sounding mezzo-soprano voice— though it is true that both Fremstad and Ponselle had darker voices than is usual for sopranos.

On the other hand, the most celebrated Carmen of all time was indeed a soprano, Emma Calvé, who had however richly colored middle and lower registers to her voice. Another highly successful soprano Carmen was Mary Garden, a remarkable singing actress. In three of the current recordings of Carmen the role is sung by sopranos, Maria Callas, Victoria de los Angeles and Leontyne Price. Only one of them attempted the part on the stage. Victoria de los Angeles late in her career sang *Carmen* with the New York City Opera. It turned out to be one of the few performances this lovely soprano gave that was an unmitigated disaster.

Of the many mezzo-sopranos who have had their innings with

Carmen one of the most notable was the Spanish Maria Gay. People who went to the Metropolitan in the thirties will remember the colorful interpretation of Bruna Castagna while those lucky enough to attend Covent Garden at about the same period will recall that of Conchita Supervia. Marilyn Horne opened the Metropolitan opera season of 1972–1973 with a highly successful portrayal of the gypsy. As the new production was mounted under the baton of Leonard Bernstein, Harvey E. Phillips, a writer and opera lover, followed its every detail. His book, *The Carmen Chronicle: The Making of an Opera*, gives a unique insight into the arduous work, time and patience that singers devote to an operatic performance. Phillips also went to the recording sessions after the premiere and noted how the performance offered to the public on discs was simply not authentic because of all the dubbing and splicing that occurred.

The dramatic soprano and the dramatic mezzo-soprano share approximately the same ranges:

Dramatic Mezzo-Soprano

What then is the difference between the two? The answer lies predominantly in the quality of the voice, the mezzo's being darker and more lush, with an emphasized lower end of the range. These attributes conjure up an atmosphere of seductiveness, perhaps used for an evil end; or even a feeling of dark, out-and-out villainy. Pity the poor dramatic mezzo-soprano, who loves but is unloved (Amneris, Eboli), who is wickedly voluptuous (Dalila, Venus) witchlike and obsessed (Azucena, Ulrica) or just plain bad news (Ortrud). Sometimes she has right on her side (Fricka) but the public considers her a scold. And sometimes she is totally ignored by operatic composers, as for instance, Puccini, who never wrote for the big mezzo voice. Since the dramatic mezzo-soprano approximates the range of the *Spinto* and dramatic sopranos, no wonder she often dreams of escaping into more elevated realms where she is good, noble even, and where above all she gets her man—if only in heaven.

Sometimes in training the singing voice an inexperienced or incompetent teacher can make a serious mistake. Hearing the full, dark lower notes of a young, exceptionally musical girl born in Sweden but who grew up in Minnesota, the first vocal pedagogue of Olive Fremstad trained her as a contralto. In doing so he emphasized the bottom and middle tones of her voice perhaps up to F'. With the immutable law in singing of sacrifice, this meant that any higher notes the handsome young woman with a splendid dramatic talent might have possessed were slighted and therefore left weak.

Let us follow Fremstad's most unusual career. Fortunately she was able to come to Europe where she sang for Lilli Lehmann, who at once advised her to train as a mezzo-soprano or even true soprano, and gave her scales and exercises that removed the stress from the low, dragging down notes of the voice. This produced a brighter quality and strengthened the upper tones of its long range. After two years of study Fremstad made her debut as a mezzo-soprano in Germany in 1895 and for the next eight years sang the entire mezzo repertory, lyric and dramatic, all over Europe and at Covent Garden.

Fremstad, one of the most dedicated of singing artists, however, was never satisfied. When she made her debut at the Metropolitan in 1903, it was in the soprano role of Sieglinde, a part which in range and tessitura lies comparatively low. That same season she also sang Venus, Brangäne and Fricka, all parts usually considered the property of the mezzo. The next year she added the marginal role of Kundry to her repertory, and the one after that found her interpreting the *Siegfried* Brünnhilde, a role that can only be sung by a true soprano. In 1907 she became New York's first Salome in a single gripping performance before the opera was forced off the boards on the charge of prurience. Finally on New Year's Day, 1908, she sang her first Isolde with Gustav Mahler as conductor. Quite literally she had turned into a soprano before the very ears of the public. The critics were amazed:

"Mme. Fremstad's voice is of indescribable beauty in this music, in its richness and power, its infinite modulation in all the shades of extremes of dramatic significance. It never sounded finer in quality and never seemed more perfectly under her control. And her singing was a revelation, in the fact that the music was in very few places higher than she could easily encompass with her voice. The voice seems, in truth, to have reached a higher altitude and to move in it without strain and without effort."

Thereafter, during a career that seems all too short* for an artist whose singing "in her highest moments . . . took on the quality of genius," Fremstad also sang the other Brünnhildes, Tosca and Elsa.

This gradual transition effected in numerous and continuing performances before the public was a most unusual feat. In subsequent years at the Metropolitan audiences occasionally heard mezzo-sopranos such as Marguerite Matzenauer and Karin Branzell in the soprano role of *Die Walküre* Brünnhilde with Matzenauer singing Isolde and the Countess in *Le Nozze di Figaro* as well. These ladies, however, did not *remain* up. One who did with fine artistic if not totally successful vocal results was Rose Bampton, who made her debut at the Metropolitan on her twenty-third birthday in November 1932 singing the mezzo part of Laura in *La Gioconda*. For four seasons she sang a limited number of mezzo roles while working to transform herself into a soprano.† This transition took place at the end of the 1937–38 season as Donna Anna. Thereafter, she slowly added Aida, Elisabeth, Sieglinde, Elsa and Kundry to her repertory. One of the biggest moments of her career was when Toscanini chose her to sing Leonore in *Fidelio* in the first of his celebrated series of broadcast operas. An intelligent, sensitive singer, Bampton's transition to a soprano never entirely worked. Neither properly a mezzo nor a soprano but something in between, she was the victim of one of those malicious tricks that nature sometimes plays on singers.

In 1943 in a performance when Bampton undertook her first Sieglinde at the Metropolitan, the ninth Valkyrie, Schwertleite, was a young American mezzo-soprano, Margaret Harshaw. By 1947 she had thoroughly established herself in the big mezzo parts such as Amneris, Azucena and Ulrica. Four years later she was engaged by Covent Garden as a soprano to sing the three

---

*She sang only eleven seasons at the Metropolitan.

†Reviewing the first edition of *The Singing Voice* a critic in the *Times Literary Supplement* wrote that Miss Bampton began "as a soprano and swiftly returned to her former vocal estate." If so, there are no public performances on record of her singing soprano *prior* to her mezzo appearances.

Brünnhildes in the *Ring*, appearances she was unfortunately prevented from making. The following year she appeared in Wagnerian roles in New York and returned to London in 1953 for her first *Die Walküre* and *Siegfried* Brünnhildes. Thereafter she dropped all her mezzo roles, usually a necessity in the process of going up, lest they drag the voice down. Like Bampton, Harshaw was an intelligent, admirable artist with a powerful, silvery voice that proved effective for a number of years in the Wagnerian soprano repertory. And yet again she never sounded effortless, never could make her voice soar with the ease and brilliance of the true dramatic soprano. Would it have been better not to have made the transition? At the time Harshaw turned soprano there was a dearth of Brünnhildes and Kundrys: certainly the dimensions of her career were much extended by the change.

The temptation for a mezzo-soprano to go up when the juicy and sympathetic soprano roles hang so temptingly near is therefore sometimes very great. Just a slight stretch (so it seems) and they are captured. Actually, stretching the compass of a voice and singing in a tessitura that is not comfortable, while possible, is also very dangerous. The two marvelously talented Garcia sisters, Maria Malibran and Pauline Viardot, appear to have been mezzos who added top notes to their voices to sing such parts as the soprano role of Norma. Whether Malibran's voice would have endured very long the treatment to which she subjected it is difficult to say as she died so young. Viardot, who at the age of thirty was described by Gounod as "already nearing her end, and singing out of tune all the time," summed it up in advice she gave to a young singer: "Don't do as I did. I wanted to sing everything and I spoilt my voice." In our own time the fine mezzo-soprano Christa Ludwig began to sing and record a number of soprano roles and seemed to be tending towards a take-over of the entire repertory. The strain, however, on her resplendent voice soon began to show in her performances and though announced to sing the *Siegfried* Brünnhilde under von Karajan, she stepped down in a return to her old mezzo ways.

Also in our time we have examples of two beautiful and gifted mezzo-sopranos who have ventured into the higher soprano realms. Grace Bumbry, who studied under Lotte Lehmann, was the first black singer to perform at Bayreuth during the 1961–1963 festivals, singing the high-ranging part of Venus in *Tannhäuser*. A splendid Amneris and Eboli, she then climbed into the soprano roles of Tosca and Salome with great success. An attempt at Leonora in *La Forza del Destino*, a part strewn with high B' flats and B' naturals succeeded less well when she performed it at the beginning of the 1983–84 season of the Metropolitan.

Early in the 1960's Shirley Verrett took second place in the Metropolitan Opera auditions singing the "Habanera" from *Carmen*. This largely self-taught artist and fine musician went on to win international recognition performing the mezzo-soprano parts in the major opera houses of the world. Then she decided to venture into the higher altitudes of Tosca, Leonore in *Fidelio* and most dangerous of all, Norma. "She is by achievement the best mezzo in the world," was the comment of the late, keenly perceptive record impresario Walter Legge. "She should be forbidden to sing Norma. Adalgisa won't harm her but Norma will. It's the last act that really kills." On the evidence of Verrett's subsequent vocal problems and frequent cancellations Mr. Legge was absolutely right.

Both glamorous divas, Grace Bumbry and Shirley Verrett, dressed to the teeth and in their best vocal estate, gave a joint recital at Carnegie Hall that included many arias from the soprano repertory and finished up to an ovation for the duet, "Mira, o Norma." As an encore they changed roles, Norma for Adalgisa and Adalgisa for Norma and sang it again. It was an afternoon of legendary singing.

Some who made highly successful transitions from mezzo-soprano to soprano, have included Edyth Walker, Gertrude Kappel, Dusolina Giannini and Anny Konetzni. More recently, the fine singing actress Gwyneth Jones started out as a lower-voiced singer. Her singing, however, of the *spinto* and dramatic soprano repertory has been afflicted by great unevenness. The same may be said currently of Renata Scotto who also began as a mezzo-soprano.

Much rarer are the cases of sopranos who have moved down to darker levels of the mezzo. In our own time we have had two examples: Regina Resnik and Helga Dernesch. Resnik made her Metropolitan debut on twenty-four hours' notice with an hour and a quarter rehearsal as Leonora in *Il Trovatore* in December, 1944, and thereafter sang many *spinto* soprano parts such as Aida, Tosca, both Donna Anna and Donna Elvira, Sieglinde and Butterfly. Her voice was full and luscious in the middle and lower parts of the range, but her top tones were often shrill and unreliable. After ten years Resnik began to make fewer and fewer performances at the Metropolitan and in the 1954–55 season dropped out altogether, only to appear the following year singing mezzo roles exclusively. Her voice by then had assumed a darker quality with more heavily emphatic low tones. Thus the career of this fine artist renewed itself. Interestingly, almost twenty-five years after her debut as a soprano her voice took on the quality of the lowest of all women's voices—the contralto.

"Une Voix Obscène.". The distinction between the mezzo-soprano and the contralto is often ill defined. The range of the contralto, however, is much lower.

Contralto

A true contralto has a dark, sometimes lugubrious sounding voice. But while the mezzo, like the sister soprano above her, strives to show off her high notes, the contralto heads in the other direction and pulls out as *her* trump card her low notes. For this reason contraltos singing recitals are often fond of choosing a song like Schubert's "Der Tod und das Mädchen" with its optional ending of D, below middle C. Marian Anderson used to bring out this note with a kind of awesome profundity. Interestingly, this great contralto tells in her autobiography that as a young girl in her teens she sang the "Inflammatus" from Rossini's *Stabat Mater,* undaunted by its repeated high C"s, which shows that she possessed a phenomenal range of almost three octaves. Having these top notes, she was occasionally advised to transform herself into a soprano. Aware of the richness and sonority of her lower range she wisely resisted the temptation and never sang, in public anyway, music that carried her much above a high A'. Thus, while her middle notes had a brighter mezzo-soprano quality, the low part of her voice had the haunting dark tones we think of as belonging to a true contralto.* Many contraltos with their much emphasized low notes and rather inflexible voices (Marian Anderson, however, possessed a beautiful trill) do not sing above F'.

True contralto roles are infrequent in opera as the voice, particularly in America, is rare. Erda, full of forebodings as she rises from the bowels of the earth, is best performed by a singer with an authoritative lower register. (The *Siegfried* Erda must sing one high A' flat, but otherwise the part lies very low indeed.) Many people prefer the role of Gluck's Orfeo to be sung by a contralto. There is some precedent for this since the part was originally perfromed by a *castrato* contralto, though Gluck later altered it for tenor when the opera was given in Paris (the French never having had a taste for an artificially created female voice emanating from a large male frame). Berlioz revived and arranged Gluck's *Orfeo ed Euridice* for the extraordinary Pauline Viardot in November, 1859, who evidently had a voice best described as a mezzo-soprano with very well emphasized low tones. It is this version that we are most accustomed to hearing today with a woman singing the male title part. The part lies low and requires a voice of great nobility and dignity; it must at the same time be tenderly poignant, a quality which is sometimes lacking in the forceful bottom of contraltos, most particularly in what one observer has described as "the dark hooting tone of the traditional English contralto."

Because of a love for oratorio as well as for the Gilbert and Sullivan operas that call for gloom-ridden contraltos to limn such parts as Katisha in *The Mikado* or Lady Jane in *Patience*, England has produced more than its share of this unusual type of woman's voice. A famous contralto of days gone by who possessed stentorian low tones was Clara Butt. "C'est une voix obscène," remarked the composer, Reynaldo Hahn, himself a singer, when he heard her. Dame Clara's voice, at least heard in records, almost completely lacked a vibrato, giving the effect of the singing of a huge mannish choirboy.

Another peerless English contralto of more recent times was Lancashire-born Kathleen Ferrier, who embarked on a professional career at the late age of twenty-nine during the height of the

---

*The black pop singer Jennifer Holiday, who made a hit on Broadway in *Dreamgirls*, has low tones that are a ghostly reminder of those of Marian Anderson.

war. She had taken two years of singing lessons when in 1943 she came to the well-known singer and teacher Roy Henderson. At that time, he writes, "the quality of the voice was rich, but rather too dark and it possessed but one colour." (This, incidentally, is a classic analysis of what irks and displeases certain people about the contralto voice: darkness and monotony.) "The range was only moderate," continues Mr. Henderson of Ferrier's voice. "The high E' tended to sharpen in pitch and lost much of the quality of the lower notes, while F' was about the upper limit and was only supported by an extra push of breath. The interpretative side of singing hardly existed."

Ten years later Kathleen Ferrier was dead of cancer. In this time she added two whole tones to the top of her range. She lightened and brightened her voice and molded it into the wonderfully expressive instrument that it became. She also mastered languages omitted in her original rather rudimentary education (she left school when she was fourteen) and she learned a large repertory of lieder, oratorio arias and other works for voice which she sang under the great conductors of her time. One of these, Bruno Walter, so admired the beauty of her voice and art that he often accompanied her in recitals. Kathleen Ferrier's last two heart-breaking appearances were in the role of Orfeo at Covent Garden. After the second performance, having smilingly received a crowd of backstage visitors and cheerily waved the last one away, when asked by her sister Winifred if there was anything she wanted, Ferrier replied, "Get me a stretcher, love." On it she left the opera house—forever.

Kathleen Ferrier seems to have had the perfect voice for Orfeo. It entirely lacked any harsh or astringent quality throughout its compass, having instead a strange kind of radiance which made her singing most moving to hear. As with Mozart, it seems as if she had some foreknowledge of the shortness of her destiny, so much did she accomplish in so little time.

THE LOWER WOMEN'S VOICES
Coloratura and Lyric Mezzo-Soprano Roles

Carmen	See discussion in the text.
Cenerentola	A luscious part for the coloratura mezzo.
Charlotte (*Werther*)	Also sung by a dramatic mezzo.

Cherubino (*Le Nozze di Figaro*)	Sometimes sung by a lyric soprano.
Dorabella (*Così fan Tutte*)	Also sung by a dramatic mezzo.
Hänsel	Sometimes sung by a lyric soprano.
Laura (*La Gioconda*)	Also taken by a dramatic mezzo.
La Cieca (*La Gioconda*)	Sung by contraltos as well.
Lola (*Cavalleria Rusticana*)	
Maddalena (*Rigoletto*)	
Mignon	Farrar and Bori, lyric sopranos, sang this part; so did Christine Nilsson, a soprano *leggiero*.
Mistress Page (Falstaff)	
Nicklausse (*Les Contes d'Hoffmann*)	
Octavian (*Der Rosenkavalier*)	Sung by lyric and even *spinto* sopranos.
Preziosilla (*La Forza del Destino*)	
Rosina (*Il Barbiere di Siviglia*)	Usually taken away from the coloratura mezzo by the soprano *leggiero*.
Siébel (*Faust*)	
Suzuki (*Madama Butterfly*)	

THE LOWER WOMEN'S VOICES
Dramatic Mezzo-Soprano Roles

Adalgisa (*Norma*)	Written for the soprano Giulia Grisi, now the role is usually sung by the contrastingly darker voice of a lyric or dramatic mezzo.
Amneris (*Aida*)	
Azucena (*Il Trovatore*)	
Brangäne (*Tristan und Isolde*)	
Dalila	
Eboli (*Don Carlo*)	"Never attempt Eboli," advised Walter Legge, ever sharp with his comments. "It is the grave of mezzo-sopranos."
Fricka (*Das Rheingold* and *Die Walküre*)	
Klytemnestra (*Elektra*)	
Magdalene (*Die Meistersinger*)	Can be sung by a lyric mezzo as well.
Marina (*Boris Godunov*)	
Ortrud (*Lohengrin*)	A very high tessitura for a mezzo.
Ulrica (*Un Ballo in Maschera*)	Sung also by contraltos, as it lies low.
Venus (*Tannhäuser*)	

THE LOWER WOMEN'S VOICES

Contraltos

Note: These roles can be sung by mezzos, but they should have very strong, deep low notes.

Dame Quickly (*Falstaff*)
Erda (*Das Rheingold* and *Siegfried*)
Orfeo (*Orfeo ed Euridice*)
Orlofsky (*Die Fledermaus*)

Also various middle-aged ladies in Gilbert and Sullivan operettas such as:

Katisha (*The Mikado*)
Lady Jane (*Patience*)
Little Buttercup (*H.M.S. Pinafore*)

THE HIGH MEN'S VOICES

"There are men; there are women and then there are tenors," is the familiar saying about these singers whose voices are scarce and tremendously in demand in the opera house. One might carry it a step further and say that there are men, women, tenors and countertenors since the male who can produce this odd, not exactly feminine but rather sexless sound is of incredible rarity. There exists a not uncommon fallacy in the public mind that a countertenor is the modern version of the *castrato*, his voice, if not artificially created, at least resulting from a lack of sexual maturation. Writing rather sourly of countertenors, Ralph Morse Brown declares that they have delicate skin, little or no facial hair and never a beard, a statement belied by the appearance of the most famous countertenor of his generation, Alfred Deller. In addition, Mr. Brown counsels the prospective teacher of a countertenor to prepare himself to deal with a person "ultra clever, highly nervous, refined and charming, peculiarly nice and correct in interpretation, and hypersensitive," or else one "stupid, phlegmatic, unreliable and a hopeless bungler"—a catalogue which would appear to cover almost all the attributes of human character.

Though the countertenor may incline to white flesh and hairlessness, he is generally no less sexually mature than his female counterpart, the contralto, who can sometimes have a sturdy, virile appearance (the famous contralto Clara Butt, was six feet tall) and possess hair on her face and body where it does not ordinarily appear in most women. The countertenor and the contralto then, share the twilight world that society seems to be tending towards today where pronounced male or female sexual qualities merge. As young men and women today dress alike and even share the same clothes, so the countertenor and the contralto share almost the same range, though the countertenor does not go quite so high but dips slightly lower:

Countertenor

Like the contralto, who by muscular adjustments within the larynx can sing the low, manly sounds of *her* extra register, the countertenor by actions within his larynx, produces in *his* extra register the high, slightly hooty tones that are correctly described as falsetto. In earlier times the high, *supported* head tones of an ordinary tenor were also called "falsetto" and there is much confusion as to the definition of the term to this day. A fuller discussion will appear in a later section.

A feminine sound, the male falsetto, emanating from a man, usually makes us laugh. Puccini asks Marcello to use it when he's pretending to be the girlish dancing partner of Schaunard in the last act of *La Bohème*. Verdi calls for the portly Sir John Falstaff to sing a few falsetto notes when he describes with comic effect how Mistress Ford has fallen in love with him. The male falsetto can also sound macabre and mad to our ears, greatly adding to the impact of an opera such as *Wozzeck*.

While the ordinary tenor or baritone voice (but infrequently the low bass) can make brief excursions into this extra male register, the countertenor uses it almost the entire time. And because he has enforced and strengthened his falsetto register to such an extent, the lower, what we might call "ordinary" light tenor or baritone part of his voice becomes weak and inaudible, just as the female pop singer using only her chest register enervates the ordinary, more feminine quality of her voice.

In an interesting passage in the biography of Alfred Deller, *A Singularity of Voice*, the celebrated countertenor discusses the existence of another kind of "high tenor who can either dispense with falsetto entirely, or use it for the top fourth or fifth of the compass, without perceptible break. Some people say this is a true countertenor; others that it isn't a countertenor at all, but merely a high, light tenor. Certainly, some singers one hears who are billed as countertenors seem to be tenors with an exceptionally high range." This type of countertenor, however, lacks the astonishing ease and effortlessness that Deller, who sings mainly in his falsetto register, possesses.

Though the world has come to accept—welcome even—a lady who belts out her songs with the raucous quality of a buzz saw, reactions to the sounds of a countertenor tend to be more ambivalent. Michael Tippett, who has composed for Deller, is quoted as saying in the same *A Singularity of Voice:* "It was the voice for which Bach wrote many of the alto solos in the Church cantatas; and Purcell, who himself sang countertenor, gave to it some of his best airs and ensembles. To my ear it has a peculiarly musical sound because almost no emotional irrelevancies distract us from the absolutely pure musical quality of the production. *It is like no other sound in music** and few other sounds are so intrinsically musical."* Along with a delight in the sound of a choirboy's voice, a particular fondness for the countertenor seems to exist among the English. In addition to Tippett, Benjamin Britten has also composed for the countertenor, including the part of Oberon in his opera *A Midsummer Night's Dream.* Can it be a national feeling for reticence, for understatement that responds to the lack of what Tippett calls distracting "emotional irrelevancies" in this type of voice? On the other hand I have heard this reaction from an otherwise unaggressive and mild-mannered Englishman, a most knowledgeable lover of music and singing. "Down with the countertenor!" he cried, turning slightly red in the face as his eyebrows worked up and down. "He always sounds unnatural, constrained and affected, as well as ugly." A taste for the countertenor voice, however, has spread to other countries, particularly Germany and America where, now that there is a demand for them, countertenors are emerging in greater quality.

In keeping with the modern crossing of the sexes, male pop singers breathing moistly and warmly on the shiny metal domes

*Italics the author.

of their hand mikes, frequently sing their numbers in the soft, veiled tones of their falsetto registers.

The public's taste in pop singers does not cease to astonish, never more than in the case of today's Number One idol, young Michael Jackson whose recent album, "Thriller," at this time of writing, has sold more than twenty-five million copies. Jackson produces entirely androgynous falsetto tones (said to be unchanged from the time when he was five years old) that are devoid of any masculine quality, which nonetheless drive his young female fans into frenzies of yearning and ecstasy. As opposed to so many popular singers and groups associated with the drug scene, this lithe, black pop artist is a member of the Jehovah's Witnesses sect and fasts once a week. Such is his reverence for *his* idol, pop singer, Diana Ross, he is said to have undergone plastic surgery in order to resemble her facially which, curiously, he now does.

Tenors: A Race Apart. Not only has it been declared that there are "men, women and tenors," but also the nineteenth century conductor, Hans von Bülow said forthrightly, "A tenor is a disease." The tenor may be short, thick-necked, fat and less than divinely handsome of features. No matter, so long as he has thrilling high notes. The tenor voice is one of the rarest of the ranges and, according to exceptionally tall and good looking Franco Corelli, who ought to have known, requires "much attention."

Why does the tenor hold such sway over his audiences? Here is one explanation offered by the vastly knowledgeable, one-time general manager of the Metropolitan Opera, Rudolph Bing: "The tenor with a secure top exerts a sexual fascination on people, not just women, men too. The best tenor has a quality, a timbre, that's essentially a sexual stimulant—that is why they are so highly paid."

As a corollary to this statement another general manager, Terence McEwen of the San Francisco Opera, claims that he can actually hear if a tenor has had sex before a performance. Luciano Pavarotti subscribes to the belief that sexual indulgence affects the voice* and abstains for twenty-hour hours before a performance.

---

*Could this be the reason for the late Lanfranco Rasponi's statement in his richly informative *The Last of the Prima Donnas* that the wives of tenors are noted for their jealousy?

Jan Peerce went further by holding off for two or even three days. (Peerce has much to say on this subject, which will be dealt with more fully later on.)

In the operatic world we have the "prima donna" and the "diva," but curiously no "primo oumino"* nor "divo." There have been many more great sopranos in proportion to their high-ranging male counterparts. In the Wagnerian repertory, for example, during the 1890's there was really only one supreme tenor: Jean de Reszke, who sang Tristan opposite no less than three superb Isoldes, Lilli Lehmann, Lillian Nordica and Milka Ternina. Later on into the twentieth century there was only one Lauritz Melchior, as opposed to Frida Leider, Kirsten Flagstad, Marjorie Lawrence and Helen Traubel. Sought after, cozzened, highly paid, indulged, the operatic tenor seems to belong to a race apart—and is well aware of it. Recently I spent several hours with a rising young tenor, a sensitive musician who promises to become that rarest of vocal artists, a leading *heldentenor*. As we were separating his hand stole to the inside wallet pocket of his jacket. "Want to see something?" he asked confidentially.

Rather puzzled, as we had not talked of his family, only intently of singing and the singing voice, I prepared to view photographs of his offspring. I should have known better. This was a tenor! My eyes beheld a likeness of the husky singer, as Otello with a gold locket gleaming on his bare chest. "It's my favorite," he added happily.

Tenore Leggiero. On an average the length of the ordinary tenor's vocal cords is around seven-twelfths of an inch† and slightly thicker than those in the throat of the female. As a result, men are far less adept at performing florid music. Handel calls upon the heavy bass voice to move with agility through such arias as "O ruddier than the cherry" from *Acis and Galatea* or "Why do the Nations" from *Messiah*, but the result is all too often a heavily aspirated and muddily articulated series of runs and skips, not at all what the composer would have wished for. The male voice most capable of a coloratura technique is the small, often rather pale-sounding tenor known as the *tenore leggiero* or sometimes

---

*The term, however, was applied to leading *castrati* of their day.
†Caruso's were said to be one inch long, the nonsensical information that tends to arise about legendary figures.

tenor bianco. His range is the same as the heavier but less flexible lyric tenor:

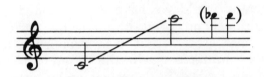

Tenore Leggiero

though this gentle, suave-sounding tenor, as Alfred Deller has noted, can sometimes extend his compass by shading his high tones off into falsetto, turning himself into a kind of countertenor. Because the *tenore leggiero* favors the middle and upper part of his range and also emphasizes lightness and agility, he usually lacks body in the lower part.

Notable examples of the *tenore leggiero* have included Alessandro Bonci, and Tito Schipa and more recently, Cesare Valletti and Luigi Alva. They have all shone in the light roles of Almaviva in *Il Barbiere di Siviglia*, Nemorino in *L'Elisir d'Amore* and Don Ottavio in *Don Giovanni*. Fenton in Verdi's *Falstaff* is also most attractive when sung by a tenor with a gentle, almost petal-like softness to his voice. These singers, however, in their search for more repertory often take on slightly heavier parts such as Rodolfo in *La Bohème*, Alfredo in *La Traviata*, or Massenet's Des Grieux. The *tenore leggiero* who sings the last named part usually fares beautifully with the evocative "Le Rêve," Des Grieux's aria in the second act that should be sung almost entirely in a finely spun *mezza voce*. But the same tenor then has difficulty in mustering the size of voice needed for the dramatic third act aria, "Ah, fuyez douce image."

At the outset of his career Tito Schipa sang in addition to the light tenor repertory some of the heavier tenor roles such as Cavaradossi and Turiddu, but soon gave them up. The glowing, youthful sheen of his voice continued to last throughout a career that endured over forty-five years.* We must not forget, too, the so-called "Irish tenor" with its light, pale quality which should properly be classified as *tenore leggiero*. The most obvious famous

---

*Schipa's present day successor, Alfredo Kraus, has continued to sing with amazing freshness while well into his fifties.

Tenor Alessandro Bonci as Almaviva in *Il Barbiere di Siviglia*. Caricature by Enrico Caruso.

example is John McCormack's sweetly flexible voice with its faultless trill.

America is a country that has not produced many light tenors of fame, yet the first black American to make a distinguished international career was not, as might be supposed, a man with a big rolling voice and expansive art to match, but Roland Hayes, who possessed a small tenor voice of extreme refinement. Against all kinds of odds and prejudices Hayes set out on a singing career in 1911, opposed by his mother, who though ambitious for her son, thought that if he became a singer it must be as a night club entertainer. A famous story is told that when Roland Hayes was commanded to perform at Buckingham Palace in 1920, he jubilantly wired his mother the news. "Remember who you are," she promptly cabled back. Like Schipa, Hayes made no attempt to enlarge his light, finely controlled voice, with the result that his career lasted thirty-five years.

A recent article in the magazine *Ovation* bewails the passing of the *tenor leggiero*. The author, Mr. Will Crutchfield, who is currently working on a book about nineteenth century singing, seems to support the theory of "the oldsters of each successive generation . . . that operatic singing has been in steady decline for a century or more." In particular he laments the "falling standards" of today's light tenors such as Rockwell Blake, or the Spaniard Francisco Araiza, who gave a delightful performance as the Prince in a telecast seen in America in February 1984 of a La Scala production of Rossini's *Cenerentola.* These singers, declares Mr. Crutchfield, are "out of touch with the needs of the music in question." He advises us to listen to reissues of the great light tenors of the past such as Anselmi, Bonci, Edmond Clément and so forth.

That this scarcity of light-voiced tenors with a coloratura technique exists at the moment there can be no doubt. But by the time we have finished our survey of the singing voice, the reader will realize that various types of voices seem to come in waves. As has been pointed out, for forty or fifty years there was scarcely a coloratura mezzo to be heard; conversely that period of vocal history encompassed a golden age of Wagnerian singers. Today we have scarcely any of the latter and also a dearth of light tenors, but the coloratura mezzo abounds. And so, doubtless the changing cycles will continue.

The Lyric and the Dramatic Tenor. When it comes to the bigger-voiced tenors the distinction between lyric and dramatic is very indistinct indeed. Much *va-et-vient* goes on, the lyric tenors pushing into heavier dramatic roles such as Radames in *Aida* or Andrea Chénier, the dramatic tenors stepping back to sing lighter, more graceful parts like Rodolfo or Alfredo. All these tenors have about the same range as their lighter voiced confrères:

Lyric and Dramatic Tenor

but considerably less agility, and in a part such as Tamino can experience difficulty with the passage in Act One, Scene Three, when he must sing embellishments of the melody he has played on his Magic Flute.

A perfect example of a true lyric tenor was Jussi Bjoerling, one of the phenomenons of modern vocal times. Bjoerling received his first singing lessons at the age of five and with his father, Carl David, and brothers Olle and Guerta sang throughout his childhood in a group known as the Bjoerling Male Quartet. He first came to the United States, not as is generally supposed, in 1937 when he made his debut with the Chicago Opera Company, but many years earlier with the quartet as a lad of thirteen. The Bjoerling family were all tenors and recordings of one of Jussi's brothers show a striking similarity of quality to that of the more famous tenor, lacking only his brilliance of tone.*

Because the careers of singers are constantly overshadowed by effects of aging, their birthdates as given to the public are open to constant suspicion. Bjoerling is usually supposed to have sung his first important operatic role—Don Ottavio—at the amazingly youthful age of nineteen. Actually he was four years older, so that by the time of his debut he had already eighteen years experience of performing. To this fact we can attribute his superb musicianship, phrasing and diction—qualities not always found in tenors of whatever sized voice.

Jussi Bjoerling, unlike many lyric tenors, never tried to move on to the bigger, more dramatic tenor parts. True, he recorded such heavy roles as Canio in *I Pagliacci* and Calaf in *Turandot* but he avoided them in the opera house. The heaviest parts he undertook at the Metropolitan were the name part in *Don Carlo* and Manrico in *Il Trovatore*, the latter reluctantly. As a result Bjoerling's crystalline sheen of voice lasted until his untimely death from heart disease at the age of fifty-three. How little his voice varied over the years, except to darken a bit, can be heard by comparing his records made in the thirties to the last, a concert in August 1960, less than a month before his death.

Ten years after Bjoerling's debut at the Metropolitan, an Italian tenor, aged twenty-seven, made his first appearance displaying a voice of the most glowing quality imaginable. This was Giuseppe di Stefano who after first singing lyric roles such as Alfredo in *La Traviata* and Rodolfo in *La Bohème* pushed on into the heavy dramatic parts with sad results. The bloom withered from his

---

*Jussi Bjoerling's son, Rolf, was also a tenor with a timbre much like his father's.

tones and eventually an increasingly pronounced wobble afflicted his top notes. By the time of his joint appearances with Maria Callas in 1973 his voice matched hers as a ruin of a vocal apparatus that was once wonderful.

As an opposite example, the Swedish-born lyric tenor Nicolai Gedda has maintained a career before the public for over thirty years holding onto his high notes as well as his freshness of voice. But this is because he has never pressed on to heavier parts than say, Don José in *Carmen*.

One who *did* press on to heavier dramatic parts (Don Alvaro in *La Forza del Destino*, Radames in *Aida* (though not Otello) with great success was the late Richard Tucker. Not quite thirty years after his debut at the Metropolitan in the winter of 1945 he was making plans to sing the demanding character part of Eleazar in *La Juive* in a new production at the Metropolitan when he was struck down by a heart attack on a joint recital tour with the baritone Robert Merrill.

The King. And what of the greatest tenor of them all? His face with its comic, wide-set eyes and broad gash of a mouth rose above a ludicrously dumpy figure, but Enrico Caruso by means of a richly dark voice, almost muscular in feeling, and a way of using it with total conviction, exerted a spell over those who heard him greater than any singer in modern vocal history. This was partly due to the introduction of phonograph records that paralleled his career, and also to the fact that Caruso happened to record extremely well. For many, he became the ideal singer through whom they could hear operatic music that had been denied them or rationed out on far-spaced occasions. But Caruso meant even more than that. He reached people all over the world, even those who were otherwise indifferent to singing. To many he was not just a singer—but a spirit. In his vocal art could be heard an accent of humanity to which the public gave its unfaltering response. Even if one had never listened to a Caruso record it is possible to understand his unique quality from his letters that Dorothy Caruso published in 1946 in her deeply moving memoir, *Enrico Caruso*. These, full of comic misspellings and grammatical errors, give the measure of the man's character and of his heart. As Mrs. Caruso points out in a little introduction to her book: "At times they are curiously Biblical."

CARUSO.   VIAFORA

Rodolfo and Mimi in *La Bohème*. Caricature by Enrico Caruso.

Caruso was no exception to the rule that boy altos are more likely to become tenors (as boy sopranos become baritones and basses). At the age of twenty-two he made his first important appearance at Caserta as Turiddu in *Cavalleria Rusticana*, a fairly heavy tenor role that he probably should not have undertaken, for during the beginning of his career he was given to breaking on his high notes. Caruso was a true lyric tenor and in his early years at Covent Garden and the Metropolitan he sang mainly the lyric roles. During this time there lay on his voice when he sang *mezza voce* that peculiarly haunting peach fuzz quality which is unique to the Italian tenor. (The voice of the young Gigli and the young di Stefano also had this gentle, vulnerable sound, not to speak of Ferruccio Tagliavini.)

Unfortunately, if the Italian lyric tenor pushes on to more strenuous dramatic parts this bloom goes from the voice, which was the case with Caruso, who by the end of his career had sung thirty-six different roles at the Metropolitan, many of them very taxing to an intrinsically lyric instrument. This, as Irving Kolodin writes, "cost him the command of his early lyric eloquence. No voice could withstand unaltered the amount and kind of usage to which Caruso's was subjected. Only his extraordinary physique and robust constitution limited what could have been deterioration to merely a change of timbre." This change took the form of a thicker, darker, certainly more dramatic quality, but with some of the sweetness gone. By performing the heavy tenor roles such as Samson or Eleazar in *La Juive*, Caruso actually strained his voice to the extent that he developed dreaded wartlike nodules on his vocal cords which had to be removed surgically.

In his pictorial biography of Caruso, the late Francis Robinson declared that the great tenor could easily have sung the lighter Wagnerian tenor parts such as Lohengrin and Tannhäuser—certainly Walther in *Die Meistersinger*. Being a completely oriented Italian, who used English, as we know from his letters, in a way totally his own, Caruso shied away from the difficulties of singing in German. Mr. Robinson, however, publishes a picture of the program of the tenor's only Wagnerian performance—*Lohengrin* in Italian at Buenos Aires in 1901 with Arturo Toscanini as conductor.

Ever since what might be described as the mystique of Caruso, tenors have been hailed (possibly by their own press agents) as a second Caruso. Mrs. Caruso is supposed to have declared that Jussi Bjoerling's voice came nearest to that of her remarkable husband whom she outlived for many years. The comparison does not seem entirely apt, but does illustrate the difference between a pure lyric tenor which Bjoerling remained and the kind of tenor who pushes his voice into more dramatic parts. Bjoerling always kept his pristine, slightly uninvolved quality; Caruso came to sound more like a baritone. In other respects, however, there were certain similarities between the two: both, as tenors often are, were short and plump, with Caruso the stouter and more massive. Both, despite the sincerity of their acting when they played romantic figures, demanded a certain suspension of belief from their audiences. (When Jussi Bjoerling sang his first, impassioned Des Grieux in Puccini's *Manon Lescaut*—one of his finest parts—at the Metropolitan, the comment was heard that he looked strangely like Lotte Lehmann dressed up in breeches. And of course some of the photographs of Caruso in costume are absurdly comic.) Of their temperaments, though Caruso appeared outwardly calm when he sang, he was not: "Of course I am nervous," he is quoted as saying. "Each time I feel there is someone wanting to destroy me, and I must fight like a bull to hold my own." Bjoerling, on the other hand, never even went through the routines of trying his voice that Caruso practiced on the day of a performance. Once when asked why not, Bjoerling replied, "If I'm well it's not necessary. If I'm not what good does it do?" Both tenors were conscientious artists, but Caruso, with far less musical background and training than the Swedish singer, had to work harder to develop his musicianship. B. H. Haggin, one of America's sharpest music critics, has this comparison to make of the singing of the two tenors on records:

"In his recorded performance of 'O paradiso' Caruso arriving at a high B flat holds and expands it from *pp* to an overwhelming *ff*, then breaks off to take breath before completing the phrase; whereas Bjoerling in his recorded performance, connects the expanded B flat with the next note as part of the continuous and beautifully shaped phrase: in the Caruso performance, then, one hears an exceptionally beautiful voice and a mastery in its manipulation; in the Bjoerling not only these but the art in musical phrasing that Caruso did not have."

Beniamino Gigli was sometimes considered a second Caruso, but his lovely lyric voice, which he pushed on into more dramatic parts, never possessed the thrilling richness and drive of his predecessor. For sheer versatility and the size of his repertory Richard Tucker came nearest to the record established by Caruso of 607 performances at the Metropolitan.

Caruso was of course the great best-selling recording artist of his time and made the fortune of what was then called the Victor Talking Machine Company. Jussi Bjoerling made over three hundred records, many of which sold extremely well. But the next tenor to surpass Caruso, in record sales anyway, was a very strange phenomenon indeed. He was Mario Lanza.

A Failed King. Born Alfredo Cocozza in the Italian section of South Philadelphia, Mario Lanza grew up to be dark, romantically handsome and the possessor of an arrestingly beautiful tenor voice. He trained with two teachers, the second being Enrico Rosati who had worked with an earlier great tenor, Beniamino

Gigli. Besides having innate musicality, this young Italian-American can also studied *solfeggio,* learned to sight read proficiently and worked at a singer's knowledge of French and German. In 1942 he spent a summer as a student at Tanglewood (with a fellow learner, Leonard Bernstein) under Serge Koussevitsky. Early in his career he gained experience singing in recital with the distinguished bass-baritone George London. With such fine musical training together with a remarkable voice, who could doubt that the young tenor would make a career that would crown him as a true successor to Caruso?

Taking the name of Mario Lanza, he did indeed succeed Caruso as the most famous tenor with an operatic voice in the world. He made thrilling records of excerpts from *Rigoletto, La Bohème, Adia,* even *Otello* (to name but a few) but he never sang in any of these operas. He dreamed of appearing at the Metropolitan Opera House and La Scala but his only live actual performances were two *Madama Butterfly*s in New Orleans.

Mario Lanza came from a working class background in Philadelphia, but his beginnings were not as raw as Naples-born Enrico Caruso. Yet unlike Caruso, Lanza couldn't manage the rocket ride to fame and fortune due to an entirely gratuitous accident in his throat—his larynx. In behavior he was boorish, sometimes appealingly boyish, generous but also meanspirited. As he and his career deteriorated, he became increasingly truculent and unreliable. His eating and drinking habits were voracious as were apparently his sexual appetites. Once when asked how he sang as he did, Lanza gave a reply that may be nearer to the truth of all great singing than he realized: "It's all sex . . . it comes right out of my balls."

At the age of thirty-eight, the warm Italianate voice of Mario Lanza was stilled forever. Even his ending in a Rome hospital has bizarre overtones. He is said to have been murdered by air being injected into a vein, a death engineered by the Mafia for his refusal to cooperate with them.

Very often a palm reader will grasp an upturned left hand and announce, "This is what you're born with," then, taking the right one, will add, "and this is what you make of it." One who prophesies the future of singers might well point to a beginner's larynx and say, "This is what you're born with," then, moving up to the forehead behind which lies the brain, add, "and this is what you make of it." In the case of Mario Lanza, born with a God-given voice, it was what he *didn't* make of it that seems so tragic.

The Throne. Who might be considered a successor to Enrico Caruso today? If the king were to return to the world today to divide up his realm, it is amazing to realize that he would not have one but two possible pretenders to his throne—the Italian Luciano Pavarotti and Spanish-born Placido Domingo. Of these he would probably crown his fellow countryman as coming closest to him in voice and personality.

Like Caruso at the beginning of his career, Pavarotti is a lyric tenor with perhaps an easier top than the celebrated Neapolitan who was prone to break on his high B's and C's during his apprentice years. It's not generally remembered, but when Pavarotti made his debut at the Metropolitan in November 1968 he was given what was called a "favorable reception" and did not receive the acclaim that he had gathered on the other side of the Atlantic. In fact he was ill with a virulent form of influenza and after singing through only one half of a second *La Bohème* he had to cancel the entire rest of his first New York season. Not until 1972 when he appeared in *La Fille du Régiment* and blazed forth with nine high C's in the first act did he make the furore that would soon turn him into a superstar. Pavarotti had the range to even sing the two D's and one F' required in the role of Arturo in Bellini's *I Puritani*.

As with Enrico Caruso, one of Luciano Pavarotti's most winning personations is the bumpkin Nemorino in Donizetti's *L'Elisir d'Amore*. Like Caruso, Pavarotti has also pushed on into some of the dramatic tenor repertory, most notably a highly successful Radames in *Aida*—though there are those who sound warnings of the dangers, pointing to the loss of quality and ease of high notes from which Caruso suffered later on in his career.

Two other comparisons are apt between the most famous tenor of yesterday and the most famous one of today. One is flawless intonation (Pavarotti has absolute pitch) and superb musicianship. The other is quite simply personality. Though much more handsome than his comic looking predecessor, Pavarotti has the out-and-out winning personality that Caruso evidently possessed, which spills out over the footlights and into the hearts of the audience. He radiates a kind of sweetness and love towards the world that the world returns in the fullest measure.*

Because Pavarotti and Domingo overlap in a few roles, stories have been put around of a rivalry between them. From the listener's point of view they in fact complement one another. If Domingo is entitled to a share of Caruso's kingdom, it is in the dominion of the *tenore robusto*, a territory where the lighter-voiced Pavarotti does not venture. Tall, with black curly hair and flashing eyes, Domingo makes an ideal romantic hero as the half-crazed poet, Hoffmann, or the tragic soldier-lover, Don José. He has also sung the jealousy-ridden Otello, a part that not even Caruso attempted. Domingo lacks a serviceable high C″ and transposes down when he sings the famous arias in *La Bohème* and *Il Trovatore* that require one. Like Caruso the Spanish tenor's voice has a rich, baritonal quality to its lower register and he, too, is a fine musician. He opened the 1984–85 Metropolitan season as Wagner's Lohengrin and also is scheduled to conduct *La Bohème*.

Domingo's vocal resources after twenty-five years before the public, though he has used them unstintingly, show little sign of diminution and he goes from strength to strength.

What these two tenors *do* share in common is promoting great singing to a larger public. Their records sell in the hundreds of thousands. Domingo has shared a disc with pop star John Denver. Pavarotti has made a movie, *Yes, Giorgio*, which while it was not critically successful, delighted thousands. Both have made numerous television appearances. As dedicated, generous-hearted artists, each has given time and effort to furthering the careers of up-coming singers. Pavarotti has not only judged competitors in the Philadelphia Opera vocal contests, but has coached and appeared on television with the winners in a *La Bohème* in that city. Domingo's master classes with young artists have also been shown on the air. The care and attention to detail that these outstanding artists give to music is a revelation to everyone, but particularly those who might take their singing as simply a gift from nature.

The Heavier Tenor. Caruso could undoubtedly have sung very beautifully some of the lighter Wagnerian roles but a tenor who

---

*Magnetic Pavarotti sold out a concert at New York's Madison Square Garden (capacity near 20,000) in August 1984 and scheduled another for November.

begins singing the Italian and French lyric roles, as Caruso did, is more than likely to remain with them. (True, late in his career Martinelli sang Tristan in Chicago, but this was exceptional for an essentially Italian tenor.) Today there are certain dramatic tenors such as Jon Vickers or Jess Thomas who switch back and forth from the German parts to French and Italian roles. Thus Vickers sings Don José, Radames, Peter Grimes, Siegmund and the exacting role of Florestan in *Fidelio*. Thomas can do most of this repertory too, also Calaf in *Turandot*, Lohengrin, and heavier Wagnerian parts such as Siegfried and Tristan. Neither of these singers, however, shades his voice down for an evening as Alfredo or the Duke in *Rigoletto*, as did Richard Tucker, who also sang Don José and Radames—but no German parts. Thus confusion and ambiguity will be seen to infect the nomenclature, "lyric tenor," "dramatic tenor," or "*tenore robusto*" as the latter is sometimes called.

So far, we have mainly discussed the Italian and French repertory. Before looking into the intricacies of who sings what in the various German operas, it would be appropriate to say a word about the German tenor himself. In certain cases, like the Italian tenor with his peach fuzz quality, the German tenor will have a peculiar national sound difficult to describe but unmistakable. It is partly innate but also compounded by the scooping, slurring way (mostly in operetta) in which the voice is employed. Richard Tauber, possessor of a glorious but unmistakably Teutonic voice, was capable of singing Mozart or lieder with impeccable style, but could also ladle out a generous helping of rich Viennese chocolate and whipped cream when he rendered such favorites as "Dein ist mein ganzes Herz" for which he was so famous. This national voice and style of singing has been apostrophized in verse by M. W. Branch in a poem called "Schmalztenor."

> O hark! 'tis the note of the Schmalztenor!
> It swells in his bosom and hangs in the air.
> Like lavender-scent in a spinster's drawer
> It oozes and percolates everywhere.
> So tenderly glutinous,
> Soothing the brute in us,
> Wholly unmutinous
> Schmalztenor.

Enchanting, his smile for the third encore
(Cherubic complexion and glossy curls),
His nasal nostalgia, so sweetly sore,
    Vibrates on the sternums of swooning girls.
    Emerging and merging,
    Suggestively urging,
    Receding and surging—
    The Schmalztenor.

The Absolute Last of the Schmalztenor
  Is heard in Vienna in lilac-time.
He's steaming and quivering more and more
    And dowagers whisper, "He's past his prime!"
    Young maidens have drowned for him:
    Pass the hat round for him:
    Open the ground for him—
    Schmalztenor.

The tenors (not necessarily German, however) who can sing the heavy German repertory consisting of Tristan, Parsifal, Siegmund, the two Siegfrieds, Florestan and Herod in *Salome* are rare indeed. In recent times audiences have been treated to the efforts of René Kollo,[*] James King, Peter Hofmann and Manfred Jung in these parts. None of their voices, however, have the size and timbre that strictly classifies them as true *heldentenors*. Nor, for that matter, did the most celebrated Wagnerian tenor of his time, Jean de Reszke, possess a voice of this heroic mold.

As is well known de Reszke began his career as a baritone singing such parts as Figaro in *Il Barbiere di Siviglia* and Don Giovanni as early as 1874. Bernard Shaw, then a London music critic, much admired de Reszke in the latter part. After appearing for three years in this guise he re-trained his voice. On his reappearance he sang what might be called the *spinto* tenor roles in the Italian-French repertory: Faust, Roméo, Radames, Don José, and then cautiously embarked on Wagnerian parts such as Walther von Stolzing and Lohengrin, but first singing them in Italian. His beautiful interpretations at a time when there was increasing excitement over Wagner, led him to push on through most of the Wagnerian repertory but then singing the parts in their original language. Some say this was fatal to his career

*Kollo began his career as a pop singer.

and that he overtaxed his voice, causing his early retirement. (He was fifty-two.) Certainly de Reszke cancelled many performances towards the end of his career, particularly Siegfried, an especially arduous role. Some say that he wasn't a tenor at all, but a baritone with high notes. But then an awful lot is said in the world of singing that is sheer nonsense.

De Reszke was not the only tenor to sing Wagnerian roles who began as a baritone. Others have included Rudolf Berger, Ramon Vinay,* Set Svanholm (who sang as a baritone for six years before going up) and the inimitable Lauritz Melchior. Outstanding tenors who sang the Italian repertory such as Carlo Bergonzi began as baritones.

For reasons best known to herself, spiteful nature usually chooses to inflict on the man with a tenor voice—he who must portray a whole series of dashing, youthful heroes—lack of height and a tendency to corpulence. Indeed, one tenor, the Rumanian-born Joseph Schmidt, possessor of a rich, soaring voice, never could make an operatic career because of being so extremely short (he was under five feet). Even in the opera house where credibility is not the commonplace of an evening, he would have looked too ludicrous. In our own day we have had such strapping and handsome six-footers as Franco Corelli and Nicolai Gedda to sing the Italian-French repertory, but they are really quite unusual. When we come, however, to that most exceptional of all tenor voices—the *heldentenor*—there can be no exception to the rule of his physique. He will be *enormous*. Not only tall, like Jean de Reszke who was six feet (though not a true *heldentenor*), but also having a chest of massive proportions, greater than photographs of de Reszke show.

During the twentieth century there have so far been very few tenors of international fame who properly fit into this category. Two of now long ago were Leo Slezak, six feet, seven inches of tenor and the Belgian Jacques Urlus, both of whom sang at the Metropolitan and Covent Garden with impressive success. In the mid-1920's appeared the greatest giant of all, Lauritz Melchior. After him as yet there have been no true successors. Some, like James McCracken, meet the physical standard but lack the untiring vocal ability of a true heroic tenor. While there have been a number of tenors to sing the Wagnerian repertory who were

*At the end of his career Vinay returned to baritone roles.

able to get through their parts such as Max Lorenz, Ludwig Suthaus, Set Svanholm and Wolfgang Windgassen, they lacked the reserve or ease that the colossal build of a Melchior might have accorded them.

Melchior, as has been said, began his career as a baritone, but one night while singing the Count in *Il Trovatore* with an observant American mezzo called Madame Charles Cahier, he added an unwritten high C' to his part. Amazed, she urged him to re-train his voice. A year later he had gone up and stayed there for twenty-five years, an incredible eye-shattering figure in the bearskin of Siegfried, a moving, but hopelessly robust and healthy-looking Tristan on his deathbed. During his career he sang opposite Frida Leider, Kirsten Flagstad, Marjorie Lawrence and Helen Traubel, sopranos with voices of prodigious size and opulence. During that time there was only one Melchior. No other tenor could be compared with him.

At this writing in the mid-1980's there are two American artists, comparatively young, who may turn out to be the leading Wagnerian tenors of the age. One, Oklahoma-born William Johns, sang a *Walküre* Siegmund to critical acclaim for the sensitivity of his portrayal in Baltimore in February 1984, and is striking for his first Tristan in Montreal in 1986. Hulking Timothy Jenkins (he is almost as tall as Leo Slezak) has already performed at the Metropolitan as Parsifal with great success and is undertaking other Wagnerian roles at that house and also at Bayreuth.

TENORS
Some Lyric Roles

Beppe (*I Pagliacci*)	The first five roles are most appropriately sung by a *tenore leggiero*.
Almaviva (*Il Barbiere di Siviglia*)	
Don Ottavio (*Don Giovanni*)	
Ernesto (*Don Pasquale*)	
Nemorino (*L'Elisir d'Amore*)	
Alfred (*Die Fledermaus*)	Most of these parts can be sung by heavier *spinto*-type tenors.
Alfredo (*La Traviata*)	
Cavaradossi (*Tosca*)	

Des Grieux (*Manon* and *Ma-
non Lescaut*)
Duke (*Rigoletto*)
Faust
Ferrando (*Così fan Tutte*)
Pelléas   Sometimes sung by a high, light
                                           baritone.
Pinkerton (*Madama Butterfly*)
Rodolfo (*La Bohème*)
Tamino (*Die Zauberflöte*)

TENORS
Spinto *or* Dramatic Tenor Roles

Andrea Chénier
Calaf (*Turandot*)
Canio (*I Pagliacci*)
Dimitri (*Boris Godounov*)
Don Alvaro (*La Forza del
Destino*)
Don Carlo
Don José (*Carmen*)
Enzo (*La Gioconda*)
Erik (*Der Fliegende Holländer*)
Forestan (*Fidelio*)
Herod (*Salome*)
Hoffmann
Julien (*Louise*)
Lenski (*Eugen Onegin*)
Lohengrin   Also sung by the heroic tenor.
Manrico (*Il Trovatore*)
Otello   An Italian *heldentenor* role.
Radames (*Aida*)
Riccardo or Gustav (*Un Ballo
in Maschera*)
Samson
Turiddu (*Cavalleria Rusticana*)
Walther (*Die Meistersinger*)

TENORS
The Heavy German Heldentenor *Roles*

All these parts have been sung by
tenors with less than heroic voices.

Parsifal
Siegfried
Siegfried (*Götterdämmerung*)
Siegmund (*Die Walküre*)
Tannhäuser
Tristan

THE LOWER MEN'S VOICES

Villain, Father or Friend. Next in order to the tenors as we descend the depths of the male voice are the baritones, usually designated lyric and dramatic, but again with a certain amount of spilling over between the two categories. What is called the "Verdi" baritone, who sings Rigoletto or di Luna in *Il Trovatore* (but also Valentin in *Faust* and Gérard in *Andrea Chénier*) requires a range of:

Baritone

It has particular power and brilliance towards the top. The baritone who sings Tonio in *I Pagliacci* must have a ringing high A flat for the "Prologue," though it isn't in the score. The baritone who sings Iago must be able to touch lightly a high A natural in the first act "Brindisi" and that *is* in the score.

This husky, virile-sounding voice with its much emphasized middle and top (to the detriment of the power of the low notes, naturally) is a comparatively modern invention, having evolved from the time of Rossini. Mozart, writing for his baritones, gives them a lower, less demanding tessitura and scarcely ever asks them to hit even a top F. This is why the higher bass singers, or bass-baritones as they frequently call themselves, have sneaked out from their usual run of characterizations—monarchs and ponderous paternal figures of other kinds—to grab the dashing role of Don Giovanni and the delightful one of Mozart's Figaro. Ezio Pinza, a high bass, was the first to initiate this practice at the Metropolitan. (The previous Don was Scotti, who sang all the Verdi baritone roles.) Since Pinza's time the baritones have continued to lose out to a series of handsome bass-baritones such as George London, Cesare Siepi and, more recently, James Morris and Samuel Ramey, all having voices bright and light enough to suit the dash and verve of these characters. Fighting back, high baritones such as Sherrill Milnes and Georges Bacquier have held on to the part of the sexy Don.

As far as leading operatic roles go the possessor of a light lyric baritone is rather restricted in the opera house. Mozart is his most generous benefactor, with Papageno in *Die Zauberflöte*, Masetto in *Don Giovanni* and Guglielmo in *Così fan Tutte*. He has a nice love duet as Silvio in *I Pagliacci* and he is onstage through most of *La Bohème*, though the role of Marcello offers him few places really to shine. This voice can manage the rewarding part of the elder Germont in *La Traviata* but few of the other fat Verdi roles. The part of Pelléas lies low in the tenor range and sometimes lyric baritones undertake it. Lacking the usual robustness of the big baritone voices, they can do justice to the grace and subtlety of this music. Above all, lyric baritones such as Charles Panzéra, Gérard Souzay and Hermann Prey have made good recitalists.

As with all voices the lyric baritone can grow in size, strength and robustness. Inexperienced in opera, Robert Merrill made his debut at the Metropolitan as the elder Germont while he was still in his late twenties. Soon afterwards he was offered the heavy and demanding part of Rigoletto but had the good sense to turn it down until he and his voice were more mature. Gradually he took on some of the other exacting dramatic baritone parts, di Luna in *Il Trovatore*, Iago in *Otello*, and, twenty years after his debut, Scarpia in *Tosca*, always retaining the freshness of his voice.

Some men are innately equipped with big "Verdi" baritone voices, but at the outset these can be thick and unwieldy. The young Leonard Warren had some trouble refining his gloriously large, sometimes wobbly voice and this was true of the Yorkshire baritone, Peter Glossop. The palm for the widest, richest, most thrilling "Verdi" baritone of all generally goes to Titta Ruffo. There is a remarkable similarity of virile tone quality between Ruffo's voice and Caruso's. Ruffo was one of the few baritone draws in vocal history (for some reason, however superb they may be, baritones don't seem to affect the box office like sopranos and tenors). While Caruso sang at the Metropolitan Ruffo did not, only appearing there after the great tenor's death. The two Italians made one record together, the duet "Sì, pel ciel" from

Otello, and it is hair-raising. A great expert on operatic voices, the conductor Tullio Serafin, once said, "In my lifetime there have been three miracles—Caruso, Ponselle and Ruffo. Apart from these there have been several wonderful singers."

So far, the baritone who sings the high-lying Italian-French repertory has been discussed. There are other artists, less comfortable in this tessitura, who devote themselves more to the Wagnerian baritone parts, Wotan in the first three operas of the *Ring,* Telramund in *Lohengrin,* Kurvenal in *Tristan und Isolde* and so forth. They will also portray the villainous Pizarro in *Fidelio* and the sanctimonious Jokanaan in *Salome,* and in the Italian repertory Scarpia in *Tosca* and Amonasro in *Aida.* Big-voiced and often dark-voiced, these are the afore-mentioned bass-baritones who have a range of:

Bass-Baritone

A fine bass-baritone of recent times whose career was shortened by illness, George London sang such bass roles as Boris Godunov and Méphistophélès, bass-baritone parts like Wotan and Eugen Onegin, and the "Verdi" baritone role of Amonasro in *Aida.* "Verdi" baritones are usually assigned the part of Escamillo in *Carmen,* which London also sang, but this is a difficult role for either type of baritone to manage. Much of the bull-fighter's music lies too low for a high baritone to project it successfully, and yet it has high notes discomfiting to the lower bass-baritone kind of voice. Walter Legge has a pithy summation to make of the part: "Escamillo is impossible for every normal baritone or bass. I've heard only two good ones in sixty-five years—(Marcel) Journet and (José) van Dam."

Another fine singing actor, the Welshman Sir Geraint Evans moved around among the bass, bass-baritone and baritone roles in a way that mocks any attempt to explain what kind of voice sings what and why. Calling himself a baritone, Evans sang Falstaff, Wozzeck and Pizarro, all considered true baritone parts. He portrayed Mozart's Figaro, a baritone or bass-baritone role, and then in *Don Giovanni* switched not to the name part but Leporello, which is almost always sung by a bass.

Currently, versatile James Morris switches between the bass and baritone repertory, making it difficult to define one from the other. He sings the bass parts, Méphistophélès in *Faust* and Colline in *La Bohème* and the higher-lying parts of Don Giovanni and Figaro in *Le Nozze di Figaro*. Of late at Salzburg and also at the Metropolitan he has appeared in the essentially lyric baritone role of Guglielmo in *Così fan Tutte*. He has been heard as all three villains in *Les Contes d'Hoffmann*, Coppelius, Dappertutto and Dr. Miracle. Of these Dappertutto is a true baritone part with his luscious aria "Scintille diamant" that ends with a flashy G sharp. In earlier times these roles were taken by Giuseppe De Luca and Lawrence Tibbett who were high "Verdi" baritones. For the type of voice that sings these three parts, then, the rule is, as usual, no rule. To add to the confusion, James Morris at this writing is setting off in another direction, towards the Wagnerian repertory. In February 1984 he sang an enthusiastically received Wotan in *Die Walküre* in Baltimore and then will go to sing the same role during an upcoming San Francisco Opera season of the same year.

Baritones are usually manly, sturdy-looking fellows, often tall, causing them to loom over the hero of the opera which the baritone, poor fellow, almost never is. Villainy is frequently his evening's work: Scarpia, Iago, Telramund, Barnaba in *La Gioconda* are all unbelievably depraved. Sometimes the baritone is a father—the elder Germont, Rigoletto, Amonasro—though his relationships with his various children never turn out to be very satisfactory due to their mismanaged love affairs. Sometimes he is just a friend like Rodrigo in *Don Carlo*, Wolfram in *Tannhäuser* or Renato in *Un Ballo in Maschera*. All too often he is in love with a lady who doesn't love him and suffers devastating rejections. Gioconda and Leonora in *Il Trovatore* both prefer to sink dead at the feet of the baritone than into his arms, while Tosca carries the rejection even further by causing *him* to drop dead at *her* feet. Even when he gets to play such a dashing symbol of sex as Don Giovanni his wooing is always interrupted, and while it is true that as Escamillo the baritone may have won Carmen between the acts, it is only a short time before he finds her, like so many of his sought-after conquests, dead at his feet.

Lowest of All. When sopranos sail up to a high C" their vocal cords or folds are fluttering at well over a thousand vibrations per second. When the very rare *basso profundo* sings a D, two octaves less one note below middle C his cords are pulsating at around seventy-six vibrations per second. Like a low pedal point held on the organ the effect is awesome and slightly forbidding. As a result the bass voice is often used to portray gods, monarchs and paternal figures, with an occasional Faustian devil (Gounod's or Boïto's) or *Siefried's* dragon (Fafner) thrown in to vary the diet.

The higher type of bass, the *basso cantante*, who sometimes calls himself bass-baritone, does not usually have the incredible low buzzing notes of the *basso profundo*, but on the other hand can reach an F or G at the top of his range, which his much darker-voiced confrères cannot:

Basso Cantante

The terms "lyric" and "dramatic" do not apply to the deepest male voices. These singers, big of stature, almost invariably have voices of a sonorousness and size that carry easily across the stretches of the largest opera houses. On the other hand, like tenors and baritones, they tend to divide up between those who sing the Italian-French repertory and those specializing in German operas. If none of them quite achieved the spectacular appeal of that former six day bicycle rider Ezio Pinza, New York has been fortunate in having a series of fine *cantante* basses including Jerome Hines, Cesare Siepi, Giorgio Tozzi, Nicolai Ghiaurov, and more recently Bonaldo Giaiotti, Paul Plishka, Ruggiero Raimondi and the up-and-coming John Cheek.

On the whole most of these singers have remained within the Italian-French repertory, dividing up such star parts as Méphistophélès in *Faust*, Don Giovanni, Mozart's Figaro, Sarastro in *Die Zauberflöte* and of course the outstanding Russian role of Boris Godunov. They also have sung less important but vivid characters such as Don Basilio in *Il Barbiere di Siviglia*, Padre Guardiano in *La*

Forza del Destino, who has much beautiful music, and Colline in *La Bohème*, with his touching apostrophe to his overcoat. If an opera house rich in first-class basses can afford to cast one of them in the relatively small part of Monterone (*Rigoletto*) or the Commendatore (*Don Giovanni*) these operas are bound to have a greater impact in performance. Those implacable men of religion, Ramfis, the High Priest in *Aida* and the Grand Inquisitor in *Don Carlo*—far more powerful than the ruling monarchs of their respective countries—offer fine opportunities to the bass who is an excellent singing actor. Of the singers listed above, it should be pointed out that Jerome Hines made a not totally successful foray into the German repertory singing the *Walküre* Wotan in which the high-lying parts proved trying to his voice, while Giorgio Tozzi demonstrated his versatility by singing both Daland in *Der Fliegende Holländer* and Hans Sachs in *Die Meistersinger* at the Metropolitan. Another versatile bass was David Ward who switched from Wotan and the Dutchman to either King Philip or the Grand Inquisitor in *Don Carlo*.

The bass who ordinarily sings German roles has a darker, rougher quality to his voice and a more declamatory way of singing. Some higher German basses, notably in recent years Hans Hotter, opted for such parts as Wotan and Hans Sachs. Others with a slightly deeper range and sometimes darker quality will stay with King Marke, the Landgrave Hermann in *Tannhäuser* and Gurnemanz in *Parsifal*. They may also perform the winning role of Pogner in *Die Meistersinger* and the stellar one of Baron Ochs in *Der Rosenkavalier*. Finally there is a truly black type of bass sometimes afflicted with a wobble who hails almost exclusively from Germany or Austria and sings mainly the Wagner villains, Fafner, Fasolt, Hunding and Hagen.

Gloom is not entirely pervasive among the basses for there is another type of deep-voiced singer who has a surprising number of delightful roles in which to shine: the *basso buffo*. Within living memory we have had the wonderfully comic Salvatore Baccaloni and more recently, Fernando Corena, who have made a specialty of singing low-voiced humorous roles in grand opera. Of these, Don Pasquale, Dr. Dulcamara in *L'Elisir d'Amore* and Falstaff (if he can manage the high-lying notes of the last named part) are star roles for the *basso buffo*. Then there are rewarding secondary parts such as Leporello or the precursor of Falstaff, the fussy, scolding

The benevolent Hans Sachs is sung by a baritone or bass-baritone.

Fra Melitone in *La Forza del Destino*. There are also the two Dr. Bartolos in *Il Barbiere di Siviglia* and *Le Nozze di Figaro* and any number of what one might call vignette characterizations: the drunken Varlaam in *Boris Godunov*; Benoit, the landlord, and Alcindoro, Musetta's elderly admirer in *La Bohème* (usually taken by the same *basso buffo*) and the Sacristan in *Tosca*. Like comedy actors who long to play Hamlet, undoubtedly a *basso buffo* would love to portray Méphistophélès or Don Giovanni. But something about his size, expression and general ambience of character dooms him to comedy in which, nonetheless, he can make a fine and busy career in the opera house.

The *basso profundo* is an exceedingly rare voice. In Russia one even deeper called the *contrabasso* used to emerge with a range down to the B,,,—two octaves and one note below middle C. These could be heard mainly in the impressive Russian liturgy since such a voice is too woolly and slow-moving to serve in the opera house. With the reduction of the church and religion as practiced in the Soviet Union during the past fifty years these rare and extraordinary voices are said to be dying out, showing again how a singing voice will evolve to serve a particular need and, equally, disappear when there is no longer a demand for it. There

The *basso buffo* sings the two Dr. Bartolos in *Il Barbiere di Siviglia* and *Le Nozze de Figaro*.

is little need for the thick, unsupple voice of the *basso profundo* in the opera house, any more than for the stolid, unpliant contralto. However the low notes of Sarastro's two majestic arias in *Die Zauberflöte* are well served by a *basso profundo*, and he can also add a proper dragonlike growl to the role of Fafner. On the whole the dark unwieldiness of his voice leaves the *basso profundo* with little opportunity for a variety of characterizations.

Outside the opera house Ezio Pinza proved that a bass could be a sexy and magnetic figure (but then so he was in it) even in middle age, when he played opposite Mary Martin in *South Pacific*. The pop singer with a bass voice seems to be something of a rarity in the history of popular music. One who never sang in an opera house—not because he couldn't have, he wasn't asked— and gave concerts of a mixture of classical and folk music, was the extraordinary Paul Robeson, the sound of whose burry, deep voice was spine-chilling. One of the most admired singers of his time, Robeson had a limited range and never aspired to be a great vocal artist. Nonetheless he was one of the great "natural" vocal artists of all time, a type of phenomenon that we will deal with in a subsequent section.

B A R I T O N E S

Belcore (*L'Elisir d'Amore*)   The first eight roles are more lyric than the rest.

Germont (*La Traviata*)
Golaud (*Pelléas et Melisande*)
Guglielmo (*Così fan Tutte*)
Marcello (*La Bohème*)
Masetto (*Don Giovanni*)
Papageno (*Die Zauberflöte*)
Silvio (*I Pagliacci*)

Alberich (*Das Rheingold* and *Götterdämmerung*)
Alfio (*Cavalleria Rusticana*)
Amfortas (*Parsifal*)
Amonasro (*Aida*)
Barnaba (*La Gioconda*)
Beckmesser (*Die Meistersinger*)   He has to sustain a difficult high A for three measures.
Count Almaviva (*Le Nozze di Figaro*)
Count di Luna (*Il Trovatore*)
Dappertutto (*Les Contes d'Hoffmann*)
Don Alfonso (*Così fan Tutte*)
Don Carlos (*La Forza del Destino*)
Don Giovanni
Enrico Ashton (*Lucia di Lammermoor*)
Escamillo (*Carmen*)   See discussion in text.
Falstaff
Father (*Louise*)   Sung by baritone and bass-baritones.
Figaro (*Il Barbiere di Siviglia* and *Le Nozze di Figaro*)
Flying Dutchman
Ford (*Falstaff*)
Gérard (*Andrea Chénier*)

Rossini's barber of Seville is sung by a high baritone. Mozart drops his range to that of the bass-baritone.

Gianni Schicchi	Can be sung by a bass as well.
Gunther (*Götterdämmerung*)	
Hans Sachs (*Die Meister-singer*)	
High Priest (*Samson et Dalila*)	Sometimes sung by a bass.
Iago (*Otello*)	
Jokanaan (*Salome*)	
Lescaut (Both *Manons*)	
Eugen Onegin	
Orest (*Elektra*)	
Ping (*Turandot*)	
Pizarro (*Fidelio*)	
Posa (*Don Carlo*)	
Rangoni (*Boris Godunov*)	
Renato (*Un Ballo in Maschera*)	
Rigoletto	
Sharpless (*Madama Butterfly*)	
Simon Boccanegra	

Beckmesser in *Die Meistersinger* is a comic part for the baritone.

Telramund (*Lohengrin*)
Tonio (*I Pagliacci*)
Valentin (*Faust*)
Wolfram (*Tannhäuser*)
Wotan (*Rheingold, Die Walküre, Siegfried*)
Wozzeck

THE BASSES

Alvise (*La Gioconda*)

Archibaldo (*L'Amore de Tre Rei*)
Boris Godunov
Don Basilio (*Il Barbiere di Siviglia*)
Méphistophélès (*Faust*)

The first eight roles are the biggest for the *basso cantante* in the Italian and French repertory. He also has the Mozart Figaro and Don Giovanni.

Padre Guardiano (*La Forza del Destino*)
Philip (*Don Carlo*)
Ramfis (*Aida*)

Arkel (*Pelléas et Melisande*)

This section lists smaller *basso cantante* roles in which there are opportunities for effective characterizations.

Colline (*La Bohème*)
Commendatore (*Don Giovanni*)
Dr. Miracle (*Les Contes d'Hoffmann*)
Elder Des Grieux (*Manon*)
Ferrando (*Il Trovatore*)
Grand Inquisitor (*Don Carlo*)

Sometimes sung by a German bass with his harsher, more declamatory way of singing.

King (*Aida*)
Pimen (*Boris Godunov*)
Sam (*Un Ballo in Maschera*)
Sparafucile (*Rigoletto*)
Timur (*Turandot*)
Tom (*Un Ballo in Maschera*)

THE BASSES
Some Basso Buffo *Roles*

Alcindoro (*La Bohème*)
Benoit (*La Bohème*)
Dr. Bartolo (*Il Barbiere di Siviglia* and *Le Nozze di Figaro*)
Dr. Dulcamara (*L'Elisir d'Amore*)
Don Pasquale
Fra Melitone (*La Forza del Destino*)
Leporello (*Don Giovanni*)
Sacristan (*Tosca*)
Varlaam (*Boris Godunov*)

Roles Usually Sung by German-Oriented Basses

Baron Ochs (*Der Rosenkava-lier*)

Daland (*Der Fliegende Hol-länder*)

Fafner (*Das Rheingold, Sieg-fried*)

Fasolt (*Das Rheingold*)

Gurnemanz (*Parsifal*)

Hagen (*Götterdämmerung*)

Hunding (*Die Walküre*)

King Henry (*Lohengrin*)

King Marke (*Tristan und Isolde*)

Kothner (*Die Meistersinger*)   Who must negotiate very florid music replete with trills in Act One.

Landgrave Hermann (*Tann-häuser*)

Osmin (*Das Entführung aus dem Serail*)

Pogner (*Die Meistersinger*)

Rocco (*Fidelio*)

Sarastro (*Die Zauberflöte*)

THE COMPRIMARIOS

There are opera singers with the various kinds of voices already described who perform only minor roles. As maids, confidantes, attendants, courtiers and messengers they are sometimes the vital means by which a plot is forwarded. These so-called "comprimario" singers are of two kinds: young artists with fine voices hoping to work their way into leading roles, and singers with unexceptional voices but who are good actors and build a career out of singing these small but essential parts. In recent years New York heard the sopranos Lucine Amara and Martina Arroyo graduate from tiny parts such as the offstage Celestial Voice in *Don Carlo* to leading lyric and *spinto* roles. Londoners can remember the occasion on which Joan Sutherland was Clothilde, maid to the Norma of Maria Callas.

Frequently, however, the singer who takes smaller roles may get stuck in them, possibly because there is too much competition

Boorish Baron Ochs in *Der Rosenkavalier* is sung by a bass or bass-baritone.

from older leading singers with the same type of voice, or perhaps because of lacking a final star quality, that mysterious combination of voice, personality and projection. Thus *comprimarios* may continue for years acting as "covers" in case the leading singer falls ill, sometimes getting a break, but somehow never quite making it to the big time. In his story, *Once More from the Beginning*, Robert Merrill tells how after having won the Metropolitan Opera auditions and a contract to sing with the company, his heart sank when he was asked to study Marullo in *Rigoletto*, the Herald in *Lohengrin* and Schaunard in *La Bohème*. With a kind of courage born of desperation lest he be singing these *comprimario* parts for a lifetime, he dared *not* to learn them. Such *chutzpah* paid off and Merrill made his debut as the elder Germont and has never sung anything but leading roles since. An earlier fine baritone, Lawrence Tibbett, made a most unobtrusive debut as Lovitzky, buried in the huge cast of *Boris Godunov*, and continued to sing small parts (with an occasional Valentin thrown in) until assigned the role of Ford in *Falstaff*. The opera was especially revived for Antonio Scotti, still the leading baritone of the Metropolitan in the 1920's. Ford's part is small but it does have the biggest aria in the whole score and Tibbett seized his opportunity. Thereafter, he never looked back until some nineteen years later he sang the part of Falstaff himself.

Some singers with fine voices have been offered contracts with the Metropolitan to sing small roles, but resist the tempting title "of the Metropolitan Opera Company" and turn their faces east to Europe. From there, having earned valuably needed experience that is so difficult to obtain in America and made a reputation, they return in triumph to New York. One of the early great and glamorous singers to establish this pattern was Geraldine Farrar, who turned down a contract with the Metropolitan and set out for Europe where she became a star of the Berlin Opera. Not many years ago the American tenor James McCracken was singing the few lines of the toymaker Parpignol in *La Bohème*. Fortunately for lovers of *Otello* and other Italian operas, McCracken threw down his basket of toys and headed across the Atlantic, whence he returned, his voice, his operatic experience and not least his physique vastly enlarged to sing the leading roles of the dramatic tenor repertory. Still another who turned down a contract with the Metropolitan was Maria Callas.

When the new production of *Carmen* under Leonard Bernstein was mounted at the Metropolitan in 1972, the soprano Jeannine Altmeyer was assigned as "first cover" for the leading part of Micaela. Altmeyer with an unusually large and mature sounding soprano had won the National Auditions at the age of twenty-one in the previous year. After that, discouragement had set in. She sang the small part of Frasquita in *Carmen* and an off-stage "Celestial Voice" in *Don Carlo* and nothing more. As she worked day after day in rehearsal blocking out the role as proxy for the scheduled Micaela, Teresa Stratas, it seemed like a real opportunity. Her hopes rose still higher when Stratas had to cancel her engagement because of the recurrence of a childhood tubercular condition. Would Altmeyer actually get to sing the part in performance? Then came a kind of one-two punch. Another soprano, Adriana Maliponte, was scheduled for the Micaela. In addition, Altmeyer was removed as first cover on the grounds that her voice was too mature sounding. She was discovered weeping backstage at the news while at the same time making plans to quit the Metropolitan to attempt a career in Europe. Just over a decade later, the still unusually young dramatic soprano was singing leading parts at Bayreuth in the summer of 1983 and could have a pick of engagements in numbers of other leading opera houses around the world.

For the number of singers with lovely voices caught in the web of the *comprimario* parts, there are ones to match them with voices lacking in sensuousness. These artists, serious, conscientious, often fine actors, have made long careers by their musicianship and their ability to assume all kinds of bite-sized operatic characterizations. One of the most famous of these interesting artists was Angelo Bada, who first sang the few, but intensely significant lines of the Messenger in *Aida* on 16 November 1908, the evening also of the Metropolitan debut of Arturo Toscanini. Bada sang his last part, Arturo Bucklaw, rejected fiancé of Lucia di Lammermoor, in March 1938. For over thirty years he never sang a leading role, nor ever even appeared as soloist in the Sunday night concerts that used to be a feature at the Metropolitan for so many years. Yet his career, based on a pale rather bleaty kind of tenor, must be accounted a notable one. Another more recent *comprimario* was the Russian baritone George Cehanovsky, who made his Metropolitan debut in 1926 and sang seventy-eight different roles for the company until 1966—a total of forty years.

Today at the Metropolitan are the mezzo-sopranos Shirley Love and Jean Kraft, the tenors Charles Anthony and Nico Castel (to name but a few), all interesting artists, who will undoubtedly achieve similar records.

Though the roles he performs may be minor, the *comprimario* does not go totally unnoticed. In the comic scene for the deaf servant, Frantz, who dusts the Munich flat of Crespel in Act Three of *Les Contes d'Hoffmann*, a clever artist as was the *comprimario* tenor Alessio DePaolis or presently Andrea Velis, could bring the house down. This same type of tenor can make a subtly evil characterization of Prince Shuisky in *Boris Godunov* and the even more sinister Spoletta, Scarpia's henchman, in *Tosca*. The *comprimario* tenor may also be given the part of Beppe in *I Pagliacci*, which includes a graceful serenade, sung, unfortunately, offstage. (A story is told that Caruso once asked the secondary tenor singing Beppe if he might perform this little aria instead, which he did. There was applause but not of the lavish kind usually accorded any rendition by Caruso, proof to him that his fame and popularity were all illusion: the audience hadn't even recognized his voice.)

There are many other outstanding vignette characterizations for the skilled *comprimario* to create in the standard operatic repertory. The mezzo-soprano who sings the blind mother pleading before the tribunal in Act Three of *Andrea Chénier* has a superb opportunity to stir her audience, and indeed so effective is the scene that sometimes a leading singer will gladly undertake the role though it is very brief. A mezzo with a gift for comedy can make much of the few lines of the Innkeeper in *Boris Godunov*. The soprano who sings the slight role of Lucia di Lammermoor's maid participates in one of the most show-stopping numbers in all of opera—the Sextet in Act Two; so does the *comprimario* tenor who sings Lord Arturo Bucklaw.

Certain operas put tremendous pressure on the *comprimario* staff of an opera company, causing the general manager to call out all the reserves he possesses. These include *Boris Godunov* with its children, servants, boyars, peasants and sole simpleton, and *Die Meistersinger* which requires a bevy of male *comprimarios* to portray the citizens of Nuremberg. Perhaps the most demanding operatic work of all in this respect is *Louise*, Charpentier's lovely evocation of Paris at the turn of the century, in which there are no less than thirty-seven tiny little parts (six, however, heard offstage). There are a number of *midinettes*, a pair of philosophers, two rag-pickers (one old and one young, the latter sung by a woman), two policemen, a variety of vendors of different foods ranging from artichokes to watercress, a junkman, a street arab, a noctambulist and a character known as the "King of Fools." A certain amount of doubling can take place, but it provides a great evening for the *comprimarios*, and if their numbers run out the hard-pressed general manager can always move in fresh supplies from the chorus.

As with the *comprimarios*, it might be supposed that a position in the chorus would be a stepping-stone to stardom for the aspiring singer. If anything, it is even less so, firmly quenching the light (if there was one) of the potential star and establishing him as a chorister and no more. True, such fine leading artists as Leonard Warren and Jan Peerce sang in the Radio City Music Hall Glee Club as a means of getting on with their careers, but that was outside the opera house. Like *comprimarios*, opera choristers can make long, full careers with usually no more than an average voice. They work hard. Only a few operas such as *Salome, Die Walküre* and *Pelléas et Melisande* give them a night off. They must memorize a large repertory and possess fine musicianship. In two operas, *Boris Godunov* and *Peter Grimes*, the chorus is really the star of the evening. Even less than with *comprimario* singers, however, does one hear of a chorister in a prominent opera company taking a leading role with a smaller one, nor, for that matter, moving into the field of concert singing. Though the singing voice remains the center of their lives they seem to become set in their ways and do not explore the musical by-paths along which their vocal art might take them.

NATIONAL VOICES

In this cataloging of voices it will be noted that certain countries or regions seem to specialize in producing certain kinds of voices. The middle-European countries and Austria and Germany are rich in high *acuto sfogato* sopranos. England is noted for its contraltos and Spain coloratura mezzos. The honeyed, almost baby-sounding tenor voice comes from Italy and the deep, deep *basso* out of Russia. In addition, certain countries may produce singers of international reputation far out of proportion to their populations. This is most true of Scandinavia. Why should three little nations with a combined population of about fifteen million have given the world scores of great singers from Jenny Lind through Christine Nilsson, Olive Fremstad, Kirsten Flagstad, Lauritz Melchior, Karin Branzell, Jussi Bjoerling and Birgit Nilsson, to name but a handful? And why should England with a population of over fifty million have produced until recently so few vocal artists of international reputation over the years?

With this discussion we once again enter the realm of pure speculation, and yet the conclusions to be drawn seem quite inescapable. Singers from a particular country are bound to be affected by its national taste and style in music, particularly folk songs. For example, the native music of Spain and southern Italy flows with Moorish-oriented runs and sinuous turns and embellishments of other kinds. Not surprisingly, a line of singers possessing remarkable agility has come from these regions, including the delightful coloratura mezzo Conchita Supervia, and later de los Angeles, Berganza and Caballé. The oratorio, beloved of the English for a century or more, usually requires a female singer with a commanding low voice. When there is a national demand for a type of voice to satisfy a particular musical taste that taste will be served, and so the English specialize in producing husky (sometimes manly sounding) contralto voices. The same has proved true in Russia where there exists a passion for the low bass voice that was once a requisite in religious services.

Next we should consider national tastes in the quality of singing voices. The German-speaking countries make an interesting contrast with those of southern Europe. Germany and Austria, besides specializing in "little girl" high coloraturas, produce a characteristic tone quality in their sopranos. These are trained towards the top of the range with little vibrato, so that sometimes a soprano like Schwarzkopf will make a sound like a mew on a high note. Above all, German and Austrian sopranos do not sing the gutsy low notes known as chest tones. The colorful, slightly aggressive vocal quality that many women singers are capable of producing is simply not taught.*

In Italy the soprano sound is entirely different, having a plentiful vibrato, and much fuller tones at the bottom which are frequently compensated by a shrillness and tendency to flat the higher notes. Among the heavier sopranos chest tones are a must. These tastes seem to match the respective national attitudes towards women. The Germans tend to keep their women subservient and dependent. The ideal is for her to be pure, girlish, with a seasoning of archness. The Italian woman, the responsible mother keeping the family together, is volatile, aggressive, full of temperament—all qualities which one hears in the Italian voice.

America, which prizes the strong, outdoor kind of male, frequently produces a kind of wholesome, clean-cut type of baritone appropriate to a not overly sensitive cowboy singing to his horse under Western skies. An American male who produced the vulnerable, almost feminine sound that proceeds from an Italian tenor singing *mezza voce* might be regarded with deep suspicion. Yet that quality matches the gentleness which often predominates in the Italian masculine character.

---

*"She did make an iron rule that the higher type of soprano, lyrical soubrette and coloratura, should on no occasion make use of chest notes even in a mixed form," writes Elizabeth Puritz in her *The Teaching of Elisabeth Schumann*. This is a characteristic attitude among all German-oriented teachers of singing.

Slavic voices can almost always be recognized by the shiver that afflicts them. I use the word "afflict" for this wiry, whirring vibrato certainly seems a fault to our ears. Yet the Russians, the Yugoslavs, the Bulgarians and the Czechs don't seem to mind. True, the characteristic Slavic voice singing central and eastern European songs and operas bothers Western ears less than in Italian or German music. This brings us to what is perhaps the most overwhelming factor of all in the shaping of national voices—language.

A Tug of War.

> No human singing can
> Express itself without
> Words that usurp the sounds
> That pour forth from the throat

In the art of fine singing an implacable war ranges constantly between the word and the tone. In certain situations one is invariably sacrificed to the other. The soprano, for instance, must never sing a long "ē" sound above G' lest she ruin her voice. To the discomfiture of the Wagnerian soprano the great composer gave the names of Siegmund, Sieglinde and Siegfried to three of the leading characters in the Ring. If one listens closely to the end of the *Götterdämmerung* Immolation Scene, Brünnhilde will really be heard to invoke her beloved "Sahgfried." "It is for the singer to defend his voice against the pitfalls of words," warns that trenchant authority Blanche Marchesi. "He must never sacrifice vocal beauty, and if anything be sacrificed let it be the words."

Pier Francesco Tosi, writing two hundred and fifty years earlier, disagrees with her: "If the words are not heard so as to be understood, there will be no great difference between a human voice and a hautboy." During the eighteenth century audiences were quite content to let the singer run along for a plethora of measures on one syllable giving no thought to the verbal content of his song; this was also true during the bel canto era of the early nineteenth century, in which Berlioz witheringly condemned the great vocal artists of this period as "performers on the larynx." (A descendant of that vocal age and one much criticized for her watery enunciation is Joan Sutherland, who by sacrificing the word—to be sure the word is often fairly inane anyway—produces floods of beautiful tone with remarkable agility.)

With the development of the so-called "art songs" requiring the voices of highly trained singers, attention to the word became increasingly emphasized. It is no coincidence that some of the most famous recitalists—singers of German lieder and French *chansons* Elena Gerhardt, Povla Frijsh, Pierre Bernac—were not noted for their voices of sensuous beauty. A fine concert singer of the 1920's and 30's, the mezzo-soprano Claire Croiza had this to say of her highly developed art: "In singing one may prefer either the sound or the word. No sound however beautiful will give me personally the joy that I get from a beautifully enunciated vowel." Certainly there have been many singers with excellent diction wedded to beautiful tone, but usually much care and hard work. has to be expended to bring about this somewhat grudging alliance. In the popular field no such attempt is made: the word almost invariably has the upper hand and the tone must adjust as best it can.

To return to the subject of national voices, two great European countries have a rich treasure house of poetry which they love and honor together with the language in which it is written. In both France and England a kind of natural instinct exists to put the word before the tone in singing, thereby causing muscles in the throat to move to positions which produce a far less pleasing quality of sound and may actually harm the singing voice. As a result in France many professional singers have reedy, nasal-sounding voices and are not often heard outside the borders of their country. England, where the word is also sacred, has continually championed the cause of opera and lieder in her native tongue since the time Handel first came to British shores— and suffered a paucity of international singers almost to the present day.* Since Covent Garden reverted to a policy of presenting opera in the original language, artists such as Sir Geraint Evans, Peter Glossop, Stuart Burrows, Gwyneth Jones, Dame Janet Baker, Margaret Price, Yvonne Minton and David Rendall have appeared around the world with superb, properly placed voices.

Since the word shapes and affects a tone of the singer's voice,

---

*Note this attitude of a celebrated English singer and teacher at the turn of the century: "Voice must grow out of language, and students must begin their studentship by singing THOUGHTS . . . No alteration of the character of the word is admissible."—David Ffrangcon-Davies, *The Singing of the Future.*

the language that a human being learns from infancy has a profound effect on the habitual position that his vocal apparatus takes when he normally phonates. Or, put more specifically, our native way of speaking requires us to put the back of the tongue and the larynx, both of which can be raised and lowered, into a particular, familiar place. Also because the language has been spoken over centuries by a native's forebears, it may have evolved a certain shape to the all-important resonator at the top of the throat, a cavity called the pharynx. It even may have sculpted in a certain way other cavities that lie behind the nose and the upper part of the face which are also resonators.

This being the case let us examine some of the languages—English, for example, the so-called Oxbridge accent. Generally considered genteel and desirable, words are spoken very far forward on the teeth and lips, so that the "t's" and labials fall upon the ears of the listener like a little shower of pebbles. Nothing could be more disastrous* for the creation of a natural singing voice, since this forward inflection draws the larynx up from the throat giving the average untrained English singing voice a white, breathy, all but toneless sound. Combine this with a terror of being rude—such as making loud noises—ingrained in the average Englishman who speaks with an Oxbridge accent and it is easy to understand why the English have produced so few natural voices. The Englishman who would become a singer must break two habits that are almost as natural to him as breathing: the way he produces his speaking voice and his mercilessly conditioned inhibitions. (The latter, of course, do not extend to the British as actors, who are superb and many in numbers, perhaps because they are dealing precisely with what comes naturally to the natives of this land of Shakespeare—the spoken word, not "rude noises.") Once out of London in the provinces, in Lancashire, say, whence emerged the great natural voice of Kathleen Ferrier, we hear an accent that places the voice further back in the throat. The same is true of the Irish brogue and though there have not been many great Irish international singers (one thinks of John McCormack and Margaret Sheridan, and

---

*The *advantage* of this placement for singers of Gilbert and Sullivan was made manifest when Joel Grey starred in a television production of *The Yeomen of the Guard*. The popular American entertainer mumbled and swallowed many of the words.

today Heather Harper and Norma Burrowes) the country abounds in lovely natural voices.

As to French it is probably the most difficult to sing of any tongue in which there exists an important vocal literature. This language, too, pulls up the larynx to a position not suited for producing a round, full tone, and in addition requires the vocalist, if he is to sing his words with an eloquent, idiomatic pronunciation, to produce some of his notes in his nose. The concept of correct singing *"dans la masque"* is well known, but *"la masque"* has nothing to do with *"le nez,"* though the two are frequently confused. The would-be French singer, therefore, has to overcome the evolution of his resonators and pharynx over generations of his French-speaking forebears together with the negative effect of the language on the positioning of his larynx. In addition there is the absolute Gallic insistence that the tone be sacrificed to the word. Finally he has to fight a certain lack of national enthusiasm for singing—certainly not the case in England.

Up until recently at the Paris Opéra and Opéra-Comique the French went through the motions of putting on works in the standard repertory with mainly native-born singers who made a mockery of the days when the Opéra could boast of such great French stars as sopranos Emma Calvé and Lucienne Bréval and, later, Ninon Vallin and Germaine Lubin; as well as the mezzos Marie Delna and Alice Raveau. In the masculine department were such superb French singers in days gone by as the tenors Charles Dalmorès, Albert Saléza, Edmond Clément, Charles Rousselière and Georges Thill; the baritones Jean Lassalle and Victor Maurel (Verdi's first Iago in *Otello*) and the sensitive recitalist, Charles Panzéra; the bass-baritones Pol Plançon (noted for his trill), Lucien Fugère, Vanni-Marcoux; and the basses Leon Rothier and Marcel Journet. Today the Opéra-Comique is no more and the demise of a whole typically Gallic style of singing will probably follow. The grand Paris Opéra, like Covent Garden, its English counterpart, has turned international, mounting productions that are no longer cast nationally. How this will affect the production of new singers from France remains to be heard. One thing is certain: The word will continue to come first in the cherished language of the French.

Cross the border at Ventimiglia and everything is reversed.

Everyone knows that to an Italian singing comes as easily as eating or making love. It is in his blood; he adores it—though doubtless there are thousands if not millions of exceptions to the stereotype of the singing, song-loving Italian. His language, of course, is beautifully conducive to singing, with its long vowels, often connecting two words in a manner which gives added line to a musical phrase such as Violetta's

Dite alle giovine. . . .

and its soft words pronounced well back in the throat. No inhibitions about rude noises in this country: the Italians thrive on noise. Nor is there any particular literary mystique here. The Italians love their language, too (though to be sure over the various sections of the country they pronounce it in a multiplicity of ways) but Dante, Petrarch and possibly Manzoni hold sway over the artistic imagination of only a few, as opposed to the way Shakespeare seems to dominate that of masses of English people.

Spain, as I have already mentioned, has supplied the world with a number of marvelous singers. Because of an idiosyncrasy of the language, Spanish vocalists can usually be detected by the aspirated way they attack certain notes in the middle and lower parts of their range. A sound like the tiniest of hiccups, it can be heard in the singing of both de los Angeles and Caballé.

Heading north again to the heavily populated Netherlands, this song-loving country has produced some, but not many, singers of international fame, probably because of the inflections of a harsh tongue. Further to the east, Germany and Austria have of course been most fecund, though not always so. "A German singer! I should as soon expect to get pleasure from the neighing of my horse!" the musical monarch Frederick the Great is supposed to have said. In an article entitled "On Dramatic Song," Richard Wagner, an informed authority on the singing voice, set down his views on the inferiority of German singing around the time of his marriage to Minna Planer (1836). The German throat, he declared, was less adapted by nature to singing than that of the Italian; nor did the majority of German singers train sufficiently before appearing in public (a complaint made to this day about singers everywhere). Hence the early loss of voice by his idol, the dramatic Wilhelmine Schröder-Devrient, Wagner's first Senta and Venus.

Perhaps because of Wagner's demand from his singers for a

more Italianate, flowing style of singing wedded to German art, a line of Austro-German giants began to emerge towards the end of the nineteenth century, including some of the first Bayreuth artists, Amalie Materna, Marianne Brandt and Albert Niemann; also the incomparable Lilli Lehmann and the equally extraordinary Ernestine Schumann-Heink. In more recent times there have been such superb singers as Maria Jeritza, Elisabeth Rethberg, Lotte Lehmann, the great Wagnerian soprano Frida Leider, and the huge, black-voiced bass Michael Bohnen. Recently Germany and Austria have supplied the international scene with sopranos such as Elisabeth Schwarzkopf, Hilde Gueden and Irmgard Seefried, the versatile mezzo Christa Ludwig, baritones such as Dietrich Fischer-Dieskau and Hermann Prey, and the late much-lamented tenor Fritz Wunderlich. German, a most expressive language, is full of harsh and guttural sounds. For this reason it produces a more declamatory kind of singer, particularly among the males. The language also puts into the voice, especially that of the tenor, a kind of taut brilliance that makes it recognizably German.

I have already mentioned the classic shiver almost inevitably heard in Russian and Slavic voices, again presumably due to language, though one occasionally hears it among Italians as in the case of the early Pinza. Certain great singers from middle Europe, however, eluded it and made international careers: from Poland, the de Reszke brothers and Marcella Sembrich; the great dramatic soprano Emmy Destinn from Czechoslovakia; Milka Ternina, a celebrated dramatic soprano of around 1900 from Yugoslavia, and her pupil Zinka Milanov. Hearing Milanov's luscious soprano with its beautifully floated pianissimi for the first time, it would have been difficult to pin down its nationality. It was a truly international voice.

Except for one or two basses, the Russians—again because of the quiver intrinsic to most of their voices—have sent few great singers out into the rest of the world. In days gone by there was the charming coloratura Lydia Lipkowska and the mountainous Nina Koshetz, whose artistry moved many in the recital hall. Today, as the world shrinks, we hear Soviet artists such as the fine baritone Yuri Mazurok and the handsome, dark-haired soprano Galina Vishnevskaya, whose slightly strident tone quality is offensive to some ears but not the artistry nor conviction of her singing. A superb mezzo-soprano without a characteristic Russian shiver to her voice is Irina Archipova, but Western voice lovers have heard her mainly through records, as she has rarely toured outside the Soviet Union.

Concerning the pronounced vibrato in most Russian voices, Howard Taubman tells a story of days gone by in Moscow at the Imperial Opera during a performance of *Ruslan and Ludmilla* when the baritone entered on a horse to engage in a scene with an old sage sung by a tenor in this case no longer young. The baritone began the parley and the tenor was just about to reply when the horse took over with a loud neigh. "The sound," says Mr. Taubman, "with its high pitch and shake and breathiness, resembled that made by the tenor. That unhappy individual tried to go on with his part of the colloquy. The horse replied in a higher key. The tenor sang again. The horse went him one better." Ultimately, of course, the curtain had to be rung down.

Of this little European tour the only area that remains is Scandinavia, comprising three countries which have given us some of the most extraordinary voices the world has ever known—way out of proportion to their small populations. Why should this be?

It is not enough to say that the Scandinavians are an intensely musical people, though musicianship of the trained, not intuitive kind, is rife among them. A myth grew up that Flagstad came from ignorant peasant stock; both her parents were in fact professional musicians, which, if living in a musical atmosphere has anything to do with it, explains why she had perfect pitch. Birgit Nilsson can memorize a score spread out on her lap in an airplane. These are not the accomplishments of some of the greatest singing stars including the late, magnetic *basso cantante* Ezio Pinza, who could not sight-read.

The true reason for the amazing flow of great singing artists from Scandinavia appears again to be a matter of language. In these countries the various tongues, somewhat interrelated, position the larynx exactly where it is best suited for singing. The "yup-yup" sound of Norwegian or Swedish and the mocking of it with such clichés as "Yonny Yonson" all instance this. "I keep the larynx down [when singing]," Marilyn Horne declares firmly of her fabulous vocal technique. For a Scandinavian the language achieves this position automatically from the moment he begins to speak.

The United States has given many remarkable singers to the world, producing at first mainly female artists, often of great physical beauty such as Emma Eames and Geraldine Farrar. With the exception of the baritone David Bispham, who had to defy his Quaker family to go on the stage, American male singers arrived on the international scene somewhat later, probably due to the American mistrust of a male artist in general and his virility in particular. (Writing in *Opera News* the tenor Jess Thomas says that as a boy in a typical midwestern small town, he had to sneak out to the garage to the Metropolitan Opera broadcasts lest he be caught in so sissy an act—and that's not very long ago.) Americans, of course, speak much further back in their throats than their English cousins and bear down on their "r's" in a way that the British have pleasure in mocking. But the curled accent of the midwesterner that seems to cling to the roof of his mouth like clotted peanut butter is far more conducive to the correct placing of a singing voice than the forward enunciation of the English- man.

America is such an ethnic mixture that it is difficult to define a strictly American voice, though fine baritones such as Lawrence Tibbett, John Charles Thomas, and recently, Sherrill Milnes would seem to be recognizably American. Chameleon-like, the American singer who trains abroad will sometimes take on the characteristics of singers of the country in which he has trained. A record by the American lyric tenor Richard Crooks, who studied in Germany and sang at the Berlin Staatsoper, of "Recondita armonia" from *Tosca* in German, would lead the most experienced analyst of national voices to think that this was a German tenor— by quality of timbre, style and inflection. Teresa Stich-Randall sang Nanetta in the Toscanini broadcast of *Falstaff* which was later issued on records. Contrast her voice then before she went abroad for training in the Austro-German methods with what it came to sound like subsequently, a totally German quality with a pure, somewhat mewed top.

The only truly recognizable American voice, or used to be anyway, belongs to the black singer—though I may be accused of racism for saying so. Marian Anderson, Paul Robeson, Dorothy Maynor all had distinctly black voices and I think today that if he did not know, a perceptive listener would instantly recognize the voice of Leontyne Price as belonging to a black. But this is beginning to change, presumably as blacks become more assimilated into America. To my ears the sweeping voice of Grace Bumbry does not sound black nor the pert one of Kathleen Battle. One thing is certain, however: now that blacks have broken the barriers that used to keep them out of the opera house, they are making an almost disproportionate contribution to the art of great singing. On the roster of the Metropolitan's 1983–84 centennial season are the accomplished *leggiero* sopranos Gwendolyn Bradley and Kathleen Battle; the splendid *spinto* Leona Mitchell and two of the most magnificent vocal artists in the history of singing: Leontyne Price and Jessye Norman. The list of black mezzo-sopranos is no less distinguished, including Grace Bumbry, Shirley Verrett, Isola Jones and Florence Quivar. If the selection of male black artists is less imposing it nonetheless includes the promising young tenor Philip Creech, and the imposing bass-baritone Simon Estes, who has also sung at Bayreuth and in other leading opera houses around the world.

In her *Manual of Bel Canto*, Ida Franca asserts that "frequently the range of the Negro singer—and especially the range of the Negro tenor—can be developed to outdo any white singer's range," and gives tables showing that the chest and head registers of black female singers are outsize compared to those of white ones. She also declares that a "tenorino" (countertenor) voice is peculiar to the black and goes on to say happily, "With appropriate training such a voice can, of course, be developed into a voice of no less power and charm than the voice of a castrated virtuoso." I do not know whether today's super pop singer Michael Jackson has had any "appropriate training." But certainly the tones that he produces could be identified as proceeding from "a castrated virtuoso."

Another somewhat ethnically crossed country is Australia, which has hatched out a number of noted singers,[*] mainly female as with the United States[†] at an earlier time. Melba, Frances Alda

---

[*]The native aborigines, supposedly because of the construction of their facial bones, usually have only rudimentary singing voices.

[†]Others of recent years have included Marie Collier, Ronald Dowd, Margreta Elkins, Elizabeth Fretwell, Joan Hammond, Albert Lance, Elsie Morison and John Shaw to name but a few.

(she was actually from New Zealand), Florence Austral, a Wagnerian soprano with a superb top to her voice, another fine Wagnerian soprano, Marjorie Lawrence, whose career was tragically reduced by polio, all made splendid international careers. Today we have two remarkable sopranos from "Down Under," both of whom can claim the title of "Dame." These are the peerless Australian Joan Sutherland and the New Zealander Kiri Te Kanawa, whose star-like tones proceed from from a blending of Irish and Maori blood.

As the world grows smaller and more international we can expect today's singing voices to emerge with fewer national characteristics. Nevertheless, as long as countries continue to preserve the precious heritage of their own individual languages, singing voices will continue to be shaped and conditioned by them.

J. von der Schlichten: The Amateur.

The Non-Operatic Voices

Of the numerous kinds of voices heard outside the opera house all belong in some way, however limited, to one of the types of operatic voices already described. In opera, despite what anyone might say, the voice comes first. With non-operatic voices there is often far less emphasis on sheer vocal beauty. New factors now enter in, such as style, personality and, in the case of the concert singer, consummate musicianship.

The Recitalists. Many outstanding concert singers have possessed voices of true operatic calibre. In the case of such artists as Lotte Lehmann, Alexander Kipnis or Elisabeth Schwarzkopf they have been equally at home in the opera house and concert hall. Other artists with big, wide-ranging voices that would seem to be suitable for opera have eschewed it for reasons of personality and a lack of histrionic flair. At one point in her career it was suggested to Kathleen Ferrier that she sing Carmen. Certainly she had the voice to do so but not the dramatic temperament. Very wisely she refused. The great mezzo-soprano Elena Gerhardt began her career with a few operatic forays (she sang Charlotte in *Werther* and Mignon) but soon realized that she must dedicate her musical life to what it was most suited for—the art of lieder singing. Other recitalists have made outstanding careers with voices severely restricted in range and tonal beauty. The much admired French baritone Pierre Bernac was never praised for vocal sensuousness. Povla Frijsh, the Danish soprano, held audiences in her sway but not because of the loveliness of her voice. In the case of a concert singer, Rossini's formula for a successful singing career—"voice, voice, voice"—does not apply. Here the necessary ingredients are artistry, musicianship and only then, lower down on the ladder, voice.

An opera singer has many supports in the distractions of scenery, costumes and his own dramatic gestures, together with a large orchestra led by a conductor giving musical cues and ready to cover over any mistakes. Not so the concert singer. He stands exposed and alone on a stage, bare except for a piano and an unobtrusive accompanist. Through the colors of his voice he has to create a different mood with each song—evoke a tiny little world in perhaps no more than three or four minutes' time. So effective must his singing be that he holds an audience fascinated for a whole evening. Small wonder that there have been fewer great concert singers than their operatic counterparts.

Successful recitalists have possessed almost every type of singing voice, but it is also true that of the various types some are better suited than others to lieder (a term that has come to mean art songs not only in German, but many other languages as well). Erna Berger, the German soprano *acuto sfogato*, was an excellent lieder singer. Exquisite in delicate songs like Mozart's "Das Veilchen" or the Strauss "Ständchen" she could not summon the darker, more impassioned accents needed in the dramatic song literature. The fine Dutch concert singer Elly Ameling with a light, soubrette soprano quality to her voice, suffers from this imposition but gives highly successful recitals as does the slightly heavier-voiced Edith Mathis. In earlier times another soubrette soprano, Elisabeth Schumann, was one of the great lieder recitalists, as were the *spintos* Lotte Lehmann, Elisabeth Schwarzkopf and Victoria de los Angeles, all singers who combined art with a great deal of charm. Who can forget an end to a de los Angeles recital when the Spanish soprano with an almost secret smile on her face would appear without her accompanist but holding a guitar? Seated on a low stool she would play and sing songs that were part of her heritage to the utter delight of the audience.

Only with the very largest soprano voices do reservations enter in. For instance Flagstad with her impeccable musicianship and marvelous vocal line, gave fine recitals and yet at times her voice seemed to overpower the songs that she sang. There was too much of a muchness and the effect something which every recitalist struggles to avoid—monotony. At a recent Carnegie Hall

T. Eakins: The Concert Singer (Philadelphia Museum of Art).

recital Jessye Norman, majestic of voice and stature, following a program that included the Wesendonk songs and *chansons* by Henri Duparc (in both cases later orchestrated by the composers), sought to lighten the evening by singing fluffy French selections of the operetta kind that Yvonne Printemps, the French star of the thirties, was famous for. These she bought off with charm and élan, though visually a suspension of disbelief was required at hearing her in this repertory.

The lower women's voices also can succeed in the concert hall, particularly in more dramatic selections such as Schubert's "Erl-könig" or "Der Tod und Das Mädchen." These songs were specialties of Ernestine Schumann-Heink and Sigrid Onegin, both of whom were equally at home on the operatic stage. Today we find the gifted Christa Ludwig switching easily between opera and lieder. In the case of the late Kathleen Ferrier, she showed less inclination to engage herself in operatic affairs.

A superb recitalist before the public today is another Spaniard, the mezzo-soprano Teresa Berganza, whose programs range from florid Mozart concert arias through subtle *chansons* by Debussy and Ravel to songs in her own language by de Falla and Granados. When opera stars take to the concert stage they often follow the easy path of putting a generous selection of arias on their programs to please their fans. The result is less than satisfactory because of the lack of an orchestral accompaniment. Berganza, though a leading opera singer, has usually kept to the subtler concert repertory. In a recent appearance, however—Carnegie Hall was again the scene—she announced as an encore the "Habanera" from *Carmen*. Then placing her right hand, palm down, on the lid of the piano and otherwise standing stock still, she proceeded to give a lesson as to how this fascinating music should be sung without shoulder-twitching, hip-wriggling and "come hither" mugging. All the aria's insouciance and suggestiveness was conveyed entirely in her way with the words and her voice.

Among the men a number of German tenors such as Julius Patzak, Karl Erb and Ernst Häfliger have proved to be outstanding lieder singers. Fritz Wunderlich was well on his way to establishing himself in this difficult branch of vocal art until his untimely death. One thinks too of the Dane Aksel Schiøtz—less so of his Swedish compatriot Jussi Bjoerling. Though the latter gave many recitals, again a certain monotony tended to creep into them—was it because of the unvarying beauty of his voice? Nor is the rich, sumptuous quality of the baritone voice as produced by, say, Leonard Warren or Peter Glossop an altogether desirable attribute in the concert hall. The most successful baritone recitalists have possessed leaner (Gérard Souzay), at times harsher (Dietrich Fischer-Dieskau), more malleable (Hermann Prey) voices that can give greater expressivity to the words with which they are so closely engaged.

From the lowest male voices one would expect a certain monotony of tone color in their need to transfer songs down to lower, darker keys. And yet the great Russian bass Alexander Kipnis brought chiaroscuro into his beautiful recitals by an ability to lighten and brighten his big, dark voice. And of course the incomparable Feodor Chaliapin also gave highly successful concerts, somewhat eccentric affairs to be sure, at which audiences were handed books containing a large collection of song texts and translations, but no announced program. Chaliapin, as if overtaken by a moment's inspiration, would then appear to decide spontaneously which one of the collection he would sing. It was noticed, however, that in fact the bass sang the same "inspired" program night after night, the way any concert singer does who puts together a fixed selection of songs for his tours.

More recently the bass-baritone Hans Hotter with his somewhat harsh vocal quality was an expressive recitalist, particularly outstanding in Schubert's song cycle *Die Winterreise*. The huge Finnish bass Martti Talvela has also proved that a deep, almost black-sounding voice, can be most effective in concert, particularly when heard in the Brahms *Vier Ernste Gesänge* or the Mussorgsky *Songs and Dances of Death*.

Laments frequently go up today that the art of concert singing is becoming lost. True, the recital series that used to be a mainstay of cultural life in cities around the United States have become fewer and impresarios are more inclined only to present big name singers like Leontyne Price (an excellent recitalist) or Montserrat Caballé whom they feel will sell the house. Yet lovers of the art song have continued to hear superbly presented programs by Dietrich Fischer-Dieskau, Janet Baker, Gérard Souzay and many other fine concert singers. And new recitalists continue to come on the scene including a pair of Scandinavian baritones, Håken Hagegård and Jorma Hynninen, who have proved to be vocal artists in the old tradition of refinement and sensitivity.

Another up-and-coming recitalist is the charming Metropolitan Opera soprano *leggiero* Kathleen Battle, who admits that one of her idols has been the equally charming lieder singer of past years Elisabeth Schumann. In the 1983–84 season Miss Battle appeared in an unusual concert series at Lincoln Center with programs ranging eclectically from a Bach cantata to Duke Ellington's "Creole Love Call." With her pert, deft voice and a personality to match, a reviewer commented on one of the three concerts, "It was one of those evenings when nobody wanted to go home."

In the challenge of holding the unwavering attention of an audience through a whole evening, singers, particularly those with operatic affinities, have been known to resort to gestures, extravagant facial expressions and even changes of costume which are entirely out of place in the subtle, intimate art of lieder singing. (Towards the end of her career, the great soprano Frieda Hempel would give what she called "Jenny Lind Evenings" in which she put on nineteenth century costume and sang the repertory of "the Swedish Nightingale." Hempel, however, was an exemplary "straight" recitalist as well.)

Ideally, nothing external should distract from the blending of word and tone in the performance of an art song. Before beginning his next selection the singer thinks himself into the mood of it. The effect on the audience can be magical as he projects this mood across the footlights before having sung a single note. Far less flamboyant than his operatic counterpart, a lieder singer, nonetheless, remains a singing actor and a show-man. He chooses songs that best display his voice and carefully puts together programs with effective contrasts of mood, tempi and rhythm—also of key signatures—in his selections. In late February 1984, just prior to singing his first recital at Carnegie Hall, Sherrill Milnes, considered to be the finest operatic baritone of his era, gave an interesting interview to the New York *Times* in which he commented on the different requirements of opera and concert singing. He described his voice as having a "brilliant" and a "mellow" side respectively. The brilliance is operatic, "what I do for the industry, [while the mellow part has] greater sway in the concert situation." In recital, Milnes says, it is necessary to break the "operatic habit of brilliant projection in favor of more introspective applications."

In this discussion of concert singing the reader may have

noticed that the word "charm" has frequently appeared. Though not an absolute requisite for success on the recital platform, personal charm is certainly a tremendous asset to the singer who stands alone and defenseless, so to speak, on a bare stage without costume or props seeking the attention of a critical audience for an hour and a half. Most of the great recitalists have projected that indefinable aura of personality that beckons and captivates others: Elisabeth Schumann, Lotte Lehmann, Kathleen Ferrier, Charles Panzéra, Richard Tauber, Victoria de los Angeles (to name but a few) all radiated waves of charm across the footlights. So did the German sopranos Irmgard Seefried and Elisabeth Schwarz-kopf though they sometimes were capable of becoming danger-ously arch. The Italian tenor Luciano Pavarotti, armed with his white handkerchief, has delighted millions over the television (an ideal medium for recitals) with the beauty of his voice, his artistry, but also that extra something—his utterly winning personality.

Writing about this mysterious element that is "charm," in his interesting *The Grand Tradition*, G. B. Steane comments, "Charm is not really a notable part of Italian singing. The French, Austrians, Spaniards have it . . . Pavarotti, however, is an exception." A German, however, who definitely does not have it, despite his enormous following, is the baritone, Dietrich Fischer-Dieskau. Because of this lack of charm, he has always had listeners who reservedly admire his artistry. Walter Legge attributes the defi-ciency to a different reason: "Perhaps it is his [Fischer-Dieskau's] *Aussprache beim Singen*, the Prussian exaggeration of consonants, particularly in Schubert, Strauss and Wolf, that slightly irritates me."

Charm aside, the singer who undertakes a recital must range the varieties of human emotion, one quickly following another, from love to rage; from ironic humor, through yearning, to deep grief. There is no greater challenge to the vocal art.

Church Voices. As we have already noted, a curious love-hate relationship exists between the Church and the singing voice. How easy and natural and thrilling for man to raise his singing voice in exaltation of the Lord, as anyone, for example, who has ever participated in a performance of Handel's "Hallelujah Chorus" well knows. Though the Church in its earliest days may have kept back the development of the singing voice, this very censorship might have given to singing an importance that it would never have possessed. Certainly the literature of vocal church music is fabulously rich, from the polyphonic master-pieces of the fourteenth and fifteenth centuries to the recent large sacred pieces of Britten and Penderecki.

Despite today's decline in religious interest, church voices are still much in demand thanks to the extensiveness and beauty of sacred music. The most perfect church voices have undoubtedly belonged to the angels, but we have no knowledge of their range and tone quality, only innumerable descriptions of their celestial beauty. Church voices as we know them today differ very little in range and volume from the various operatic voices already described. The pure, limpid tones of a lyric soprano are particu-larly suited to the ethereal atmosphere of much sacred music, and if the voice possesses flexibility as well, it will do justice to the florid runs of "Rejoice greatly" in *Messiah* or the closing "Alleluia" of Mozart's *Exsultate Jubilate*. The bigger-voiced sopranos also fare well in church vocal literature ranging from a time long before Bach to the present century. Only the very largest type of dramatic soprano voice, the kind needed to sing Gioconda or Isolde, is not so welcome as a church voice, except when called upon to perform in the Italianate, quasi-operatic *Stabat Mater* of Rossini or Verdi's *Requiem*.

Mezzo-sopranos and contraltos, serene, sometimes sorrowing, are heard to advantage for example in the beautiful arias such as "O erbarme dich" that Bach wrote for them. A nineteenth-century favorite is "O rest in the Lord" from Mendelssohn's *Elijah*, demanding a voice with accents of tranquillity and rever-ence.

Like his dramatic soprano counterpart, the heavy tenor voice with an emphasized vibrato does not sound appropriate in most church music except that of the synagogue, perhaps because a more dramatic note is struck in the Jewish liturgy. Not surprising-ly, outstanding tenors like Jan Peerce and the late Richard Tucker have made an easy transition from the temple to the opera house. Worst off as a church voice is the baritone. Even Verdi, who very much fancied this type of voice, failed to write a baritone part in his *Requiem*. Indeed, when singing hymns in a church choir the baritone has to choose between taking the second tenor line or that of the first bass, neither of which lie comfortably for his voice.

One other, very definitely non-operatic yet church voice that should be mentioned here is the one belonging to the gospel singer. In the religious fervor of this kind of singing, bel canto goes out the window, and we are involved with a shouted kind of vocal production, rising at moments of exaltation high into the soprano register.

Finally there is the voice of the choirboy, who often at the insistence of his parents but to his shame and humiliation (particularly in America) is made to lift up his angelic voice in church and eke out the family income. The choirboy's voice usually has a compass:

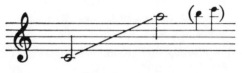

Boy Soprano

The slightly rarer alto approximates the range of the ordinary contralto and uses, just as she does, a chest tone. Vibrato-free and innocent-sounding, the voice of the choirboy to many people's ears is the most perfect of all church voices.

This is particularly true of the English who have a passion for the pure, sexless sound of the boy's voice. English boys' choirs such as the one of King's College, Cambridge, are famous. Choirmasters are revered in England and as in no other country tomes are published with titles such as *Training the Boy's Changing Voice*. No wonder then that a record made in 1927, just after the coming of the electrical recording technique, should turn out to be a best-seller. It was of a boy soprano singing Mendelssohn's "Hear my prayer."

The singer, Master Ernest Lough, was six months short of his seventeenth birthday, an unusually advanced age to retain the silvery tones heard on the record made "on the site" at the Temple Church, London. "I have never heard such a beautiful voice," declared Sir Compton Mackenzie in the *Gramophone* Magazine, this at a time when sopranos such as Ponselle, Galli-Curci and Elisabeth Rethberg were raising their voices in song. The record created a furore. Visitors, even from overseas, stormed the church to hear Master Lough in his boyish person and tickets had to be issued. The church fathers, as though they had been caught betting on a winning horse, were embarrassed by the huge royalties received. While from all around England mothers and fathers, hoping that they had propagated a rival to Master Lough, besieged the record company with requests for auditions.

Amazingly, Master Lough continued to record for another year and a half until he was overtaken by what all choirmasters fear and dread—the voice change. The usual rule is that alto boys' voices become tenors and sopranos turn into the lower-voiced male ranges, as was the case with Master Lough. In manhood he acquired an adequate bass voice and was transformed into a sometime chorister of no particular distinction, but even now the record of his boyhood days continues to sell.

Though emphasis is laid upon a serene, devotional quality in rendering church music, this does not mean that church singers are never expected to sound dramatic. One thinks of the many anguished passages in the *Passions* of Johann Sebastian Bach, particularly *St. John*. Handel calls for a bass with a highly developed sense of drama combined with a coloratura technique to sing the aria "Why do the Nations"—though alas! he is not always available. Many of the later oratorios and masses—Mendelssohn's *Elijah*, for example, or the arresting *Glagolitic Mass* of Janáček—have also been highly dramatic. As for the Requiems of Giuseppe Verdi and Benjamin Britten—they are pure theater.

Many an aspiring opera singer has gained experience and cash by fulfilling often very lucrative church engagements, but on the whole those artists who have appeared to greatest advantage in sacred music have usually been less successful on the operatic stage. This was said to be true of the noted nineteenth-century English soprano, Clara Novello. Jenny Lind made her sensational success as an opera singer, but retired from the boards at a comparatively early age never having morally approved of the theater. Her piety and religious faith illuminated the church music which she continued to sing. In more recent times this same spirit of reverence was deeply apparent in Marian Anderson's renditions of religious arias, or perhaps even more so in her singing of the spirituals with which she usually ended her recitals, as has been the custom of many black singers since. In a recent interview the black soprano Kathleen Battle was asked by music writer Will Crutchfield whether she thought that "the era of spirituals as genuine folk music might recede so far into the past that it could no longer offer the enrichment it has brought to the singing of people like Marian Anderson or Leontyne Price." Miss Battle didn't think so, "particularly if blacks keep in touch with the pop music that has sprung directly from their folk heritage." Then this rising star of the Metropolitan Opera added rather astonishingly, "I was brought up on it, you know—not on opera. In college I didn't even know who Callas was."

The Pop Voices. When the first edition of this book appeared, the surprised reaction of some was that along with comments about great singers such as Caruso or Flagstad a section on pop singers had been included. What was Frank Sinatra or gravelly voiced, off-pitch Billie Holiday doing in the company of the great exponents of bel canto?

The answer is that many of these so called popular artists have voices of fine quality and sometimes of tremendous range. We usually do not think of Sara Vaughan as a noted coloratura-mezzo, but with her compass of almost three octaves (from the D, below middle C to the B' just below High C") and her "scat" technique, that is what she is. Nor do we readily recognize this description by Henry Pleasants in his *The Great American Popular Singers*: "The voice covers about two octaves and a third, from the baritone's low G, to the tenor's high B, with an upward extension in falsetto to at least a D' flat" as belonging to Elvis Presley. When fans told me excitedly that no book about singing today could appear without mention of their idol Michael Jackson none of them added that the young black pop star was a countertenor—or, to use another term, a "tenorino."

There are several basic differences between the qualities of pop stars and those of concert and opera singers. One has to do with the microphone which, since a pop vocalist relies on it totally, did away with any need for formal voice training. Before the invention of electrical amplification the voices of the stars that our grandfathers admired—Lillian Russell, Anna Held, George M. Cohan, Julia Sanderson—were much nearer to opera or at least operetta voices. The microphone made it possible for a singer to make a career with a wisp of a voice, providing the personality was abundant and the way with a song original and appealing. The introduction of the microphone coincided with a vogue for cute, "little girl" mannerisms in the female. As a result the first women pop singers of our modern amplified age, such as Ruth Etting or Helen Morgan, sang with small, almost helpless sounding soubrette soprano voices. Nowadays we no longer hear this girlish, innocent quality (except in folk singers) because of a change in taste combined with a peculiarity of women's voices.

The peculiarity I refer to is the fact that many women are capable of singing the notes from A, below middle C (and lower) up to C' (and even higher) in two different qualities of tone. One sounds warm, round and what we think of as feminine. The same notes can also emerge with the tough, gutsy, more masculine quality of what is known as the chest register. Opera and concert singers use this second bold-sounding tone with great effect, but sparingly and rarely above E', knowing that if the chest register is carried higher it will drag down the rest of the voice and ruin it. Sometime in the 1920's, however, coinciding with a period when women gained greater freedom, a taste for females singing entirely in their masculine sounding chest registers came into being and has been with us ever since. Thus because they have the range (though usually more limited) and emphasize low notes, female pop singers of today can be regarded as contraltos, even though their voices may sound more abrasive than those of the true operatic and concert contralto.

One of the first of these brash, almost raucous-sounding vocalists was Sophie Tucker, who had a voice as ample and handsome as her presence. She called herself the "last of the Red Hot Mamas" but her voice, which sounds like that of a real contralto on records, calls more readily to mind the idea of a golden-hearted madam.

Another great star of her time, Ethel Waters, was an innately tasteful vocalist who said of her own singing that she could "riff and jam and growl, but . . . never had that loud approach." Nevertheless she sang entirely in her mellow chest register and, lacking a trained technique, brought her notes in that register up perilously high, something that a singer properly trained in a vocal studio learns never to do. As a result at the height of her career, Ethel Waters developed the pimple-like protruberances on the edges of the vocal folds known as nodes that are caused by strain. After delicate surgery was performed in London in 1930, she resumed her career singing as well as ever and six years later

Sophie Tucker, "last of the Red Hot Mamas."

would be heard in the unforgettable "Takin' a Chance on Love" in *Cabin in the Sky*.

Two other supremely successful popular singers, Ethel Merman and Judy Garland, both sang entirely in their chest registers. Of her non-existent vocal technique Merman wrote in her autobiography, "I just stand up and holler and hope that my voice holds out." Both singers had a suprisingly limited range for the size of their careers. But then they were unique in reaching out and capturing their audiences by the immensity of their personalities.

Other celebrated singers in the popular field have called upon all the registers of the voice with which the female is commonly endowed, and some even which are very rare. The sopranos Cleo Laine and Maureen McGovern, appearing before the public today, have in fact the compass of the soprano *acuto sfogato* hitting notes as high as the G″ above high C″. Interestingly, Miss McGovern, a late-developer, started out her career singing entirely in the chest register in imitation of the average pop singer, and didn't even know that she possessed the altitudinous notes at the other end of her range. Now in an evening of songs she switches from dizzying coloratura to scat songs, from simple ballads to a vocalise set to music of Fauré, proving that bel canto is to be heard in the supper club as well as the opera house—though always with one basic qualification: all the singers discussed in this section use amplification. Their voices would simply not be *heard* in an average-size auditorium where the concert or opera singers appears without a microphone.

Another great popular star with a large range (from a low D flat to the B′ flat under high C″) is the inimitable Ella Fitzgerald. Like almost every pop singer Ella never had formal vocal training but slides intuitively from register to register and at the top of her voice even into falsetto. The result is a range of honey-sweet, equalized tones that she uses with supreme art. "But while she may be for the jazzman a musician's musician," writes Henry Pleasants about her, "and for the lay public the First Lady of Song, she has always been more than anything else a singer's singer."

Another pop singer with a huge following, a cast in her eye and a voice of lovely quality capable of a great range of color and subtlety is Barbra Streisand. With this singer, however, rather as in the case of Maria Callas, we plunge into a world of contention.

"Miss Streisand remains the most affected, synthetic, self conscious, over-stylized singer in music," thundered a reviewer in an issue of *High Fidelity* a number of years ago. To which came a rejoinder two years later in *Stereo Review* from the not always fulsome Rex Reed: "Her voice can transform a piece of music into something more demanding and really rewarding than it seemed possible it could be." Even more oddly the lady who provokes such disparate comments on her vocalism would say of herself, "I'm not a singer, I'm an actress." (She is also a movie director as evinced by her film, *Yentl*.)

Again, as did Callas, Streisand seems to suffer from the folly of excess. She has subjected her malleable, totally untrained voice with a range from a low E to G' below high C" to more than its share of pressure with brayed nasal high tones and melodramatic whoops and hollers that her detractors find so off-putting. The comparison with Callas continues also to be apt if one considers her not as a pure singer but a singing-actress.

Over the years opera singers have occasionally invaded the pop field, usually with unsatisfying results. The effect of a large, somehow formal-sounding voice close up to the microphone is disquieting, like watching a dignified middle-aged woman trying to "get with" the latest youthful dance. Helen Traubel appeared both in the movies and in night clubs, and there was some novelty in hearing one of the great Wagnerian sopranos of her day belt out numbers in a hearty style, but little else. Eileen Farrell put out records which showed that she had an amazing grasp of a jazz style, and of late, the incredible Leontyne Price has done the same thing. Pop purists will cavil (they always do) but certainly one or two of her selections are absolutely authentic.

Barbra Streisand with her usual *chutzpah* reversed this procedure of classical to pop by putting out in 1975 an album called "Classical Barbra" that included a song each by Robert Schumann and Hugo Wolf, Debussy and Fauré as well as two arias by Handel. Devotees of this repertory found the results tentative (except for a sweetly rendered "Berceuse" from Canteloube's "Songs of the Auvergne") while her regular fans more or less ignored it. Nonetheless it is another example of this enormously talented performer's desire to extend her abilities.

When a classical singer makes the attempt to "cross over" into popular music and (very rarely) the other way around, it emphasizes another basic difference between the pop and classical singer. The latter is a servant of the music; the pop vocalist uses the music as a servant—or rather a jumping off place to vary the rhythm, the tone values, even the notes themselves. This free approach to the basic music becomes synonymous with what is known as the pop artist's "style." That is not to say that the opera or concert singer does not employ *rubato*—"a device by which time is stolen from one note and given to another"—or, particularly in the case of coloratura singers, even embellishments. But a singer of classical music, though he may possess personality or a kind of panache, does not develop a "style" in this sense. The operatic or concert singer always obeys the commands of the composer as set down in the music that is performed.

With the male pop voices as well, there was a certain amount of shifting between the singers of operas and concerts and those who appeared in operettas and musical comedies until the introduction of electrical amplification. The handsome young Canadian tenor Edward Johnson made a sensational success as the lead in Oscar Straus's *Waltz Dream* on Broadway in 1908. Eschewing what could have been a continuing popular career, he went to Europe as Edoardo di Giovanni for further vocal training and when he next sang on Broadway it was at the Metropolitan on Fortieth Street just south of the "Great White Way," appearing opposite Lucrezia Bori in Montemezzi's *L'Amore dei tre rei*.

That was in 1922. A few years later came "the mike"—or as one of the first pop tenors to sing in a new way, Rudy Vallee, would call it, "the electronic megaphone." As Vallee wrote in his autobiography, "My use of the megaphone came through absolute necessity," since his voice was "not penetrating nor strong." This remains true almost without exception of pop singers to this day: their voices would be weak, insignificant things without the electrical boost that gives them strength and the ability to be heard by many ears.

This invention of the microphone brought a highly significant change in the history of singing. Hitherto, there had always been words and music. But the words, particularly in public performances before large audiences, were often lost to the listeners, as they still are today in opera houses where amplification is not used. Now, with electronic boosting, each and every syllable could be clearly understood. More than that, the singer no longer needed to "throw" his voice using techniques of deep breathing combined with adjustments to his larynx. He could almost talk his songs. Singing as softly as a mother in a lullaby to the babe in her arms, he could sound intimate, confidential. Among the male pop singers who emerged in the early 1930's including the pioneer, Rudy Vallee, and Russ Columbo and Harry Richman, this style of vocalizing into a microphone came to be known as crooning. And among the crooners the greatest and most famous of them all was Bing Crosby.

Crosby's legendary fame was partly due to the many movies he made but also because of his unique voice, round, mellifluous, having a special quality of its own which is not always the case in the pop world where second-rate vocalists can and do sound alike. There have been successors to Crosby with round, smooth baritone voices and emulating his casual, rather uninvolved style. Some of these direct descendants include Dick Haymes, Perry Como, Dean Martin and currently well-favored Engelbert Humperdinck, all of whom sing the baritone or bass-baritone range as did Bing Crosby. But none of them has had quite the honey of "the Groaner" in their voices that made his so unique.

The invention of the microphone not only produced a taste for the aforementioned "little girl" voices possessed by Ruth Etting and Helen Morgan, but also it developed a vogue for light lyric tenors. Some of these were Latins such as Tino Rossi and Tito Guizar, who on the radio airwaves held sway over thousands during the 1930's. Nino Martini's voice was sufficiently large for him to make a modest career as a *tenore leggiero* in the opera house. Another tremendously popular "radio tenor" was Lanny Ross, not to speak of Kenny Baker and Dennis Day, all of whom required electronic enhancement as has in later years Sergio Franchi.

Tenors with tiny voices like Johnny Mathis, who resorts to a lot of breathy falsetto, could not survive without amplification. And how would Tiny Tim ever have tip-toed through the tulips without aggrandizement of his neuter-sounding tones? The same is true of today's number one pop star, Michael Jackson.

In what might be called sexual quality, Jackson's voice sounds the exact opposite of the male leads who appeared in Broadway musicals of the 1940's and 1950's. Alfred Drake, Howard Keel, Robert Goulet—strapping, macho-looking men with strapping, macho-sounding baritone voices—stirred audiences during the golden age of such shows as *Oklahoma!*, *Annie Get Your Gun* and *Camelot*. Alfred Drake, with an aspiration for opera, failed to win the Metropolitan Opera auditions, but certainly conquered Broadway many times over. Another, who did actually begin his career in opera (he appeared with the Philadelphia Opera Company and actually sang the Drum-Major in Alban Berg's enormously difficult *Wozzeck*) was popular Nelson Eddy, the cinematic vocal apotheosis of the virile hero in the 1930's and into the forties. All of these singers had voices that could have been heard in spacious auditoriums without amplification. One, however, with a voice of limited range and small size, who could never have carried the huge places where he has appeared without a mike—is "the Voice," Frank Sinatra.

To Frank Sinatra is often attributed the development of what has come to be known as a microphone technique. Unkind critics said of his early appearance as a skinny lad with protruberant ears, that he needed the fixed, standing microphone before which he sang in those days to hold himself up. Let it not be forgotten that during those younger days in an engagement at the Paramount Theater in New York over eight hundred policemen with the aid of twenty radio cars and two emergency trucks had to be called out to control a queue of ten thousand teen-agers standing six abreast waiting to hear the fragile-looking singer. Another twenty thousand milled about in Times Square. At that time intellectuals on *The New Republic* and the London *Times* solemnly sought to analyze Sinatra's power over his audiences. Loretta Young, the apparently never ruffled movie actress of many years, seemed to know: "What is there about that boy," she is supposed to have said, "that makes you feel he is singing to you—and you alone?"

Sinatra's evolution of a microphone technique made the mike become, in the acute words of Henry Pleasants, "an instrument on which he played as an instrumentalist plays a saxophone, or a trombone—in other words, an electronic extension of his own vocal instrument." Sinatra never had any formal vocal training and never learned to read music. Yet being of Italian origin he has approached singing in a bel canto, non-crooning way and with attention to the line in music that is also a characteristic of the great violin *virtuosi* such as Fritz Kreisler or Heifetz.

Sinatra sings the baritone range, but his voice is weak and poorly focused at the bottom. It also lacks the round, rich quality of many other pop baritones. He sings up to an F, the note where a tenor must make a certain change in his throat to reach his high notes, leading to the suspicion that possibly in his early days there was a whole set of untapped tenor top notes to his voice. The reader may be slightly startled when I say I hear a distinct similarity between the way of singing of Frank Sinatra and Kirsten Flagstad. Both, when they attack a note, often begin it without vibrato and then gradually let it come in. Both sing on the consonant "n" using the resulting resonance whenever possible to add a connecting line through their singing.*

Close to seventy now, Frank Sinatra continues his astonishing career before cheering fans who could and do date back a half a century.† As with most singers, his voice has thickened and lost some of its boyish glow. Being mercurial of personality, his voice has often reflected his temperament. In 1950 he got into serious vocal difficulties, suffering a throat haemorrhage during an engagement at the Copacabana. This seems to have been due to nervous tension over his tempestuous romance with Ava Gardner and when that came to some kind of resolution, Sinatra's career continued unabated. Fine musicianship, exceptional phrasing, total involvement with his material which in turn he communicates to his listeners, in short, the attributes of a great singer, have made Sinatra's career what it is—together with shrewd showmanship and the pugnacious charm of his personality. To quote Henry Pleasants once more: "I dislike hyperbole and usually manage to avoid it. But with [Sinatra] I cannot restrain myself from saying that I rate him with the greatest singers of my experience, especially with John McCormack and Richard Tauber, and well above any other American popular singer."

This writer cannot but concur.

Another remarkable male pop singer who came to fame after Sinatra in the 1950's is Ray Charles. Blinded by glaucoma at the age of five he studied by Braille classical music (most unusual for a pop star) as well as jazz and country-and-western. Originally an

---

*Surprise and amazement was registered by a number of reviewers when I published these comments on the singing of Flagstad and Sinatra in the first edition of The Singing Voice. I see no reason to modify nor alter them.

†For a Sinatra concert in June 1984 at New York City's Carnegie Hall fans, both old and young stood three hours or more to buy tickets.

instrumentalist (the piano, saxophone, clarinet), he took up singing in an arresting, hoarse (a quality that would make any classical singer shiver) range that goes from a low A, flat two octaves up to the baritone's high A flat, ascending from there into stratospheric falsetto heights. Of his technique Ray Charles says that he sings "by my own crazy contortions." The results have been described graphically by Whitney Balliett: "Charles can shape his baritone voice into dark, shouting blocks of sound, reduce it to a goose-pimpling whisper, sing a pure falsetto, resemble Nat Cole at his creamiest and growl and rasp."

The career of this notable black singer has been crossed by heroin busts, numbers of marriages and bouts with the bottle. Always handicapped by his blindness, he has nonetheless through his musicianship and unique style of singing (he has been called the greatest of gospel singers without singing gospel) continued to delight legions of fans through the years.

Surveying today's up-coming popular singers, the voice would appear to be losing out more and more to the visual and the electronic. Even more curiously it is losing the attribute that the singing voice is inherently equipped to express—sexuality. A recent hour-long television program previewing the candidates for the Grammy '84 Awards—"Record of the Year," "Song of the Year," "Best New Artist," etc.—offered viewers a selection of video discs beginning with Michael Jackson's "Beat It." This introduced a world of leather-clad gangs, black and white, violent-looking virile males intercut with a shot of a diminished looking Michael Jackson lying in bed and singing in the voice of a schoolboy asking his mother for a glass of milk. Indeed the voice sounds so faint and unsupported that it seems as if this leading pop star must be deprived of oxygen. Is vulnerability this young man's appeal to the female?

The next selection on the program presented Billy Joel (who sings the high baritone range) in company with an all-male chorus done up as gas station attendants. This number called "Uptown Girl" had curious reverberations of an old-time operetta.

Further along the viewer was returned to the androgynous world with a group called the "Eurhythmics" offering a song entitled "Sweet Dreams." This was led by a singer with a crew cut dyed a vivid orange who though low of voice turned out rather surprisingly to be a girl. With excellent enunciation and pitch she gave her audience the sado-masochistic message that there are some who "want to use you" while others "want to be abused."

A final exercise in sexual confusion was served up by a singer called Boy George done up in pigtails, who with a costumed group celebrated life on what appeared to be a distinctly English river in a steamboat in the 1870's complete with a crooked gambler and a "pickaninny."

Though this program was a celebration of the best in pop singing the overall effect to this listener was that the larynx and a pair of lungs had been entirely eliminated. Instead, the performers seemed to have swallowed some electronic device that did the singing for them, and not very well at that since sung words were often out of synchronization with the viewed lips. All the immediate, direct effect of the singing voice upon the listener was absent: singer (and audience) had become dehumanized.

The Rock Singers. If reviewers cavilled at my giving a place to pop singers in an earlier edition of this book how will they react to a new section on rock singing? Yet surely any proper survey of the singing voice must at least offer a passing consideration to these stars who excite millions by their so-called singing, even if the sounds that they produce are more an electronic phenomenon than a vocal one.

With rock singing we are about as far removed as we can get from the deeply moving, ennobling art of Orpheus, the first singer. In fact one can fancy that rock singing with its shrieks, its howls, its raging cries, sounds like the protests of the Furies that Orpheus had to overcome with his own matchless vocalism as he made his way through Hades to recover his beloved Eurydice. Hellish indeed are the noises that the rock singer frequently makes and frightful the din created by his mass of amplifying equipment. Of rock music Frank Sinatra, one of the great singers of all time, has this to say:

"Rock music is the most brutal, ugly, vicious form of expression . . . sly, lewd—in plain fact, dirty . . . [a] rancid-smelling aphrodisiac . . . martial music of every delinquent on the face of the earth."

The first and still the most famous of the rock singers, with his insolent stare and sneering lips, was of course Elvis Presley.

Though some commentators have acknowledged that Presley had at least a passing baritone range with a pleasing quality in the middle of the compass, he himself said, "My voice alone is just an ordinary voice. What people come to see is how I use it. If I stand still while I'm singing, I'm dead, man." Note his use of the word "see." Paradoxically the effect of rock singers on their huge audiences is as much visual as vocal. Hence the outrageous get-ups and the suggestive sexual gyrations. Also distracting from the usual paucity of the rock singer's voice are the deafening, electronically swelled "back-up" arrangements over which the vocalist, clutching his microphone like a baby's rattle so close to his mouth that it seems the hard metal may knock out his front teeth, presents his song.

In the next section the reader will find listed some of the physiological functions other than phonation with which the larynx serves the human body. Rock singing, however, demonstrates the extraordinary range of sounds that the larynx can produce. "Wails, moans, screeches washing dizzily against a distortion as angry as an amplified hive of buzzing instruments" is the way the singing of Janis Joplin has been described, her voice "like a bow stuttering on a sooty viola." Cackles, squawks, yowls, the noises of the entire animal kingdom will proceed from the vocal folds of a rock singer such as Bruce Springsteen. (His biographer, Dave Marsh, nevertheless refers to him as an "artiste.")

Springsteen's story is typical of the rock singer, many of whom have been English (Springsteen, however, hails from New Jersey), in rebellion against a dreary working class background. "Rock and roll reached down into all those homes where there was no music or books or anything," Springsteen has said. "And it infiltrated that whole thing. That's what happened in my house." Thus rock singing for the rebellious, usually ill-educated adolescent becomes less a song than a way of life. Springsteen fervently proclaims that if there were an Eleventh Commandment it would say, "Let it be rock."

Springsteen writes songs, but like almost all rock singers has had no musical training, hence the dreariness of these compositions which often rely totally on the tonic, dominant and sub dominant chords and scarcely range an octave. Springsteen's hit "Born to Run" is "locked into an America of screen doors, fast cars and casual violence" according to Dave Marsh, but most of these songs have to do with *extreme* violence, blood and despair. Lately increasing attention has been paid to teen-age suicide. Rock songs and the destinies of the singers who perform them seem to reflect this drive to self-destruction, as in the examples of such terminal superstars as Jim Morrison, Jimi Hendrix and Janis Joplin.

As long as there are teen-agers, there may continue to be a demand for and response to rock singing. To lovers of the singing voice and the wondrous beauties of which it is capable, this vocal manifestation can only be regarded as a degradation of the powers of the larynx.

The Composer As Singer. Pop singers of late such as Bob Dylan and Bruce Springsteen to name only a few who have taken pride in calling themselves "singer song-writers." The idea of the composer as singer, however, dates back in fact to Homer who is believed to have sung (or at least intoned) his great epics. As Rossini once said, "He who wants to write well for singers must be a singer himself," and though not generally realized, the history of music confirms that this is often so.

The first (and some say finest) era of bel canto was ushered in with the operas *Dafne* and *Euridice* by Jacopo Peri. Peri was also a singer as were a number of the sixteenth- and seventeenth-century Italian composers who came after him. Today, vocal students working to perfect the long, flowing line that is one of the secrets of beautiful singing practice the *Arie Antiche*, songs and arias by composers who understood the voice because they themselves were singers.

An opera that survives from this same period is Henry Purcell's *Dido and Aeneas*, and here again we learn that Purcell was an excellent singer, first as a countertenor, a type of voice for which he wrote many compositions, and later, oddly enough, a bass. Purcell's performance of his ode "Hail, bright Cecilia" was praised by a local music critic of the day for the "incredible graces" which he bestowed on the aria " 'Tis nature's voice."

This bond of composer and his own singing voice as inspiration continued into more recent times. Though Mozart sang duets with his sister as a little boy, post-pubescence does not seem to have left him with an impressive vocal organ. And yet his preoccupation with the voice, his rare understanding of it which makes his vocal compositions such a delight to perform, suggest that he had the sensibility of a remarkable singer if not his physical equipment. Quite the opposite is true of Beethoven, who wrote ungratefully, almost aggressively for the singer. It is said that Beethoven himself could not sing in tune—though this may have been due to the affliction that attacked his hearing so early in his life. Even then Beethoven seems to have resorted to a kind of singing to assist him in composing. A friend, Ferdinand Ries, relates how once while out walking, Beethoven "had constantly hummed or almost howled up and down the scale without singing definite notes. When I asked him what it was, he replied that a theme for the last allegro of the sonata [Opus 57] had come into his head."

Not surprisingly then, those who have written most sympathetically for the voice and specialized in vocal music have been the most proficient singers themselves. This is borne out by the case of Rossini, who as the son of a soprano and the husband of another, thoroughly understood the technique of singing, besides having a fine high baritone voice of his own. In December 1823, Rossini endured the torments of seasickness to cross the Channel to England, where as a famed operatic composer, he was taken up by the fashionable as well as the musical of the day. Though ostensibly engaged as impresario at the King's Theatre for a "Rossini season" the composer, never at a loss for expediency, capitalized on his lionization by singing and playing one of his own *buffo* arias at the Brighton Pavilion before George IV. He also rendered (I'm certain smiling inwardly) Desdemona's "Willow Song" from his *Otello*, singing it in falsetto, which caused an uneasy stir in the audience to whom this *castrato* sound was now decidedly unfashionable and even scandalous. As the rage of London, Rossini was asked to many of the houses of the elite, for which he usually charged a fee of £50. He also gave singing lessons to the aristocrats of the day, among them, the Duke of Wellington. Another would-be singer was the King himself, and Rossini, already beginning to bulge, found himself in the company of this monstrously corpulent monarch, clinging to the tenor part of a *buffo* duet, while George IV wandered around hopelessly underneath in the bass. Thanks mainly to Rossini's singing he amassed a fortune of 175,000 francs during his six

J. Ingres: Portrait of G. Rossini.

months' stay in England, a fortune which enabled him to retire and—ironically—almost entirely give up composing.

Rossini was renowned for his generosity towards other musicians, and about this time in Paris he was introduced to a young Irishman who had learned the violin as a child but had now developed a voice that he hoped was suitable for opera. Impressed, Rossini loaned him money for further singing lessons and subsequently arranged for his debut at the Théâtre des Italiens in *Il Barbiere di Siviglia*. Thus did Michael Balfe, future composer of *The Bohemian Girl*, not yet twenty, make his entrance into the important musical world of Paris in the early nineteenth century. According to contemporary reports Balfe possessed a voice of great sweetness and flexibility. One of his best roles was Don Giovanni which he sang *"con amore."* Balfe also appeared in several other Rossini operas including *La Gazza Ladra and Cenerentola*, the latter with the fascinating Maria Malibran, who also arranged for his engagement at La Scala. Ultimately Balfe returned to London to become manager of the Lyceum Theatre, for which he wrote a number of operas, largely forgotten with the exception of the sprightly *Bohemian Girl*.

About this time Hector Berlioz, sent by his father to medical school in Paris, had secretly begun to study music. When the medical training became unbearable Berlioz announced to his family that he was quitting in order to become a composer. Their bourgeois reaction was to cut off his financial support. Berlioz, who had already studied the flute and could sing at sight, applied for work at the Théâtre des Nouveautés. When an opening occurred for a chorus singer he was summoned for an audition. His rivals, he discovered, included a blacksmith, a weaver and a chorister from the Church of St. Eustache, each of whom sang a selection of his own choosing. Berlioz's turn came and when asked what he had brought to sing, the future composer replied, "Nothing." Nothing? Had he no music with him at all—not even an Italian vocal exercise? "Nothing," repeated Berlioz. The next question was what operatic arias he knew by heart. Berlioz's reply is characteristic of a man who never did anything halfway. He had memorized the entire standard operatic repertory, the Gluck operas *Orfeo* and the two *Iphigénies*, the Spontini *La Vestale*, etc.

Dazed, the manager asked Berlioz to sing a selection from this vast list and the next day the aspiring composer learned that he had triumphed over the blacksmith, the weaver and the chorister from the Church of St. Eustache, and was engaged at a salary of fifty francs a month. Thus as a vaudeville singer did Berlioz embark on his extraordinary musical career.

Of the two towering operatic composers of the nineteenth century, Verdi and Wagner, no description exists of how Verdi sang, but George Martin in his rich biography of this most vocal of composers holds the theory that Verdi as he wrote most certainly sang, though not necessarily out loud. Or to put it another way, Verdi responded within his own throat to his music as he composed it. To support this idea, Mr. Martin points out that in the years around 1844, Verdi, a man of excellent health and great energy, was constantly beset by sore throats and hoarseness. It is this period of his life that the composer with all the commissions he could handle referred to as his "galley years" during which he worked at an exhausting pace turning out one opera after another. Mr. Martin believes that as Verdi wrote, he unconsciously sang or felt in his throat the many difficult roles that were pouring out of him, and his sore throats and hoarseness were really the result of straining his voice by "over-singing." Later, when Verdi slowed his rate of work, these throat ailments disappeared.

Of Richard Wagner it has been said that he would have been the greatest singing actor in the nineteenth century but for one deficiency: he lacked a voice. This did not prevent him from singing large sections of his music dramas, often taking all the parts, male and female, to stunned friends and admirers. Léon Carvalho, director of the Théâtre-Lyrique at Paris, gives us this description of Wagner's personal audition of *Tannhäuser:*

"I can still see Wagner, wearing a blue jacket with red braid, and a yellow Greek cap adorned with a green fringe . . . With a fire, an *entrain* that I shall never forget, he began by giving me the first part of *Tannhäuser;* then, dripping with perspiration, he disappeared, to return this time in a red cap decorated with yellow braid, his blue coat had been replaced by a yellow one embellished with blue braid. In this new costume he sang for me the second part of his opera. He howled, he threw himself about, he hit all kinds of wrong notes, and to crown it all he sang in German! And his eyes! The eyes of a madman! I did not dare to cross him; he frightened me."

Another of Wagner's famous performances was an audition in Paris of the second act of *Tristan* in which he sang Tristan to the Isolde of the remarkable Pauline Viardot. Present was an audience of two, Madame Kalergis, a wealthy patroness of the arts, and Hector Berlioz. Wagner hurled himself into his role with his usual intensity while Viardot, who at that time had some reservations about the composer's music, "rendered most of her part in low tones," as Wagner sourly observed afterwards. It is typical of him to complain of her not doing justice to his music when she was reading her tremendously difficult role *at sight*. Of Wagner's singing, Berlioz could only find words of praise for the warmth of the composer's delivery. Nonetheless, whatever his voice lacked, Wagner's performances must have been thrilling and deeply moving.

Another celebrated operatic composer of this period, Charles Gounod, also liked personally to audition his operas. The comic actor E. Got heard Gounod sing and accompany himself through the entire score of his first opera, *Sapho*, and commented characteristically, "no voice, but what charm!" And a worshipful fan, Marie Anne De Bovet, writing to Gounod in 1891, two years before his death, gives us this lavender description of the composer's song in old age:

"His tenor voice, once so sweet, which he manages with infinite skill, not of professional technicalities, but of intention and feeling, is now impaired by age; at times he can hardly sing at all." Nonetheless, she goes on to relate that "No one can sing Mozart as he does, it is with him a question of expression, of suppressed feeling, of intense vibration . . . With a voice that hardly carries beyond the piano, he will give Marguerite's appeal to heaven, 'Anges purs, anges radieux' or render the ecstatic triumph of Polyeucte after his baptism, so as to reveal beauties which the most applauded vocalization of a prima donna, or the highest notes of a fashionable tenor have never equalled."

Gounod seems to have understood well the nonsensical images awash in the average singing teacher's studio. Though Gounod never gave singing lessons, he pretended to let his daughter bring a friend to him for advice. "Child, you want to sing?" the composer is reported to have said with mock solemnity to the trembling young woman. "Well I'll tell you what to do. Place your bow *(archet)*, let the urn of your voice pour out its contents and give me a mauve sound in which I can wash my hands."

Still another composer with a less than special singing voice was Georges Bizet, who maintained that he would have been a great singer if nature had endowed him with one. Bizet's father, Adolphe, was a singing teacher, also his mother's brother, the eccentric François Delsarte. An accomplished pianist, Bizet put singing before all. As his pupil Edmond Galabert recalled, "He . . . used the voice, particularly when he was playing an orchestral piece, to imitate by singing or humming the timbre of the different instruments, filling out or underlining the details and counter-melodies." Galabert also remembered Bizet's accomplished interpretation of various operatic roles in which Bizet would sing the female parts in a tenor voice, the male roles in a baritone or bass range. This prodigally gifted composer also suffered from throat ailments all his life. Was it for the same reason as Verdi—over-singing?

A little known, unfinished opera by Georges Bizet called *Don Rodrigue* was commissioned by the most celebrated baritone of his day, Jean-Baptiste Faure, who also composed himself. One song of his still survives, the well-known "Les Rameaux" ("The Palms"), a great favorite of baritones and basses. The Venezuela-born composer, Reynaldo Hahn, who wrote what might be described as slightly perfumed songs and operettas, was also an accomplished singer. His vocal art resembled his compositions, utilizing a slight, pastel *tenore leggiero* not unlike in quality that of Tito Schipa or Alfredo Kraus.

In modern times the relationship of the composer to his singing voice remains as powerful as ever. Poulenc, like Wagner or Gounod, used to give premières of his vocal compositions to friends with overpowering effect, even though he had no voice. Leonard Bernstein resorts instantly to his own limited voice to illustrate a passage in either his own or someone else's compositions. Samuel Barber, who wrote so felicitously for the voice, was a trained singer and even recorded his evocative "Dover Beach" for RCA Victor.

The composers of popular songs as singers are also many. Anyone who ever heard Irving Berlin or Harold Arlen sing one of his own hits, quickly realized that they could not be interpreted more perfectly despite the limitations of the composers' voices. Still another pop singer-composer, even though she couldn't read a note of music, was Billie Holiday. An idea for a song such as "Bless the Child" would come into her head and she would then hum it to her accompanist who would pick it out on the piano. Billie Holiday shared in the writing of the famous "Strange Fruit." "La Vie en Rose," one of Edith Piaf's most famous numbers, was written by herself.

At this writing we still have with us the amazing Alberta Hunter, born "around 1895," who sings songs in six languages but is also a composer of a number of blues songs. For her "blues are what the spirit is to a minister." When a new song comes into her head, frequently at three or four in the morning, she has to hold onto it until she can find someone to set it down for her since she can't read a note of music.

Many of these composer-singers possessed scarcely any voice to speak of yet sang with telling conviction. This brings us to the category of some of our most successful singing artists who have made wonderful careers with very little vocal equipment.

The Non-Voiced Singers. Paradoxical but true, some of our greatest non-operatic singers have had really scarcely any voice at all. Among concert singers not generously endowed vocally I have already mentioned Povla Frijsh and Pierre Bernac. One who only half sang, half spoke her repertory with a shred of a voice was the great *diseuse* Yvette Guilbert. And later on came Lotte Lenya who, by merely approximating the pitches of the songs of her husband, Kurt Weill, such as "Jenny" or "My Ship," could hold an audience riveted.

In the strictly popular field there have been so-called vocalists who made great careers by their way of projecting a song, by their magnetism or personal beauty, but not by their singing voices. One of the all-time greats was Billie Holiday who had an extremely limited voice which she lacerated by the intensity of her cigarette and drug habits. Another example of a non-voiced singer was Mabel Mercer, who held legions of fans in her thrall for years even though her voice was practically non-existent and her intonation not always precise. And what of another great singer with a voice sometimes out of tune—Marlene Dietrich? Yet to hear one of her concerts was an absorbing, even moving experience, as when she sang "Where Have All the Flowers Gone?"

In this category too belong the dancing singers Fred Astaire and Gene Kelly. With no voice to speak of, but confident that if their song wouldn't win the girl they could resort to their wonderfully deft feet, they put over with charm and simplicity some of the loveliest melodies of Irving Berlin, Jerome Kern, George Gershwin, and other great song writers.

As the voice diminishes with age the art grows. This was true of the concert singer or of entertainers such as Sophie Tucker or Maurice Chevalier, who in their seventies or eighties talked more than sang their numbers. Even in his prime the versatile and charming Rex Harrison never seems to have possessed more than a feather of a voice, but that didn't stop him from making his way with infinite aplomb through one of the most successful musicals ever written, *My Fair Lady*—occasionally hitting some notes but rarely sustaining them. Another who never pretended to have a voice at all yet made one of the most endearing and enduring vocal records of all time was the superb actor Walter Huston. In the 1938 Broadway musical *Knickerbocker Holiday* Huston sang Kurt Weill's "September Song" in tones dusted with rue, and later recorded it. In 1984 the record, a continuing best-seller, entered the American Record Hall of Fame.

The successful folk singers also belong in the category of non-voiced singers, usually having true, sometimes quite pretty voices (though this can scarcely be said of Bob Dylan) but small, thin in quality and limited in range. Here again the word is all important. The singer with a big, sumptuous voice would swamp this kind of vocal literature, as often happens when opera singers attempt popular songs. Style, very personal phrasing, clarity of diction and an intimate approach is what's wanted—not voice.

The Amateur Singers. Since singing comes as naturally to most people as breathing, the amateur voice is the most common of all. It comes in every range and quality and can be heard from all ages, beginning at two and all the years thereafter. There are those unfortunates who, though they may love music, sadly proclaim that they "have no ear" and "can't carry a tune." Actually the "trick" of matching one's singing voice to a conceived pitch is a mental process and if it does not occur naturally can be painstakingly learned. However, such is the love for singing of some out-of-tune vocalists that they join choirs and choruses anyway and stand close to a helpful neighbor to keep them on pitch.

The school chorus or glee club, the Sunday School choir, then the church choir, later high school and college musicals, later still choral societies, performances of *Messiah*, "barber shop" quartets, and at all stages of existence Christmas carolling, song-fests, bathroom vocalizing—amateur singing is threaded through our lives. Who has not known the thrill and delight of raising the

C. Guys: A Victorian musical evening.

singing voice in the company of our fellow human beings to produce a soaring block of massed sound? When he wished to express musically the brotherhood of man, Ludwig van Beethoven turned to the singing voice. Upliftingly, it rings out in the last movement of the Ninth Symphony:

> *Alle Menschen werden Brüder,*
> *Wo dein sanfter Flügel weilt.*

Until the invention of the phonograph a requisite for a properly furnished house was a piano, even if it was a simple upright one pushed against a wall. This friendly musical instrument in the parlor was a center and a bond, uniting the family in a way that the television that now dominates our living rooms does not. In her autobiography, *My Life,* the great mezzo-soprano Marilyn Horne describes with deep feeling what a big role music played in her family life growing up in the 1930's and forties when there was radio, movies and recordings. Because her father had a fine tenor voice and sang in the church choir, he instilled in her musicianship and musical integrity from an early age, to which she attributes much of the success of her career. In addition she had an older sister with a fine voice. Encouraged by their ambitious father, the Horne sisters, little Gloria and Marilyn, would appear in school programs, or during World War II at bond rallies and patriotic rallies where they would harmonize in lusty renderings of "Over there" or "It's a grand old flag." What better training for her later years when Miss Horne puts her head as close to Joan Sutherland as she can get (they are like Mutt and Jeff in height) and the two rip off in thirds and sixths the exhilarating duet "Mira, o Norma?"

Among the well-to-do of an earlier age one of the most desirable accomplishments of a young lady was her ability to sing, and voice lessons were given a high priority in her otherwise limited education. Natasha, heroine of *War and Peace*, possesses a lovely contralto voice and is studying when we first meet her. Elizabeth Bennet suffers agonies over the inadequacies of her sister Mary's singing at the Bingley dance in *Pride and Prejudice* and finally persuades her father to make Mary desist.

Amateur singing extended to royal circles as well. The Empress Maria Theresa is reputed to have been a gifted singer. While still princess, the contralto-voiced Victoria, a life-long devotee of opera, took singing lessons from the most renowned bass of his day, Luigi Lablache. It is on record that Her Highness performed the difficult duet "Mira, o Norma" with her mother, the Duchess of Kent, taking the other part—but unfortunately not on a phonograph record.

Though *jeunes filles* of these and later times often took vocal instruction, there was usually no thought of doing anything so vulgar as going on the stage and making a professional career. An amateur, whose singing nevertheless gave her a fabulous career in the glittering salons of Paris during the 1850's and 1860's, was the amusing Lillie Moulton, born Greenough in Cambridge, Massachusetts. After studying in London with Garcia, who said she reminded him of his sister, Maria Malibran—except that Lillie had brains and Maria did not—she moved on to Paris with a note from him to his younger sister, Pauline Viardot. "Do all you can to persuade her to go on the stage," he wrote. But in this project the powers of the fascinating Madame Viardot for once failed. Instead Lillie married the scion of a wealthy American diplomat and plunged into the rich and varied life of Paris in the Second Empire.

"This was a great occasion seeing and hearing Rossini, Gounod and Auber at the same time . . . I wonder that I had the courage to sing before them," she wrote home to her New England relatives.

Or, on another evening, "I sang some of Massenet's songs, accompanied of course, by Massenet. Liszt was attentive and most enthusiastic. He said Massenet had a great future, and he complimented me on my singing, especially my phrasing and expression."

Or again, "Jenny Lind and I performed the duo from (Auber's) *Le Premier Jour du Bonheur* . . . She put her arm around my waist while we were singing, as if we were two school girls." How many professionals during the same period could have boasted of such performances before the musical elite of Europe?

Lillie's amazing penchant for being on the scene of an important musical event produced this interesting item written from Cambridge to her sister in June 1877: "There is also another invention, called phonograph, where the human voice is reproduced, and can go on for ever being reproduced. I sang in one through a horn and they transposed this on a platina roll and wound it off." On hearing the playback her reaction was similar to many people who hear their voices reproduced for the first time. "The intonation—the pronunciation—I could recognize as my own, but the *voice*—Dear me!" To Lillie de Hegermann-Lindencrone (she had remarried after the death of her first husband) must go credit for being the first person known to have recorded the singing voice.

Not generally known is the fact that James Joyce was the possessor, like his father before him, of a light, sweet tenor voice. Joyce grew up in an atmosphere of singing, as he recalled evenings in his childhood in *A Portrait of the Artist:*

One by one the others took up the air until a full choir of voices was singing. They would sing so for hours, melody after melody, glee after glee, till the last pale light died on the horizon, till the first dark night clouds came forth and night fell.

In 1904, Joyce, discouraged in his attempts at writing and desperate to earn money by some means other than drudgery, decided to enter the Feis Ceoil, a musical competition held annually in Dublin. (The previous year it had been won by a nervous nineteen-year-old named John McCormack.) Joyce sang an aria from Sullivan's *The Prodigal Son* and an Irish air and would have won the contest but for the rules requiring each contestant to read a song at sight. Joyce refused, declaring grandly that it was not worthy of an artist to sing music unprepared. In fact he could scarcely read music and was near-sighted to boot. As a result Joyce only won second prize, a bronze medal which he is said to have thrown into the Liffey. On the strength of his appearance, the best voice teacher in Dublin offered to teach him for nothing, but the future author of *Ulysses* preferred to take the position of the great singer "who might have been."

Joyce continued to sing throughout the whole of his life, and a friend recalls him performing three ballads on his forty-sixth birthday "more beautifully than I had ever heard him, his voice charged with feeling." The author's love for singing illumines everything he wrote. "The human voice, two tiny silky cords," he once said, "wonderful, more than all the others."

In recent times when there has been no stigma attached to going on the stage, two amateur singers and presidents' daughters, Margaret Wilson and Margaret Truman, attempted unsuccessfully to make professional careers. By means of the radio the whole country was able to gauge the essentially thin and tentative quality of Miss Truman's voice.* Further study improved it and gave her more assurance in later appearances but she never really rose above the status of an amateur.

Another who qualified as an amateur singer was the late Thomas E. Dewey, governor of New York and presumptive president of the United States until expectedly defeated by Harry S. Truman. As a young man Dewey trained his baritone voice with a well known teacher in the Verdi Square (Seventy-second Street and Broadway) area of New York City where vocal pedagogues are most abundant. On the morning of his first concert appearance he awoke with incipient laryngitis but decided to sing anyway since important musicians and critics were to be in the audience. All went well until in the middle of Schubert's "Der Doppelganger" his voice seized up on him—the

---

*Her father, the President, denounced a Washington D.C. critic, Paul Hume, for pointing this out.

vocalist's nightmare. Thereafter, Dewey and his handsome wife, Frances (herself a singer with an operetta soprano kind of voice), performed strictly in private.

It is perhaps not generally known that the young Agatha Christie, before turning to mystery story writing, studied singing in Paris, as did the young Diana Trilling in New York before she became a trenchant critic and essayist. Paul Horgan, author of some forty books including novels, biographies and a major history in two volumes, began as a singer, training his baritone voice at the Eastman School in Rochester, New York.

Over the years there has also been the kind of aspiring amateur, usually female and very rich, who has tried to "buy" a singing voice. One of the best known was Polish-born Ganna Walska, who by various alliances, including marriage to the Chicago millionaire Harold McCormick, gained a fortune. All her life she tried to gain a voice as well, going to any number of teachers including Jean de Reszke, Frances Alda and Frank LaForge. When these did not provide the alchemy to produce vocal gold, she also went to spiritualists, psychiatrists, astrologers, hypnotists, telepathists, Brahmin scholars and even the ouija board—all of which is recounted solemnly in her autobiography, *Always Room at the Top.*

Of these attempts Frances Alda, just retired to teaching from a long career at the Metropolitan Opera, writes amusingly in her autobiography, *Men, Women and Tenors*: "I did my level best to teach Ganna Walska to sing. I demonstrated, I repeated, I praised wherever I honestly could praise. I scolded. . . . But work as I did I could not teach Ganna Walska to sing.

" 'No, *No,* No!' I'd say to her. 'Not like that. You're singing like five million pigs.' "

One who sang like ten million pigs to the delight of her screaming fans was Florence Foster Jenkins, who annually would hire an auditorium in New York City's old Hotel Ritz and offer a program of songs and arias that she could perform scarcely even on pitch. The audience thought it wildly funny, and a record of one of these recitals—surely one of the cornerstones of camp— used to be produced at parties to provide a moment of mirth for the guests. At the risk of being charged with stuffiness, this writer's spirits, far from being lightened on hearing her, were agonized; but that was not a typical reaction. Did she herself know how comic her listeners found her? Did she realize how excruciatingly awful her singing was? These, of course, are questions which the amateur, if she is wealthy enough, does not have to raise.

The era of the rich amateur singer who buys her audiences would appear to be dying out, yet up until a few years ago, a soprano whose vocal endowments were decidedly limited would nonetheless hire a New York recital hall and give programs of serious contemporary songs, some of which she herself had commissioned. Thus, buried in the joke of a rich singer buying her audience was a serious effort to help the cause of new music.

There is the amateur singer longing for the voice which nature never supplied, and there is the opposite number: the person endowed with a beautiful natural instrument and musicianship besides. These favored people may even undergo vocal training besides but then for economic or personal reasons or for just plain lack of ambition choose to remain amateurs all their lives. To this category belongs my next-door neighbor Mrs. Norma Gorovoy. The first time I heard her luscious, finely equalized soprano soaring in the long phrases of George Gershwin's "Summertime" I couldn't believe my ears. Breathing, accuracy of pitch, musicianship were all there. She is a handsome woman and also possesses that indefinable asset so important to a singer—projection. Then why? Why no career?

"Oh," she shrugged when I asked her later. "I thought of it. I studied six years. When I was sixteen I went after school to Juilliard. I even studied with Estelle Liebling who taught Beverly Sills. But there were other things." She shrugged again but this time her eyes also smiled with fun. "You know. Boys. Having a good time. Marrying. Babies."

"Was there music in your house when you grew up?"

It seems there was not, though she was raised in New York City. Yet none of the musical aspects of that metropolis had much interest to her parents. Not until she was in high school and met a gifted student pianist did she discover music. "We used to go to my friend's house and sing and play every night." But without the drive for a career that comes from early influences, Mrs. Gorovoy remained an amateur.

As with the thousands and thousands of fine singers like her, she may be asked to dinner and "to bring her music." Though musical evenings with gifted amateurs* holding forth in the home are perhaps less prevalent than they were in the days of our grandfathers, they still persist wherever people delight in lifting up their voices in song or hearing their non-professional friends and neighbors do so.

As Hugo von Hofmannsthal wrote: "Singing is near miraculous because it is the mastering of what is otherwise a pure instrument of egotism: the human voice."

---

*The theme of an amateur singer buying a career was thoroughly, agonizingly explored in Orson Welles's classic film *Citizen Kane*.

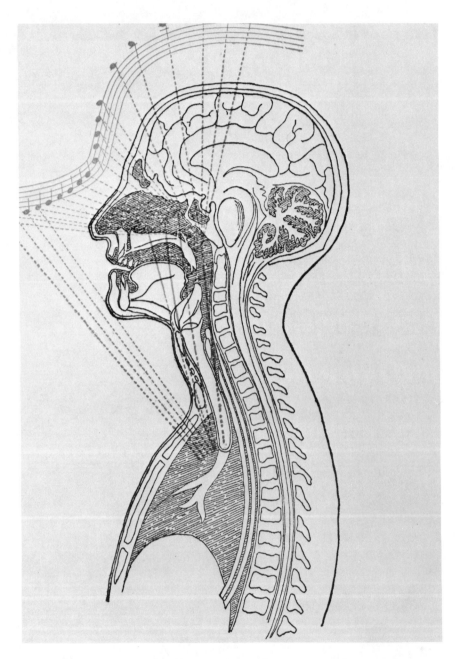

Dotted lines denote vocal sensations of soprano and tenor singers.

Singing: Illusion or Science?

Have not poetry and music emerged, as it seems, out of the sounds the enchanters made to help their imagination to enchant, to charm, to bind with a spell themselves and the passers-by?

—W. B. Yeats

Out of Sight. Orpheus, the first great singer, was also a magician and often the spell that a singer casts upon his audience seems utterly magical. To a person watching and listening it all looks so easy. Singers simply open their mouths and a flood of tone comes pouring out capable of stirring up in us all kinds of emotions. We too can open our mouths and let forth a singing voice of a sort, but no such spell is engendered by our song—except sometimes a kind of self-hypnosis when the walls of a bathroom give back the voice in an enriched form. What then do great singers do that is different from when we sing?

Outwardly, our eyes detect nothing except perhaps an occasional odd, comic grimace on the face of a singer. At a piano recital we can see how a pianist holds his hands—with wrists held high, or, depending on his technique, with flattened wrists and fingers. In the same way our eyes can see a ballerina set her toe in a blocked shoe in a certain precise manner onto the floor of a stage, her arms held in various positions any of which again are demonstrable. But when it comes to singing it was God's little joke to place the larynx, the hard-surfaced kernel of the voice containing the vocal cords, *just* out of sight of any normal visualization of what is going on in the throat during vocalization. Ask a professional singer how he produces the easy flood of rich, powerful tone that emanates from his mouth and he may give an

175

elaborate explanation of his sensations while singing. But he can only *tell* you—he cannot physically show you. And so we are in a world of mystery, where all is unbeheld sensation, and nothing apparent. No wonder that singing seems to be accomplished by magic.

When for the first time, in 1854, a human eye viewed living vocal cords vibrating in the throat of a human being it was believed that a basis for a scientific understanding of how the voice functions had finally been established. Before that much had been guesswork. In ancient Greece, Aristotle understood empirically that the larynx by some mysterious means played a part in the production of the voice, but thought that alterations in the length of the trachea (the windpipe) must control the changes of pitch of the voice, as though there were a set of organ pipes built into men's throats. (Aristotle also believed that the true source of the voice was the heart, and though this may have been scientifically inaccurate no one can gainsay its essential importance to great singing.) By the second century A.D., Galen, the Greek physician, had named and described the larger cartilages of the larynx. Hundreds of years later Leonardo da Vinci made the first known drawings of the larynx in profile, including the vocal cords, though he did not realize their importance and still believed the voice to be produced by a column of air vibrating in the windpipe.

In 1636 by citing the laws of sound which were now understood, a French scholar gave the lie to this organ-pipe theory. Man would need to have a trachea or windpipe of giraffe-like proportions to produce a range of two octaves or more, he declared, and decided that the vocal cords, as revealed by dissection, must produce sound by vibrating.

A hundred years later another Frenchman, Antoine Ferrein, published the startling results of his experiments on a human larynx taken from a cadaver. By blowing air through the tiny organ he discovered that the two tweezer-shaped bands, joined at one end and attached to the front of the throat, but free to open or close at the back of it, could be made to come together and vibrate, thus producing a sound. He also showed that the greater the speed and the pressure of the air forced across these bands, the larger would be the volume of sound. Air playing on the vibrating ligaments, said Ferrein, had the same effect as the action of a bow on the strings of a violin and so he named them *"cordes vocales"* or "vocal cords" or "strings" a term familiar to us to this day.

Frequently and nonsensically, however, they are referred to as vocal "chords." Present day laryngologists and vocal experts also feel that the word "cord" is inaccurate, since the wiry, immensely strong ligaments fluctuating across the larynx are really tapered membranes shot through with muscular fibers. They prefer to use the term "vocal folds."

During the early part of the nineteenth century scientists worked in increasing numbers to establish somehow that the voice functioned on the basis of one of four types of musical instruments. At the same time attempts were made to see into the throat, particularly the fascinating glottis, the space within the larynx that contains the vocal cords or folds. All experiments to arrive at a means failed until curiously, not a doctor, but a grave, quietly charming vocal pedagogue with a scholarly turn of mind and a cracked singing voice succeeded in the fall of 1854 at Paris. This was Manuel Garcia II—a name held in reverence by many vocal teachers to this day.

Unaware of earlier unsuccessful efforts to see into the throat with a mirror, and with but one overwhelming desire—"If only I could see the glottis!"—Garcia went to a surgical supply place in Paris and happened on a new kind of long-handled dentist's mirror. Once home he warmed the instrument in hot water and placed it against the uvula at the back of his mouth and the top of his throat. (This operation, incidentally, must be performed with great delicacy, for the slightest excess of pressure will cause an instant reaction of gagging or even vomiting.) Taking up another larger hand mirror he stood by a window and caught a ray of the sun which he flashed onto the tiny mirror in the depths of his mouth. And there for the first time the glottis of a live human being containing its precious treasure—the means by which man communicates to his fellow man—was first beheld by the human eye. Manuel Garcia II had invented the laryngoscope. Now an exact science of voice production was at last assured.

Or was it?

At best the laryngoscope made it possible to view the top of the vocal cords only. Their undersides were, and still are, out of sight of the eye of the scientific observer. And then there was, and is, the vexing problem of the mirror inserted into the back of the mouth above the throat. Everyone knows what a dismal bleat emerges when a doctor places a wooden depressor on the tongue and asks us to say "Ah." How much more difficult then, to semi-swallow a mirror and be called upon to sing while the scientist makes his observations of the changes in the vocal cords. At best he sees only an approximation of their appearance during vocalization for the simple reason that there cannot be proper singing when the mouth is stopped up with bits of glass and metal. In more recent times we have had remarkable high-speed photographs taken of a singer's glottis in performance* but even these had to be made with the ever-present mirror reflecting light down into the throat. Nor do these pictures show what is happening on the underside of the cords. Still more recently, in an untiring quest to see what occurs during the vocal process, laryngologists have considered the possibility of inserting elec-trode needles into individual muscles within the larynx and obtaining what are known as electromyograms. But as a doctor with a wryer sense of humor than some of his colleagues remarked of the idea, "This causes some discomfort to the subject, which he does not always recognize as necessary."

The invention of the laryngoscope, however, did corroborate certain principles either suggested in the dissecting room or arrived at empirically. A great wave of optimism combined with a surge of medical inquiry swept through the vocal world. This Victorian invention coincided with the belief that technology could solve all of man's problems and it now seemed certain that an exact scientific method of singing could be evolved. But following from 1854 no new race of vocal giants appeared in the musical world, only the usual fluctuating proportion of great singers that arrive on the scene with each new decade. Garcia, his simple little mirror always at hand, continued to produce a number of noted singers in his vocal studio; so did his sister, Pauline Viardot, and his pupil Mathilde Marchesi. Though the laryngoscope might confirm certain theories about the changes in the vocal folds during singing and could reveal inflammation in a

---

*A film of a soprano's vocal cords as she sang "Poor wand'ring one" from The Pirates of Penzance was shown on a national television program about the human body in February 1984. It did not, however, yield up the secrets of a perfect vocal technique.

strained pair of vocal cords, the fact was that the instrument made it no easier to teach someone to sing. Confusion continued to exist concerning the vocal process and the arguments became, if anything, more heated than ever.

Indeed half a century later in 1909 an Englishman, Ernest G. White, published a book called *Science and Singing* in which he put forth the theory that the vocal cords did not produce sound at all. Illustrated with the skulls of snakes, sheep and giraffes, the volume gravely and apparently plausibly put forth the proposition that the tones of the singing voice are produced in the sinuses, with the result that a whole school of "sinus tone production" evolved in London and spread to the United States. White's book and several later volumes elaborating the theory are available in some libraries to the innocent voice student who might chance upon them, despite the comments of today's experts such as Elster Kay in *Bel Canto and the Sixth Sense*: "First prize in idiocy goes to the writer who said that vocal tone originated not in the vocal cords but in the sinuses. This particular book reached a very wide student public and was made the basis of an elaborate teaching method, which, hardly surprisingly, collapsed when after the passage of some years it produced no singers at all."

As late as 1950, not quite a century after the introduction of the laryngoscope, an emboldened Frenchman put forth a theory that rocked the laryngological world and set the scientists rushing to their sound laboratories. The larynx, maintained M. Raoul Husson, was not the sole vocal organ in the human body, but part of a system controlled from an acoustic center in the brain. Quite the opposite from the idea that a column of air rises from the lungs and pushes against the vocal cords making them flutter, this acoustic center sends nervous impulses—"coup par coup" as he put it—directly to the cords, which by their vibrations set in motion the column of air. This chicken-before-the-egg theory set up a tremendous fuss and was denounced by many as utter nonsense. However, to disprove it a considerable amount of research had to be accomplished with the result, as one noted voice doctor says, "we learned more about the physiology of voice in that decade than in any other, thanks to Husson's erroneously but sincerely conceived challenge."

The Theory. Then what is really and truly known about the basic principles of voice production? Put very elementally, this much seems almost certain:

Air having been taken into the lungs is expelled back through the larynx. At the same instant the vocal cords come together, or, more accurately, approximate. Such is the pressure of the breath on these tiny ligaments that a portion, or the whole of them (depending on the pitch of the note being sung) is forced apart, letting through a tiny puff of air. This causes the cords or folds to vibrate, and since they are capable of changing their length and thickness these amazingly adjustable ligaments produce a series of notes ranging over two or more octaves.

Up from the larynx lie the resonators. These include the pharynx—the soft palate above the throat—also the arched roof of the mouth called the hard palate, and certain cavities that lie behind the nose. They vibrate in sympathy with the note giving it a special tone quality. It is believed that the larynx is also a resonator, and that in addition on certain notes the upper part of the chest also vibrates, though the idea of the chest as resonator has been disputed. The infinite varieties of these resonators, like the features of a face, give every voice a unique sound and character.

Battlefield Number One. "The voice," said Seneca, "is nothing more than beaten air." How right he was has now more or less been proven. Since there can be no singing without air let us examine the first of the basic factors in singing: that apparently simple and natural function called breathing. Immediately we are plunged into a battle in which the hue and cry is deafening. If nothing else, the vocal experts, those who set themselves up as absolute authorities on how to sing, are unabashedly vocal in their claims to know right from wrong.

Some vocal teachers pay no attention to a breathing technique, merely asking their pupils to take in air the way they ordinarily would. The subject is not raised. Other pedagogues believe that a good singing technique depends almost entirely on breathing correctly. But what is "correct" breathing? Here the bickering and strife break out in fearful force.

On one point only does there seem to be agreement: man can take breath in one of three basic ways. (He can also breathe in a combination of these ways, but for some reason dogmatism obtains in the manuals of singing, and the point is rarely stressed.) When we have been running and badly want breath, we take in air in a series of very short, quick breaths as our shoulders rise and fall. This is called clavicular or upper chest breathing, and though it feeds fresh supplies of oxygen to the lungs quickly it does not supply them with very much and only to the upper part of the body. Athletes mainly breathe in this fashion, but almost without exception the vocal experts condemn it as inadequate and unsuitable for singing. It should be pointed out, however, that a cunning singer falls back on this type of breathing when a very long phrase cannot be managed. Not wishing to break it, he takes a barely perceptible half or "catch" breath.*

A second kind of breathing goes under such names as "lateral" or "intercostal." Air is drawn to the bottom of the lungs which are enclosed by the eighth to the twelfth ribs of the thorax or rib cage. Unlike the upper ribs rigidly attached to the sternum and back bone, these lower, so called floating, ribs make it possible for a large expansion of the lungs. If the abdomen is held in as a kind of base or support, this expansion will cause the ribs to push out in front and to the sides in the area just above the navel. Thus a fanatic believer in this type of breathing for singing, issues these exhortations to her students:

"1) Draw in the abdomen below the navel, as well as the navel itself, and keep them thus always, for the rest of your life." (In heavy black print.)

She also has a few other suggestions to the aspiring singer:

"2) Put yourself in the physical and spiritual state of one who is about to take a dive into the sea, or is training for the championship in running, jumping, and so forth.

"3) Be happy, radiantly happy; please!"

Dividing the rib cage from the abdomen is a muscle known as the diaphragm which exerts an up and down force within the torso. Shaped like an inverted saucer, the diaphragm can be made to flatten out by taking a deep breath. This exerts pressure on the

*Sometimes this gulp can be noisy, as was the case of Lotte Lehmann's singing.

abdomen forcing it to protrude. The downward movement of the diaphragm creates a partial vacuum within the rib cage into which air rushes and we have what is known as deep abdominal, but sometimes diaphragmatic, breathing.

Women who have taken courses in natural childbirth will understand well these three different kinds of breathing, particularly the intercostal, in which they learn to keep pressure off the top of the uterus during labor, and the upper chest, or clavicular, practiced during the last moments of birth.

Assertions are made that intercostal breathing was the choice of the early great bel canto singers and of the wondrous *castrati*. The words of Manuel Garcia II that the chest should be lifted and the abdomen drawn up and in while taking breath are also frequently quoted by his fervent disciples in support of the intercostal breathing method. In 1855, however, one year after Garcia's discovery of the laryngoscope, a mettlesome doctor named Mandl, writing in the *Gazette Médicale*, published in Paris, dared to say that if the diaphragm was made to descend as deeply as possible more air would be taken into the lungs, providing always that the abdomen pushes out during this action. Soon after, his theories were taken up and taught by noted singing teachers in both England and America. The intercostal forces, uttering bel canto cries that *theirs* was the true method of the Italian master, rallied at once and the battle was conjoined. It continues to this day. Here is a section of a review published in *Opera* magazine by Rupert Bruce Lockhart in 1966:

> I once attended in Paris a meeting of the Union des Maîtres-Chanteurs and the subject for the evening discussion was "Breathing." In the auditorium were over a hundred professors of singing or speech and on the platform three doctors (throat specialists) and one physical-culturist. I was taken by one of the most famous musicians and singing professors in Paris. We laughed helplessly all evening. There was almost a free fight. No two people in the entire assembly seemed to agree on a method of breathing. Insults were hurled around and two of the doctors finally turned their chairs back to back and refused to speak to each other. The evening ended with the physical-culturist illustrating an entirely different method from anything that had been exposed by the singing fraternity.

Caught in this continuing fray is the student anxious to learn a correct breathing method that will enable him to take in three or four more times as much air as he uses in average quiet breathing. If this student turned to the literature, what might he find? I made a random survey of twenty-eight different books or manuals published in the last hundred years purporting to treat the subject of breathing authoritatively. (There are dozens and dozens more but these happened to be on my shelves.) I found that twelve experts advocated intercostal breathing with the abdomen drawn in, ten, abdominal breathing with a relaxed abdomen, three that counseled a kind of combination of the two, and three that advised breathing in any way that seemed comfortable but was at the same time supportive. Gentleness is simply not in most of the authors. J. C. Veaco announces his position with the thunderous title, *Why Abdominal Breathing is Fatal to Bel Canto.* Another declares that this kind of breathing may do dreadful harm to certain organs in the female abdomen. Herman Klein, in whose family's London house Manuel Garcia II gave singing lessons, declares that not only is abdominal breathing the only desirable method, but adds, "This I believe to be the old Italian system of breathing, as it was taught by Manuel Garcia II." What *are* we to believe?

The experience of great singers ought to reveal the truth. One book informs us that Melba, Eames, Nordica, the de Reszke brothers and Pol Plançon were all advocates of intercostal breathing, raising their chests high and restraining the lower and middle parts of their abdomens. On the other hand, a legend says that if Caruso stood next to a grand piano he could move it as he drew in breath and his abdomen pushed out. The celebrated coloratura soprano Marcella Sembrich is supposed to have built her vocal career on the use of half breaths, which suggests that she used the clavicular, high chest method of breathing. Sembrich studied with the noted teacher Giovanni Lamperti and tremendous squabbling goes on to this day as to whether he taught deep abdominal breathing or the intercostal system; if the story is true about the way Sembrich breathed, it suggests he taught neither. Going to the present authority of one who has been called "probably the greatest singer in the world," Marilyn Horne declares, "The principle of (breath) support is simple: you stand erect . . . and as you inhale air and the muscle across your diaphragm expands you push out and shove to keep it there. Breathing in is really breathing out, in singing—a yoga principle as well."

Other legendary singers have made enigmatic comments on breathing. Lilli Lehmann says that in the earlier part of her career she always had a sensation of taking in too much air and, feeling stifled, wanted to let some out before she sang a phrase. Kirsten Flagstad is quoted as saying that the subject of breathing is "almost impossible to learn or understand and almost impossible to teach."

And yet it is breath and breath alone that makes it possible for singers to emit long, beautifully controlled phrases and sustained high notes that are part of the art of great singing. Singers can and do begin a note pianissimo, swell it out to a forte and then back again to its previous softness in a manner known as a *messa di voce* that leaves the audience, if only out of identification, literally breathless. All this is made possible by the support given their tones by breath (a support, by the way, that is far less needed in closely miked popular singing). Thus, because correct breathing is a necessity to fine singing, the experts continue to argue the merits of the various methods while students often undergo real physical torments practiced in vocal studios trying to learn how to breathe. Belts may be fastened around their waists or the lower part of their abdomens more and more tightly constricted. A pile of bricks or large books will be piled on the belly as they lie on their backs on the floor. Blanche Marchesi writes amusingly of a teacher who would make the student place a large tumbler of water on her chest while lying on her back. If the pupil breathed right the glass would remain in place. Most of the lessons, however, were spent in wiping up herself and the room. I had thought that by this time enlightenment might have put some of these barbarous teaching practices to rout, when to my amazement, on striking up a conversation with a student lyric soprano employed at Schirmer's in New York, she said that she had left her previous teacher because *he had stood on her belly* to strengthen her abdominal muscles.

It would be unsuitable—and highly dangerous as well—for this writer to enter the intercostal versus abdominal breathing battle, but there does seem to be one commonsense element to consider about the two methods. In the intercostal technique the abdomen is held in, creating a firm base for the air to spread out in a lateral way across the body just above the navel. People naturally wide in this part of the body would presumably find this method of breathing more congenial to the way they are built. Is this why women with their wide hips and abdomens containing organs that men do not have are naturally inclined to breathe in the intercostal manner? Equally a tall bass, say, with wide shoulders, a long torso and relatively narrow hips, might well find that deep abdominal breathing would provide him with a powerful, vertical column of air to sustain his tones. Could this be the reason, as has been established, that men take more instinctively to abdominal breathing?

Another smaller but vexing point of dissension exists among the breathing experts: is it preferable to take in air through the nose or the mouth when singing? "Whenever possible, breathe through the nose, as that ensures a deeper breath as well as being kinder to the throat." "Breathing through the nose is inefficient because 1) it is stilted and awkward, 2) it prohibits the swift and quiet inhalation of requisite amounts of air, and 3) it is inclined to lead to a high chest position, which induces throatiness." These two opinions written within six years of one another in the 1950's show that as with almost all aspects of technique, concord and peaceful agreement is unknown among the experts. The advocates of nasal breathing point out that not only is it natural, but also ensures that outside air, which may be cold and contain particles damaging to the larynx, will be warmed and filtered before being drawn into the lungs. The mouth-breathing exponents emphasize the impossibility of taking in air through the nose quickly enough to meet the ordinary demands of singing. Certainly it is true that if air is drawn rapidly into the nose the resulting sound can only be described as a sniff. (This was a noise that marred the singing of the volatile, red-haired soprano Ljuba Welitsch.) Herbert Witherspoon, a bass of some renown at the Metropolitan during the early part of this century, advises the readers of his manual to take breath through *both* nose and mouth.

Is there then one proper breathing technique? I can only cite the result of tests made to determine how eight important famous singers breathed which was published in 1948. Dr. E. Froeschels, a prominent laryngologist, found that *each one of the eight singers breathed differently.*

Attack! Up from the lungs rises the breath, having been taken in whatever fashion. Hurtling into the trachea, or windpipe, it encounters an extraordinary nut-sized organ known as the larynx which is the Greek word for "throat." Though we have come now to think of the larynx as the "voice box" there is every reason to suppose that while earliest man possessed one he had scarcely any voice at all. If one considers the matter, speaking and singing are not absolute requisites for survival, though many of us, once having known them, would not be much interested in an existence that did not include the use or the sound of the voice. A number of years ago the Doctors Jackson, professors of bronco-esophagology at Temple University, listed some of the truly important uses of the larynx that enable us to live:

1) Regulatory. The larynx is not just a passageway through which air flows into and out of the lungs. This tiny organ, a skeleton of cartilages bound together by ligaments and membranes, exerts a "delicate and co-operative" effect on the regulation of the interchange of carbon dioxide in the bloodstream, so that the level remains constant during all phases of breathing. The precision that the larynx possesses in controlling our respiration is vital to our survival.

2) Circulatory. Working like a valve, the larynx maintains a control of lung pressure. This in turn exerts a pumping action on the blood flowing through our thin, elastic vessels as well as on the heart itself. Another absolutely vital function.

3) Fixative. The next time you lift something slightly heavy, note how the larynx, probably quite unnoticed by you, locks air in your chest cavity. Try lifting something of comparable weight while continuing to breathe in and out and it will readily be seen what an important aid this fixative function of the larynx is to man's physical actions. Studies show that persons who for one reason or another have had their larynxes removed and with them the power to lock in air within their bodies, are practically incapacitated for manual labor. This same fixing ability of the larynx also works during defecation, enabling straining at the stool.

4) Protective. Day and night the larynx keeps vigilant watch against the entrance of any matter into the air passage. In the event that a large crumb should enter the windpipe instead of the esophagus (the second pipeline in the throat down which food descends to the stomach), the tiny folds within the larynx instantly snap shut, blocking any further descent of the un-

wanted crumb. At the same time air pressure builds up in the thorax below the larynx. With equal rapidity, the tiny little ligaments now fly apart and the compressed air rushes out, blowing the crumb before it with a sound we describe as a cough. Without the vigilant larynx our lives would be in constant danger of "swallowing the wrong way" or of death by choking.

5) Emotional. Not everyone can sing and we all have to learn to speak. The larynx however provides a basic means of expression of our more animal emotions such as grief or terror through its ability to make a noise of sobbing or moaning or of crying out in delight.

Only this far down on the list of essential functions of the larynx do the Doctors Jackson place the voice, which they, while admitting that it has become rather vital in modern times, still say is not "an absolute necessity under ordinary circumstances."

To return, however, to the singing process, expelled breath, as has already been said, rushes into the versatile larynx. At the same time, solely by direction of the brain, wedge-shaped folds within the larynx dart out from either side and all but block the passage of the breath up to the mouth. Such is the pressure of the air that the ligaments are forced to give way in all or part of their length and a puff of air escapes through. In what is known as the "Bernoulli effect" the ligaments immediately resume their former position until the pressure of the air rising from below once again forces through a minute puff. This breath, chopped up at an incredible rate of speed, becomes sound. (Certainly it is no longer air. As has been pointed out, a properly trained singer can stand before a candle flame, and having taken a deep inhalation of air will expel it in the form of a wave of lovely sound; the flame close to the singer's mouth does not move.) The vocal cords or folds which have shut like gates across the glottis must however swing together smoothly, firmly and at the *exact* instant that the air strikes them in order to achieve what is known in singing as a perfect "attack."

"It was not an attack at all. She just opened her lips, and the tones dropped out like the pearls from the mouth of the princess in the fairy tale," wrote the vocally astute W. J. Henderson of the way Nellie Melba began a vocal phrase. "Or one might liken an attack of this kind to the beginning of a flow of water when a faucet is turned." Critics at the time that Melba was in her prime seem to make more of the attack than they do today. (Henderson says in the paragraph following his description of Melba, that the attack of the fabled, all but legendary Lilli Lehmann, "was imperfect throughout her career.") Possibly, vocal authorities of that time had become preoccupied with the attack because of another violent controversy that had broken out due to a confusion that has plagued the singing world ever since.

When in the middle of the nineteenth century Manuel Garcia II wrote in French a manual describing the mechanism of the singing voice he called the coming together or approximation of the vocal folds "le coup de glotte" or in English the "stroke" or worse still "blow of the glottis." To explain more clearly what he meant, he wrote, "By slightly coughing we become conscious of the existence and position of the glottis, and also of its opening and shutting action." The inevitable conclusion seemed to be that the great Garcia, inventor of the laryngoscope, god of vocal pedagogy, had advocated a method of attacking notes with a hard "h" sound like a very quick clearing of the throat. Immediately a whole school of teaching arose around this idea and pupils were instructed to strike their tones with a tiny edge to them. Nothing could be more disastrous for the voice. In order to make this sound like a catch in the throat the vocal cords have to bang together tightly an instant *before* the air from the lungs reaches them. The pressure then literally blows them apart. Such a violent process injures the vocal apparatus in a very short time. Yet this kind of attack was solemnly taught in the name of Garcia.* Actually when a note is correctly attacked a singer should have no feelings in his larynx at all.

Certain languages, however, demand this forceful, ejaculated way of striking a note. In good German a kind of rough click is imposed on vowels that begin words—for instance *"aber"* or *"echt."* As a result German voices often have a harsh quality from the violence with which the vocal folds are treated by the language. Spanish also calls for a sound like the soft clearing of the throat. Careful listening to the singing of Victoria de los Angeles and Monserrat Caballé will reveal this characteristic little Spanish clutching sound when these sopranos attack certain notes.

---

*Later, Garcia, appalled, was to write: "The meaning of the term, 'stroke of the glottis' which was invented by the author . . . has been seriously misrepresented and its misuse has done a great deal of harm."

An "h" placed before a tone that is sung on a vowel will give the note a certain focus that it might otherwise lack, and we often hear a series of "ha-ha-has" rising from the throats of baritones and basses when, lacking agility, they come to grips with some of the florid music devised for them by Bach, Handel or Mozart.

Another faulty kind of attack also exists, less dangerous to the vocal apparatus, but scarcely welcome in the art of fine singing. In this case a tiny volume of air escapes past the edges of the vocal folds *before* they have come together. The result is a breathy tone as though the note being sung had been preceded by a tiny whisper. This kind of soft, aspirated singing we often expect to hear from sexy pop singers of today.

A Voice That Trembles. Air rising from the lungs forces its way through the gate-like folds across the glottis. Because of the tremendo̶us pressure that blows them apart the number of vibrations of a note that a singer intends to hit rises fractionally higher than the precise frequency of the note. As the folds snap back to their original approximated position, the number of vibrations sinks a tiny bit below the true frequency of the note that is in the singer's mind. This deviation of frequency in the human voice, occurring with lightning-like speed, is known as vibrato, and means that in fact no singer sings precisely on pitch. Because this slight swerving of each side of the true pitch is small and, ideally, *regular* most ears hear the tones produced by a fine singer as being in tune.

Responses of people to vibrato in a singing voice are as varying and subjective as tastes in physical types. There can be no doubt that a vibrato invokes an atmosphere of the sensual, the voluptuous, though why this should be so is difficult to say. Witness this passage in George Moore's *Evelyn Innes*, a novel about a Catholic soprano, who, remorseful over the sinfulness of her career and her love affairs, seeks to return to the Church:

> Evelyn hummed the plain chant under her breath, afraid lest she
> should extinguish the pale voices and surprised how expressive
> the plain chant was when sung by these etiolated sexless voices.
> She had never known how much of her life of passion and
> desire had entered into her voice and she was shocked at its
> impurity . . . Her voice, she felt, must have revealed her past
> life to the nuns, her voice must have shocked them a little; her
> voice must have brought the world before them too vividly. For

all her life was in her voice, she would never be able to sing this hymn with the same sexless grace as they did. Her voice would be always Evelyn Innes—Owen Asher's mistress.

Of singers in earlier times there is the usual speculation which voice buffs seem to find so enjoyable as to whether they employed vibrato in their singing. Some musical historians claim that the vocal music of the Renaissance was sung with a so-called "straight" tone, but that the vibrato was cultivated and used to ornament or embellish music. Today, when this music is re-created for us, singers who possess relatively vibrato-free voices or the ability to make them so, usually perform it, though there is no actual proof that the early voices sounded in this manner. Writing of singing in the eighteenth century, no less an authority than Mozart has this to say about vibrato in a letter to his father: "Meissner, as you know, has a bad habit in that he often intentionally vibrates his voice . . . and that I cannot tolerate in him. It is indeed truly detestable, it is singing entirely contrary to nature." Then he adds, "The human voice already vibrates of itself, but in such a degree that it is beautiful, that is the nature of the voice."

Mozart lived in a relatively relaxed time when it came to sexual mores. A century later, with Victorian morality the dominant influence in parts of the Western world, there is much inveighing against the vibrato. It was sweeping "through Europe like the influenza" complained the young music critic George Bernard Shaw, who was not without his prudish side. "I have the voice of a choirboy," Nellie Melba once proudly proclaimed, comparing her silvery tones to those piping singers who lack pulsations to their tones. Phonograph records of Melba and other singers of her time attest to the fact that many used much less vibrato than we are accustomed to today. "The vibrato is popular among the Latin races, while the Anglo-Saxons will not tolerate it." Dr. Holbrook Curtis, a noted American laryngologist, who treated the throats of many singers at the Metropolitan, wrote this in 1909, adding, "No great singer has ever succeeded in securing recognition in the United States . . . who has attempted to secure his effects with a vibrato quality." Given the time he was writing and his familiarity with the artists at the Metropolitan, it was an odd statement to make. If ever there was a singer who secured "his effects" with a glorious vibrato quality it was Enrico Caruso, then in the prime of his adulation both in New York and London. Even as late as 1923 the singing teacher and authority on voice Herman Klein denounced vibrato as a "sin."

Oddly enough it was in the American midwest, where "sin" does not go unremarked, that a psychologist at the University of Iowa attempted to make "an objective analysis of artistic singing" during the late 1920's and into the thirties. Among Dr. Harold Seashore's discoveries was the fact that "individual differences in the capacity for hearing vibrato are very large. In a normal population one individual may be 50 or 100 times as keen as another in this hearing . . . Each individual has his own illusion," he adds, "and his individual sense of the vibrato determines what shall be good or bad for him." This statement renders arguments between the fans of various singers over the tone quality of their favorites absolutely ludicrous, since it appears that *no two people hear the same voice the same way.* Measuring an aesthetic response is a dubious undertaking at best, but Seashore declared that a voice to sound beautiful should possess a smooth, *regular* (sic!) vibrato of between five and a half to eight pulsations a second—the ideal being about six and a half. Such a conclusion, presumptuous as it may seem to measure beauty of tone, is given credence by the analysis of the vibratos of a number of famous singers of the time made by another investigator. Here are a few of the results:

Singer	Rate of Vibrato per second
Galli-Curci	7.4
Caruso	7.1
Martinelli	6.8
Gigli	6.3

He also found that when these singers performed concert selections and were not fighting a large-sized orchestra, the rate of the vibrato usually dropped by as much as one full vibration per second. Equally in climaxes or long-held notes, the swing either side of the true frequency increased to almost as much as a whole tone and the rate picked up to anywhere from eight to ten per second. Most ears interpret this wider swerve and increased rapidity of vibration as greater brilliance and excitement in a tone and applaud all the harder when the singer has left off.

When an accomplished vocalist alternates two notes that are a half-tone or even a whole tone apart very rapidly and (again most important) evenly, the effect is known as a trill, or by the more olf fashioned word "shake." Coloratura sopranos have a particular fondness for the trill and may sometimes hold one for what seems like hours to the ears of an astonished and delighted audience.* Because the lower voices have longer and thicker vocal cords they take less readily to the trill, but the ability can be acquired through practice, though few low-voiced singers seem to have the patience to learn it. There are more trills for men's voice in opera than is perhaps generally realized. Walther von Stolzing in his Act One aria "Am stillen Herd" in *Meistersinger* has a whole measure's trill; Verdi writes a trill for the manly Rodrigo, friend of Don Carlo in the Third Act aria "Per me giunto." Handel and Rossini did not neglect to write trills for the bass voice as well, but these usually emerge as blobs of sound when performed by today's artists.

Among those able to trill there is often discussion as to how to begin one—whether from the top note to the lower one, or the other way around. Not the least of the many amusing scenes in the memoirs of Lillie (Moulton) de Hegermann-Lindencrone is her morning call on Jenny Lind-Goldschmidt, living in retirement at a villa on the French Riviera. The two ladies fell to discussing singing, and eventually the Swedish Nightingale asked the gifted American amateur to sing her a trill.

"I looked about for a piano to give me a note to start on," writes the ubiquitous Lillie. "But a piano was evidently the thing where the Goldschmidts had drawn the line. I made as good a trill as I could without one.

"'Very good!' said she, nodding her head approvingly. 'I learned my trill this way.' And she made a trill for me, accentuating the upper note.

"Pointing her finger at me, she said, 'You try it.'

"I tried it. Unless one had learned to trill so it is very difficult to do; but I managed it somehow . . .

"Twelve o'clock sounded from a cuckoo-clock in the next room, and I felt that my visit, fascinating as my angel was, must come to

---

*A singer named Bernardine Hamaekers, who appeared at the Paris Opéra between 1857 and 1870, is supposed to have sung a trill at the end of "Caro Nome" that lasted one minute.

an end. I left her still standing on the verandah in her white brocade, and as I walked off she made the trill as an adieu."

A trill can be learned and some of the great singers have taken the trouble to do so. John McCormack was the possessor of a beautiful trill and even a soprano with the immense voice of Kirsten Flagstad could trill, as a record she made of the aria from Weber's *Oberon* "Ozean zu Ungeheur" attests. She was less successful with the sustained high F' sharp trill that Wagner demands of Brünnhilde in her enormously difficult opening "Ho-jo-to-ho" at the beginning of Act Two of *Die Walküre*. Indeed, though one usually thinks of a trill in association with the florid music of Donizetti or Rossini, Brünnhilde has to sing several trills in the course of the *Ring*, particularly in *Siegfried* where the tenor is supposed to join her in these rapidly vibrating notes of ecstasy during the Awakening Scene.

Producing a trill can be learned by deliberately acquiring the agility to alternate two notes in the voice. It is also possible to gain the skill of taking vibrato *out* of a tone, though oddly this is not a vocal exercise but a mental one. The singer has to think dead center of the note and then imitate it with his voice. William Vennard, a distinguished voice teacher whose pupils included Marilyn Horne, made the interesting suggestion that singers who wish to obtain a perfect vibrato-free tone should apply to the public relations department of the Bell Telephone Company for their record of a baritone computer singing, "Daisy, Daisy give me your answer, do." À propos of the machine's performance he adds dryly that automation seems to be "less a threat to the arts than to any other profession."

Unlovely and Unwanted. So far we have discussed the vibrato, which, except by those who might almost be accused of pruri-ence, is considered a virtue in today's singing voice. High on the list of what constitutes bad singing is that quality of tone which resembles a quaver, or the slow turning over of a car motor on an icy morning. This unattractive, undesirable effect goes under various names, most commonly "tremolo," but also "wobble." (The word "judder" turns up in a British manual of singing, though it does not appear in the shorter version of *The Oxford English Dictionary*.)

Here again we are caught in a tangle of confused semantics. It was Dr. Seashore's idea to do away with the term "tremolo" and call it "bad vibrato," since each listener has a varying concept of what is "bad" vibrato to his ears. A later writer on the subject declares that "there is no such thing as having a 'bad vibrato' and the term is self-contradictory." In his *Bel Canto*, Cornelius L. Reid states instead that the term vibrato stands for exactly one thing, a cycle that "is completed about six and a half times each second with absolute consistency." The tremolo, which some people refer to as excessive vibrato, often has as many as eight pulsations per second; the slow moving wobble is made up of four vibrations per second. What makes these sounds unattractive to the ear is the fact that the pulsations are irregular and the swerve to either side of the pitch uneven. Just as a singer works to achieve a smoothness of tone quality throughout his range, in the case of the vibrato, evenness of periodicity and frequency fluctuation is essential.

As I have mentioned elsewhere an intense vibrato or shiver seems to be innate to the voices heard in eastern Europe and Russia, nor does it offend the ears of audiences. In Western climes the voices of black singers like Leontyne Price often have a pronounced vibrato, a quality which some people find not to their taste. But then vibrato *is* a matter of taste. The tremolo or wobble, however, must be accounted a distinct vocal fault caused by too little breath support, nervousness, which of course affects the breath, or old age, which diminishes it. Muscular tensions within the throat, a kind of tensing and clutching at the tones, may also be a cause of tremolo. A mainly involuntary vocal fault, it is not an easy one to correct. Sometimes the more the unfortunate vocalist struggles to eliminate a tremolo, the more likely he is to make it worse. Breathing exercises, singing pianissimo and above all trying to establish in the singer's mind the idea of a tone free of tremolo or wobble are some of the means of correcting this unlovable, unwanted sound.

Another Battlefield. Within the tiny cave of the larynx, breath expelled from the lungs is chopped up by the pulsating vocal folds, creating a basic sound. Curiously, that sound, though born of musuclar action, is "thought" into being. That is to say, the brain directs the cords to produce the tone of every note sung in whatever infinite variety of tone color and loudness. Even more curious is the fact that while singers experience a number of different sensations as they perform, they do not, or at least *should* not, feel them in the larynx, where in fact their song is being produced. Most vocalists, except for light sopranos, are aware of vibrations at the base of the neck and the top of the chest while singing low notes. Tones in the middle of the range produce a feeling of fullness at the back of the mouth and the top of the throat. And in the top part of the compass singers have very real sensations that their high notes are proceeding from somewhere behind the nose or eyebrows or even out of the top of the head.

The most uninformed amateur can feel these basic changes of sensation by singing "ah" up the scale from a note comfortably situated in the middle of his voice. If he tries to maintain this same comfortable feeling as he continues higher and higher, he will find it increasingly difficult to keep his original vocal position. Moreover the sound that he makes as he attempts to force his way upward will become "shouty" and unpleasant. Finally, if he continues to push on in this same vocal position there will be a sudden sound like a truncated cackle and his voice will have "broken." Let him repeat this experiment, however, but at the note which begins to strain his voice, make an adjustment to the level of his larynx, letting it sink back very slightly, and he will then be able to continue up the scale feeling a different set of sensations, much more, now, in the head. The tones, too, particularly if he is an amateur, will have a different timbre.

The most uninformed amateur can also hear the sharply differing tone quality of the husky chest tones in women's voices, just as they recognize the fluty, comic sound that men can make known as falsetto. In both cases different sets of sensations accompany the singing of these odd types of tones. The variety of physical feelings that a singer experiences when producing a variety of different kinds of tone quality brings us to the phenomenon of registers—a subject over which rages full scale warfare.

As far back as the seventeenth century the singing voice is mentioned as having two basic qualities of tone. Since within the voice two sets of notes had a distinctive quality they came to be called registers like the registers of an organ with its series of pipes that make tones resembling one another in quality. In an early manual on singing, Giambattista Mancini wrote in 1774: "The voice in its natural state is ordinarily divided into two registers, one of which is called the chest, the other the head or falsetto." In his use of the term falsetto, Mancini unwittingly stirred up the most frightful turmoil among those seeking to understand the registers of the voice, for to others, falsetto meant not the ordinary top part of a singing voice, but an artificial voice, high and ludicrous sounding (to most ears) when emitted by a man, and eerie and unhuman when emerging with a peanut whistle sound from the few sopranos who have ever managed the trick of producing it. As a result, even modern manuals of singing emulate the use of the Mancini term and divide up the voice into chest and falsetto registers, leaving baffled or frustrated those who understand falsetto to be a separate, higher register found in all male and female voices.*

Even before his invention of the laryngoscope Manuel Garcia II had defined a register of the voice as "a series of consecutive homogeneous sounds produced by one mechanism, different essentially from another series of sounds equally homogeneous . . ." A view of the cords seemed to prove this; they could be seen to take on a specific shape and density and vibrate during one section of notes or "register" in the voice and change quite definitely when the singer used another set of tones with a different quality.

In the early 1880's, Emil Behnke, a voice teacher with a sound knowledge of anatomy, succeeded in obtaining the first photographs of the glottis in song, in this case his own. These showed that at the bottom of the range the edges of the vocal folds were thick, dense and impenetrable to light; also that they vibrated throughout their entire length. Singing the middle notes of the compass caused the folds to lengthen slightly and become thin, tense and translucent. In this phase they still continued to vibrate for their entire length. When Behnke sang his top notes the vocal folds did something extraordinary. A portion of them came together at one end and locked tight, so that the breath could only

---

*Viktor Fuchs relates that at the Third Congress of the International Society for Logopaedia and Phoniatry in Vienna in 1920 a professor gave a talk on "The need for a generally acknowledged nomenclature for the physiology, pathology and training of the voice. Unfortunately it was impossible to please all the members of the Society and the fine plans were abandoned."

pass through a partial aperture between the folds. This had the effect of shortening the vibrating lengths and raising the pitch of the note being sung. In addition Behnke was able to observe that if he attempted to sing his high notes while retaining the position of his middle register, the folds, usually a pearly white or pale pink in color, turned bright red in anger at such abusive treatment. Behnke also confirmed a theory of Garcia's that there were two subdivisions to the lower and medium registers of the voice. In partnership with a distinguished laryngologist, Lennox Browne, he published his findings in a book called *Voice, Song and Speech*. To enrich the brew of confusion, however, these men along with several others changed the nomenclature to read for Garcia's chest register, "thick reed"; for the medium, "thin reed"; and the head, "small." To the subregisters they gave the names, "lower thick" and "upper thick" and "lower thin" and "upper thin." This book setting forth their scientific theories with a relative amount of clarity sold widely (an undated secondhand copy in my possession is marked "Twenty-third edition") and the "method" was taken up and taught on both sides of the Atlantic.

Unfortunately the glottis as seen by the camera settled absolutely nothing. In the first place, disclaimers asked if these were accurate pictures of the folds in normal singing, considering that the singer had to vocalize half choking over an object in his throat. They also pointed out that they were pictures of a vocalist who sang by a certain method. Would photographs of the glottis of a singer who sang in another way be the same? And what of the great teachers and singers of the past, demanded those ever wistful for the golden age of bel canto? They had described only two registers. Why now were there thought to be three?

The threats and denunciations mounted. Investigations continued and scientific manuals poured from the press propounding new theories illustrated by vaguely obscene looking drawings and photographs of the vocal apparatus. All claims were put forth with absolute authority and conviction that brooked no contradiction nor any other possible explanation.

Well over a century after the invention of the laryngoscope, that supposed shiny key to a scientific understanding of the voice, how do we stand today in our knowledge of the registers? Here are excepts from important manuals on the technique of singing, almost all of which have either been published for the first time or re-published from older editions *within the past fifty years.*

"Register changes are no more inherent in the anatomy of the vocal cords than they are in the construction of a violin . . ."

"According to natural laws the voice is made up of only *one* register, which constitutes its entire range."

"As Mancini categorically stated, 'all voices divide themselves into two registers,' the first duty of the teacher is to recognize this condition and to take proper steps necessary to establishing them in their divided form."

"Most teachers and singers now believe that both men's and women's voices consist of three registers—chest (lowest), middle and head (highest)."

"There are altogether four resonance walls and consequently four registers."

"All five registers are usually present in the contralto voice."

". . . it is not surprising that some pretend to tell us that there are two, three, four or five registers. It will be much more correct to call every voice by the name of a new additional register, for in the end every tone will and *must* be taken in a different relation."

"As the whole conception of voice registers is a hazardous one it is best to disregard their existence altogether."

Of two authoritative *medical* manuals on the voice published in the last three decades, one ducks the entire question of registers altogether, while the other gives this tentative advice: "Use the terms *upper* and *lower register* to refer to the two vocal ranges. . . . In some cases we might sub-divide to upper, middle and lower registers. One is thus committed to no theory of function."

This little survey omits the scorn and vituperation heaped upon one expert by another for enumerating the registers differently, or for declaring or denying their existence, nor does it convey the often astonishing amount of self-praise that rises like heavy scent from the pages of these books. *"I have proved that there is but one continuous register in a voice—any voice,"* triumphantly proclaims the author (italics hers) of one such manual, finishing up her treatise with a paean to the "youthful freshness, quality and power" of her voice for more than forty years, not to speak of her praiseworthy musicianship.

On the subject of registers, G. B. Shaw with his superior insights into matters of singing had this to say:

The laryngoscope has proved that the old tradition of three voices coming from the chest, the throat and the head respectively had, in the registering mechanism, a foundation of physiological fact; but as to how many registers can be made, how many *should* be made, whether any at all ought to be made, whether the old names should be retained, which is which and what practical conclusions the singing master should draw; on all these points there exist not only differences of opinions, but feuds— deadly, implacable vendettas—in which each party regards all the others as imposters, quacks, voice smashers, ignoramuses, rascals and liars.

Shaw's words are as fresh and pertinent today as when he wrote them a century ago.

Tell Me No Lies. Then what, if anything, are we to make of this mass of contradictions? Ever hopeful of enlightenment, let us review these conflicting theories of the registers in more depth, beginning with perhaps the most complicated one, that every note of the singing voice is a register unto itself. It is a concept that contains more than a little truth. Certainly with the sounding of each note in the range of a human voice, subtle, tiny muscular changes must take place within the larynx. No two notes of a different pitch, quality or volume are produced exactly alike. Therefore in one sense every note *is* a register. The idea, however, begs the question of the obvious basic changes in the vocal mechanism, as high speed photographs have shown of some of the different positions that the vocal folds take during singing.

Next, there are those who believe that there are only two registers to the singing voice: the chest and the head. Some, tradition-bound to "bel canto" theories, even cling to the old terminology and refer to the normal top of the voice—not the strange, artificial one sounded an octave higher—as falsetto. The two-register advocates point out that the major break in the male voice, when it goes into a head tone, and the female voice, when it changes to a chest tone, occurs within the same range: approximately D to F above middle C, *on exactly the same pitches*— not, as might be supposed, an octave apart. In the main, the male voice uses the chest register up to this break, after which it goes into the head register. The head quality, however, can be brought down and imposed on notes lower than where the break occurs, creating a nice blend of the two kinds of sound.

The two-register believers also assert that the higher women's voices use the head register for the top two-thirds of their compass and pass down through the break into the chest tone. They contend that this head quality can be brought into the chest tone, smoothing over the break or disparate quality of the two registers. It is *universally* agreed that for both men and women to take the chest register up beyond its natural range will be fatal to the voice, causing the high notes to go flat or be lost altogether. Finally the disciples of the two-register theory point out that the tenor and the contralto, who share a goodly number of the exact same pitches, will have the most difficulty in adjusting their two registers as they pass over the area of the break and attempt to make all their notes sound with an equalized quality.

The three-register school, to prove their theories, will point to photographs of the vocal folds, showing how they are thick and comparatively slack when the chest register is being sung, how they become thinner and tense looking in the medium register, and how only part of the ligaments vibrate in the top register. To prove their thesis they might also take as an example an untrained dramatic soprano. This young woman may possess heavy contralto-like tones, joined to a veiled, weak middle part of her voice in which she finds it uncomfortable to sing. On the top will be a high soprano of a light, almost fluty quality; in short, three distinct vocal sounds. Three voices, three registers say the supporters of this school. Three voices or three registers which must somehow be made to melt into one another to produce an evenness of quality throughout the compass. Even in a well-trained dramatic soprano these separate qualities of tone are sometimes exposed. One of the best arguments for the three-register theory I know of is to listen to the three different qualities of tone in the voice of the dramatic soprano Ina Souez singing "Come scoglio" from the old Glyndebourne recording of *Così fan Tutte*. The records of Maria Callas would also seem to define the three-register theory, so differentiated in quality are the upper, middle and lower parts of her range. This would also explain why the dramatic soprano is such a difficult voice to train.

Those who opt for the three-register idea are merely saying that beside the basic break which the two-register devotees acknowledge, there is another one approximately an octave higher in the woman's voice, when she goes into her head tone. Some who subscribe to this idea also say that a man has only two registers, and this is why the woman's voice is more difficult to train in general. Others believe that the male and female voices both have three registers and the break in the male voice occurs anywhere from A, to C,. If a man wants to produce a true chest tone he can do so by using a kind of belch—rather the way a female can sound her chest tones by imitating the quacking of a duck. Otherwise the male chest tone merges more simply with his medium register than does that of the female.

Those who assure us that the singing voice has five registers are in fact closely allied with the three-register school. By subdividing the chest and medium into "upper" and "lower" registers they maintain that it is possible to sing the same note in two different positions, so that the singer experiences different sensations when he does so. Hence the upper chest overlaps the lower medium, and the upper medium merges with certain notes of the head register. This more elaborate concept is aimed at smoothing out the *two* breaks they claim exist in the voice, which are the bane of many student singers.

The four-register man is rather a loner compared to the multitudinous disciples of some of the other theories. He allies himself with the three-register idea but points out that we are forgetting a fourth—the strange, unnatural sound of the falsetto. In the male it is a quality of tone easy to recognize and one that usually brings forth laughter. His sensations when singing falsetto are entirely different than when producing tones in his other registers. There is an odd feeling of letting go and blowing through the open glottis, which then creates this curious hooty sound. Photographs of a vocalist's throat while singing falsetto confirm that the larynx assumes a high position and that only the very edges of the vocal folds vibrate to produce this distinct quality of sound, which is another way of saying a separate vocal register. Whatever they may be, this series of notes exists as an entity, and therefore may legitimately be considered another register in the male voice.

The odd sounding fourth register at the top of a man's voice is useful to the tenor, who when diminishing his pianissimo high head tones, if he is skillful, can merge them into a falsetto without most ears being able to detect the change. For this reason the falsetto is sometimes referred to as the "tenorino" register. Overuse of these high, crooned falsetto tones, however, may be dangerous to the tenor's low tones. Richard Crooks, the much admired somewhat stolid American lyric tenor, who sang at the Metropolitan during the thirties, is supposed to have over-used the falsetto register thereby diminishing the rest of the range of his voice and shortening his career.

Not so much is made of the fourth "whistle" register in the female voice that is the equivalent of the male falsetto. The highest notes in the voice of Lily Pons, her F″ and G″ above high C″ which required that the Mad Scene in *Lucia di Lammermoor* be transposed *up* for her convenience, were not produced in the same way as the tones around high C″. To sing these highest notes, far from opening her mouth wider as do most singers when emitting their top tones, Pons half closed her mouth and let out her pure, if thin altitudinous sounds, looking slightly startled as if she didn't quite know where they were coming from. Indeed in the opera house they seemed to emerge from somewhere behind her. The production of this whistle-like tone has been compared to the violinist's technique of playing a harmonic, which he does by not pressing a particular string down the whole way so that it vibrates an octave higher.

At the Sistine Chapel in Rome, the great soprano Emma Calvé heard a Turkish *castrato* named Mustafà utter "strange, sexless tones, superhuman, uncanny" which he called his fourth voice. "You have only to practice with your mouth shut for two hours a day," he told her when she asked how to sing these tones. "At the end of two years, you may possibly be able to do something with them." Determined, Calvé went to work and after three years mastered the use of this fourth voice. Its notes, as one listener commented, were "very sweet with a noticeable difference in timbre from the usual tones of the singing voice, and with a distinct bell-like quality—a reflection, delicate and evanescent, rather than an echo of the other voice." In her memoirs Calvé admits that she was never able to pass on the secret of producing this falsetto or fourth register to any of her pupils.

And what of the idea that there is only one register in the voice? This is often put forth by authorities who agree that there may be changes in tone quality in different parts of the voice, but don't want singers, particularly novices, to become selfconscious about these so-called breaks. It is certainly true that some singers from their student days on have no trouble in knitting up changes of tone quality so that the voice seems to possess only one register. The late, much-mourned Ethel Merman never took a singing lesson in her life, yet as Luciano Pavarotti points out admiringly in his *Pavarotti, My Own Story,* "her voice is all one register. She never has to shift gears but can sing right up to the top of her range in the exact same vocal quality that she has with the middle or lower notes."

Other vocalists have had to work for years to smooth away the abrupt transition of tone quality in their voices known as the *passaggio* or "break" that is considered aesthetically displeasing in the art of song. Therefore the one-register idea has validity if only as a teaching method: if no attention is called to the mechanism that produces changes of tone quality in the voice, then hopefully the notes will emerge naturally equalized. Viktor Fuchs quotes Professor Martienssen-Lehmann, a teacher of singing, as writing: *"One register is not a starting point but a goal."*

"There are rare examples," writes Mancini, "in which one has received from nature the most unusual gift of being able to execute everything in the chest voice." It all depends what he meant by "everything." Many female pop singers belt out their songs entirely in the chest register, which makes them one-register vocalists, but the range of the music they perform is not great. The extraordinary Kirsten Flagstad with her warm, voluminous lower tones produced them by bringing down her medium or head register (depending on whether we go by the two- or three-register theory) deep into the region where an ordinary dramatic soprano must use the chest tone if the notes are to project. Flagstad, then, under the two-register theory, was a one-register singer.

And finally there is the no-register concept. But surely this is another way of saying that every note is a register unto itself; and we have come full circle.

Vibrations of Sympathy. Two basic factors then, breath and the vibrating vocal folds, produce tone within the larynx. These, however, are not enough to produce the beautiful sounds of a singing voice as we ultimately hear them. In experiments on patients about to undergo removal of the larynx because of cancer, an incision was made in the windpipe just above the voice box and they were then asked to phonate. The resulting sounds were small and weak. Access had been cut off to the third essential factor in the singing process—the resonators.

This term refers to cavities close to the larynx which vibrate in sympathy with the basic tone set up by the fluttering folds. Of these resonators one of the most important is thought to be the cavity above the throat known as the soft palate, or pharynx. Also influential is the mouth with its bony arched roof and rows of teeth having hard resonating surfaces. For this reason singers are fearful of tooth extraction or any kind of oral surgery. Below the larynx lies the trachea, a cartilaginous tube believed by some to add sympathetic and enriching overtones to the voice. Finally there is the larynx itself. A number of authorities think it may be an even more important resonator than the pharynx.

In the past, a good deal of attention has also been paid to the chest, the nose and the sinuses behind the nose as important resonators, simply because singers feel vibration in these areas when they perform. But the chest or top of the thoracic cage where the vocalist has definite sensations when he sings low notes contains a kind of insulating material which far from adding richness to the tone would seem to deaden it. The nose too, is lined with soft unvibratory membrane and we are all familiar with the unlovely sound it can produce when we direct vocal resonance into it. The nose is the last place where a singer wants to sing to produce a lovely tone. Some evidence exists that the various sinuses behind the nose and under the eyes may vibrate fractionally with the note that is produced in the singer's throat. But though the singer may have pronounced sensations in his head (the feeling of singing his so-called "head tones"), there is strong reason to believe that he hears these vibrations by conduction to his ears, and that *the audience does not,* as these vibrations have no way of getting out and mixing with the tones emerging from the singer's mouth. This is one of the explanations why singers, and of course non-singers as well, are often surprised and shocked when their recorded voices are played back to them.

It is the singer's resonators then that add the final beauty and power and quality to the tone produced. Much is written of the importance of "placing" a voice. This term refers to these all-important resonators which vary in shape and size in every person, thus creating the infinite diversity of tone that singing voices possess. We hear constantly about singers who have found the right teacher to "place" their voices (and many more who have not) as though this was a conscious physical process learned by the student vocalist. The teacher tells the student to direct his flow of sounds towards the arch of his mouth, his front teeth, his cheekbones, his forehead—or whatever. Actually, though the singer may seem to feel sensations in these places that add brilliance or a ring to the voice, they are entirely illusory. It has been shown scientifically that it is impossible to consciously direct a stream of sound to one portion of the anatomy or another.

Nonetheless if the vocal student grasps the teacher's "method," whether through the use of imagery, imitation or however, the tones will begin to take on (magically) a new brilliance and ring and ultimately the voice will be "placed."

Coda. So once again in this necessarily short survey of the theories of vocal production we have returned to such words as "illusory" or "magical." When the first edition of this book appeared over a decade ago a distinguished reviewer, himself a singer, criticized it for only enumerating the theories of how the voice is produced without giving the documentation or essential reasoning behind them. Since the documentation and reasoning lying behind one theory is very often contradicted by the documentation and reasoning behind another this would be a futile exercise, particularly in what is only set forth as a brief survey. Let it be pointed out once again that many aspects of vocal production are not clear, have to be guessed at or are not understood at all. Why else is there so much argument among the experts and why are they so contentious?

Though the glorious sounds poured out by a singer are invoked by a *mental* concept combined with *illusory* sensations, we have hundreds of years of evidence that the singing voice can be "placed" and trained. But a scientific understanding of how man brings about his wonderful song is about as elusive as a scientific comprehension of how he produces the effects of his soaring imagination. As the inimitable American writer Willa Cather says: "The voice simply is the mind and is the heart."

P. A. Renoir: Young Girls at the Piano

PART FIVE

The Ages Of Voice

And one man in time plays many parts,
His acts being seven ages. . . .

—Shakespeare (*As You Like It*)

I

. . . . At first the infant,
Mewling and pewking in the nurse's arms.

They tell a lovely tale in the world of the singing voice that the
first cry of the newborn Adelina Patti was a perfect F″ above high
C″. Less gifted newborn babies utter their first cries at a pitch of
around A′ or B′ and do so to rid the glottis of that curse to all
singers, an accretion of mucus. For this reason the first human
sounds are apt to be hoarse in quality. Immanuel Kant devoted a
long chapter of his *Anthropologie* to the first cry of an infant,
declaring that it may well have been a dangerous characteristic in
primitive man, since these first sounds would betray the mother
weakened by childbirth and her helpless infant to beasts of prey.
Actually the cry is a sign that the infant will live, for with the
viscous phlegm cleared from his throat he can now take a proper
breath.

Experts, as usual, disagree over the length of the vocal folds of
the newborn infant, though all admit that they are very tiny
indeed—anywhere from three to nine millimeters long. At
between two and four weeks old, according to one authority, Dr.
Paul J. Moses, an infant emits "about six to eight half tones in the
middle soprano range . . . interspersed with high notes, occasionally as high as high C″." At fourteen weeks he starts to make
sounds not unlike singing. Over the next months his range
develops mightily, and another scientist in a paper with the

delightful title "An Acoustical Study of the Pitch of Infant Hunger Wails" declares that by the time a baby is nine months old it can produce sounds ranging between 207 to 2631 vibrations per second—a compass calculated to excite the envy of the most richly endowed coloratura soprano. In addition, he breathes perfectly and has a faultless vocal technique, so that he never develops hoarseness nor other flaws of tone quality that mar the song of older singers. In later life vocalists sometimes have to learn to "throw" their voices, so that they project to the back of theaters and auditoriums in which they sing. Not so the infant—as we all know. His voice, with its unforced vocal production, carries perfectly.

II

And then the whining schoolboy, with his satchel
And shining morning face . . .

At the age of four, the same year that Freud has stated that a child's sexual impulses are at a heightened state, the voice loses something of its infantile piping quality and begins to strike a slightly more personal and sexual note. There is little if any differentiation between the male and female tone or range. From this age children can be trained to sing and by the time they are seven will have a compass of anywhere from ten to thirty-one half tones. Besides continuing to develop, the vocal folds are constantly subjected to shouts and shrieks and other violent shocks inflicted by their youthful possessors. For this reason the voices of pre-adolescent boys and girls will sometimes be heard to "break"; but this is not the true mutation that comes with puberty. Children, particularly by the time they have reached eleven or twelve, often have extensive ranges and love to squeak out very high notes as a kind of game. The rare, extremely high falsetto or "whistle" register heard occasionally in the *acuto sfogato* soprano (whose voice very often has a childish quality) is thought to be a leftover from these pre-adolescent days.

Sometimes if children have naturally beautiful voices and are musical, their enthusiastic or ambitious parents will take them to voice teachers. This is particularly true in England of boy sopranos. Most authorities seem to think, however, that except for instilling musicianship in a child, to impose extra strain on the delicate, still-developing vocal apparatus may do it irreparable harm. Such was not the case with two of our greatest American sopranos, Beverly Sills and Marilyn Horne.

Beverly Sills, rather astonishingly, first sang before the public at the age of three and by the time she was seven had learned in phonetic Italian all the songs and arias on her mother's collection of records by Amelita Galli-Curci. When her ambitious mother made an appointment with Estelle Liebling, one-time pupil of the great vocal pedagogue Mathilde Marchesi, and walked in with a seven-year-old child, the aghast teacher said, "But I don't teach children," adding after a pause, "I don't even *know* any children." Her response to little Beverly Sills's rendition of "Il bacio" was a burst of laughter at the absurd Italian pronunciation. Nonetheless Miss Sills remained for thirty-four years with Estelle Liebling who became her teacher, mentor and second mother.

From the ages of seven to twelve the child soprano took one lesson a week from Miss Liebling. She also studied the piano, learned French and appeared regularly on the "Major Bowes Family Hour" over the radio, thus gaining invaluable experience at performing before the public. Perhaps the wisest moment in her career came when at twelve years old she "retired" professionally. Her voice had begun the often not very evident mutation that every female larynx undergoes. She did not appear again in public for three years.

Marilyn Horne made her public debut as a singer when she was four and by the time she was eight, pushed on by her ambitious father, she was working with her third voice teacher, a Miss Edna Luce. Fortunately none of these pedagogues harmed the child's basic equipment (as all the world knows). In the case of Miss Luce, Marilyn Horne learned the principles of breath support that she relies on to this day.

After a move to California Marilyn Horne joined the Roger Wagner Chorale, which was employed to dub in musical backgrounds for movies. Though she never stopped singing during her vocal change (which would have been wiser), again fortunately she does not seem to have pushed her voice into more strenuous solo singing that might have caused it damage.

On the whole, children's lungs (however our ears may tell us differently) simply do not have the capacity to sustain the line and volume required for fine singing. As a result there have been very few celebrated pre-adolescent vocalists. In the thirties when child movie stars were the vogue, Shirley Temple piped her untuned ditties in a "cute" but scarcely inspiring voice. We also had a boy soprano movie star named Bobby Breen. (As his contemporary I remember hating him, for not only was he a goody-goody but I was certain that my voice was much better than his.) One exception, however, did exist, if we can believe the mass of material written about her.

The Prodigy Diva. In the spring of 1850 at a charity concert in New York City, a seven-year-old girl with round brown eyes stood on a table and with the same self-assured manner that never left her throughout fifty-five years of appearing in public, sang "by ear" the enormously difficult "Casta diva" from *Norma*. Moreover she gave it with all the interpolated ornaments and embellishments fashionable at the time. For the next five years Adelina Patti made a successful and lucrative career as a child soprano touring the United States and Cuba, sometimes performing alone, or jointly with the celebrated pianist Louis Gottschalk, or the equally well-known violinist Ole Bull. Charming audiences wherever she went, she was most charmed, we are told, by her dolls waiting for her in her dressing room. "Correct breathing, scales, shakes, ornaments, fioriture of every kind, all came naturally to her," writes Patti's contemporary Hermann Klein, and whatever she needed to be taught, "thanks to a marvellous ear, she could instantly repeat." These were the P.T. Barnum years and in a country inclined to applaud the prodigious more than the artistic, one wonders how childish in quality little Adelina's voice actually was. Obviously a musical marvel and a born imitator the way most prodigies are, did she have the physical strength to sing plausibly the long, sinuous phrases of the "Casta diva" that have exhausted in their time the sturdiest of prima donnas?

Yet here is part of an account by another contemporary, the conductor and composer Luigi Arditi, who with his musical friend Bottesini, received a call from the little girl in the company of her mother and her doll. After the child had "demurely placed her music on the piano," she asked him to accompany her in the Rondo of *Sonnambula*.

"How am I to give an adequate description of the effect which that child's miraculous notes produced upon our enchanted senses? Perhaps if I say that both Bottesini and I wept genuine tears of emotion, tears which were the outcome of the original and never-to-be-forgotten impressions her voice made when it first stirred our innermost feelings, that may, in some slight measure convince my readers of the extraordinary vocal power and beauty of which little Adelina was, at that tender age possessed. We were simply amazed, nay electrified, at the well-nigh perfect manner in which she delivered some of the most difficult and varied arias without the slightest effort or self-consciousness."

Remarkable she certainly must have been—which makes one wonder how many other "mute inglorious" Pattis have existed in musical history unheard and undetected because they were born into non-musical families or backgrounds. Both Patti's parents were in fact singers: she was born at Madrid an indecently short time after her mother had sung the role of Norma at the Royal Opera House. Her sister, Carlotta, also sang professionally. (A rival prima donna of Adelina's is not reluctant to declare, "if the truth must be told, many people found Carlotta the more satisfactory singer of the two.") At any rate the little girl was surrounded by musicians who were there to "discover" her when she sang her first phrase.

They were also there five years later to advise on what was probably the most important single step she ever took in her extraordinary career. At the age of twelve Patti "retired" from the public for two years presumably because her astute and vocally experienced family forbade her to sing during the most dangerous of vocal ages—adolescence.

SINGING FAMILIES

One thinks of a beautiful singing voice as an accident, a very rare occurrence. And yet there have been families of singers. Here are a few instances:

> Emmy Strömer-Ackté—mother of Aino Ackté, soprano, and her sister the mezzo-soprano Irma Tervani
> Andrews—three famous sisters
> Carl David Bjoerling—father of three singer sons including Jussi, whose son Rolf was also a singer
> Boswell—two sisters including Connie

SINGING FAMILIES

Castagna—two sisters
De Reszke—two brothers and a sister
Willi Domgraf-Fassbänder—a daughter, Brigitte
Garcia—father, mother, son, two daughters
Judy Garland—daughter, Liza Minnelli
Giannini—father, two daughters including Dusolina
Gigli—father and daughter
Grisi—two sisters
Homer—mother and daughter both named Louise
Selma Kurz—and her daughter Desi Halban
Konetzni—two sisters
Karl August Lehmann—a tenor married to Maria Theresia Lehmann-
     Löw, also a singer. They were parents of Lilli and Marie
Anton Ludwig—a tenor married to Eugenie Ludwig-Besalla, a contral-
     to, had a daughter whom they named Christa
Manski—mother Dorothee, daughter Inge
Marchesi—father, mother, daughter
Nevada—mother and daughter
Patti—father, mother, two daughters including Adelina
Pickens—two sisters, including Jane
Pinza—father Ezio, daughter Claudia
Ponselle—sisters Rosa and Carmela, brother Tony
Quilico—father Louis, son Gino, both baritones
Ravogli—sisters Sophia and Giulia
Rysanek—sisters Leonie and Lotte
Frances Saville—niece Frances Alda
Simon—sisters Joanna, Linda and Carly
Sinatra—Frank and his son and daughter
Tetrazzini—sisters Eva and Luisa
Van Zandt—Jennie, mother of Marie (the first Lakmé)
Weber—sisters Josepha and Aloysia
Fritz Windgassen—a tenor married to the mezzo-soprano Vally van
     Osten, the parents of tenor Wolfgang. His aunt was soprano Eva
     von der Osten
Albert Wagner—oldest brother of Richard was a light tenor and father
     of the celebrated Johanna Wagner, a soprano

III

. . . . And then the lover,
Sighing like a furnace, with a woeful ballad
Made to his mistress' eyebrow.

The awkward age—all arms and legs, stumbling over things, gawkiness—and the voice with its unexpected cracked tones, one note that of a child, the next of an adult. During adolescence a youth's vocal folds grow with the same astonishing rapidity as his body. Within six months they may lengthen a whole centimeter, as well as thicken. Is it any wonder that the bewildered adolescent presented with these new, seemingly enormous ligatures, "trips" on them much as he does over the newly acquired length of his hands and feet? Just as with his members, he has to retrain or even develop a whole new set of muscles to control the odd, new sounds that now arise from his throat.

Aurally the process is less evident in the female, whose speaking voice, which sounds slightly husky during the period of mutation, drops only two or three tones in pitch whereas a boy's will usually deepen a whole octave. This is because the vocal folds of the adolescent girl lengthen only three or four millimeters. Nonetheless she too has to learn to manage the changed apparatus of her speaking and singing voice, and mutation for her—a process which in the female usually takes place two years earlier than the male—is also a critical vocal age, lasting the same length of time, a minimum again of two years.*

What high school anywhere in the Western world is without its choral group or glee club? Considered wholesome and beneficial, group singing brings together confused adolescents trying to sort out a hundred different identities and gives them a communal one in a shared love for singing and music. Ironically, there is good reason to suppose that this same much approved activity may mar or even destroy many incipient fine singing voices; ironic too, to consider that the average high school music teacher in discovering an attractive or interesting voice, singles it out for attention and (quite naturally) piles extra strain upon it, rather

---

*During her voice change in her early teens, Luisa Tetrazzini, who had sung soprano as a child, thought she was a contralto. She always had a pronounced break in her voice.

than asking its possessor to keep silent until the process of mutation has definitely taken place. Various books have been written, usually by choirmasters reluctant to lose years of training to the inexorability of nature, explaining how the young male may sing through the time of his voice break supposedly by simply singing the old boyish top tones, now cracked, an octave down in his new man's register. But with the exception of one or two whose passion for the boy's voice blinds them to good sense, all the authorities warn, even thunder against adolescents singing during mutation. Of course boys and girls have sung while their voices were changing and developed into fine singers. It is interesting to note, however, that in England, where choirboys are frequently urged to continue singing after the breaking process has begun, a study showed that out of a selected number who had sung well as boys about two per cent turned into good adult singers, a fact "attributed to the irreparable damage contracted in adolescence."

The strange change that takes place in the human throat confirms how directly connected are the singing voice and sex. As most people know, if a boy fails to mature sexually or is castrated before adolescence he will retain his child's small larynx coupled with a man's body; surgery which prevents a female's sexual development will cause her to retain her "little girl's" voice too. A woman's menstrual cycle also appears to be connected with her voice. Swelling often occurs in the sinuses causing the voice to sound husky just before the onset of a period. For this reason a woman singer may have a clause in her contracts excusing her from appearing during this period, a practice, however, more common in Europe than the United States. Sometimes this swelling adds resonance to a voice and it will sound enriched.

The sexual characteristics and the voice that young men and women develop during pubescence very often are directly linked. Thus women with deep contralto voices may have large bodies, heavy features and excess facial and body hair, while men with high tenor voices frequently turn out short, fleshy and without much need of a razor. The eunuch-like Pardoner in Chaucer's tale was one of these:

> A voys he hadde as small as hath a goot.
> No berd hadde he, no nevere sholde have,
> As smothe it was as it were late y-shave.

"In both sexes those who mature early have high voices, and those who mature late are inclined to have low voices," writes an authoritative laryngologist, Irving Voorhees. But it must be pointed out that he uses the word "inclined" and that there are definite exceptions to his statement. He also tells us that "nearly all boy sopranos become baritones or basses,"* but again there is that qualifying "nearly" which makes this a general rule rather than a fixed one. Sometimes, indeed, boys' voices don't turn into anything at all, but keep their treble quality. This may be due to some kind of pubescent atrophy of, or accident to the testes. Very rarely, a web of membrane stretched across the glottis allows the breath to pass but inhibits growth of the vocal ligatures. When this membrane, an accident of birth, is divided or removed, the voice will develop properly.

For one who has a pleasing voice as a child and has begun to dream of becoming an adult singer, waiting through pubescence to see what kind of voice will develop adds yet another agony to these frequently tormented years. "All last winter I could not sing a note. I was in despair; I thought I had lost my voice," the thirteen-year-old Marie Bashkirtseff, never one to conceal her feelings, reported to her journal. "Now it has come back again, my voice, my treasure, my fortune . . . I said nothing but I was cruelly grieved. I did not dare to speak of it. I prayed to God and he has heard me! What happiness. What a pleasure it is to sing well!"

But in fact if there is a voice and talent to go with it the pains of adolescence are nothing compared to those of making a career.

IV

. . . . *Then a soldier.*
. . . .
Seeking the bubble reputation,
Even in the cannon's mouth.

What are the necessary basic requirements for an aspiring singer to go out into a treacherous world to fight for fame and fortune? Rossini is said to have answered, "Voice first, voice second, voice third." (This plump, neurasthenic composer much given to *mots*

---

*The voice of the celebrated Luigi Lablache is said to have dropped overnight from high soprano to deep bass.

is also reported to have said of Adelaide Kemble, one of England's first international singers, "To sing as she does three things are needed: this"—touching his forehead—"this"—touching his throat—"and this"—laying his hand on his heart.) Surprisingly, the doyen of singing teachers, Manuel Garcia II, who might be thought to have put voice before all, gave his three basics for a singing career as, "First character, secondly character and thirdly character."

Voice, heart, mind, character—the list grows,[*] and to it must be added several more fundamentals. The most beautiful voice in the world is nothing without a basic ability to sing in tune and at least some kind of musical ability. The most beautiful voice in the world combined with acute musical sensibility is still little or nothing if these are contained in a body that is diseased or frail. Still another element enters into the careers of singers, one which they are intensely aware of—luck.

However, to return to Rossini's requirements for a singing career: "Voice first, voice second, voice third," they raise the question as to whether there have ever been any great vocal artists who were simply born with great "natural" voices and never required any training at all. In the history of singing it is difficult to find an example. Adelina Patti certainly almost qualifies as a "natural." Yet she is said to have trained with her half-brother, Ettore Barili, though it is possible that the training only consisted of exercises to increase the brilliance and flexibility of her voice. When asked throughout her long career for the technical explanation of her exquisite singing she would smile disarmingly and reply, *"Ah, je n'en sais rien"*—"Ah, I know nothing about it."

In later times after World War II a handsome six-foot-one tenor possessed of a beautiful natural tenor voice entered the conservatory at Pesaro for vocal training. Within a few months he lost the entire upper part of his range. Dismayed, he withdrew and never thereafter put his voice under "expert" instruction. This was Franco Corelli, who became one of the most successful and important tenors of his time. Nonetheless Corelli was by no means endowed naturally with the exciting voice that audiences were later to hear. Instead by continual and painstaking imitation

[*]Caruso's requisites included, "A big chest, a big mouth, ninety percent memory, ten percent intelligence, lots of hard work and something in the heart."

of the records of Caruso, Gigli, Lauri-Volpi and Fleta he taught himself to smooth out the coarseness of his middle register, to extend his top to an easy High C" and ultimately to sing *pianissimi*. This self-training continued for many years including a time while he was appearing before the public. Thus though Corelli did not formally train his voice with a teacher, neither did he have a "natural" voice that required no training at all.

There was one—and so far in the history of singing—only one who did.

A Miracle. "Perhaps the geneticists can explain it; I know I can't. All I know is that from about age fourteen I had a fully rounded, opera-like dramatic voice." So recalled Rosa Ponselle in her autobiography, *Ponselle: A Singer's Life*, written with James A. Drake. "As far back as I can remember, I never had what I would call a 'girl's voice'—the light, breathy-sounding, high-pitched voice we normally associate with young children. My singing voice was big and round and I could sing almost three octaves. I never recall the slightest trouble swelling or diminishing a tone anywhere in those octaves." Further on she says of this voice that was described as "colorful," "golden," "ductile" and compared to "warm alabaster," "I never had a singing lesson in my life."

On the evening of November 15, 1918, just short of her twenty-second birthday, Rosa Ponselle made her debut at the Metropolitan Opera House in the long and demanding part of Leonora, the heroine of Verdi's *La Forza del Destino*. Appearing opposite her was the most celebrated singer in the world, Enrico Caruso. The debutante had no formal vocal training, and had only attended three operatic performances in her lifetime: a *Tosca*, a *Madama Butterfly* and Montemezzi's *L'Amore dei tre rei*. In any case she could not have been familiar with the Verdi work because this was the first time that the Metropolitan had ever presented it.

The totally raw young soprano was instantly hailed as a new star, the gold of her voice noted by one critic, its voluptuousness by another and Rosa Ponselle's "fine musical quality" by a third. The whole story seems incredible for in addition to the God-given (in the true sense of the term) untrained voice, she possessed many other assets required to make such a success including musicianship, proficiency in Italian and a dramatic sense and quality of projection. From the age of seven she played the piano

Rosa Ponselle at the time of recording in her home, Villa Pace.

by both sight reading and ear; her parents were emigrants from Caserta; and the miracle continues with her inherent dramatic sense and projection. Fortune favored her in one more important way. Her much older sister, Carmela, also had a fine voice, was ambitious and went into vaudeville to which she introduced her baby sister, Rosa, in a "sister" act. By the time of her debut, Rosa Ponselle had faced audiences around the country and even in the number one theater on the circuit, the Palace on Broadway— though never of the kind to fill an opera house. Thus the Deity appeared to have endowed her with every possible attribute for the greatest operatic career in the history of singing, but he also sent down one grievous affliction: this was "nerves."

Rosa Ponselle always attributed her morbid stage fright to reading bad reviews on the day before her debut of the first performance in America of a well-known Italian tenor, Giulio Crimi. If the critics could condemn a famous European artist, what would they do to a *vaudeville* singer? Heavily sedated, equipped with prayer cards and monotones of Christ and the Virgin Mary and comforted by the ever kind Caruso, she was shoved out from the wings of the stage on that November evening.

Yet after her sensational success, Rosa Ponselle's nerves continued to bedevil her throughout her lamentably short career. All singers suffer to a lesser or greater extent from nervousness when they perform. But Ponselle was almost phobic. On evenings of her performances at the Metropolitan she would walk around the dreary building several times before summoning the courage to get herself through the stage door. Why such fears when she was so remarkably endowed? The explanation might be that since she was entirely a "natural," she had no technique: quite simply she had no insights into how she was producing her voice. *It just came out.* This in contrast to, say, Marilyn Horne (the two singers have been compared), who trained for years learning her marvellous technique and who claims never to be nervous. As a corollary, note that in later years Franco Corelli, self-taught, without formal training, rivalled Miss Ponselle in his nervousness before a performance.

Rosa Ponselle retired at what seemed the criminally early age of forty. The reasons given are a quarrel with the Metropolitan Opera management and that she had found true love and the marriage of her dreams. It seems more likely that she found vast relief in escaping from the fearful nervousness to which her career had condemned her for two decades—miraculous phenomenon though she was.

Rosa Ponselle lived out her retirement years in the Villa Pace outside of Baltimore, Maryland, a house that sonically wasn't all that peaceful with the voices of her many students and the barking of more than a dozen little poodles. What also sounded in the mansion was her singing voice. In 1954 when she was fifty-nine and refused to travel, the RCA Victor Company came to her with its engineers and equipment and recorded her in a program of various songs. Her renditions of Schubert's "Erlkönig" and songs by Donaudy and Tosti give testimony to the vocal and musical miracle that she was.

What about a young person in the grip of a passionate desire to sing, yet not born with an unusually beautiful voice? In other words, is it possible to make one? Let us turn to the pre-phonograph years where all is speculation—always a great pleasure to the voice buff—and study the careers of the two remarkable Garcia sisters, Maria and Pauline.

A Chain and a Silk Thread. Surely in all of musical history no one can have been more obsessed, more fanatic about the singing voice than a handsome, curly-haired, violent Spaniard—some say of gypsy descent—named Manuel del Popolo Vicente Garcia. He was born in Seville in 1775 the illegitimate child of a mother who died when he was six. Fate in the form of a pretty singing voice and musical talent saved him from the beggar's lot of an orphan of those times and he entered the choir of a cathedral. Thereafter singing was all. Garcia grew up to become one of the leading operatic tenors of his day and the first Count Almaviva in Rossini's *Il Barbiere di Siviglia*. When in the course of time three children were born to the singer, Manuel (1805), Maria (1808) and Pauline (1821), with a zealousness that seems almost to border on the insane, he determined to make singers of them too, whether they possessed naturally good voices or not.

The fate of Manuel II was irony itself: forced by this fanatic and at times cruel father to sing during the voice change, his vocal career was lost forever. Of the charming, highly strung, impulsive second child, Maria, there is the oft-repeated story of two friends passing under the window of the Garcia house in Paris and one expressing alarm at the screams issuing from it. "It is nothing," says the other; "just Garcia beating trills into his daughter." When reproached later by his daughter's friend the Countess de Merlin for his harsh treatment of Maria, Garcia replied that she could "never become great but at this price: her proud and stubborn spirit requires [it] . . . to be bound by a chain."

Garcia had already subjected the highly gifted dragonfly of a little girl to rigorous musical studies before beginning to train her voice seriously when she reached the age of fifteen. Here, according to the same Countess de Merlin, who was about the same age as Maria and often sang duets with her, was the material that the obsessed father had to work with:

"Maria Garcia's voice was at first feeble. The lower tones were harsh and imperfectly developed, the upper tones were indifferent in quality and limited in extent, and the middle tones wanted clearness. Her intonation was so false as to warrant the apprehension that her ear was defective . . .

"One evening Maria and I were practicing a duet into which Garcia had introduced some embellishments. Maria . . . was vainly endeavoring to execute a certain passage and at last uttered the words 'I cannot.' In an instant the Andalusian blood of her father rose. He fixed his large eyes upon her and said, 'Did I hear aright?' In another instant she sang the passage perfectly. When we were alone I expressed my surprise at this. 'O!' cried she, clasping her hands with emotion, 'such is the effect of an angry look from my father, that I am sure it would make me jump from the roof of the house without hurting myself.'"

Thus Garcia through tyrannical domination turned his daughter into the most celebrated singer of her time. Indeed, more than a singer, she represented the impetuous, impassioned force of romanticism itself that brooked no limitation until the welcome release of death. A creature of the moment, Maria Garcia (or Malibran as she came to be known after her married name) would become so carried away in a performance that her acting bordered on what might be described as the sensational. Another apostle of the romantic movement but a critical opera-goer, Eugène Delacroix, remarked to his journal after witnessing Malibran rip up her handkerchief and tear her gloves to shreds as the despairing Maria Stuarda in Donizetti's opera: "That, again, is one of those effects to which a great artist will never descend: they are of the sort that delight people in the loges and win an ephemeral reputation for those willing to indulge themselves in that way."

There is no reason to suppose that the voice which Manuel Garcia managed to wrench from his daughter's throat ever possessed the beautiful quality of that of, say, Monserrat Caballé. The astute English music critic Henry Chorley recalled that it was a mezzo-soprano stretched in both directions, so that it ranged over two and a half octaves and was weakest in the middle. Her dazzling rendition of ornaments and embellishments, her ability to leap from the highest to the lowest notes in daring fashion, together with an almost exhausting conviction with which she sang, seemed to completely distract her adoring audiences from the deficiencies of her vocal quality. Thus showmanship, musicianship drilled into her by her father, sensibility (it is said that on hearing Beethoven's Fifth Symphony for the first time she had to be carried unconscious from the hall) combined with great charm of appearance if not classic beauty, all aided in building one of the most sensational careers in musical history of a woman who had quite literally "made" a voice.

A story is told that Maria Garcia Malibran was standing talking to a friend on a Paris street when a carriage drove by containing her sister, Pauline, thirteen years younger, who leaned out the window and blew kisses to her. The friend asked who the little girl was. "That child is someone who will eclipse us all," replied Malibran.

"That child" was completely different from her sister; calm, contained, highly intelligent as her brother, Manuel Garcia II, had to admit that Maria was not. From an early age Pauline showed precocious musical talent and when eight years old could play the accompaniments for her father's teaching sessions. The daughter of much older parents, she seems in fact never to have been a child, possessing from very early on a kind of grave assuredness that when she sang was transformed into a quality of nobility. Of his three children the elder Garcia treated only this last one gently and with tenderness. The disparity, which must have been difficult for the older children to accept, he explained to the same Countess de Merlin: "Towards [the] younger sister, on the contrary, I have never had cause to exercise harshness, and yet she will make her way," adding that she could be led as easily as "though by a silken thread."

Pauline was just short of eleven when her father died in June 1832, after which Malibran became the bountiful provider for the family. By the time Pauline neared her fifteenth birthday she was studying with Franz Liszt, her mind firmly set on a pianist's career of her own. Occasionally she accompanied her sister in concerts. In a biography of Pauline Viardot, as she afterwards came to be called, April Fitzlyon says that on Pauline's fifteenth birthday her mother shut the case of her piano and told the astonishingly plain girl with heavily hooded eyes and a long, arching upper lip that she was to become a singer. Pauline Viardot was a woman of tremendous character and will and one wonders what might have ensued between mother and daughter over this choice of a musical career to be imposed on the latter. Two months later all possibilities of conflict were removed: Maria Malibran while out riding in the early stages of pregnancy fell from her horse and died shortly after, at the age of twenty-eight. There was now only one Garcia left to sing. This strange, sacred trust had been handed to Pauline and she took it up.

No contemporary account exists of the raw material with which this second Garcia sister diligently went to work to make a voice. The descriptions of the end result tell enough. "Unevenness," "harshness," "feebleness," are some of the words used to describe its quality. Even at her London debut, aged seventeen, it was never a "young" voice, according to Chorley. Camille Saint-Saëns had this comment: "Hers was not a voice of velvet or of crystal, but a voice just a trifle harsh and occasionally was compared to the flavor of bitter-sweet oranges." The twenty-five-year-old writer Ivan Turgenev fell under the spell of this plain, magnetic young woman when she came to sing at St. Petersburg and became enmeshed in a *ménage à trois* that lasted all his life. Seeking at one point to escape the enslavement of it, he fired off this little poem to Pauline Viardot which speaks eloquently of the beauty of her voice and face:

> *Corbeau, corbeau*
> *Tu n'es pas beau*
> *Mais tu viens de mon pays*
> *Eh bien! retournez-y.*

> (Crow, crow
> You are not beautiful
> But you come from my country
> Well—go back there.)

Yet her career was as remarkable as her sister's short-lived one and, though less sensational, founded on far deeper artistic principles. How then did she do it, without voice, without

The plain but fascinating mezzo-soprano Pauline Viardot.

physical beauty? One explanation was her unremitting capacity
for hard work. Her friend George Sand modelled a rather
preposterous novel called *Consuelo* after her, in which however
the author observes of the heroine singer: "Consuelo enjoyed one

of those rare and happy temperaments for which labor is an enjoyment, a sort of repose, a necessary condition and to which inaction would be an effort." Charm and fascination we know she possessed in abundance. In addition to magnificent musicianship and conviction one final element must have been movingly apparent in her singing. Her admirer, Alfred de Musset, put it this way:

"She possesses, in a word, the great secret of artists: before expressing something, she feels it. She does not listen to her voice, but to her heart . . ."

Can a voice be made then? These two instances are, of course, most extraordinary. Overshadowed always by the will of another, the self did not have to provide the entire impetus toward making a career. Yet it is apparent that much can be done and a career made, provided that the singer has the force of personality and musical temperament to triumph over what nature failed to provide. The usual puritanical price will be exacted however. Gounod described Pauline Viardot at the age of thirty "as already nearing her end" and a musical paper of the same period declared that "every note that comes from her voice is an ear-splitting cry." Such "made" voices fare infinitely better in the intimate spaces of the concert hall where they do not have to fight a heavy orchestra. While Viardot's operatic career was cut short at a relatively early age, she was still able to perform with telling effect in small auditoriums and at private parties, including her own.*

The Singer as Musician. "Voice first, voice second, voice third," Rossini may have declared to be the requirements of a singing career, but he was much given to facetiousness. Obviously the most beautiful voice in the world such as the one possessed by Trilby in George du Maurier's novel is of little use to the world if the singer can't stay in tune, as poor Trilby could not expect by the aid of hypnosis. In the matter of faulty intonation it is interesting to note how much more tolerant were our forebears. Giuditta Pasta, the first Norma and often conceded to be the greatest singing actress of the nineteenth century was evidently much

---

*Madame Viardot's "musical parties are rigidly musical and to me, therefore, rigidly boresome especially as she herself sings very little. But when Mme Viardot does sing, it is superb. She sang last time a scene from Gluck's *Alcestis*, which was the finest piece of musical declamation, of a grandly tragic sort that I can concieve." Henry James in a letter to his father, April 11, 1876.

given to off-pitch singing. "Never before have we had a Tristan able to sing the declamatory music . . . with correct intonation, to say nothing of the duet of the second act," wrote the critic Henry Krehebiel of Jean de Reszke's first Tristan. That was in 1895. A great star of the 1910's and 1920's was Amelita Galli-Curci with her exquisitely pure tones which her most extravagant admirers declared were always in tune. Less loyal ears, however heard her tendency to go flat, undoubtedly due to a goiter growing in the soprano's throat. Nowadays, almost without exception, any singer who does not have a sure sense of pitch is almost certain to displease his listeners.

As to actual musicianship, this is obviously extremely important too, though singers have a reputation in the musical world for being self-indulgent and sloppy exponents of their art. Certainly there have been great stars who counted on the beauty of their voices to gloss over the fact that they hadn't bothered to learn their music properly nor interpret it with distinction. The great *basso* Ezio Pinza could not read music and had to learn all his parts by ear, drilled into him by a *répétiteur*. Nonetheless this singer who thrilled thousands was wonderfully musical, shaping the phrases of his numerous roles with intuitive insight and threading them through with a most beautiful line. This line, or *legato*, is a requisite of the finest singing. It has been compared to a "telegraph or telephone wire where you can see the line going through and the consonants are just perched on it like the feet of sparrows." Many great singers, such as Kathleen Ferrier, who only began her career when she was thirty years old, possess this line innately. Others have learned it, frequently by taking the example of great violinists such as Fritz Kreisler or Jascha Heifetz.

It is also a fact that musicianship can be drilled into those who do not possess the gift altogether naturally. A tough coach can stand over a vocalist and make him dot a quarter note as the composer has written it or teach him to count through the two measures of rest until his next entrance. Some singers have been what is known as a "slow study," artists who have had great trouble in committing to memory the words and music that they must perform. Joan Sutherland has problems with memory and it is said that a similar affliction kept the dramatic soprano Eileen Farrell from singing Wagnerian roles when she finally came to the Metropolitan, though she was eminently equipped to do so.

"High ideals and application"—a motto that any aspiring singer might well adopt—were the watchwords of one of the first great American sopranos, Lillian Nordica. Her career was an interesting one. Endowed with promising basic material, she had to undergo long, extensive vocal training before her voice emerged in its full richness and beauty. The first American to sing all three Brünnhildes at the Metropolitan, she was an immensely slow study. To learn her long, difficult roles, the Maine-born diva with her sparkling eyes and determined chin would work six hours a day with a coach, going over the scores two pages at a time. Sometimes when she felt it physically unwise for her to continue she would lie down while the coach continued to play the passages under study over and over again. This gluttony for hard work enabled her to endure the daily grind of learning Elsa at Bayreuth under the supervision of the dragon herself, Cosima Wagner. But Nordica was the first Bayreuth Elsa and the first American to sing there. She also managed to learn some forty other operatic roles besides.*

Curiously, the next American soprano to sing the three Brünnhildes at the Metropolitan, Helen Traubel, also had the same slow approach to learning her roles and throughout her career worked three hours a day with her coach, painstakingly going over every phrase in the music. In total contrast was her counterpart, Kirsten Flagstad, who learned the long, arduous part of Kundry in *Parsifal* in eleven days.

Some singers then are innately musical. Many, such as Placido Domingo or Leontyne Price, are proficient at a second instrument, the piano. The much beloved Polish coloratura soprano Marcella Sembrich was accomplished on the piano and the violin as well. When the operatic career of Sembrich came to an end, not surprisingly she moved effortlessly and most successfully into a career of lieder singing and also teaching.

Mens Vox, Mens Corpus. Given a lovely voice (or the ambition to make one) combined with basic musical talent, there is still one other absolute requisite the hopeful singer must possess before considering a career. I speak of good health and a strong, even

---

*According to her contemporary Ernestine Schumann-Heink, Nordica "sang as nobody I ever heard sing—nobody." But by tackling the most difficult German roles "it robbed her of her beautiful voice too soon."

ironclad constitution. The human body is the case of the singing voice and if there be any cracks or weaknesses in it the voice no matter how lovely will not endure. Singing is a mental process too, with the voice highly responsive to imagination and nerves. So there must also be good mental health. In an attempt to sing against poor physical health, the nervous tensions can become stretched so that the psyche and soma interact, precluding all possibility of a career. Such was the case of Mark Twain's beloved first daughter, Susy.

"Madame Marchesi said she had a grand opera voice— 'Marvellous voice' was one of her expressions," Mark Twain wrote proudly in his notebook of the famous old teacher's pronouncement on Susy's singing. Mathilde Marchesi's daughter, Blanche, also a voice teacher, concurred with her mother's opinion, saying that Susy's "voice was competent for the parts of Elsa and Elisabeth in *Lohengrin* and *Tannhäuser;* and later she added Isolde . . ." Susy, however, with her poignant eyes and poetic, nervous sensibility, had always inclined to frailness. Earlier that year at a previous audition Blanche Marchesi had detected a formidable tremolo in her voice "which did not only come from forcing the high notes, but which seemed to have its source in a physical weakness." She had suggested a treatment of baths in Austria and Bavaria which Susy, eager to become a singer in her own right and not merely the daughter of a celebrated author, underwent. Returning to Paris, she began her training with high hopes only to have them immediately destroyed.

"After the second lesson what she [Blanche Marchesi] calls my 'general anemia' took hold of my breathing power and ever since, my breath has been so short and weak that all my volume of voice has gone," Susy wrote to her sister Clara, later to become the wife of the pianist and conductor Ossip Gabrilowitsch. "I am frightened to death for fear this will last, in fact, I am entirely broken hearted. Cold douches, eating, walking, sleeping, *nothing* helps . . ."

Blanche Marchesi blamed Susy's lack of strength on her poor living habits. "I found that she slept very little and ate next to nothing, and her education, as is frequently the case in America, seemed to have been taken in hand by the girl herself, the question of food being thrown aside as very uninteresting. Here was a case of voluntary self-starvation, and she laughingly confessed to have lived chiefly on mixed pickles, ice cream, candies and similar foods." Mournfully, in her next letter to Clara, Susy wrote, "For the present I'm stopping all the hard exercises, and everything, and may have to stop the lessons . . . I'm paying now for my past sins."

Eventually she allowed herself to be thoroughly examined by a doctor in Paris in the hope that medicine might come to her aid. Of this, Mrs. Clemens wrote to her husband who was in America trying to repair his broken fortunes: "He says that one great trouble with her is that she is not sufficiently developed, particularly her chest. The doctor prescribed gymnastics and massage. I hope now she will be soon on the road to health. It has been very pitiable to see her look so miserable."

Mark Twain, who could spot a fool at a hundred paces but was always ready to believe in some magical solution to the problems of life, soon after became convinced by Mrs. William Dean Howells that hypnotism was the answer to Susy's health. "The very source, the center of hypnotism is *Paris*," he wrote excitedly to his wife. "Dr. Charcot's pupils and disciples are right there and ready to your hand . . ."

But of course it was hopeless. Nothing could give Susy the physique and stamina required of a singer. Finally she faced the truth and returned to America where shortly afterwards, to Mark Twain's unassuageable grief, she died unexpectedly in August 1895 of meningitis. On her deathbed she imagined that she was singing again.

Some indications as to who should and should not attempt a singing career for physical reasons are given by the basic body types as categorized by Dr. W. H. Sheldon. There is the plump, jolly endomorph, particularly happy at the dinner table, sometimes simple and elemental away from it. He laughs easily, doesn't mind playing a comic role and basks in the attention of it when he does.

There is the husky, muscular mesomorph, vigorous, outgoing and usually an excellent athlete. This type, according to Dr. Sheldon, is often highly ambitious and, in his desire to achieve his aims, likely to be self-centered.

The third type is the tense, narrow-shouldered ectomorph, a bundle of nerves and sensitivity. Often this type lacks physical strength, has a small, unresonant voice and is likely to be self-critical and inhibited.

Of these various shapes of body obviously the possessor of the third body type, the ectomorph with his narrow chest and shrinking ways is least suited to a singing career. Having a generous covering of flesh to pad his nerve endings, the endomorph will be happy before his public and know no fear of it. The burly mesomorph may be subject to nervousness but will overcome it in order to accomplish his ends. And of course his excellent physique will be a bulwark in sustaining the athletic rigors of a singer's life. What a pity though, that neither type possesses in such marked degree the ectomorph's sensitivity. On the few occasions when this third body type have become singers, they are usually artists of rare subtlety and insight.

Of course most people are a mixture of body types, but in the case of a pronounced ectomorph here is the baleful advice of Judith Litante, who takes Dr. Sheldon's theories very seriously in her *A Natural Approach to Singing:*

"If the ectomorph clings to the idea of being a singer let him do it for his own pleasure and that of his friends. He would be far wiser to choose some other lifework, and that as early as he can. Otherwise he may suffer the painful awakening of finding himself a square peg in a round hole too late to remedy the tragic error. Worse, *he could become a candidate for a mental institution* [italics mine]."

Singers often seem to come in standard sizes—short tenors, tall basses etc. There are of course exceptions in anything where the laws of nature are concerned. Very rarely does a big, dramatic voice proceed from a petite woman or a slimly built man. There have been dramatic singers of small stature but not girth. Giulietta Simionato with her large, opulent voice, was very short but built like a bubble. A big chest and accompanying lung capacity are inevitably associated with a big voice. Kirsten Flagstad points out in her memoirs how as she progressed from the light, lyric soprano roles to the heavy Wagnerian ones, which she did not undertake until she was close to forty, her body enlarged and seemed to thicken, as the photographs in the book attest. Weight, therefore, a subject so much on the modern mind, is a necessary adjunct to the big voice, literally shoring it up like a bulwark.

In a sensible little manual called *Hints to Singers,* the American diva Lillian Nordica wrote almost a century ago: "With progress in one's career, and when one has a reputation to sustain, the nervous strain becomes increased, and one evidently needs one's nerves covered with fat to shield them. Singers who have banted* or taken medicine to reduce their flesh have more frequently paid for it dearly. One of my colleagues told me that she had banted for six weeks, and could not sing for three months; she had no strength."

That was a period when fleshiness or *embonpoint* was acceptable and even admired—certainly not regarded with the repugnance that it is today. Singers for the most part were stout and in the case of Caruso, Schumann-Heink, Tetrazzini, even ridiculous looking. There are those who claim that singers of this age also sang better. Could it have been because of their weight?

At least one star of that particular golden era, however, fell victim to overweight. In his *The Grand Tradition*, J. B. Steane is puzzled why the career of the Czech prima donna, Emmy Destinn, whom he describes as a lyric soprano (*spinto* would be more appropriate) declined at such a relatively early age. The reason was that this otherwise marvellous singer became so immense that her weight impeded her vocal production. By her early forties she had virtually stopped singing before the public.

By the 1930's the cult (and some say the curse) of keeping thin had settled in to stay, and Metropolitan Opera stars such as Grace Moore and Gladys Swarthout, and later comely Risë Stevens, were svelte enough to appear in the movies. With the exception of the Wagnerian roles audiences were less and less prepared to suspend their disbelief at grossly stout singers.

When Maria Callas made her debut at La Scala in 1951 she weighed 210 pounds. Two years later she began to diet and with everything this complex artist undertook there were no halfway measures. In under twelve months she lost over sixty pounds. How had she done it, asked a fascinated world? One theory held was that she had gone to a sanitarium where she had ingested a tapeworm. Her husband, Signor Meneghini, declares in his memoirs that she did just the opposite: in the bathroom of a Milan hotel she expelled and killed a tapeworm, and this explained, moreover, why up until then she had always liked uncooked meat (presumably the worm's favorite diet). Soon after, a doctor who claimed to be the personal physician of Maria Callas declared

*New Englanders (Nordica came from Maine) use "bant" to mean "diet."

Maria Callas as Violetta in *La Traviata*.

in an advertisement that he had put her on a diet of a certain brand of pasta, and this had caused her dramatic weight loss. Callas denounced this statement as utterly false and sued.

Nothing, it seems, connected with "la divina" was ever simple. The next section of the story of the singer's figure finds her rising from kissing the Pope's hand at an audience in the Vatican to hear the soft tones of His Eminence asking if she would not settle the suit as the president of the pasta company was his nephew. Accusations of impropriety against one who bore the name Pacelli impugned by indirection the person of another with the same name, the Pope himself. For a number of years the suit went underground until 1958 when the Pope died and Callas instantly insisted that the case be reinstituted in the law courts. As her husband writes in his often rueful memoirs: "I was upset by this decision she made the very day the Pope died. Instead of thinking of his death Maria was thinking about her lawsuit."

But that was Maria Callas, who by the time she opened the season at La Scala late in 1954 had reduced to 144 pounds. Of her voice the noted critic B. H. Haggin wrote soon after: "By now its original bloom and loveliness are gone, it has a bad wobble and as often as not it produces a climactic note off pitch . . ." Though only her most idolatrous fans ever claimed that Maria Callas possessed a voice of innately lovely quality, what she did have was certainly undermined by this reckless loss of weight. Her vocal production was no longer consistent, and in addition because the flesh covers and pads the nerve endings, this exceptionally tautly strung artist performed under increased agonies of tension.

Typically in the world of singing, where everything always seems to be arguable, there are those who claim that a loss of weight does not affect the singing voice. Yet take another, little publicized example: this was Renata Tebaldi, supposedly the great rival and arch-enemy of Maria Callas, though this seems never to have really been true of the beautiful and eminently gracious prima donna.

Possessor of a ravishing *spinto* soprano, Renata Tebaldi's career took wings when Arturo Toscanini chose her, relatively unknown, to appear in the gala concert in May 1946 that re-opened La Scala, Milan, after it had been bombed during World War II. Tebaldi became an international and much loved star, though by

1960 a New York critic noted that her voice was becoming heavier, with the chest tones more emphasized. When the Metropolitan Opera season of 1961–62 was shortened by a strike she cancelled her appearances and, remaining in Europe, put herself on a drastic diet that caused a weight loss of forty pounds in less than a year. When she returned to the Metropolitan in Cilèa's *Adriana Lecouvreur*, which was especially revived for her, her voice had deteriorated with a "steely" and forced top. After six effortful performances she bowed out of the rest of the season and went to re-study with a teacher who claimed that her vocal problems stemmed from "a small breathing defect."

A year later Renata Tebaldi, more glamorous than ever, resumed her career, but her voice never regained its former loveliness though, as is often the case when a voice loses quality, her artistry and acting ability increased. There was never the fuss made, however, in the case of Tebaldi's weight loss, over the damage to her voice as with Callas.

Weight then, in this age when audiences demand believability in that place of unbelievability, the opera house, is a vexing problem for the opera singer. Their profession is a physical one and tremendously arduous; their appetites are legendary not to speak of their capacities. Yet even with today's standards of thinness and looking fit, there are superstars who defy them such as Luciano Pavarotti: song, soul and avoirdupois are all of a piece that audiences enthusiastically accept.

There is another exception. In the mid-1960's this writer was present at the Metropolitan Opera Auditions in the old house on Broadway when a black soprano, aged twenty-four, walked out on the stage to sing Elisabeth's "Prayer" from *Tannhäuser*. So enormous was the girl she seemed to come in two sections. So enormous and beautiful was the voice that this listener was left gasping. Musicianship and the all-important line were also evident in her singing. The auditionist, however, did not receive an instant contract with the Metropolitan (as winners did at that time)—only scholarship money for further study.

When I published the first edition of this book in 1971 I ruminated on the destiny of this physically immense, immensely gifted singer: "I couldn't help wondering," I wrote, "whether she was handicapped not, happily, because of the color of her skin, but by her exceptional girth. Today's audiences would find it

H. Toulouse-Lautrec: Mme. Cocyte in Offenbach's *La Belle Hélène*. Most singers have a weight problem.

difficult to accept her as Aida or Tosca, roles that she gave evidence of being able to sing most effectively. In time she might certainly grow into the heavy Wagnerian repertory in which with the help of abundantly draped costumes combined with Wagnerian concepts of character, girth would not seem such a prob-

lem. But here is a case where physical appearance might proscribe
an operatic career, though not one made in the concert hall."

Readers may have guessed that the young soprano who sang
that one and only time before an audience at the old Metropolitan
Opera House was Jessye Norman who went on to Europe for long
years of training. What I wrote over a decade ago has largely
come true. Jessye Norman has made so far a limited career in the
more static operatic roles: Elisabeth, Ariadne and Dido or
Cassandra in Berlioz's *Les Troyens* in which she made her debut
with the Metropolitan in September 1983 to great acclaim, though
she is unrivalled as a concert singer and recitalist. At this writing
it seems more than likely that she will continue to eschew the
volatile Italian roles such as Aida and Tosca, though we may
expect one day to hear her as a superlative Isolde. In whatever
repertory her career proves that with the case of a truly extraordinary vocal artist excess poundage peels away under the spell cast
by the tiny larynx.

What about other aspects of physical appearance that might be
essential to a career? Obviously beauty is a great help, especially
in the field of popular singing. If a visage or body shape be
markedly odd or comic this may limit an opera singer to
humorous or character roles. Such was the case of Thelma
Votipka who sang only *comprimario* parts at the Metropolitan for
twenty-five years, despite the fact that she possessed a voice of
outstandingly beautiful quality. Lack of stature limited the career
of the Rumanian tenor, Joseph Schmidt, to concert and later, film
appearances: he was simply too short (under five feet) to meet
even the undemanding credulousness of operatic audiences.
Another who might have made a fine operatic career, the baritone
Emilio de Gogorza, was prevented by another physical reason: in
the days before the invention of contact lenses he could not enact
operatic roles because of short-sightedness.

Though glamour and beauty are much emphasized in the field
of popular singing, Fanny Brice with her tragic-comic "funny
face" made in her younger years a marvelous singing career.
Edith Piaf, with looks generously described as *"gamine,"* became
one of the most successful popular singers of her time.

From another point of view it is well that singers be robust and
eat heartily. This is because of the sheer physical endurance
required of them, long hours of rehearsals, the equally lengthy

performances,* the strain of incessant travel that is part of their careers. The Wagner operas make particularly heavy demands on the strength of those who perform them. A story is told of an aspiring dramatic soprano who on being introduced to Flagstad gushingly asked this great artist if there was any particular advice that she could give out of her experience of singing Wagner. "Yes," Flagstad replied calmly, "get a sensible pair of shoes."

Voice, musical aptitude, a strong constitution—even these elements would not be enough to make a career without overriding ambition to accompany them. Many a fine potential singing artist has existed who for one reason or another refused to take on the rigors of a professional life—and perhaps rightly so. It is an unnatural, arduous and not always rewarding existence. But for those with the necessary qualifications, who cannot stop themselves from attempting a singing career, the next step is one of the most vital—but potentially horrendous—moments in the vocal ages: the choice of the right teacher.

Svengalis. Fresh, pulsating with youthful vitality, the female voice at seventeen or eighteen, the nineteen or twenty-year-old one of the male, is now ready to go out into the world to find fulfillment. But what a perilous, sometimes cruel world it is. For each sensible, intelligent, above all judicious teacher of singing there is his regrettable counterpart, lurking spiderlike in a studio, door wide open, awaiting his victims who are for the most part young men and women with little money at their disposal, desperately anxious to believe that the master—for he is literally that—to whom they have committed their vocal destinies possesses the "true method" of producing a beautiful voice. The embittering fact is that anyone—the singer of bit parts with the Riga Opera Company in 1971, a Texas church soloist, young singers studying themselves and trying to pick up extra money on the side, failed singers, not even singers at all but the maid or valet of a famous opera star, coaches, hack accompanists, ex-instrumentalists, throat doctors, out-and-out charlatans—anyone can hang up a sign and claim to be a teacher of singing. No license has to be displayed, no qualifications produced. The only

---

*Mrs. Caruso writes that during a performance the tenor usually lost three pounds.

requirement is faith which at this vulnerable moment the student singer unwittingly gives because he *wants* to believe.

Because of this unwholesome situation that leaves open the field of vocal pedagogy to any and all comers, singing teachers as a group have scarcely enjoyed a very good reputation. As far back as 1906 a number of thoughtful vocal instructors in New York City banded together (an unusual occurrence in a profession where one self-proclaimed expert is often inclined to snub or vilify another) and formed an association to establish certain standards of teaching and a code of ethics. In addition it began a lobbying operation at Albany in an attempt to have legislation passed requiring all singing teachers to be licensed. By 1924, when nothing had come of this effort, the New York Singing Teachers' Association decided to ask its members in answer to a questionnaire to register with the Association their qualifications for teaching. The questions were simple and logical enough. What, where and with whom had the teacher studied voice and for how long? Had he a thorough musical education? Could he play an instrument? And so forth. Out of the hundred odd members about half chose to register their qualifications; the others abstained—presumably because they lacked them.

A national organization with similar aims was founded in 1944. Called the National Association of Teachers of Singing, it accepts as voting members voice teachers who have completed two years of continuous teaching. Applicants have to set forth their qualifications in full, together with recommendations from two other NATS members. In addition they pledge in writing their adherence to the code of ethics of the Association.

At this writing the organization has about four thousand qualified members around the United States, most of whom belong to regional chapters. NATS sponsors summer workshops at various campuses throughout the country that offer recitals, lectures, coaching and all that can further a knowledge of the art of singing among both teachers and singers. A national convention is held every eighteen months at which two winners of the Artist Awards are announced, chosen from regional auditions held around the country (first place, three thousand dollars; second place, fifteen hundred dollars). In addition five times a year NATS issues a handsome bulletin with articles by laryngologists, acousticians and of course voice teachers. Anyone who is interested in the voice in depth ought to read this regularly. They also have leaflets on important vocal subjects "on request" from their headquarters at New York University, 35 West 4th Street, New York, 10003, administered by the executive secretary for the past ten years, Mr. James F. Browning.

The idealistic aims of the National Association of Teachers of Singing are of course extremely commendable, but in summing up the organization's first twenty-five years of existence a former president, Bernard Taylor, sounded a trifle rueful over what NATS had accomplished in that time: "Members and non-members are certainly more aware of what a code of ethics means to the profession," he wrote in the October 1968 bulletin, "altho' [sic] I would not, nor indeed could not say that there has been a complete and unqualified adherence to the ethical code on the part of even our own membership." As to the NATS objective of establishing and maintaining "the highest standards" of teaching principles he was silent.

Nevertheless, the aspiring singer who chooses to study with a member of NATS knows that he is going to a person with certain important qualifications for teaching and a minimum of two years' experience in the profession. Otherwise the fact remains that a chiropodist or a masseur each requires a license to practice, but not so a voice instructor, even though he is concerned with a highly delicate and complex mechanism of the body. And yet were legislation to be passed, what would be the criteria to obtain a license? A previous professional career in singing? The experience of having studied singing? Thorough scientific knowledge of the vocal process? Historic knowledge based on vocal "methods" set down by great teachers of the past? Experience gained from having long been connected with singers and their world? At this time there are teachers who believe they are qualified to teach singing and who fit each one of these categories.

On the face of it singers who have made long, successful careers founded on a secure vocal technique should make the best voice teachers. Though the analogy is inexact, this does not work out any more than that fine authors should be able to impart a fine style of writing to their students. Out of the many great stars at the turn of the century only a handful chose to teach: Jean de Reszke, Emma Calvé, Lilli Lehmann and Marcella Sembrich. But not Patti, Eames, Mary Garden or Farrar,[*] all of whom lived on to become very old ladies. From outward evidence, Lilli Lehmann appears to have been a fine teacher, perhaps because she didn't subject the voices of her students to the drillmaster routines, hours of singing even when hoarse, through which she put her own. Sembrich, a superb musician, was also a fine teacher, though judging from her records her voice was not equalized in the lower part of its range.

Nor did the great stars of more recent years turn to teaching. Flagstad never considered it, nor did Melchior. Lucrezia Bori, though she busied herself with helping found the Metropolitan Opera Guild, never made any attempt to impart her vocal secrets to the generations succeeding her; neither did Lily Pons. Two exceptions who, while they did not exactly teach singing, at least coached were Lotte Lehmann in a studio on the West Coast and Rosa Ponselle at her home, the Villa Pace, just outside Baltimore, Maryland.

As she was to her audiences, Lotte Lehmann appears to have been an inspiration to all the singers with whom she worked. Her help to Jeanette MacDonald as an opera and lieder singer has been described. Grace Bumbry gives her unstinting credit for similar kinds of help. Marilyn Horne, who took master classes with Lehmann, writes with more reserve in her autobiography that while the great German soprano had her "dark side" and was "one very tough lady" she also "opened the doors of singing lieder for me. Her instruction is inextricably woven into my own interpretation. As exponent and teacher, she was incomparable and inspirational." Lotte Lehmann was often described as a teacher but what she taught was really interpretation, not vocal production.

The same was more or less true of Rosa Ponselle. At least four internationally known opera singers—Raina Kabaivanska, Beverly Sills, Sherrill Milnes and James Morris—"worked with" her as did a number of other lesser artists. James Morris describes how in his student years he actually only studied voice with her for four or five months, when she made him sing scales and exercises that placed his voice *"dans la masque"* ("in the mask"), that portion of the head fronted by the cheekbones and the bridge of the nose. Thereafter, he only worked with her on interpretation. In her

*Farrar studied with Lilli Lehmann.

autobiography Rosa Ponselle, who it must be remembered, never had a voice lesson in her life, describes how she gave Kabaivanska humming exercises that again would place the voice "*dans la masque.*" The mask was the secret of Rosa Ponselle's vocal "method."

Beverly Sills, who at the age of twenty-four actually went to live with the great soprano gives a telling account of her "teaching." Ponselle was then in her late fifties and still in possession of her extraordinary voice, the effect of which "was overwhelming," as Miss Sills reported many years later in an interview.

"I tell you, for a young girl to hear this voice that was completely in the mask . . . I've never heard anything like it. It went up to the high C and it was still in the mask, never in the back of the throat, never the top of the head. . . .

"It was an inspiration to me, and of course, little Beverly had to have it in the mask also. . . .

"A little problem. First of all Rosa's face was like five inches broader than mine. Second of all, Rosa had what I think was the creamiest, richest Italianate sound that I've ever heard. Mine has always been, at its best, a French voice. . . . There I was, walking around with my hands on my cheeks, trying to get the voice into the mask. . . . Miss Liebling (Estelle Liebling, Beverly Sills's famous teacher) would talk to Rosa and say, 'With that little face she's never going to get it in the mask.' And I never got it in the mask, although Rosa would say:

"'Stop it, stop it! Get it in the mask, get it in the head.'"

This illustrates perfectly why the very greatest singers with an impeccable technique do not make excellent teachers. The pupil with a differently constructed vocal apparatus will invariably try to imitate the star, while the star, who has made a triumphant career singing in one particular fashion will invariably try to impose it on the pupil. "There are many teachers, each with their own teaching system," says Arrigo Pola, teacher of Luciano Pavarotti. "This is unfortunate. The only right method is the one that adapts to the student."

Therefore it is the opera singers of slightly less stellar quality, the ones who lacked the ultimate opulence of voice and sweep of personality to make them great stars, who seem more likely to teach after retirement, and often with very good results. In this category we might put Margaret Harshaw and Rose Bampton, each of whom taught at universities with fine music departments. Both, oddly enough, were mezzo-sopranos who made the difficult and not altogether successful change to sopranos; both made careers distinguished by intelligence and musical discrimination. Others in this category have been Queena Mario, Dorothee Manski and Mack Harrell, all of whom could put "formerly of the Metropolitan Opera Company" after their names, as today can the amazingly versatile Eileen Farrell on the staff of the University of Indiana, and the mezzo-soprano Nell Rankin at the Academy of Vocal Arts in Philadelphia.

To facilitate the flow of students through the studio, this kind of "name" teacher may employ assistants, many of whom are either unknown singers or not even singers at all and who often give the entire lesson into which the teacher may drop in or not at his pleasure. Such was the practice of Mack Harrell, my first so-called singing teacher, who paid a call on exactly one lesson during a summer term at the Juilliard School of Music, though ostensibly I was studying with him. (Perhaps he was only sparing himself needless pain, for to be sure after auditioning for admission to the fall term the school turned me down.) Sometimes these assistants go on their own using the name of the well-known Metropolitan Opera singer with whom they have once worked as a magnet to draw in students, though they themselves may have had little or no voice training.

Then there are singers who turn to teaching after a short and not particularly notable career. Probably the best example is Manuel Garcia II, who sang in his father's opera company—he was America's first Figaro in *Il Barbiere di Siviglia*—but too much too soon with the result that he had "not the ghost of a voice." Another to fit into this category of the one-time professional singer who enjoyed a limited career is Mathilde Graumann Marchesi, a pupil of Manuel Garcia II. As a mezzo-soprano she sang concerts for a few years on the Continent and in England before settling down in Vienna to impart the methods of Garcia at the Conservatory. In a second incarnation she opened up a school in Paris. Marchesi accepted only women and her classes were unique for being just that—classes. She rarely gave private lessons, only to the most advanced students or the miraculously gifted such as Nellie Melba, who did not have to make her way up from the beginner's clases as did Emma Eames, much to the latter's annoyance. This method of having to sing before their fellow students and (naturally) most merciless critics wiped away any inhibitions at appearing before people. In addition the pupils could easily be taught ensemble singing. It is a system having considerable merit but little practiced today.

The list of Marchesi famous pupils, almost all sopranos, is impressive indeed: the eccentric coloratura Ilma di Murska who always toured with a menage of animals and birds; Etelka Gerster who broke down mentally during a marvelous career, and Gabrielle Krauss, "the most compelling dramatic soprano who ever existed," according to Mathilde Marchesi's daughter, Blanche. There were the two American coloraturas, Emma Nevada and Sybil Sanderson, the latter possessing the extremely rare soprano *acuto sfogato* range. Nellie Melba is probably Mathilde Marchesi's most famous pupil, but the latest biographer of this flamboyant prima donna believes that much more credit for Melba's flawless technique should be given to her teacher of six or seven years in Australia, an Italian tenor named Pietro Cecchi. Emma Calvé is always listed as a Marchesi pupil, but she left her after six months because the aging woman had lost her voice and gave her pupil nothing to imitate. Another pupil, the beautiful blue-eyed Emma Eames, with her flaring nostrils, writes coldly of Marchesi as being an "ideal Prussian drillmaster" who "fortunately did not attempt to change my natural singing voice, and as my voice was a healthy one, she did it no harm, but neither did she show me the absolute vocal security which I was to gain for myself later."

The personalities of Marchesi—"an old, curt, haughty woman who came forward like an empress and just deigned to bow to you"—and the young Mary Garden completely failed to mesh, particularly as the famous teacher then in her seventies wished to make Garden into a coloratura soprano, the last thing the young girl wanted. After a few lessons she wrote to Marchesi that she would not continue. "Mary Garden," came a note in return, "A rolling stone gathers no moss. Don't cry till you come out of the woods. Mathilde Marchesi." In her eighties, Marchesi taught Frances Alda, her last pupil, whom she called "her Benjamin." Alda, not known for her graciousness, leaves a generous portrait in her memoirs of "a czarina . . . who altered the course of my life."

Mary Garden, a soprano who stepped into the part of Louise at the Paris Opèra and rocketed to fame.

Inherent in the authoritarian, parental role of the singing teacher is the often desperate dependence on the part of the pupil not only for vocal, but total personal approval. It is this interaction in the teacher-student relationship that perhaps explains why a teacher is successful with one pupil and fails with another. Marchesi evidently mothered her girls or as Emma Eames puts it "got a hold over them." She criticized the way they dressed,

Viviane Thomas, a soprano who stepped into the part of Aida with the Connecticut Opera.

made sure they lived in a suitable section of Paris and generally oversaw their deportment even though they might have with them their own mothers as chaperones. Mary Garden, a strong-willed young woman, could not accept the domination of the older one and so the teaching attempt quickly proved a disaster. Alda, orphaned at an early age, and indeed brought up by a grandmother, fitted into the psychological climate of Madame Marchesi and there was rapport.

A good example of the "motherly" tone frequently adopted by a teacher toward her student is conveyed in this chiding letter from Erminia Rudersdorff, who was a pupil of Manuel Garcia II, to Emma Thursby, one of America's earliest sopranos. (Thursby, who in turn taught Geraldine Farrar for a time, held views against the stage and never appeared as an opera singer.)

"My naughty little speranza, after heartily thanking you for your ready assistance yesterday, I am going to scold.

"My child, you did *not* sing well yesterday. That was not the singing of a faithful student and a great artiste. It was very unfinished, often downright blurred—and—the worst—out of tune. The last cadence was so and you finished quite a quarter of a tone flat.

"That must not happen again. You have no excuse, you had all your changes and cadences written three weeks ago, and you owed it to yourself to have studied them faithfully. You have not had so many engagements as to render study impossible, moreover to those who *want* to study, study is *always possible*."

In more recent times Florence Page Kimball looked after her "girls" such as Leontyne Price and Veronica Tyler, coaching and grooming them in matters far exceeding the vocal. Estelle Liebling, perhaps in imitation of the ways of *her* teacher Madame Marchesi gave her young pupil Beverly Sills tickets to the opera. She also invited her to dinner parties at which the guests might be Maria Jeritza, Grace Moore or Lauritz Melchior thus introducing the fledgling soprano to the way her life as a future star would be, hob-nobbing with the greats of the operatic world.

HIERARCHIES OF TEACHERS

Here are a few examples of a teaching "method" being handed down over the years:

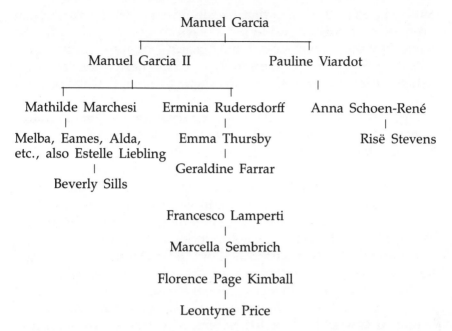

Manuel Garcia

Manuel Garcia II — Pauline Viardot

Mathilde Marchesi — Erminia Rudersdorff — Anna Schoen-René

Melba, Eames, Alda,
etc., also Estelle Liebling
Beverly Sills

Emma Thursby
Geraldine Farrar

Risë Stevens

Francesco Lamperti

Marcella Sembrich

Florence Page Kimball

Leontyne Price

Lacking the magic title "formerly of the Metropolitan Opera Company" or "Covent Garden" the teacher who can describe himself more vaguely as the internationally famous "Madame X" or "Signor Y" still has a fly of sorts that can be cast on the water to hook students. Just where and how the fame of Madame X and Signor Y has been achieved is usually rather vague and the student in all probability too intimidated to ask.

Then there are singer-teachers who have no "name" at all. Sometimes they are young and studying themselves while they pick up extra money by passing on to beginners what they themselves are still trying to learn. Such were two young women on the faculty of a well-known music school in New York which the writer entered after his Juilliard rejection. I began lessons with one of them because her fee was half what the "names" on the faculty charged, and also because the "names" may well not have been interested in teaching anyone who produced the sounds I was making at that time. My teacher proved to be kind, young, extremely musical and pleasant to be with. Her voice, a soprano, sounded attractive enough, though I was aware that she had trouble with her top notes just as I did. In my case "trouble" was a euphemism. I didn't *have* any top notes. Not too long out in the winter I began to realize that I really wasn't making very much progress with this agreeable and always encouraging person. The magic key that would unlock the "beauty" of my voice in which all students have to believe simply wasn't in her possession. And yet, not knowing what else to do or who to go to, I drifted on with her.

One day she came to me in great excitement: a famous singer (whom I had never heard of) was joining the faculty of the school. She was going to study with him herself and she would arrange for him to give me a few lessons at not much more than the fee I was paying her. My heart jumped up. A student passionately trying to find the secret of a beautiful singing voice is like a person cursed with some malady and searching for a cure. All common sense goes; in its place comes unjudgmental belief.

The former great singer turned out to be elderly and paunchy; he wore an obvious toupee of pale orange and more astonishing to my American eyes, his lips were of a rosier hue than any I had ever seen on a male. When those lips parted to demonstrate the sounds that would lead to the loveliness of my own voice I nearly fell to the floor. Raspy, blatted tones pressed on the room, mounting higher and higher with excruciating intensity. I was appalled. Could this be the way to glorious song? And yet because I so *wanted* to believe—I believed, at least for a time.

Common sense would seem to dictate that the person who teaches singing should have studied voice for a number of years and have knowledge of the sensations of the vocal process—even if they have never made careers. There are however, many, many teachers who never attempted to sing. Often they are coaches or *répétiteurs*, who after a number of years of being around singers and drilling them in repertory, diction and so forth, feel that they understand enough about vocal technique to teach it. Some go to the manuals and give vocal instruction by the Porpora or Garcia method, simply putting their students through the course of exercises left behind by these great pedagogues, certain that they will benefit each and every student. Throat doctors or men and women who have acquainted themselves as best they can with all the physical intricacies involved in singing also set themselves up as teachers without ever having sung themselves, using a strictly "scientific" approach to the achievement of a beautiful singing voice. Still another kind of non-singer teacher is one who has assisted in the studio of a celebrated teacher and now carries on that great antecedent's "method."

Strangely, to this last category belonged my next teacher, a middle-aged man with a leonine head and a belly that pushed out his shirt over the top of his trousers. I had been sent to him by a handsome, gifted dramatic soprano who believed that he could help me as he had her. By this time I was in a desperate state. I had discovered that under the G.I. Bill I could qualify for several thousand dollars worth of free vocal training if the American Theater Wing which supervised the program considered me to have sufficient promise. The Theater Wing after hearing me audition did not. But they were prepared to give me one more chance in three months' time, if by some fluke my new teacher could make something of my voice.

I cannot remember much of the first half hour with this somewhat awe-inspiring figure except the usual terror that accompanies all such moments in the life of a would-be singer. Almost all voice teachers sing, or at any rate make noises of some sort, however distasteful. Imitation is one of the basic elements in vocal instruction. To my amazement this teacher was silent. He looked as if he was going to sing: that is, he fixed me with purposeful, glaring little eyes and then quickly dropped his jaw so that I could see into the rosy interior of his mouth. But no sound came forth. I was told to do as he had done, except to sing, which I did, and for the first time sang the F sharp, G, and A flat, the high notes of the baritone range which I did not believe were in my voice. How or why this alchemy was accomplished I shall never understand. At the end of two lessons a week for six weeks I returned to the Theater Wing for another audition and was promptly accepted. It was, one of the judges remarked, the greatest piece of teaching he had ever heard.

"There is nothing more strange than this question of voice teachers," wrote Sidney Homer,[*] who certainly ought to have known. When he first met his wife-to-be, beauteous Louise Beatty from a suburb of Pittsburgh, she had already studied with three teachers. But her large, low voice continued to remain woolly and ungainly and she could not shade it down. In Boston she went to her fourth teacher, William Whitney, who had taught Lillian

---

[*]Sidney Homer was a professional musician and minor composer, yet curiously, both his parents were deaf mutes.

Nordica by what was known then as the "Italian" method. Again she made no headway. Sidney and Louise Homer married, had a baby and on borrowed money went to Paris where she studied with a noted teacher called Jacques Bouhy. This pedagogue succeeded in diminishing the size and brilliance of her voice and making it sound muffled. Teacher number six, an out-going Italian, Signor Juliani, restored its volume and freed the high notes at a cost to the bottom of the range where the once full and sumptuous tones emerged sounding breathy, hollow and flattened out.

While still studying with the Italian, Louise Homer met a vocal coach at the Paris Opèra named Fidele Koenig who was married to an American from Cambridge, Massachusetts. He asked to teach her, a move that Sidney Homer opposed. Ostensibly, Louise Homer went to work with him on interpretation but secretly practiced head tones in a daily lesson. A few months later she made a stunning debut in Donizetti's *La Favorita* at Vichy and the rest is operatic history. (Not only did Louise Homer wrest an operatic career from the instruction of seven teachers but coming from a deeply religious family, she had to defy her parents by marrying an agnostic and going on the stage which they regarded as "a sin.")

Of his wife's long search for the right vocal method, Sidney Homer wrote a forgiving summation: "I have long made up my mind that when a pupil does not make progress it is not necessarily a reflection on his teacher. Another pupil will do wonderfully under his care and the unsuccessful pupil will get on famously under another master. There is an alchemy about it, a reaction of personalities, a mysterious mutual helpfulness, an unexplainable sympathy."

One of the most celebrated singing teachers of the nineteenth century was François Delsarte, uncle of Georges Bizet. Delsarte turned to teaching after his own voice had been ruined in training at the Conservatoire. That delightful reporter Lillie (Moulton) de Hegermann-Lindencrone who went to study with him, has left an account of his methods.

"He is not a real singing teacher, for he does not think the voice worth speaking of," she writes; "he has a theory that one can express more by the features and all the tricks he teaches, and especially by the manner of enunciation than by the voice . . . ."

On Delsarte's walls "were hung some awful diagrams to illustrate the master's method of teaching. These diagrams are crayon-drawings of life-sized faces depicting every emotion that the human face is capable of expressing such as love, sorrow, murder, terror, joy, surprise, etc.

"It is Delsarte's way, when he wants you to express one of these emotions in your voice, to point with a soiled forefinger to the picture in question which he expects you to imitate. The result lends expression to your voice."

The method of a total charlatan one might suppose, and yet it evidently proved effective. One of his last students was the young Lillian Nordica who felt that she learned much from him. Here again is a connection of magic with the singing voice. "Svengali" has become a commonplace in today's vocabulary. We should not forget that Svengali was a singing teacher, who by using the highly irregular vocal method of hypnotism was able to make "Trilby, the tone deaf, who couldn't sing one note in tune! Trilby who couldn't tell a C from an F" into a marvelous singer. *Trilby*, George Du Maurier's novel, is farfetched.

"Well, we both taught her together—for three years—morning, noon and night—six—eight hours a day. It used to split me to the heart to see her worked like that! We took her note by note—there was no end to her notes, each more beautiful than the other—velvet and gold, beautiful flowers, pearls, diamonds, rubies—drops of dew and honey; peaches, oranges and lemons! . . . She could run up and down the scales, chromatic scales, quicker and better and smoother than Svengali on the piano, and more in tune than any piano! and her shake—ech! twin stars, monsieur! She was the greatest contralto, the greatest soprano the world has ever known!" Though the story is ridiculous the fantasy of the singing teacher who by some magical means can elicit the most beautiful voice in the world from his pupil is a very real one in the mind of almost every student who steps hopefully across the threshold of a teacher's studio.

What Am I? Unless his family happens to move in musical circles the aspiring singer looking for a voice teacher is as defenseless as the newly hatched baby turtles on the Galapagos Islands, making their frantic dash to the safety of the sea while frigate birds hover relentlessly above waiting to snap them up. Who can the incipient

Trilby under hypnotism.

singer turn to for advice? His high school music teacher will
probably be interested and sympathetic, but in a small town will
have little experience or information. One possibility is to enroll
in a music school or a college with a good vocal department and
then move on from there to private instruction. More impatient
students who want private instruction from the outset but do not
know to whom to go, sometimes boldly write a favorite singer
and ask for advice. Others simply contact a teacher on the
strength of his label "Formerly Metropolitan Opera Company," or
his claims to have taught a number of celebrated singers.

In finding the right teacher the would-be singer is confronted
with an element that will influence his entire career: this is, quite
simply, luck.

Roberta Peters, at the age of thirteen, went to a teacher who
made her sing bending over or holding out a medicine ball
weighing ten pounds in front of her. At eighteen she made her
debut at the Metropolitan. He was her only teacher.

Birgit Nilsson worked at Stockholm's Royal Academy with her

first teacher, who in three years made her huge voice small. Another teacher made her sing high C's for a quarter of an hour and tried to develop a big chest voice. After that, in her rueful words, "I started to find my own way."

The fine bass-baritone James Morris studied with a number of teachers but credits his first high school instructor Forrest Barrett with the rudiments on which his solid vocal technique is based today. At the University of Maryland Morris worked with a teacher who tried to train him as a tenor, which Morris resisted. But suppose that teacher had been the one at high school? What irreparable damage might have been done to Morris's fresh, untrained voice as was evidently wreaked on Franco Corelli's unschooled tenor by his first and only teacher?

Luck then hovers over the hopeful singer's application to a teacher. This will involve an audition for which in the cases of the grander ones a fee will be charged. The nervous student brings out his music—a song, an aria that brought down the house in high school, while the teacher, wondering if an exciting new talent has happened into his studio, slips to the piano—unless he employs an accompanist. The introduction sounds and at the moment of entrance, like plunging down the first fall of a great roller-coaster, the hopeful singer utters his opening note. Now there is no going back . . .

The last note dies away. An anxious silence follows. Will the teacher ask to hear more? "Have you something else? Something a little simpler?" come the welcome words. And then, "Will you sing me this scale slowly up and back down again?"

In the case of an aspiring singer who manifestly could never make a career, how difficult for all but a truly kind teacher to say the truth. And even the most experienced judgment could always be at fault. Easier to say, "I'm not accepting any more pupils at the moment—but if you want to call me in six months' time . . ." The more unscrupulous teacher given such a prospective pupil will delve immediately into his victim's ability to pay, murmuring in a prophetic way, "There is potential. It will take work, a great deal of work. But there is definite potential."

"You don't have a voice anymore," was Manuel Garcia's comment to the eighteen-year-old Jenny Lind when she auditioned for him in Paris in 1841. Already a famous singer in her native country she had sung herself into a state of vocal fatigue through incorrect methods and performing too much. Shattered, she begged Garcia to help her, to which he replied doubtfully that if she went away and rested her voice completely without speaking for six weeks, it might be saved. Jenny Lind, always a hard worker, used the six weeks' enforced silence to teach herself French and Italian. All the world knows the result, but contemporary reports of Jenny Lind's voice always speak of a veiled, husky quality in the middle of its range, suggesting that in fact she had done it permanent harm. How many teachers would prescribe such treatment today, one wonders, or indeed students endure it?

If the young hopeful shows promise and the teacher has time as well as interest, the new pupil will be accepted and an hour appointed for the first lesson. Before leaving the audition the gratified student may ask eagerly, "What kind of voice do you think I have? My music teacher always said I was a contralto but I have some very high notes as well."

Unless the classification is a most obvious one such as a deep bass or a high, light coloratura, a scrupulous teacher will reply that this must remain to be decided, perhaps only after several months of lessons. The classifying of a voice can be most misleading and tricky and even experienced teachers have been known to make mistakes. I know of one gifted singer who started off her training in her teens as a coloratura soprano, though there were rich contralto tones in her voice as well. Later she went to Europe to study with the noted contralto Sigrid Onegin. One of the pitfalls of working with celebrated singers is that they tend to think of their pupils as images of themselves, so that the former coloratura soprano was turned into a contralto. In the end her voice was correctly classified as a dramatic soprano. With some voices the quality and range will make it perfectly obvious what they are: with others, it is more difficult. In all cases the note on which the singer must change into a different register is a helpful clue. If a man, for instance, can sing an open "ah" no higher than E flat, and possibly not even this, it suggests that he is a baritone or bass. If on the other hand he can carry the "ah" up to an E natural or F, this arouses suspicions—however rich and baritone-like his voice may sound—that he could sing tenor.

There is another, by no means certain, but intriguing clue.

A friend of mine engaged the noted German baritone Hermann Prey to sing a private recital at his house in Philadelphia and asked me to drive down from New York to hear it. Prey sang beautifully a program of lieder in a lyric, not overly-rich baritone slightly weak and without fullness of tone at the bottom. On the other hand the baritone's transition note of E flat he sang openly and with consummate ease and it seemed to me that he could have easily gone higher in this same register without having to make the requisite change for his high notes. The intimacy of a beautiful reception room in a private house made it possible to study the shape of Prey's face closely: it is round, not long, with wide-spaced eyes, prominent cheek bones, and a short space between the lower lip and chin.

The next day my host asked me if I would give the singer and his wife a lift back to New York, and in the car somewhere along the New Jersey Turnpike I realized that I felt under compulsion to ask Mr. Prey a question which at best might be construed as rude, and at worst insulting. From observations over the years I had long held the theory that the shape of a singer's face gives a clue to the range of his voice. It had struck me that a face which was wide across its top half, often with knobby cheekbones, and then tapered sharply to a chin set not far beneath the lower lip produced a high voice in either sex—soprano or tenor. These faces were also likely to be convex. Baritones and mezzos were inclined to have longer faces, and the low basses and contraltos an oblong shape to their heads. Catching sight of Mr. Prey in the rear view mirror and remembering his vocal quality of the previous evening, also the ease of his high tones, I could contain myself no longer. "Mr. Prey, do you think by any chance you're really a tenor?"

"Oh yes," he replied calmly. "I could sing tenor."

"Then why—?"

"It would mean studying again." I saw in the mirror the reflection of his smile and a shrug. "Why should I?"

Soon after, much to my delight I came upon medical confirmation of my totally empirical theory. In his highly informative *Keep Your Voice Healthy*, a practicing oto-laryngologist, Friedrich S. Brodnitz, quotes from the writings of a fellow throat expert, Dr. Deso A. Weiss. Dr. Weiss "who examined a large number of successful singers believes that a definite body type can be associated with the high and low voices. According to him, singers with high voices have: round faces with short noses, a convex profile with small delicate details, short necks, round or quadratic chests, high palates with delicate soft palates; while the deep voices are characterized by: long faces with long noses, straight line profiles with massive details, long and narrow necks, long and flat chests, broad palates with massive soft palates. A flat palate or a sharp angle between the floor of the mouth and the neck was rarely found in a singer with a good voice."* To which I would add, again totally from observation, that one does not see a singer with a decidedly undershot jaw or what might be described as a "weak" chin.

Here is another description of a classic tenor face. "The depth, width and height of the roof of the mouth, the broad cheekbones and flat even teeth, the wide forehead above wide-set eyes—that spacious architecture gave him his deep resonance of tone." Thus Mrs. Caruso describing her husband. Naturally, the theory that the shape of a face tells what kind of a singing voice is behind it cannot be expected to operate with one hundred per cent accuracy. An exception that comes instantly to mind is Joan Sutherland, long of face and long of jaw, scarcely typical of a soprano. Nevertheless just as the soprano *acuto sfogato* is most often doll-like and petite, and the bass tall and commanding, the shape of the face is one more guideline to vocal identification. Almost four hundred years ago the playwrights Beaumont and Fletcher had already recognized the fact when they wrote:

> Come sing now, sing; for I know ye sing well,
> I see ye have a singing face.

AAH-OOH-AAH. Excitedly the student singer arrives for his first lesson eager to learn the secrets of his new teacher's method. This will have one of several definite orientations.

Most common is some kind of physical approach, though as has been pointed out a demonstration of how to sing is perforce very limited. Still there are certain muscular actions that a student can learn to control and regulate. It is possible, for instance, to slightly raise or lower the level of the larynx while singing, thus increasing or decreasing the size of the resonating pharynx at the back of the throat. There have been teachers who made the pupil

---

*Caruso could hold an egg in his mouth without anyone realizing it was there and the teacher of Kathleen Ferrier declares that "one could have shot a fair-sized apple right to the back of her throat without obstruction."

stand with the back of his head forced hard against a wall and by this extra pressure push down the larynx in his throat. The result, as anyone can find out by doing so, will be a dark, thick tone, which may also sound lugubrious and lacking in vitality. Then there are teachers who demand that the student bring the tongue forward, which has the effect of raising the larynx. The resulting tone is usually a "white," bleaty kind of tone. (I have seen the adjective "chicken" applied to it.) Somewhere between these extremes lies the best level of adjustment. But one must ask where? And isn't it possible that a desirable level will vary from singer to singer?

Some teachers emphasize the shape of the mouth and going back to the early song manuals cite Mancini, for example, that the mouth should be in the shape of a smile. W. J. Henderson gives this confusing report of various singers in the golden age at the turn of this century: "Some teachers and some singers believe that the secret of good tone lies in pushing forward the lips. The mouth is resolutely opened in the form of the letter O, the lips being compelled to protrude somewhat. Sbriglia of Paris is the most ardent advocate of this style, and Jean de Reszke who studied with him for a time* discarded it in the very beginning. Madame Nordica employs it and is a firm believer in it. Madame Sembrich, on the other hand, employs the horizontal oval, or letter O laid on its side. This lip formation, the old masters asserted, gives the tones a beautifully soft sonority, suitable for the expression of feeling."

Other teachers lay great stress on the tongue. Should it be humped—or flattened? Blanche Marchesi writes in her *A Singer's Pilgrimage* of mechanical devices used to control this organ, the action of which most of us take perfectly casually. She mentions in particular a kind of mouth cage that the teacher sold to each of his pupils. Smaller at the back and flaring out in front, it was supposed to flatten the tongue. This unpleasant contrivance came in but one size—which certainly cannot be said of the human mouth. She relates another story of a teacher in Dresden who made the pupil balance a large round piece of lead on the tip of the tongue, thus forcing it down. Fear of swallowing the lump of metal naturally caused the mouth to dry out and the muscles in the larynx to tense. The lead did slip down the throat of one

---

*Sbriglia is generally given credit for training Jean de Reszke from baritone to tenor.

Blanche Marchesi, soprano and renowned singing teacher.

unfortunate student whose life was despaired of until the metal
was ultimately retrieved. But such ordeals and worse are often
the lot of those who strive to achieve a beautiful singing voice.

Still other teachers have evolved often mad-sounding theories
concerning movable parts of the face, the mouth and the throat
over which we have some control. "Cause the cheeks to become
hollow from without inwards, pout the lips as far out as possible

in trumpet formation. This will add to the resonance of the voice, as the space between the teeth and the lips is the real resonator." Try it!

Or, "Lie crosswise on your bed. Let the arms hang down on one side and your feet on the other until the body feels well stretched. Extend the arms in the shape of a cross. Let the mouth open by letting the head fall down instead of lowering the jaw. Sing AH! This will send the voice in the head, take the strain off the throat, widen the chest."

Or here is an injunction from a well-meaning authority claiming to impart the secrets of Elisabeth Schumann's vocal technique: "With teeth closed, lips pressed firmly against them and cheeks well raised (the upper teeth will be clearly visible), the singer must blow on to a lowish note through the consonant sound 'v,' taking care that only the diaphragm and not the throat does the pushing. After a time he must release the teeth just sufficiently to make a real note instead of merely a buzzed hum. This will be 'a small note' and will as yet have no vowel shape."

The great tenor Jean de Reszke, when his voice began to fail turned to teaching, and the result was another muddle that seems so often to beset singing and its instruction. Together with the American laryngologist Dr. Holbrook Curtis they concluded that the aforementioned "coup de glotte," which Garcia had so unfortunately named, was fatal to a proper singing technique and that the only way to avoid the quick striking together of the vocal folds or lips within the glottis was by preceding each tone with a kind of hummed "n" sound. This was conveniently demonstrable to the most inexperienced student, but it also had the effect of putting the tone undesirably in the nose. De Reszke taught this method for years in his studio at Nice, in which the composer Reynaldo Hahn was for a time *répétiteur*.

Meanwhile in 1909, Dr. Curtis, a doctor but never a singer, brought out his manual *Voice Building and Tone Placing* in which we find this excerpt: "On welcoming my dear friend Jean de Reszke to my house after his fourth return to our shores I said to him: 'Jean, have you any new facts for my poor book? Have your studies during the past year taught you anything which may be of use to me?' 'Yes,' he responded. 'I find that the great question of the singer's art becomes narrower and narrower all the time, until I can truly say that the great question of singing becomes a question of the nose—la grande question du chant devient une question du nez.'"

There remain a few other demonstrable movements of the face which may also be called on in the struggle for a beautiful voice. Hopeful students are frequently instructed to flare their nostrils as though an offensive odor had been thrust beneath them, or perhaps to lift the eyebrows in an effort to "think high." The position of the head can obviously be varied so that for every would-be singer who is taught to lift his chin and throw back his head in order to obtain a high ringing note, there is another instructed to bow his head in what is known as a "goose-neck" position, which some believe aids in placing the high notes.

Finally there are the physical devices to which teachers will resort in the hope of training the voice to ring with all the resonance that is inherent in it. Thus to prevent singing in the nose, a teacher will force a pair of corks up the nostrils of the student. And though it would seem that in our supposedly enlightened age such artificial methods might be harmful, there is a singing manual written only a few years ago and available in shops specializing in music which advises the beginner to place "a small, *clean* [italics mine] cork between the front teeth, separating them one half to three quarters of an inch," so that he may learn how wide apart the jaws should be when singing.

Absurd and ludicrous as these instructions may sound, strangely enough there is always a chance that they may be of help, and some muscular action, however little related to the vocal process provide a singer with a kind of crutch towards reaching a desirable tone quality.

Another kind of teacher will decry this physiological approach to vocal instruction, believing that it makes the student self-conscious about the muscles used in singing, and ultimately tense. Instead he advocates a psychological approach. The voice is all in the mind, he declares; if one simply conceives a pleasing tone mentally, the proper muscular action will result automatically. In the studio of this type of teacher images and metaphors shower down like petals blowing off a fruit tree that has just given up flowering.

"Think of the tone as a ping-pong ball riding on a jet of water."

"Make a foolish face in order to relax. Then place the hands behind the back, bend, and chase an imaginary dove around the room."

"Think of *stinking fish* to produce the head voice."

"Sing high notes with a *black snore*."

Caruso is said to have been much amused by a vocal teacher of whom he said, "He knows more than me. When he teaches he takes an umbrella and when he opens it the pupils sing 'EEE-EEE-AAAA' and when he closes it slowly, slowly they go 'AAA-AAA-EEE.'"

Students are frequently instructed to think of a "pear-shaped" tone, to lift their upper jaw (impossible, as it is rigid), or to feel the tone coming out of the roof of the head (where it is not nor ever could be). The relentlessly disciplined Lilli Lehmann provides a scary looking chart in her book *How to Sing* of a head in profile with red lines flying out from the skull to indicate all the different places where a singer must feel his head tones—again all fantasy. In certain cases this chart has actually been helpful to singers in extracting the marrow, as it were, from their resonators; to others, Frau Lehmann's manual, a miasma of the sensations she felt when she sang, is incomprehensible to the point of nonsense. Here is a characteristic excerpt:

"As I have said before in speaking of the attack, in order to make the vowel sound ā, the larynx is with energy brought in closer relation with the nose. By dilating the nostrils a preparation is made. The sensation is then as if the larynx were under the nose in the chin. If we then sing ā energetically we soon become conscious of an inherent strength which is created partially by the energetic opening of the epiglottis in the pronunciation of ā and partially by the position of the larynx which makes possible the attack of the breath on the hard palate," etc.

Making desperate attempts to bring out resonance in the tones of their students, the metaphors of teachers sometimes exceed the hallucinations of a "trip." Elster Kay in his *Bel Canto and the Sixth Sense*, gives this splendid example of metaphor run riot.

"One is required to think of a ladder (two ladders) in one's head, a biscuit-mold and Hoover in one's mouth and a chimney in one's throat . . . The upper jaw has to be thought of as a pointed bird's beak which, during singing, stabs into an apple. And of course, during singing one must relax completely body and soul."

And yet again these images, strange and ludicrous as they may seem, can perhaps have meaning to one person, and that person translate them into the tones of a lovely singing voice. Many a singer has produced his song within the realm of his own vocal fantasies, feeling sensations to which he gives names or comparisons that have no meaning to another person.

Another approach is the "natural" one. A runner doesn't think how his leg muscles are functioning as he sprints for the finish line—so there is no talk of anatomy. Emphasis is placed on the involuntary and spontaneous, with no thought to any kind of muscular control. Such teachers often liken singing to speaking and put much emphasis on the pupil's speaking voice; if the speaking voice is perfected, they believe, the singing voice will automatically follow.

Whatever the approach (or combination of them) the student will eventually, if not right away, be asked to vocalize during his lessons. Some teachers give their pupils scales and exercises only, believing that when technical mastery is gained over the voice then and only then can it be applied to the art of singing. These pedagogues divide up still further. Some believe that the same set of exercises, perhaps as prescribed by Manuel Garcia II or Mathilde Marchesi, will invariably benefit every voice that practices them. Others, perhaps wiser, tailor the various scales, arpeggios and *vocalises* to the individual voice of the student and its problems. This type of teacher may keep his beginner student singing scales and exercises and nothing else for a number of months, or he may start the pupil off right away on a song used as an exercise. The various *Arie Antiche*—Italian seventeenth- and eighteenth-century songs with long, flowing lines and accommodating open syllables—are particular favorites of teachers in this respect. Over the decades how many multitudes of hopeful singers have attacked the Giordani "Caro mio ben" or the charming "Nina," supposed to be a lament by Pergolesi for his cat—but now, in this age of disillusion declared to be neither by him nor for his pet.

The Making of a Singer. And so time passes—time which the aspiring singer quickly comes to feel as a nemesis to his career, insistently there and having to be overcome, only later to be held back. With each lesson questions bedevil the student's mind. Am I making progress? Am I on the right track? If the temperaments of teacher and pupil mesh and there arises a strange, almost mystical comprehension between them, and if the teacher is an experienced and intelligent one, then one day, magically, the student may suddenly feel his voice ring out free and easily in a way that it never has before. Here at last is a kind of break-through. Excitedly he returns for the next lesson but now this exhilarating, soaring tone is lost. At the next lesson it returns briefly, only to disappear again. I have found no better description of the manic-depressive life that a student singer leads than this passage from the memoirs of Clara Doria Rogers, an English singer who studied in Milan almost a hundred years ago:

> There is no ecstasy like that experienced at the sound of one's own voice when it fulfills one's ideal, as there is also no depres-sion so profound as that induced by the loss of it—even when one believes that loss to be temporary! I was frequently and painfully subject to these fluctuations, and my alternate spells of ecstasy and misery cannot be gauged by any ordinary standard of human emotions. I was constantly seeking for a way to clinch my triumphant tone. The word which expressed it for me was "it." Yesterday "it" was mine to keep forever, as it seemed; today "it" was gone and I as helpless as an owner of a pet bird that had flown from its cage! In vain did I plead with my teacher for help. "If you could only give me some advice what to do, how to practice to get a permanent tone-emission! If you would only tell me why I have no voice—no breath—no anything today, when in the last lesson I had all of these and you were so pleased with me."
>
> All I could expect from him was a kind, sympathetic smile, and "You are tired; you have been overdoing and have exhausted your vitality; stop singing and you will find your voice again." He was invariably right! Still I was not satisfied. I ached to dis-cover the why and wherefore of this tantalizing state of things. I went searching—searching—day after day. I shut myself in a little studio, trying every sort of experiment with my voice—all in vain, till I would bury my face in my hands on the keys of the piano in utter despair.
>
> There my poor dear little mother would find me and in anx-ious tones say, "For God's sake, Clara, don't work so hard. Do you know that you have been singing for four hours? You will kill yourself if you go on in that way!"
>
> To which I would answer, sobbing, "Oh I have lost my tone-emission; I have lost 'it.'"

Melodramatic and typically nineteenth-century as this may sound to those who have never studied voice, it is an all too agonizing and true experience to those who have. As a result, in the quest for "it" many students leave one teacher for another, and that one for a third, taking up a nomadic life which for some never becomes settled.

In desperation some students try to teach themselves and turn to the manuals of singing. These exist by the hundreds and range from cheap paperbacks to thick volumes filled with complicated, often disgusting looking diagrams of the throat and head, strange symbols such as might be used in a calculus problem and of course vocal exercises. The pages are thick with interjections: "ee!" "aw" "OH"—and the prose denser still:

"By means of the tongue thus raised, the closely but flexibly held larynx, and the free and slightly covered nose, the two bright vowels partially remain, and combine with them the dark vowel, thus making a complete singing tone. . . ."

Or: "Thus an increased tension of the abdominal muscles causes the vocal cords to vibrate at greater amplitude horizontally, the greater adduction of the vocal cords means that less breath volume is needed to vibrate the same depth of vocal cord vertically."

Or: "Be it noted: If the singer *thinks* 'back of the vertical,' at a certain angle, the throat obeys the thought, releasing the parts concerned and assuming the right shape; whereupon the sound beam will *of itself* soar upwards into the head cavities at the correct angle with respect to the vertical. It is really all very simple."

Presumably publishers wouldn't go on printing these books unless there was a market for them among people to whom they have meaning. Again it is a question of a word, a suggestion, an image striking the student-reader's sensibility in such a way as to help him.

One most unusual book is worthy of comment here. Called *Great Singers on Great Singing* and published in 1982, it is a series of interviews conducted with famous singers and compiled by the bass Jerome Hines, veteran of thirty-eight seasons at the Metropolitan, concerning their vocal technique. What is impressive is the *consistency* of response to various questions about singing that he raises. Invariably, for instance, correct breathing—support or, in Italian *appoggiare*—was considered the fundamental of good singing. Yet not unexpectedly, there were differences among the thirty-nine inteviewees as to how the best breath support was obtained: in the abdomen or by expanding the rib cage (intercostally). They concurred almost unanimously that breaths were never taken in the chest.

Mr. Hines repeatedly asked what the term "open throat" meant to these artists. With a little coaching most of them agreed that it felt like the "beginning of a yawn" and that it was this sensation that accompanied their singing. Most also agreed that to smooth out the break or *passaggio* that occurs in every voice it helped "to think a little bit nasal."

Whether a student can teach himself from a manual is doubtful. But to find a volume in which experts are quoted as agreeing on the basics of vocal production when they are so often at each other's throat (no pun intended) is most unusual. This book could certainly have rewards for the thoughtful reader-cum-vocalist.

Students also attempt to teach themselves by imitating records of famous singers. This was the method of Amelita Galli-Curci who claimed to be self-taught, as does Franco Corelli. There is a recording of Maria Callas singing "Tu che invoco" from Spontini's *La Vestale* which is a ghostly imitation of Ponselle's rendition of this aria, suggesting that the one diva learned from the records of the earlier one.

While self-teaching may be beneficial to a voice student, it is also true that every singer needs a second pair of expert ears to overhear his vocal work since he cannot hear himself physically or critically as others do. On this subject Ernestine Schumann-Heink, one of the all-time great singers, tells in her biography *The Last of the Titans* how her second husband, Paul Schumann, an actor, worked with her on the acting and interpretation of her roles: "Such criticism as he gave is of the highest value to an artist. One can never either hear or see themselves, and it is a necessity—if one would make real progress in art—for constant criticism. Any young artist who does not realize or disdains this can never reach the greatest heights."

Let us assume, however, that our hypothetical student is making excellent progress with his or her teacher. By this time a rapport will have inevitably grown up between them. The pupil feels the teacher's backing and confidence in his emergent voice and art, while the teacher grows more and more involved in the promise of this particular student.

To his growing knowledge of vocal technique other skills must be acquired by the student to make a singing career.* As the voice develops the teacher will recommend that the pupil study one or more of the three languages that are a requisite—Italian, French and German. Here again, background plays such an important factor in the life of the would-be singer. If for one reason or another he has heard one of these languages spoken at home he is that much ahead of the game. Perhaps he has had good instruction in French in high school, or simply possesses a facility for languages that others do not. These factors will be of immense help. Many English-speaking singers never do become fluent in all three languages, content to go over the words of their repertory with coaches who drill them in the pronunciation and meaning of the texts.

Another essential soon needed in the pursuit of a singing career is an accompanist. Some teachers, afraid that beginners will go on repeating mistakes in vocal technique, do not allow them to practice except under their own supervision or possibly that of an assistant. Others expect them to practice outside the studio but not seated at the piano—a position less conducive to good singing than standing up. Therefore an accompanist is required. As the voice develops and can undertake more difficult music an accompanist (a good one is perhaps even more of a rarity than a good singer) becomes yet more of a necessity. Only the most musical voice students can play for themselves the quick, dancing accompaniments of a Mozart aria or make their way through the complexities of a song by Richard Strauss.

The finest vocal technique properly only serves musical art, and a conscientious teacher will eventually recommend that his promising pupil go to a coach, who will supervise points of interpretation, or work on tricky ensemble passages in the various operatic roles that by this time he has begun to study.

Having to work privately with all these different mentors puts a crushing load of expense on the student singer. Well-known teachers charge seventy-five to one hundred fifty dollars per hour. A good coach asks forty-five to sixty, while a plain accompanist's

---

*"For singing, I should like the students to have a wide knowledge of music; exercises in voice production; very long courses in *solfeggi*, as in the past; exercises for singing and speaking with clear and perfect enunciation." G. Verdi.

fee will be from fifteen to twenty-five dollars. The fee of the language teacher will depend on his specialized knowledge of song and operatic literature in his particular tongue. Thus an aspiring singer may find that he is spending hundreds of dollars a week before he has taken up a forkful of food or put his head down on a pillow. In addition he must have a room with a piano where he can practice; he has the expense of purchasing necessary scores and sheet music and he also should attend as many live vocal performances as he possibly can.

How to finance the study of the singing voice thus becomes a major problem. One often hears the complaint that singers don't study as long as they ought to, that they should remain in the studio on the average several years longer than they usually do. What forces them out prematurely is this overwhelming financial pressure that causes them to take a job singing in the chorus of a musical or as hard-working church soloists when their voices are not yet ready to undergo the strain. Yet how else are they to support their studies? If they are lucky they may find a patron, as did Leontyne Price from a Mississippi family for whom her mother was a domestic. Geraldine Farrar borrowed money from a wealthy woman in Boston and proudly displays a photograph of the debt marked "Paid in Full" in her memoirs. The sum came to $30,000—and that was at the beginning of the century!

Another solution, though an arduous one, is to take a full time non-vocal job, which necessitates dashing for lessons in the lunch hour or after work and practicing and studying in the evenings, a killing schedule but in some cases the only possible one. Sometimes success in a job and the resultant security will weaken and eventually undermine the ambition of an aspiring singer and he abandons the idea of a career altogether. Louise Homer saw the dangers of this as she became more proficient and better paid as a court stenographer in Philadelphia. Eventually she threw over her well-paying job and the dangerous safety it offered in order to go to Boston to study.

There are also many stories of kind and generous teachers who have waived their fees or at least reduced them for promising pupils without the ability to pay. There are equally unpleasant tales of pedagogues who make the student sign a binding contract that he will pay a percentage of his future earnings—sometimes *for the rest of his life*.

HOW THEY BEGAN

In order to support themselves while studying singers have held a wide variety of jobs. Others were already equipped for an entirely different profession before discovering their voices.

Albert Alvarez, tenor, was leader of a military band.

Peter Anders, tenor, was an accountant.

Francisco d'Andrade, baritone, studied law.

Hendrik Appels, a Dutch tenor, was first a practicing dentist.

Salvatore Baccaloni, the *basso buffo*, studied architecture.

Alfred von Bary, tenor, was a qualified neurologist before his voice was discovered. He returned to medicine for a time after failing eyesight terminated his musical career.

Don Beddoe, a Welsh tenor, was first a miner.

Eugenii Belov, baritone, started out as an engineer.

Erna Berger, coloratura soprano, was a governess.

Ingrid Bjoner, soprano, worked in an apothecary shop.

Beno Blachut, a Czechoslovakian tenor, was an ironworker.

Alessandro Bonci, tenor, was a shoemaker's apprentice.

Kim Borg, bass-baritone, began as an engineer.

Giuseppe Borgatti, a tenor and the first Andrea Chénier, started out as a mason.

John Brownlee, baritone, worked as a bookkeeper.

Aloys Burgstaller, the German tenor, studied to become a watchmaker.

Florencio Constantino, tenor, was a ship's engineer.

Régine Crespin, soprano, studied to be a pharmacist.

Charles Dalmorès, a noted French tenor, was also a horn player.

Peter Dawson, Australian bass-baritone, began as a professional boxer.

Nelson Eddy, baritone, was a reporter.

Pablo Elvira, baritone from Puerto Rico, was a trumpeter in a dance band.

Kathleen Ferrier, contralto, was a telephonist.

Mario Filippeschi, bass, started as a police official.

Miguel Fleta, tenor and first Calaf in *Turandot*, was a miner.

Alfons Fügel, German tenor, began as a tile-setter.

Beniamino Gigli, tenor, worked in a pharmacy.

Alexander Girardi, a popular Austrian operetta tenor, was a locksmith.

Tito Gobbi, baritone, earned money as a sidewalk artist.

Apollo Granforte, the celebrated Italian baritone, began as a shoemaker.

Joseph Hislop, Edinburgh-born tenor, was a press photographer.

Samuel Hybbinette, Swedish tenor, was principally a surgeon, director of the Seraphiner Hospital in Stockholm and physician to the King. He appeared frequently in concerts and was said to have the most beautiful tenor voice in Scandinavia.

Morgan Kingston, English tenor, was a miner.

Walter Kirchoff, German tenor, began his career as a cavalry officer.

Dorothy Kirsten, lyric soprano, worked as a telephone operator.

Mario Lanza, the popular tenor, was a truck driver.

Emanuel List, Austrian bass, learned the tailor's trade.

Cornell MacNeil, baritone, was a machinist.

Emilio de Marchi, tenor and first Cavaradossi, began as a lieutenant.

Queena Mario, soprano, was a journalist.

Sherrill Milnes, baritone, worked on the family farm till he was twenty-five.

Oscar Natzka, New Zealand bass, was a blacksmith.

Alfred Piccaver, the tenor idol of Vienna, worked in the laboratory of Thomas A. Edison before his voice was discovered.

Ezio Pinza, *basso cantante*, was a professional bicycle rider.

Paul Plishka, bass, drove a truck.

Helge Roswaenge, tenor, started out as a chemist.

Charles Rousselière, French tenor, began as a smith.

Mario Sereni, baritone, trained first as a mechanic.

Leo Slezak, the great Austrian tenor, was a gardener and a locksmith.

Thomas Stewart, baritone, worked in a government laboratory doing mathematical-physics research.

Martti Talvela, bass, was a school teacher.

Jess Thomas, tenor, started out as a child psychologist.

Jacques Urlus, the Wagnerian tenor, began as a metalworker.

Walter Widdop, English tenor, began as a wool-dyer.

Erich Zimmermann, a *buffo* tenor, painted porcelain at the Meissen factory.

And so these difficult, intense studies continue—training the voice, developing musicianship, improving memory and concentration, learning how to act, to project, to move on the stage, and all this accompanied by—God willing—an unfolding of the soul without which there can be no great singing.

How long do the studies last? A purist would reply, as long as the career itself, for a true artist never ceases to continue to perfect his technique and his art as long as his career endures. As I have said, nowadays laments go up that young singers do not study long enough and by singing in public with an imperfect technique soon throw away their voices. There are the usual references to the golden age of bel canto when one *castrato*, Nicola Porpora, taught another, Gaetano Caffarelli, the same set of exercises for six years, at the end of which he is supposed to have said, "Go, my son, you have no more to learn. You are the finest singer of Italy and of the world."

Tetrazzini in her memoirs claims that she studied only one year, though she grew up in an atmosphere that exposed her to opera throughout her childhood. The great tenor Richard Tauber studied a mere two years before his debut in Freiburg, Germany, as did Jerome Hines when he first appeared in small parts with the San Francisco Opera. Mary Garden had two teachers and three years of training before her dramatic substitute debut in Paris as Louise on Friday the thirteenth of January 1900. Eames studied about five years. Melba worked six or seven with a teacher in Australia before coming to Mathilde Marchesi, who seems to have done little more than polish her. Flagstad credits three teachers over a six-and-a-half-year span for her flawless vocal technique, though in addition both her parents were musicians. The Italians Renata Tebaldi and Luciano Pavarotti both devoted approximately six years of their lives to vocal study. The Canadian tenor Edward Johnson went through five singing teachers in over a dozen years before making a successful operatic debut in Italy at the age of thirty-four. To train her enormous, sumptuous soprano voice, Helen Traubel declares that she studied seventeen years with one teacher, her "second mother," Madame Vetta-Karst, performing the same scales and exercises throughout this entire span of time. There seems no ready answer then, to the question of how long a singer should pursue his studies before appearing in public, since it depends much on his original vocal endowment, together with his musical background, education and general aptitude.

Meanwhile as the training progresses, the feelings of a fine teacher who succeeds in molding a lovely voice and vocal art can readily be imagined. This voice beomes his creation, like a child whom he has come to love and whose every need he understands perfectly. Because the teacher-student relationship is such a close one, it can be subject to all the strains of intimacy itself, but with one difference; at any time a promising student with a voice that the teacher cannot help feeling he has created, may take that voice away and never bring it back, leaving the teacher to feel as betrayed as a rejected lover. A number of reasons can bring about this for the teacher disillusioning and embittering defection, the simplest being that the student decides after several years that the demands of a career are too great. Or perhaps the money for his training has run out with no possible source of any more. Female students marry and give up the idea of singing professionally in the interests of a husband and a family. Impatient students may develop their voices to a point and then leave the teacher for easy money in show business. Such is the close relationship between teacher and pupil that an ill-judged criticism, a tactless personal comment can send a sensitive pupil in flight from the studio never to return. Every singing teacher of any merit will have his stories of students who might have been a glory in the singing world, but who betrayed or were lost forever through pressure of outside circumstances.

Spending several hours each week in a fervent joint search for a vocal technique and art, it is not surprising that the closely closeted teacher and pupil often develop a strong personal relationship. As has already been pointed out, some women teachers tend to play a motherly role with their students. In the case of the male pedagogue, he too may be cast in an authoritarian paternal image, but he can also enact another part. In "Mr. Reginald Peacock's Day" Katharine Mansfield has left a biting portrait of a vain, unctuous, lecherous voice teacher presumably drawn from her first husband who taught singing. Sometimes, however, out of this situation a meaningful and lasting relationship can arise. One thinks in recent years of Mary Curtis-Verna who married her teacher, and Astrid Varnay, who married Hermann Weigert, her vocal coach.

MARRIAGES BETWEEN SINGERS AND TEACHERS, COACHES, CONDUCTORS, ETC.

Singers often choose mates who are in some way connected with their careers but are not vocal rivals. These marriages would appear to be particularly felicitous, but obviously not always.

Singers	*Spouses*
Adelina Agostinelli (soprano)	Giuseppe Quirolli (teacher)
Emma Albani (soprano)	Ernest Gye (impresario)
Frances Alda (soprano)	Giulio Gatti-Casazza (impersario)
Rose Bampton (soprano)	Wilfred Pelletier (conductor)
Fedora Barbieri (mezzo)	Maestro Barzoletti (impersario)
Louise Beatty (mezzo)	Sydney Homer (composer)
Xenia Belmas (soprano)	Alexander Kitschin (conductor)
Cathy Berberian (soprano)	Luciano Berio (composer)
Teresa Berganza (mezzo)	Felix Brambilla (accompanist)
Lillian Blauvelt (soprano)	Alexander Savine (composer)
Theresa Brambilla (soprano)	Amilcare Ponchielli (composer)
Jean Browning (mezzo)	Francis Madeira (conductor)
Muriel Brunskill (mezzo)	Robert Ainsworth (conductor)
Marion Claire (soprano)	Henry Weber (conductor)
Isabella Colbran (mezzo)	Gioacchino Rossini (composer)
Hedwig von Debicka (soprano)	Pietro Stermich de Valcrociata (conductor)
Anton Dermota (tenor)	Hilde Berger-Weyerwald (pianist-accompanist)
Blanche Deschamps-Jehin (contralto)	Léon Jehin (conductor)
Mignon Dunn (mezzo)	Kurt Klipstaetter (conductor-coach)
Ludmilla Dvoráková (soprano)	Rudolf Vasata (conductor)
Minnie Egener (soprano)	Louis Hasselmans (conductor)
Elise Elizza (soprano)	Adolf Limley (teacher)
Cato Engelen-Sewing (soprano)	Henry Engelen (impresario)
Birgit Engell (soprano)	Hans Erwin Hey (teacher)
Dietrich Fischer-Dieskau (baritone)	Irmgard Popper (cellist)
Thérèse Foerster (soprano)	Victor Herbert (composer)
Helena Forti (soprano)	Walter Bruno Iltz (*régisseur*)
Amelita Galli-Curci (soprano)	Homer Samuels (pianist)
Marguerite Giraud (scprano)	Albert Carré (impresario)
Alma Gluck (soprano)	Efrem Zimbalist (violinist)

Singers	Spouses
Marie Gutheil-Schoder	Gustav Gutheil (conductor)
Marilyn Horne (mezzo)	Henry Lewis (conductor)
Maria Ivogün (soprano)	Michael Raucheisen (accompanist)
Helen Jepson (soprano)	George Possel (flutist)
Barbara Kemp (soprano)	Max von Schillings (composer-conductor)
Auguste Krauss (soprano)	Anton Seidl (conductor)
Annelies Kupper (soprano)	Joachim Herrmann (accompanist)
Frida Leider (soprano)	Rudolf Deman (violinist)
Zélie de Lussan (soprano)	Angelo Fronani (pianist)
Maria Malibran (soprano)	Charles De Bériot (violinist)
Lucille Marcel (soprano)	Felix Weingartner (conductor)
Edith Mason (soprano)	Giorgio Polacco (conductor)
Susan Metcalfe (contralto)	Pablo Casals (cellist)
Zinka Milanov (soprano)	Ljubomir Ilic (teacher)
Audrey Mildmay (soprano)	John Christie (impresario)
Caroline Miolan-Carvalho (soprano)	Léon Carvalho (impresario)
Anna Moffo (soprano)	Mario Lanfranchi (*régisseur*)
Agnes Nichols (soprano)	Hamilton Harty (conductor)
Elena Nikolaidi (mezzo)	Tanos Melos (teacher)
Lily Pons (soprano)	Andre Kostelanetz (conductor)
Elena Rakowska (soprano)	Tullio Serafin (conductor)
Delia Reinhardt (soprano)	Georges Sebastian (conductor)
Jane Rhodes (soprano)	Roberto Benzi (conductor)
Leonie Rysanek (soprano)	Rudolf Grossmann (teacher)
Therese Schnabel-Behr (contralto)	Artur Schnabel (pianist)
Grete Schneidt (soprano)	Jacques Stückgold (teacher)
Elisabeth Schumann (soprano)	Karl Alwin (conductor)
Renata Scotto (soprano)	Lorenzo Anselmi (coach)
Irmgard Seefried (soprano)	Wolfgang Schneiderhan (violinist)
Maria Stader (soprano)	Hans Erismann (conductor)
Hanny Steffek (soprano)	Albert Moser (impresario)
Giuseppina Strepponi (soprano)	Giuseppe Verdi (composer)
Joan Sutherland (soprano)	Richard Bonynge (conductor)

Singers	Spouses
Tarquinia Tarquini (mezzo)	Riccardo Zandonai (composer)
Viorica Ursuleac (soprano)	Clemens Krauss (conductor)
Astrid Varnay (soprano)	Hermann Weigert (coach)
Galina Vishnevskaya (soprano)	Mstislav Rostropovich (cellist)
Carolina White (soprano)	Paolo Longone (teacher)

The years have passed. A fine teacher has been found and a vocal technique mastered, so that the voice is free and ringing and beautiful. The singer now possesses some knowledge of three languages different from his own. He has committed to memory the words and music of a number of operatic roles, as well as a quantity of songs and labored to interpret them persuasively and with sensitivity. He may even have found time to fit in lessons in acting and stage deportment as well. And most miraculously, he has been able to lay his hands on the money to pay for all this expensive training. One might suppose his troubles were over.

The Cold, Cold World. It is one thing for the student singer to work in the teacher's studio—criticized, yes, but also cosseted and given an almost parental feeling of support and belief by the instructor. This is true of a coach. There may be hours of methodical repetitions of phrases, of remonstrances even—"No, no. Not like *that*." Yet always the work will be contained in an atmosphere of approval and with a sense of progress—"Now, now we're getting somewhere."

But once faced with auditions or actual engagements, however small, that involve working with a strange accompanist, conductor, stage director or fellow singers, some of whom may be competitive and even hostile, the fledgling singer discovers what a cold place the world can be outside the studio.

Of all the unnerving aspects of a singing career, auditions are probably the worst. The bare stage, the all-but-empty auditorium in which sit the supreme judges often looking glazed and disinterested, the whole baleful feeling of "it's now or never" is enough to make the young aspirant ask "why, *why* did I get myself into this?" With one aria or song, not even five minutes in length, a singer soars or is grounded. If the voice at that particular moment fails to respond there will only be a chilling "thank you" and that is the end of it. Unless a sensitive listener happens to hear the potential of a voice through the cloudiness that nervousness has laid on it, rarely does a singer have a second chance. (Thomas Stewart, a leading Wagnerian baritone, declared on a recent Metropolitan broadcast, "I've never sung a good audition in my life.")

Even when a singer feels he has sung well there is no applause, none of the response that he has worked so hard to achieve. Instead usually a voice calls out, "Thank you very much. We'll be in touch with you." And that is that.

Auditions in the field of popular singing can be even more degrading. Nothing is more awful than an open call for the casting of the chorus (perhaps twelve male and twelve female singers) in a Broadway musical. Among the several hundred or more who show up, there will be every kind of singer from opera to pop, all seeking the same two things: the security of a good salary for singing eight times a week, and possible recognition. With such a multitude to be heard the auditionist is not permitted to sing through a whole number, though many hopefuls do not know this and look surprised and pained when they are cut off halfway through their song. The experienced auditionist usually begins with the return of the refrain of his number in order to include a top note that he wishes to show off. Sometimes at these auditions, which frequently require a whole morning or afternoon's wait on the part of the hopeful singer, high notes or indeed any kind of notes don't seem really to be on the mind of the producer or casting director at all. Even the men may be asked to strip to the waist and judged on the strength of their less than vocal "cheese cake."

Yet as an introduction to a bulletin entitled *Career Guide for the Young American Singer* in its wisdom points out: "No one likes audition; but no one has found a more satisfactory way for singers to demonstrate their talents efficiently to opera producers, conductors and directors."

This booklet, published by the Central Opera Service of the Metropolitan Opera, Lincoln Center, is an absolute must for the young trained singer embarking on a career. It lists the opera companies of the United States (there are close to a hundred) and

Canada, the names and addresses of the managers and directors and when auditions are held. There are also sections devoted to grants and to vocal competitions. In the latter category there are over ninety. These have varied requirements, residency within the state or region where the competition is taking place being the most common. The prizes range from one hundred dollars and a possible engagement with the local opera company to twenty thousand dollars offered in the name of the late tenor Richard Tucker. There are other great singers so honored: The Rosa Ponselle Awards, the Lauritz Melchior Heldentenor Awards (open to tenors or baritones, prize ten thousand dollars), the Bruce Yarnell Memorial Award (prize one thousand dollars) in honor of the handsome bass-baritone who made a career on Broadway and in films. He died in a plane crash at age 38.

An unusual contest goes under the name of "International Competitions for Excellence in the Performance of American Music." Here the singer must perform "diverse American music . . . written after 1900." The rewards are exceptional, first prize being a "ten thousand dollar cash award for one year; possible five thousand dollars for second year, management and concert tour; and recording contract." Another exceptional contest is a "Music Competition for Blind Artists" held in Fort Worth, Texas which offers a first prize of two thousand dollars.

All this bespeaks a much greater activity on the American vocal scene than one might have supposed. This same Central Opera Service, directed by the apparently indefatigable Maria F. Rich, keeps track of the live operatic performances in the United States during a year. In 1983 these numbered over ten thousand. Many of them were very modest productions indeed put on by the hundreds of workshops and opera groups around the country. Nonetheless for every production there has to be a cast of singers who thus acquired all important vocal and dramatic experience.

Indeed the enthusiasm for great singing in America has never been so great. Though the recital series that used to be so common in local cities may have been cut down, what has taken place are the extraordinary presentations of great singers over television. Who would have guessed it a decade ago? Not this writer; not Karl Trump, president of the National Association of Teachers of Singing whose words were quoted in the first edition of this book published in 1971:

Television is a medium that has shown itself to be stubbornly uninterested in good singing. Its viewpoint remains primarily visual. Though it may occasionally find a place on a variety program for a Birgit Nilsson, it has no confidence in her ability to hold the viewers with her art; it garbs her in exotic gowns and plumed headdresses and distracts our listening as it offers us a kaleidoscope of angle and distance shots that have no relationship to what she is singing. Or it dreams up some way to prove that artists are "just folks": I have not yet forgotten the disappointment I felt when I turned on the television one evening last winter and saw Eileen Farrell and Marilyn Horne disporting themselves with Carol Burnett as the Three Little Pigs!

In the thirteen years since those words appeared millions have come to gather before their television screens with an additional boost of fine sounding simulcast from their stereo sets, to see and hear live opera performances, recitals offering Leontyne Price and Marilyn Horne singing duets, or Luciano Pavarotti or Placido Domingo in fascinating coaching sessions with young singers. Not long ago millions watched a program of young artists from the Metropolitan Opera Studio, the possible singing stars of tomorrow. What made the event particularly special was that the concert was presented by Leontyne Price and took place at the White House before the President and the First Lady thus calling attention to the art of fine singing in an unprecedented way.

Television performances of opera are unique because they offer the viewers details and close-ups that would be lost in the larger stretches of a theater. In addition audiences can follow the operas with subtitles so that people who were never really attracted to Wagner's *Ring*, for example, were absolutely riveted when they could follow the story by captions on the television screen. A spin-off from subtitled performances of opera on television is the use of what are known as "surtitles" flashed above the proscenium in the opera house while the work is presented in the original language.

There is no doubt that these television programs have created a greatly increased interest in opera and singing throughout the country. During the past decade many new local opera companies have been born in the nation, doubtless due in part to the influence of television. In 1931 when the Metropolitan Opera broadcasts began there were those who warned that the box office would suffer when millions could have free access to a live performance. In fact the effect was just the opposite: millions now wanted to attend a live performance of opera. Today the same is true of television. Opera companies, old and new, around the country report that should they schedule a work that is shown nationally on television from the Metropolitan or the New York City Opera, it seems only to encourage people to want to come and see a performance in the theater.

Nevertheless despite these many operatic performances around America and the greater interest in fine singing, aspiring vocalists think big and to them the opportunities in the United States often seem small. "Big" means, of course, the Metropolitan—then the New York City, San Francisco and Chicago Opera companies, all of which have seasons lasting at least a decent portion of the year. After that, the number of performances presented by say, the Baltimore or the Tulsa Opera Companies are much fewer in number—certainly not enough to support a singer in residence even with supplementary concert engagements. For this reason the aspiring American singer may look to Europe as a place offering more opportunities to get ahead. (Again the ever useful *Career Guide for the Young American Singer* lists grants for study abroad and a suprisingly large number of international competitions open to young artists from the United States.)

In Europe, particularly in Germany where there are many opera houses offering a ten-month season in almost every city of any size, he will then have much more of an opportunity to find engagements. Some of today's well-known stars such as Evelyn Lear, Thomas Stewart and Jess Thomas have made their fame and fortune via this road. Tatiana Troyanos and Jessye Norman, both American born, went to Europe, made careers and returned to their native country as stars of the first magnitude. James McCracken, the burly tenor, and Jeannine Altmeyer, a comely soprano, both threw over their contracts with the Metropolitan Opera that called for appearances in small parts and went to Europe. Mr. McCracken became a leading singer in demand for such parts as Otello and Tannhäuser while Miss Altmeyer is a star at Bayreuth. Indeed, there are a number of Americans who have yet to be called back to their native land to sing professionally but are enjoying very respectable European careers.

In years past the young artist who aspired to the more subtle and musically demanding career of a lieder singer, would usually somehow raise the money to hire New York City's Town Hall, or the small recital auditorium in Carnegie Hall. London's equivalent is of course Wigmore Hall. They would have programs and tickets printed, pay for as much publicity as possible, paper the house and sing an afternoon or evening's concert of songs. On the strength of the (hopefully) favorable reviews, they would then attract the attention of one of the concert agents and obtain bookings in all parts of the country. Unhappily, the formula for launching a concert career has begun to change. Agents find increasing difficulty in selling recitals by even the top stars around the country, let alone unknowns. There seems to be altogether less demand for concerts of lieder, with the inevitable result that there are fewer and fewer artists proficient at the art. Nowadays would-be concert singers are advised to try to make some kind of name for themselves in opera, however much they may feel themselves unsuited to it; but with a background of operatic appearances agents feel that they can then obtain for them engagements in the musical field that they find more appealing.

Breaking into the world of church-singing is perhaps simpler than obtaining entrance to some of the other branches of the professional singing world. The young oratorio singer who manages to get a position with an important New York church virtually has it made, for these appearances will inevitably lead to calls from other parts of the country for his services in performances of oratorios and other religious musical works. Like aspiring young opera singers, it is important that the church soloist know the standard repertory such as *Messiah* or *Elijah* and have worked with a coach who specializes in this type of music. Another way for a church singer to get his break is to be taken on by a church agent who will help him to get engagements.

So far we have considered only the training and subsequent struggles to gain notice of the singer of so-called classical music. What about the huge flock of hopeful pop singers?

With the age of the microphone the actual vocal training of a pop singer is unnecessary, providing the voice possesses some kind of appealing or arresting quality. The training of a pop singer consists much more in developing a definite style, a "way" with the words and music of his songs, which, however, most of the great entertainers seem to possess naturally. I have read somewhere the earnest declaration that singing off the beat can be taught—but if this essential timing that is the pulse of any good pop singer's interpretations has to be painstakingly learned, it seems to me that the would-be Frank Sinatra or Ella Fitzgerald had better call the whole thing off.

Ideally the hopeful pop star should have musical training and be able to read music at sight. Many in this hectic age never do, but these are usually the ones who though they may come on strong for a moment or two, vanish with equal rapidity. To make a career that does not burn itself out overnight a pop singer should have coached extensively with a professional who will concentrate on his timing, his expression and teach him an all-important microphone technique to bring out the best in his voice. The pop singer also needs an accompanist with whom he has rapport and an arranger who understands and suits his style. Arrangements are a big expense for a pop singer. In addition to the mandatory photographs and résumés of his appearances, he must also circulate among the powers who control the pop vocal world tapes or demonstration records of his singing and his songs.

We have seen too many movies about the struggles of the unrecognized pop singers to break into "show biz." Unfortunately the difficulties are all too true. It is a big, highly competitive, unfair and very often corrupt business requiring the utmost toughness and determination from the singer hopeful of becoming a star.

Just One Break. With a number of successful auditions that have led to engagements with say the Utah and Hamilton, Ontario, Opera Companies—or if the career is made in Europe, a season at Karlsruhe—the aspiring opera star would seem to be on the way at last. Yet all too often the way seems steep and progress maddeningly slow. The reviews may be good, much experience gained, a large repertory increased. And yet the crown of real stardom still has not been bestowed. In the back of every singer's mind there is another way to glory.

We are in London. A performance of *Madama Butterfly* has been announced for that evening in the fine old opera house at Covent Garden. That afternoon the General Administrator and his staff have been listening to auditions, among them one by an unknown American whom I shall call Lucy. Lucy has a well-trained lyric-*spinto* soprano and unusual dramatic talent. She auditioned for the New York City Opera and they were most encouraging, but since they already had two *spintos* on the roster and a repertory with only three operas calling for this type of voice, they proffered no contract. And where else? Lucy herself realizes that she is not ready for the Metropolitan. She has no experience whatsoever and at best, if they liked her voice, she might be taken on in *comprimario* parts, a potentially dangerous dead end.

So Lucy with the blessing of her teacher and the backing of her family has decided to try her luck abroad. Through a fortunate connection she has obtained an audition with the Covent Garden management, though in England as is true in almost every country, perference is given to a native-born singer. At Covent Garden Lucy has chosen to sing Leonora's last act aria in *Trovatore* to show off the lovely, limpid high *pianissimi* that her teacher has given her. Evidently everything has gone well, for a voice out of the shadowy auditorium has asked Lucy for another aria. In contrast, this time she picks the *Butterfly* "Un bel di" which gives her a chance to display dramatic intensity as well as the beauty of her voice. When this is sung, the same polite British voice thanks her and asks her to leave an address where she can be reached. Nothing more. Gathering up her music, Lucy reminds herself in her disappointment that she is American; with a growing wealth of fine English singers, as in every country, native talent must be served first. But the thought is poor consolation. Returning to her hotel, which is cheap and smells vaguely of mutton fat, she contemplates a lonely dinner, not knowing anyone in London. On the following day there is the prospect of setting out for the Continent and the unknown. Weary from the strain of auditioning, she kicks off her shoes and stretches out on the bed. . . .

In the semi-darkness a telephone is ringing and ringing, mixed with the clack of shoes on the sidewalk below the window. For a moment Lucy cannot think where she is. Then the now strong, permeating smell of the fat rushes into her nostrils: London, and the sound of tapping feet. It must be the rush hour . . . *My telephone?* . . . But no one knows me in London. A vaguely familiar British voice speaks her name in inquiring fashion. "Yes. This is Lucy—" The voice is identified as belonging to the assistant General Administrator of Covent Garden. He was much

impressed by her audition that afternoon and wonders—"Yes?"—
the soprano scheduled to sing Butterfly that evening at Covent
Garden has been struck down by flu. Her "cover" so far cannot be
reached; no one seems to know where she is. The only other
soprano in the country at the moment who knows the part is
unfortunately committed to a concert in Manchester. The management wondered if by any chance Miss—"But I—"would
consent to fill in. "But I—" It is now close to six with the
performance announced for seven-thirty. The curtain could be
held for at least a quarter of an hour.

"I'll be right there."

On the stage of the opera house she is shown the first act set
and where she must make her entrance singing Cio-Cio-San's
difficult music that rises sequentially higher and higher. Photographs of the second and third act set—fortunately the same—are
handed to her together with blocking outlines of her positions
onstage throughout the opera. Also she is shown her props, her
fan, the few possessions that Cio-Cio-San brings with her on her
wedding day, and the knife with which she will eventually stab
herself.

Time begins to run short. The costumes of the ill soprano—
unfortunately a woman larger than Lucy, who still commands a
shapely figure—have somehow to be fitted to her. A man in
American naval uniform comes up and says in broken English
that he will whisper to her where she must go and what she must
do whenever he can. For a moment in the daze of it all Lucy
wonders how the United States Navy has come to hear of her
plight and send rescue until she realizes that this is her Pinkerton
for the evening. A friendly Suzuki with a brisk British accent
appears to wish her luck and say that she too will give guidance
whenever she can.

The nervous opening music of the opera strikes up and before
she knows it, as if time had accelerated, Lucy hears the tremulous
high strains of the violins that signal the entrance of Cio-Cio-San.
She nestles behind the other girls with their parasols as slowly
they begin to move out onto the stage. Still in the wings Lucy
takes breath:

Ancora un passo or via . . .

Next morning she is the talk of London. All the newspapers on
the Continent and in America have carried accounts of her

triumphant feat. She is launched, on her way to a fabulous career . . . stardom. . . .

A crash, a tinkle of glass of two taxis colliding in the rush hour. The clack of heels on the paving stones and from far off the sound of Big Ben striking the hour. Our student stirs on her lumpy bed. Of course it was all a dream.

Many years ago in Paris, Mary Garden did just what Lucy dreamed, and went on without a rehearsal in the third act of *Louise* as an absolute unknown never having appeared on the operatic stage before. But now in this age of the jet such dramatic substitutions are almost unheard of. When the tenor engaged to open the 1983 fall season of the San Francisco Opera became ill at the last moment, Placido Domingo flew out from New York, bucking head winds, while the curtain was held until he arrived to save the performance—and an unknown who might have stepped in and become famous overnight was done out of the opportunity.

In recent operatic history an unknown soprano, Linda Zoghby rushed in to cover a Mimi in *La Bohème* when Teresa Stratas was indisposed. But she did not achieve fame and fortune. When the Connecticut Opera recently staged a gala *Aida* in the huge Hartford Arena, an Italian soprano was engaged to sing the name part. A truncated version in English as a special children's performance was assigned to the American *spinto* soprano Viviane Thomas who having gained considerable European experience singing seasons at Berne and Karlsruhe had returned to the United States to try to sing her way to stardom in her native country.

On the afternoon of the Italian prima donna's second performance she became ill and the frantic management called Miss Thomas in New York City to ask if she could sing the full version of the opera in Italian and without any rehearsal. Miss Thomas could and did—triumphantly, and this at a time when experts were lamenting that there were no sopranos around any more who could sing Aida.

Hartford is located within the Boston–Washington megalopolis. Viviane Thomas's huge success did not go unnoticed. And yet no flood of offers came in; there was no triumphant rise to the stardom of every artist's dreams. Engagements continued in Toronto as Chrysothemis in Strauss's *Elektra* and Lady Macbeth in

Reno. But only a year later was she finally engaged by the New York City Opera, a major company with a long season thus making a big advance in the long struggle to the top.

So, struggle it is. And even when artists achieve fame in one particular country, the ultimate international recognition may still be denied them. In this respect the history of the Metropolitan Opera Company has always been puzzling. Too often very great artists have been hired only late in their careers if at all. One of the finest basses of all time, Alexander Kipnis did not sing with the New York company until he was forty-nine. And the remarkable Beverly Sills, possessor of a peerless technique combined with rare dramatic ability only made her debut at the Metropolitan in 1975 when she was just short of forty-six. "I simply did not care very much for her," is the rather lame explanation General Manager Rudolf Bing offers for her exclusion in his memoir, *A Knight at the Opera*. He also had on the roster two other stars who sang Miss Sills's repertory, Joan Sutherland and Monserrat Caballé. This brings us back to the element of luck that continues to fly over every singer's career either like a lovely dove or an evil raven.

Keeping Out. Even a company with as long a season as the Metropolitan has a place on its roster for only a certain number of singers of each kind of voice. And when a star has become established and is a favorite with audiences, that star tends to keep out others who sing the same repertory. During the years that Caruso reigned at the Metropolitan, for example, a number of gifted tenors who had to all intents and purposes "made it"— the American Riccardo Martin is a good example—sang at the famous theater but did not achieve careers of long endurance. During more or less the same seasons, Louise Homer dominated the mezzo repertory and no one could depose her. One who tried was another American, Edyth Walker, a fine artist who eventually became a dramatic soprano. But not at the Metropolitan. She returned to Europe and made a distinguished career there mainly in Germany. Another American mezzo with a fine voice, Florence Wickham, tried to buck Louise Homer at the Metropolitan for three seasons before giving up and turning to light opera. In Reginald De Koven's *Robin Hood* she made "O promise me" famous.

A soprano who did not feel called to compete against such potential rivals as Nordica, Eames, Fremstad and Gadski was the San Francisco-born Maude Fay, who made a very fine if not international career, again almost entirely in Germany where she was dubbed "Königliche Bayerische Hopofersangerin" by the Prince Regent of Bavaria. A singing actress of great magnetism, she is said to have been the model for the improbable novel about a Wagnerian soprano called *Tower of Ivory* by Gertrude Atherton.

This "keeping out" trick of destiny runs through the whole history of the Metropolitan Opera. The great Italian baritone Riccardo Stracciari sang only two seasons in New York. He was kept out by Scotti and Amato. The superb basso Tancredi Pasero lasted only five years because Ezio Pinza dominated the repertory. The fine lyric-coloratura Toti Dal Monte sang but a single season because Galli-Curci was already ensconced. There can be no doubt that the presence of Kirsten Flagstad on the roster, not to speak of Marjorie Lawrence, delayed the debut of Helen Traubel in Wagnerian roles at the Metropolitan until she was forty. Fate, however, gave Traubel's career a second important twist.

In the same year that she made her debut, 1939, war was declared in Europe. Two years later Flagstad decided to go back to her native Norway to be with her husband; Marjorie Lawrence was stricken with polio and Helen Traubel gained the entire Wagnerian repertory to herself. Since World War II dried up any possibility of the Metropolitan engaging European-trained singers, this turn of history undoubtedly gave many relatively inexperienced American singers such as Eleanor Steber, Risë Stevens, Jan Peerce and Leonard Warren the opportunity to show what they could do.

As has been mentioned, since there are just so many operas in the repertory and just so many roles in these operas, the jockeying for leading parts can well be imagined, also the feelings between rival singers who after all are not people of exactly inhibited emotions. Fremstad and Gadski who sang more or less the same repertory appeared together one night in *Walküre* during which Gadski managed to draw literally the blood of the other diva. Fremstad's clever retaliation during the curtain calls was to put her arm around the German soprano, thus calling the attention and sympathy of the audience to her wound besides thoroughly staining her colleague's costume. Was it Gadski then who sent Fremstad a note containing sneezing powder to her dressing room just before curtain time, knowing that one sneeze can loosen floods of unwanted phlegm and wreak general havoc to the singing voice for several hours? The teller of this tale does not say. Nor does Helen Traubel in her memoirs hint at the name of the person who mixed ground glass into a jar of cold cream which she was about to use to make up for her evening's performance.

The world of pop singing is not immune to unpleasantnesses either. Ethel Waters relates how when she appeared on the same bill with Bessie Smith she was prevented by the older star from performing her different "non-shouting" style of blues singing. The audience clamored for it, however, and Bessie Smith had to relent. Later, after the engagement she called the younger singer to her and said, "You ain't so bad. It's only that I never dreamed that anyone would be able to do this to me in my own territory and with my own people. And you know damn well you can't sing worth a ******."

Ethel Waters doesn't seem to have been any more generous to upcoming rivals and bumped Billie Holiday from a show in Philadelphia because she auditioned "Underneath the Harlem Moon," a Waters specialty.

As long as there are superb singers who sing the same repertory there will be rivalries and jealousies which the public very much enjoys (such as the supposed enmity between Callas and Tebaldi). Similarly the keeping-out process will continue to take place. Recently there was much comment as to why the Metropolitan debut of Samuel Ramey, the American bass-baritone who had made a fine career in Europe and also at the New York City Opera, had been so long delayed. But the company already had a particularly rich selection of basses and bass-baritones including John Cheek, Simon Estes, Nicolai Ghiaurov, Bonaldo Giaiotti, Jerome Hines, James Morris, Paul Plishka, Ruggiero Raimondi and Martti Talvela. When Ramey at last did appear in the Metropolitan's first production of a Handel opera, *Rinaldo*, in January 1984, it turned out to be the triumphant debut of which every singer dreams.

Debut. As has been said it is the fantasy of many young singers struggling to gain recognition that they will be "discovered" under dramatic conditions and gain stardom in one night. The last such happening of this kind occurred at the Metropolitan in November, 1950 when a nineteen-year-old soprano was thrust into the part of Zerlina on five hours' notice and with no orchestra rehearsal. She had worked the part thoroughly with the stage director, Herbert Graf, the previous autumn, but she had never before set foot on an operatic stage. This was Roberta Peters who instantly proved that she was born to it. On the other hand if she had made her debut as scheduled there is no doubt that she would have gained equal, though less sensational recognition of her vocal and histrionic talent. Her real break was in 1) making a successful audition at the Metropolitan and 2) that the company in this season was giving a number of student performances of *Zauberflöte* and needed an exceptional soprano voice such as Peters possessed to sing the Queen of the Night as well as to cover the regular performances of Erna Berger, the reigning coloratura at the Metropolitan of the time.

For most singers a debut will be inconspicuous in America, at best, with the New York City Opera; in England, with the National Opera. Both companies have proved to be an accommodating stepping stone to the larger New York and London houses for a number of singers. In America a debut can also be made with local companies, which however present only a few performances and therefore provide only limited experience for young artists anxious to sing as many times as possible. This, as I have already pointed out, is the advantage of going to a country such as Germany, with its numerous opera houses, to gain a start. The pay in the various theaters is mostly not much and very often young singers find themselves called upon to sing in unknown operas such as *Der Liebestrank* or *Bajazzo*—until they discover that these are none other than the familiar *L'Elisir d'Amore* and *Pagliacci* as performed in German. The pervasive and disciplined musicianship of the Teuton, above all the experience of singing evening after evening before the public returns ample rewards and also offers total immersion in at least one language vital to a singer.

In Europe the young artist need fear far less the rut of *comprimario* roles than he might at the Metropolitan. The soprano who sings Violetta's maid one night may quickly make her way to Musetta the next and perhaps Mimi six months later. Thus, some small European opera house is probably the best and most likely place for the debut to be made—quietly, undramatically and probably with no stupendous response from the public. The extraordinary, long-lived baritone Sir Charles Santley as far back as 1857 made his debut in the tiny role of the Doctor in *La Traviata* at Pavia. Giglio Nordica, as she called herself in 1879, made her debut with an inferior opera company at Milan singing Donna Elvira in *Don Giovanni*, which at that time was considered a secondary role. The nervous debutante was the only one of the Don's pursued and pursuing ladies not to be hissed. Melba made no great splash in her debut role of Gilda at La Monnaie, the theater in Brussels, while Louise Homer first tried out the experience of singing and acting on stage with a full orchestra in the pit at Vichy. Of the great English-speaking singers in that era only one, as she puts it, seems to have gone on stage "a nobody" and found herself "the next day the talk of two continents." This was Emma Eames who made her first appearance in a theater anywhere at the Paris Opéra, 14 March, 1889 as Gounod's Juliette, having been coached by the composer himself. Two other Marchesi pupils, Suzanne Adams and Bessie Abott, also debuted in this role at the Opéra but neither achieved the glowing stardom of Eames, though judging from their phonograph records their voices were lovely. Geraldine Farrar, offered a contract to sing small parts at the Metropolitan, turned it down for European training and experience, confident that one day she would sweep back across the Atlantic as a reigning prima donna, which of course she did.

It was really not until 1918 in her triumphant debut at the New York Metropolitan Opera House that Rosa Ponselle proved that it wasn't absolutely essential for English-speaking singers to undergo European training and experience, but she of course was a phenomenon. Earlier, however, an attractive soprano from New Jersey, Anna Case, had already broken the shibboleth when she made her debut in 1909 at the Metropolitan singing small parts. In 1913 she was much admired as Sophie in the New York premiere of *Der Rosenkavalier*. Over the years singers who had never soaked up the atmosphere of Europe began to trickle into the Metropolitan, including Lawrence Tibbett, Gladys Swarthout, Helen Jepson and Helen Traubel, to enumerate some of the stars of the late nineteen-twenties and thirties.

Since extra strain accompanies a debut certain roles are often favored to introduce new singers. Mimi is a graceful, untaxing part in which to introduce the lyric or *spinto* soprano. Heavier voiced sopranos often make their bows as Sieglinde, while the *leggiero* or coloratura may be heard first in the relatively undemanding part of Gilda. Gilda's Duke and Mimi's Rodolfo are popular tenor debut roles, while a new baritone may appear for the first time singing the smooth, non-arduous music of the elder Germont in *Traviata*.

Whatever the part and wherever it is sung, the debut, even if it earns splendid critical acclaim, is just that—a first appearance, a beginning. Now the singer is faced with yet another challenge, that of establishing himself.

Drop-Outs. "The following season [after her debut] Miss Ponselle slipped slowly backward. When she sang with Caruso in the memorable revival of *La Juive*, we said: 'Miss Ponselle did not fulfill her promise of last season. Her voice sounded much more constrained and less noble in tone, while her action was primitive indeed . . .'

"Miss Ponselle continued her descent for a considerable period . . ."

These were comments in retrospect by an astute vocal critic, W. J. Henderson, on the career of one of history's greatest singers. What happened to Ponselle, thrust totally inexperienced before the public in a leading opera house and expected to fulfill all that her debut had promised, is, on a less flamboyant level, the experience of many singers after their initially successful debut. As has been pointed out, until the debut the singer has led a life in the studio, protected and encouraged by his teacher and his coach, his faults scolded but forgiven, his virtues touted. Now he is out in a chilling world, facing audiences that may be sympathetic but who after all have paid their admission prices and expect a reasonable degree of professionalism from the fledgling singer. In the studio a faulted note, a muffed entrance can be repeated—not so in performance. And should mistakes occur during rehearsals there is the far from tolerant conductor to deal with besides the weary scorn of the other, more experienced singers, who do not relish having to repeat duets or ensembles because of the rawness of their new colleague.

The first professional years, the ones after the debut, then, require tremendous physical and psychological adjustments on the part of the singer launched on a career. For the first time he realizes that he no longer quite owns himself: one part now belongs to the opera house that holds him under contract, and another belongs to the public itself. His life is partly planned by the General Manager as to what days he must sing, or to stand by covering other performers* in case of an indisposition. There are also rehearsals and even if he does not participate in them he may be required to sit out front and watch the blocking of the part currently being performed by an older leading artist, a role, naturally, to which the young singer aspires. Of the two, the junior singer will probably think bitterly and often rightly that he possesses the fresher voice, but he finds that maddeningly, the management will not scrap older, experienced artists no longer in their prime, but who have served the company faithfully and well, in favor of raw youth. So he must sit there fuming, prevented from appearing for lack of experience, but having no other means of obtaining it.

In these first arduous professional years, the young singer's voice is also subject to far rougher treatment than in the days of its training when his various masters handled it with sympathetic care. Now he may be asked to learn a role that does not lie well for him but which he dares not refuse. Singing the whole time with orchestra, too, is quite different from letting the voice soar over a single piano. He may be called upon to rehearse the day before or after the evening of a performance or sometimes on the very day itself. In these years he learns how to husband his voice, to sing through a rehearsal *piano*, and "mark" his high notes, which means to sing them an octave down. (Melba never sang her high notes while practicing or in rehearsal, believing like a penurious miser that she only had so many and when one was spent it was gone forever.) Because of this extra strain singers who reveal fresh, lovely voices at their debuts sometimes go "off" in the years that immediately follow. Due to over-singing and the strain of numerous public appearances in a competition-ridden opera

---

*The Metropolitan requires that "covers" be no further than twenty minutes from the opera house until the last entrance of the singer for whom they are covering. For this service the stand-by singer receives a fee.

house, the quality may become shrill or coarse and the voice sound strained and fatigued.

There have also been young singers who have made it to the top, but finding the grind and discipline not rewarding enough have turned to show business or night club work. In former times both Fritzi Scheff and Lina Abarbanell sang at the Metropolitan but left it for fame and stardom in operetta. During the season of 1943–44 Christine Johnson, a young American with a luscious, beautifully trained contralto voice made her debut at the Metropolitan as Erda in *Das Rheingold*. The reviews were very favorable and much was expected of her. Offered an attractive part the following year in Rodgers and Hammerstein's new musicial *Carousel*, Miss Johnson became the first of many to give out the joyous "June is bustin' out all over." But after the run of the musical she was never heard at the Metropolitan again and her career simply dissolved.

The reaction of her teacher, one of the most distinguished and conscientious in the field, can be imagined.

Sometimes young singers burst upon the musical scene—a "meteor" is usually the image conjured up in connection with them—and after a few years before the public burn themselves out. One of these whose memory is still revered was the great French singing actress Marie Cornélie Falcon who made a sensational debut in 1832 when not quite nineteen at the Paris Opéra and thereafter attracted an adoring public every time she sang. Five years after her debut, she was appearing opposite the tenor Nourrit in an opera based on the life of Alessandro Stradella when at the end of the first act she opened her mouth to sing and nothing came out but a kind of strangled cry. The soprano went white and Nourrit is said to have gripped her by her shoulders in order to hold her up until the curtain could be rung down. Falcon went to Italy in an attempt to retrain her voice but it had been irreparably damaged by singing too much with a faulty vocal technique, as a single reappearance in 1840 gave sad testimony.

Another in more recent times who came and went amid the most tremendous publicity was the young coloratura soprano, Marion Talley, who made her debut at the Metropolitan in February 1926 at the age of nineteen—one for which she was patently not ready. Though youthful and attractive in voice and appearance, her technique was faulty and her musicianship insecure. Talley lasted four seasons at the Metropolitan, each one with successively fewer appearances—and was not heard from again.

In the 1960's a dynamic *spinto* born of a Russian mother and a

Giuseppina Strepponi, soprano and wife of Giuseppe Verdi.

Greek father burst on the operatic scene while she was still in her early twenties. This was Elena Suliotis, who made a particular success at La Scala in the excruciatingly difficult part of Abigaille*

---

*The soprano Giuseppina Strepponi, later Verdi's wife, apparently ruined her voice in the same part.

in Verdi's *Nabucco*. Forcing her voice injudiciously, this highly gifted artist soon vanished, not to be heard again.

V

> . . . .*And then the justice,*
> *In fair round belly with good capon lin'd,*
> *With eyes severe and beard of formal cut. . . .*
> . . . .
> *And so he plays his part.*

Once the precarious period of adjusting to the strains of professional life is safely past, the existence of the singer settles down into a more predictable pattern, but one which to ordinary people would seem very strange and irregular. Now the singer's life is completely dominated by the demands of his voice: it is the master he must serve, the sometimes querulous mistress that he must humor and cajole, the child that must be tended and coddled and looked after with loving care. The entire being of the dedicated singer is concentrated on his next performance, and when it is finished the one after that. In between there is daily practice which varies from singer to singer. Some spare their voices and sing for themselves as little as possible; others believe it efficacious to vocalize regularly up to an hour a day or even more. (To maintain the flexibility of the voice a coloratura or mezzo-soprano for the length of her singing career is a slave to exercises; not so other singers.) Then there are rehearsals* and sessions with coaches at the opera house or work with the singer's own coach and accompanist. Scores already committed to memory have to be reviewed and new ones learned. Nowadays, costumes are usually part of an overall operatic production and supplied by the opera company; in former days they were not, but expressed, exclusively, the singer and his tastes. In any case costumes have to be tried on and fitted. Women singers also require flattering dresses for their concert appearances. Interviews and public appearances have never been thought harmful to a singer's career; letters must be answered, photographs autographed and managers and agents dealt with, particularly if the artist is a big star. All of these activities come together in a

---

*In former times stars often avoided rehearsals to spare their voices. It is said that Patti never went to a rehearsal in her whole career.

kind of lump which provides a routine for a singer—albeit a knobby, irregular one—but a routine that requires a very strict kind of discipline.

If the singer should try to forget all these impositions on his life by say, going to a party, it is not easy to relax totally. Among a large group may be some traitor with a cold. Drink, a usually reliable provider of relaxation, has to be taken judiciously and rich food regarded with suspicion. A full night's sleep, naturally, is essential to a singer's vocal health.

From these pressures and feelings of not really belonging to themselves, there is no surcease for the man or woman who has chosen to become a serious, dedicated singer. On the one hand he is owned by his voice; on the other he is possessed by his public who are free to applaud or withhold their approval as they see fit. Only a decision to take a month or two off and totally "forget" can provide a singer with temporary relief from this unusual human condition in which he has worked so hard to embroil himself. But even then, relaxing somewhere in the country and not singing at all (a hiatus, by the way, that can have a most salubrious effect on the voice of a hard-working artist), the thought of next season cannot be totally forgotten: new roles . . . perhaps an engagement in a different, more important opera house . . . an increased number of recital dates . . .   ·

Tremors and Terrors. Throughout a singing career there is one ever-present nemesis: nerves.

"I have never been nervous in all my life and I have no patience with people who are," declared Mary Garden in her autobiography. Caruso's opinion then cannot have been very high of her (their careers coincided, but they did not sing together) for he is on record as saying, "The artist who boasts he is never nervous is not an artist—he is a liar or a fool." Singers obviously vary in their capacity for nervousness, just as people do. We have already discussed Rosa Ponselle's psychological state before a performance. Another who trembled and shook prior to and upon her first entrance was the thin, petite coloratura soprano Lily Pons. Her voice always wavered noticeably until she gained assurance. Was this because like a whippet she had so little flesh to cover her nerve endings? Franco Corelli's nervous state was such that he could not attend concerts by *other singers* lest he raise sympathetic spasms of tension in his own throat. Corelli also suffered terribly from insomnia. Carlo Bergonzi sometimes cancelled out of fright.

When it comes to nervousness nature sets a cruel and cunning trap for a singer. Anyone who has ever undergone an "attack of nerves" knows that the two immediate reactions of the body are a shortness of breath and trembling, both of which immediately affect the quality of the voice. In addition, nervousness inhibits the glands that lubricate the mouth with saliva, so much so that the tongue can stick to the roof of the mouth. The larynx also needs its lubrication of mucus and this too dries up under conditions of fear. Any or all these reactions can and do have a disastrous effect on the singing voice.

Nor does the plight of the nervous singer end there. As a British laryngologist points out: "The larynx to the singer is what the hands are to the surgeon, limbs to the dancer or eyes to the marksman. But unlike the latter, the singer's throat is subject to a multitude of strange sensations which he usually tries to analyse, often with the handicap of very erroneous ideas of structure, function and what he calls 'voice production.' Almost assuredly he becomes obsessed with such notions, which serve only to increase his anxiety and may lead to injurious habits or treatments."

In short the nervous student singer or professional is trapped by a vicious circle. One or two lessons, or performances, when the voice has not come out with a free and ringing tone but sounds labored and of poor quality will set him to worrying. Something has gone wrong with his vocal technique, he decides (particularly if he does not possess a particularly secure one). In this state of worry he works to correct what is wrong and by his anxiety only makes matters worse.

The ordinary tensions and problems of everyday living can also affect the voice. A teacher with a promising pupil who suddenly goes into a slump will do well in his role as counselor and confessor to inquire gently into the circumstances of the student's life. He may not at all be surprised to discover the damaging presence of an unhappy love affair, or perhaps extreme worry over finances. Heightened emotions also affect the voice so that it trembles and becomes distorted. For this reason during a performance singers must never lose themselves completely, say, in the tragedy of Violetta's plight or the angers of Otello, lest the quality of the voice be too much affected. Singers must sometimes sing over the griefs of real life. The day after the dress rehearsal of the Vienna première of *Arabella* Lotte Lehmann's mother died. There was no cover for the part, so, in her own words:

". . . I sang at the première . . . There were moments when I forgot the sorrow I bore, whose magnitude only those can realize who have been attached to their mother as I was to mine . . . I was no longer Lotte Lehmann, a daughter bowed down with grief. I was Arabella . . .

"Immeasurable boon of being an artist!

"Only when I got home did I break down and weep."

With the approach of each performance the same unconscious questions begin to mobilize: "Am I in voice?" "Am I sure of my words? my music?" "How will the audience react to me?" To make a singing career is to have to undergo the exactions of nervous tension until the last note is uttered.

On Stage! The day of the performance finds the singer trans-formed into a monastic figure, refusing human contact as much as he possibly can. Mrs. Caruso describes grippingly how the famous tenor passed the slow, stretched out hours before an appearance: "On the day of a performance there was no music in the house and Enrico rarely spoke. Through the silent hours he played solitaire, drew caricatures and sorted the rare collection of gold coins he had begun in 1907 . . . The only occupations that relaxed and amused him were those in which he could use his hands. . . ."

Many artists do not sing or even speak on the day they are to appear, contenting themselves with a few scales in the morning to confirm that the voice is "there." Two noted Wagnerian sopranos made an exception to this routine of silence. Frida Leider would get her voice up early in the day with soft arpeggios, then study her role of the evening silently, after which, as she says in her autobiography, "I would sing the most difficult parts. The arduous training in the morning made me feel secure for the evening performance, *if I was in good form* [italics mine]"—that conditional clause which inevitably qualifies the performance of every singer. Helen Traubel, even more astonishingly, says she would go over the whole long Wagnerian role that she was to sing in the evening at full volume—a practice that would appall most

singers. Wildest of all pre-preformance routines is one attributed
to the mercurial Maria Malibran who thought nothing of staying
up the entire night before a performance dancing at a ball. Then
she would sleep to noon and ride horseback all afternoon.

The problem of what to eat is also a vexing one. A singer needs
his strength; on the other hand a full stomach restricts deep
breathing, while any kind of digestive disorder will of course
disrupt song entirely. Usually then, singers on the day of a
performance will restrict themselves to a light, simple meal in the
middle of the afternoon. Beverly Sills, Leontyne Price and Jan
Peerce all report that they would have a steak and salad around
four P.M. Again, the redoubtable Traubel describes how she
shocked a fellow singer by devouring a bag of peanuts and an ice
cream cone not long before a Hollywood Bowl concert. Even she,
however, imposed on herself the recluselike standards to which
most singers resort, refusing to see anyone or talk on the
telephone.

Finally the time for departure to the theater is reached. Many
singers like to get to the dressing room early to make sure that
their costumes are perfectly in order, to warm up their voices and
commune with or propitiate whatever gods they feel have control
over the quality of the night's performance. Much has been
written of the dressing room rivalries on evenings when an opera
such as *Don Giovanni* is presented, involving three prima donnas
and perhaps a single star dressing room. At the old Metropolitan,
Geraldine Farrar obviated any competition by having her own
dressing room fitted up for her. It was little larger than a cubicle
but it was hers and she kept it padlocked when not using it. At
the old Metropolitan too, Rosa Ponselle used to cause consterna-
tion among the other singers, ever fearful of catching cold, by
demanding that the steam heat, which she disliked intensely, be
shut off.

Within the dressing room the final, sometimes very odd,
routines are accomplished. Caruso, for example, on seeing his
wife, who came later when his make-up was already in place,
would become calm and ask "for a cigarette which he smoked
slowly in a long black holder.

"When he had finished the cigarette he went to the washstand
and filled his mouth with salt water, which he inhaled—or
seemed to inhale into his lungs, then spat out before he strangled.

The temperamental and volatile Maria Malibran, who died at the age of
twenty-eight.

Mario (his valet) held out a box of Swedish snuff from which he
took a pinch to clear his nostrils; then he took a wineglass of
whiskey, next a glass of charged water and finally a quarter of an
apple. Into the pockets that were placed in every costume exactly
where his hands dropped, he slipped two bottles of warm salt

water, in case he had to wash his throat on stage. When all was ready Mario handed him his charms—a twisted coral horn, holy medals and old coins, all linked together on a fat little chain . . . Just before he left the dressing room he called upon his dead mother for help, since the thought of her gave him courage. No one ever wished him luck because, he said, that was sure to bring disaster."

With all their training and experience during these last moments before their entrance many singers lapse back into faith in spells and superstitions. All has become totally fatalistic. Tetrazzini's barometer was a dagger that she used in *Lucia di Lammermoor* and which one night when she was singing at her best had fallen from her hand and stuck upright in the floor. Thereafter the tormenting test had to be made before each performance: if the dagger landed flat—*downfall!* Some singers rely on fetish objects such as a doll or a toy animal to bring them luck. These have to be touched before leaving the dressing room or else worn or carried during the performance. Others spread out photographs of their families and solemnly kiss the faces of the loved ones before going off to perform the night's vocal work. An amusing story of a singer's superstition is told by George Marek in his collection of little pieces called *A Front Seat at the Opera:*

"Selma Kurz, the Viennese coloratura, believed that she would sing well if she saw a chimney-sweep before the performance. Her manager used to hire one to saunter accidentally past the stage door. On one occasion, seeing the sooted man, she called him over, reached into her purse, and gave him a tip; whereupon the honest fellow said, 'Not necessary, Madame. I have already been paid.'"

As the time of the performance approaches most singers now try out their voices at full volume in a series of whoops and howls that have been much mocked over the ages. Each artist will have his own pet way of warming up—scales, arpeggios, hummed notes or singing odd-sounding syllables—"oh Oh! OH; Tee-Tee-Tee" sounded on different pitches. Others may sing snatches of a song or even a bit of the role they are about to perform. This process of warming up as with an athlete loosens and tones up muscles connected with the vocal process and brings blood into the throat, increasing the resonance and ring of the singing voice.

Certain operatic roles give the singer no opportunity to get the feel of his voice onstage before he must launch into a famous and difficult aria. The tenor cast as Radames leads off with the recitative of "Celeste Aida" having sung a bare fifteen measures before the aria. The mezzo portraying Azucena doesn't even have that: she simply begins "Stride la Vampa" without any vocal introduction of any kind. This same mezzo must also begin her entrance as Carmen with the tricky melodic pattern of the "Habanera" made even more difficult by the fact that she is usually positioned up a flight of steps far back on the stage so that it is difficult to hear the orchestra. On these nights when the singer must jump into a famous aria "cold," extra warming up may take place in the dressing room. Pity the poor soprano who sings the *Siegfried* Brünnhilde; no matter how much preliminary vocalizing she may have done, she still has to lie for many minutes silent on her rock,* while her hero accomplishes her rescue and puzzles over the fact that she is not a man.

Finally the moment of the entrance is at hand. In a concert or recital naturally it will be applauded—not so in every opera house. If a star has come to rely upon a burst of applause to bolster his confidence, he will be very upset in a theater such as Covent Garden to be greeted by silence. It is the reverent custom in that theater usually not to interrupt the music and many singers appearing there for the first time have been seriously shaken by this cold lack of greeting.

Once out on the stage and actually performing, the singer, if he is an artist as well, loses himself in the role he is portraying—or the song he is singing—but only a portion of himself. Another vigilant part of his artistic being must stand off watching, listening, alert to any mistakes and critical of lapses in musical and dramatic taste. In an operatic performance time is the despot; everything must be performed to cues in the music moved on relentlessly by the conductor. Yet among the most faithful opera goers who can ever remember a performance, however complicated, being stopped because a singer has lost his way? It seems remarkable that it almost never happens. A singer, terrifyingly, may make a wrong entrance, skip a number of measures of his role, get out of time with the orchestra, but

---

*To accommodate a new production at Bayreuth in 1983, Hildegard Behrens was strapped to and suspended underneath the rock during the entire long first scene of *Siegfried's* third act until it was flipped over for the second.

somehow with the help of the conductor and the prompter, he will right himself again and very often few in the audience are even aware of the mistake. The singer knows, however.

Occasionally in recitals an artist can lose the way with his accompanist and make a false entrance. If worst comes to worst the error can be glossed over with a charming smile, a word of explanation and recommencement of the song. Popular vocalists have been known to muddle the words of a number or fail to mesh with their accompanying band in some way, but again these mistakes can be glossed over or the song begun again. The only time I have ever read of an operatic performance coming to a halt in a major opera house is this incident related by Blanche Marchesi of a performance of *Die Walküre* at the Paris Opéra with Paul Viardot, son of the great Pauline, as conductor:

"In the first act, Sieglinde got out of control, and Viardot had to stop the orchestra. After a deadly silence in which the audience dared not breathe, he had to restart the scene. Such an incident is so terrifying that it can never be forgotten," she continues in true operatic style; "dying in front of a cannon seems a joke compared with it. That night Paul Viardot could not continue his conducting, being too ill, and Monsieur Mangin, accompanist of my mother's opera class, a person for whom music had no secrets, took his place without ever having rehearsed the opera, and carried it through without a hitch."

Act after act the opera progresses. The physical as well as the nervous strain can be tremendous. Sweat from the tension, the heat of the lights and the heavy costumes flows freely. A tenor performing the prostrate, dying Tristan was once temporarily blinded by perspiration pouring off the faithful Kurvenal leaning over to tend him. Another potential source of moisture, particularly in German opera, is a pointedly enunciated interchange between singers involving such spit-spraying words as "Mutter" or "Freude." Opera singers also run the risk of being gassed by garlic or onions when playing an intimate scene with a fellow artist.

In between the acts the voice must be rested, but the excitement and energy generated in the performance kept at the highest possible peak. Singers at Glyndebourne, the tiny English opera house set so unexpectedly among the downs of East Sussex, find that amid ideal rehearsal conditions and a satisfying repetition of an opera with the same cast, there is one drawback to performing there. The operas are usually given with a single interval of seventy-five minutes duration, which means that a singer with his voice warmed up and energy mobilized for the first part of the opera must repeat the whole process for the second time in one evening.

When the final curtain falls there is a burst of applause. This is the moment for which every singer, however selfless and artistic, waits. Applause, for all singers, becomes like a habit-forming drug, life-giving, stimulating, essential. In the opera house I am always amused by the various styles of taking a solo curtain call as practiced by singers. There is the exultant approach, when the singer strides quickly out onto the stage, arms raised, sweeping the audience with the proud, happy gaze of a warrior who has conquered. Then there is the "modest" style, in which the singer glances shyly, almost timidly around the theater with an expression of dawning awareness as the applause continues—for me?— all this for ME? which is followed by a girlish curtsey or a boyish bow. Still another type of curtain call might be entitled, "Overwhelmed." Here the star, delaying fractionally the moment when the excited audience expects to glimpse the singer, moves gravely before the curtain, exhausted, drained, still in a trance from the role that has been interpreted. Clutching at the edge of the curtain for support the artist scarcely seems to see the audience until the roars of approval and the sound of beating hands breaks through to conscious awareness. Completely overcome, the singer sinks down in a long deferential curtsey or bow while the applause washes over this humble figure. Just the opposite is the jaunty, casual—"Aw, anyone could have done it"—style of accepting the acclaim of the audience, accompanied by a grin and perhaps a little wave of the hand. Any of these approaches is more than acceptable, particularly if the singer puts them over with apparent sincerity. It must never be forgotten that mixed in with all the necessary ingredients for becoming a great star is the final one of a certain innate showmanship.

With the last bow made, all the excited energy generated by the performance must be allayed. Some singers will go out with friends and wolf down a large meal, having had little to eat that day; others fearing not to sleep on a full stomach will try to calm themselves down in other ways. Olive Fremstad was so keyed up after a performance, according to her one-time secretary, that she had to cool off before she could even eat a bite of supper prepared by "a cross and sleepy cook." After the meal the young Mary Watkins Cushing had to read aloud to the diva "a rubbishy detective story, usually, so that her mind could relax . . . If insomnia plagued Madame, as it often did, she would call me an hour or two later to come and talk to her."

Willa Cather in her novel *The Song of the Lark,* which is supposed to be based on the character and career of Olive Fremstad, gives an episode in which the prima donna heroine, Thea Kronborg, keyed up but desperate for sleep, agitates over whether or not to have a hot bath (sometimes the effect is a rousing one), decides to, and having soaked for half an hour gets into bed. There, in order to calm herself still more, she re-enters in her mind the old house in Moonstone, her midwestern home town, passing from room to room until she climbs the back stairs to her own bedroom under the roof. After which she sleeps ten hours.

"My poor Willa," was Fremstad's comment on *The Song of the Lark.* "It wasn't really much like that. But after all, what can you know about me? Nothing!"

What we, the public, *can* know about the existences of great singers is what they choose to tell us. Placido Domingo says that after a performance he does not get to sleep until five in the morning. The superlative artist Leontyne Price *does not sleep at all.* She stays up and thinks over how she has performed and the unwinding process lasts for two days.

Indisposed. How often has it happened in opera houses around the world that audiences gather expectantly to hear a favorite singer, only to have, as the time of the performance is at hand, a figure inevitably bowed with guilt step before the curtain to announce that Madame X or Signor Y "is indisposed. The part will be sung instead by . . ." The groans that go up! The sighs of desperation! (Occasionally though, such a situation provides a young singer with a chance to appear in an important leading role before the public.) On rarer occasions audiences have arrived at the opera house and because of a plague of indispositions heard an entirely different work from the one they expected. Sometimes another kind of announcement is made: "Though suffering from a cold Madame X or Signor Y has graciously consented to appear in tonight's performance."

(There have been occasions when a star not wanting to sing a performance or wishing release from a contract may feign indisposition. The management, if suspicious, usually has the right to require a doctor's certificate as proof.)

Bugaboo of all mankind, the common cold is the singer's particular nightmare. He lives in constant dread of it, fleeing from rain, drafts, cold—indeed, it sometimes seems, in constant flight from all weather. Obviously for a singer the worst type of cold is the sore throat which strikes at the very core of his vocal apparatus. Under examination the vocal cords, normally a pearly white (though in some singers, because of so much use, they sometimes show up a pale pink), will appear a brilliant red. In other cases, the top surfaces of the cords, the only ones visible to the laryngoscope, may look perfectly normal, but the degree of the singer's hoarseness will lead the doctor to suspect that the underneath surfaces which cannot be glimpsed may be acutely inflamed. Should a singer against the advice of a physician or plain common sense attempt to perform when suffering from such an acute inflammation (and singers under pressure or out of inexperience have been known to do so) the result, as one distinguished laryngologist thunders, "may entail weeks or months away from the stage and has been known to ruin a larynx permanently."* When in the grip of such an affliction, that most distasteful of all conditions to a singer, silence, is the best recourse.

Curiously enough a head cold may actually add resonance to a singer's voice and many a student singer has thought he has at last won through to his teacher's method with a sudden enrichment of tone, only to discover the next day what he has really acquired is a stuffed-up nose. If no evidence of any inflammation of the larynx exists, it is also possible for a vocalist to "sing over" a head cold. This however is not possible if the inflammation sinks to the chest causing the lungs to throw up a glutinous coating of phlegm over the vocal cords, making the voice soft and weak.

Female singers have also to deal with the problem of menstruation. Cramps can greatly affect their vocal performance. Some contracts are written that a woman does not have to perform

---

*This is supposed to have been the case with Ljuba Welitsch, whose career terminated prematurely.

during her period, though this practice is more common in Europe than America. Menopause, since the voice and the sexual processes are so closely allied, may also affect the vocal quality.

Even when in perfect health a sudden surge of phlegm into the throat, familiar to us all, is the bane of the singer's existence, causing imperfections or even the breaking of tones. "How often it happens that one comes to a concert in splendid trim only to be met by a cool wind at the very first entrance," writes Lilli Lehmann in *How to Sing*. "The difference in temperature between the artists' room and hall very often with the first inhalation causes a clearing of the throat, loosening small particles of phlegm which in the constantly out-flowing breath move to and fro completely spoiling one's pleasure in the concert . . . If they are happily situated they are sometimes quite loosened with the first number" (hence the veiled or uncertain sounds that some singers make on their first appearance) "very often, however, not for half, or even all the evening . . . Sometimes even a single little thread lying across the vocal cords may spoil everything . . . One can't clear or cough it away, neither during the concert, nor during the singing."

Small wonder then if an evening's performance can be affected by a simple temperature change that a singer must be highly self-centered or at least self-protective. On the morning of a day when he is to appear, one basic question will absorb his mind: am I in voice? As with any ordinary human being, supine through hours of sleep, phlegm will have collected in his throat. But will it be gone by curtain time? "You never can tell early in the day how you are going to feel in the evening," Lilli Lehmann writes with the intent to comfort—but the sentence can be read another way as well. It's interesting how many speak of "the voice" as something outside themselves, a capricious, willful creature whose whims are innumerable and not simple to satisfy. Yet this is understandable given the invisibility of the vocal apparatus and the number of outside factors—dust, humidity, temperature— that can affect it. One would think that a brisk walk with a friend on a crisp winter's day would relax and divert a singer facing a performance that evening. In fact nothing could be more ruinous than cold, dry air being taken into the throat while conversing, and some doctors advise their vocalist patients always to wrap a scarf around their mouths when going out in the wintertime.

And what about those vices, drinking and smoking, much beloved by most of the world? Certainly great singers have been drinkers. Kirsten Flagstad was very fond of her dry martinis (though never before a performance). Another Scandinavian, Jussi Bjoerling, was a heavy drinker but not the slightest alcoholic vapor ever seemed to cloud the purity of his voice. This was not the case with the superb American baritone Lawrence Tibbett whose voice and career deteriorated from drinking to excess. Most laryngologists and teachers agree that in the long run alcohol can be injurious to the voice and should be taken with great moderation.

As to the use of tobacco, certainly on the face of it hot smoke drying out the secretions of the mouth and larynx and ultimately (as we are now certain) limiting the smoker's lung capacity, would scarcely be thought to bestow any benefits on a singer. Yet many vocalists find tobacco a relaxation and support to the nerves and have smoked throughout their entire careers. The suave, handsome nineteenth-century tenor Giovanni Mario frequently laid down his cigar to go out and sing before an adoring public, and took it up again as soon as he re-entered the wings. Another tenor, the immortal Enrico Caruso, was also a heavy smoker. This seems surprising since he was an acute hypochondriac having been born in a Naples slum as the eighteenth child in a family where not *one* of the seventeen preceding infants had survived. Also when twelve, he survived a cholera epidemic that swept the Italian city. It is no wonder that the great tenor took two baths a day, gargled incessantly and was terrified of germs. Yet daily he smoked two packs of Turkish cigarettes using a holder. A cigarette was rarely absent from the elegant hand of the Russian bass Feodor Chaliapin, while the legendary tenor Jean de Reszke actually gave his name to a brand of cigarettes that the manufacturer claimed would not harm his voice. If these examples are to be followed, then smoking would not appear to be injurious to the singing process at all; yet common sense declares that singers would do well to avoid the habit if they possibly can.

Formerly, singers travelling about to fulfill engagements would have a rest forced upon their vocal cords by the slowness of train or boat travel. Walter Slezak in his amusing *What Time's the Next Swan?* gives an account of how a great opera star travelled in former halcyon days. When his father, the tenor Leo Slezak, tremendous as a vocal artist and tremendous of size, was engaged by the Metropolitan, his contract stipulated that transportation costs would be paid for the entire "entourage." This all-encompassing word meant naturally, the tenor, but also his wife, the two children, the singer's accompanist (and wife), Frau Slezak's maid, the children's governess, a Czechoslovakian cook, two Maltese terriers, a canary bird and a parrot, plus the luggage containing everyone's clothes as well as all the out-size (he was six feet, seven inches) costumes including "a special long casket-like trunk" that "contained the swords, lances, daggers, scimitars," and "a large valise . . . for make-up, wigs, beards and the stage jewelry."

Today a singer can and does appear one night in London, the next in Milan, and perhaps rush to New York on the following evening to substitute for an ailing colleague. In addition there is the call of the recording studio with repeated takes during sessions. Goaded by ambition and the desire for fees, many a young singer of today is threatened by the annihilating gust of the jet. In general the public thinks that singers spend hours and hours of the day bellowing out scales and whooping up and down arpeggios. In fact singers, teachers (the intelligent ones) and doctors all warn against the dangers of over-singing. The vocal cords are not like the ligaments of an athlete which must be worked out to keep their elasticity. Precisely the opposite: tired or overworked or strained because they are not correctly manipulated, these extraordinary bands of tissue that singers call on to make lightning changes in length and tension lose their ability to do so. Sensing this, the singer forces them on, bringing their two delicate edges together violently while attacking a note. Loss of brilliance, flexibility and the ability to stay on pitch—these are the first warnings of an over-used voice. The next consequence may be hoarseness, and then, most dreaded of all, the eruption of a node or nodule on the vocal cord.

Tiny, pimple-like protuberances, they are sometimes called "screamers' nodes" because when they develop, a singer can no longer properly diminish his tone nor sing softly, particularly his high notes, but must shout or scream them. This causes the cords to fly together still more violently, exacerbating the nodes (usually there are two, exactly opposite one another) until the cords are prevented from approximating, leaving a space through which air rushes, creating breathiness or hoarseness. Nodes, which often develop in the throats of people who put a heavy strain on their voices such as clergymen, schoolteachers, or even ebullient children, can usually be seen with the aid of a laryngoscope by throat doctors, who refer to them as chorditis nodosa. Recognized early enough, they give warning to student singers of imperfections in the technique that they are acquiring, and to professionals of over-singing, or performing music too exacting for their voices. Rest, refraining from singing and a correction of the abuses that caused the nodes will usually cure them. In more serious cases surgery is sometimes advised, but this is a tremendous decision for a singer to take, since the slightest nick of the delicate ligaments by the scalpel will permanently scar the voice. Even a perfect operation may leave the vocal cords less malleable than they once were. Blanche Marchesi says that because Caruso, the possessor of an essentially lyric voice, invaded the dramatic repertory and at the same time sang as many as five times a week at the Metropolitan, he developed a node on one of his vocal cords, which he had removed. This operation was a complete success. But when a second nodule occurred and had to be excised, he never was able to sing a lovely high pianissimo as before.

The high voices, particularly those of sopranos, are most prone to nodes; indeed, laryngologists have found tiny chronic protuberances on the cords of professional women singers, which because they are so minute, have not impaired their careers. Melba, who kept at least a semblance of a voice for nigh on forty years, was aware of the danger of high notes sung loudly, and reserved them only for performances. Yet even she, because she once invaded the dramatic repertory to sing the *Siegfried* Brünnhilde with her light, silvery voice, developed a node and had to cancel all her appearances for a year. Fortunately her voice was restored to her and when she returned to the lyric parts for which it was suited, nodes never afflicted her again.

After three seasons of charming audiences at the Metropolitan, Lucrezia Bori was forced to retire and undergo surgery for the removal of nodes on her vocal cords by a specialist in Milan. Terrified of the experience, she later discovered that Caruso had gone to the same doctor, a fact that might have provided her with some comfort, only by that time it was too late. For two years thereafter, Bori lived the existence of a mute hermit in the mountains of her native Spain. Eventually she gained courage to try her voice and found that it still existed. Her first reappearance in opera was at Monte Carlo: the strain and nervous tension can be imagined. In January 1921, after an absence in all of five seasons, she was joyfully welcomed back to the Metropolitan. Her most astute critics, however, always declared that her voice was never quite what it had been.

Marilyn Horne has an interesting passage in her autobiography on this singer's affliction—the dreaded nodes. When she was performing during her apprentice years with the German opera company at Gelsenkirchen in the Ruhr Valley, she found herself having to take two or even three breaths to sing a phrase where one ought to have sufficed. A throat specialist, Dr. Kriso of Vienna, not only found a "swollen spot" on one of her vocal cords but pinpointed the cause of it. Had Miss Horne recently sung a performance when suffering from a very bad cold? The young prima donna, who was then singing soprano roles, recalled the exact occasion—a *La Fanciulla del West* at Frankfurt.

Frequently the nodules are excised surgically, but in this case the doctor treated the surface of her throat with ultrasound waves, a deep-heat therapy, and ordered her to keep as mute as possible, which she did and the spot went away.

During these medical visits, Marilyn Horne learned that when Dr. Kriso, as a young man, was assisting a Vienna throat specialist of an earlier age, one of their cases had been her vocal coach, Lotte Lehmann. Nodules had been discovered on the great soprano's vocal cords and though she was advised to have them removed she refused "on the grounds that she would lose the special quality of her voice" that these tiny calluses seemed to give it. But since nodules have the effect of making the singer require more air to stretch out and shut the vocal cords, this was the explanation for the shortness of breath and gulped phrases that marred her singing.

When the first edition of this book was published a doctor who had cured many cases of nodules wrote me a most interesting letter on the subject: "Nodules are only one of a number of vocal disabilities from which singers suffer," he said, adding in a thunderous tone, "If *they had been taught proper vocal production* [italics mine] they would never have developed nodules." This is

Marilyn Horne as Rossini's Cenerentola.

obviously an informed, sensible statement, but then the doctor raised the real problem by adding a quotation from the music writer Carleton Smith on the subject of voice teachers: "One thing is universal, the ignorance of singing teachers . . . they know nothing about anatomy, physiology, physics or music." In short, let the singer achieve the "right" vocal method and he will never suffer from nodules. So we are returned to the vexing problem of what is right.

Of the vocal cords, Blanche Marchesi has written: "One can

pinch, burn, pull or cut them, but they have never been known to tear." Small comfort this, to the singer, considering all the additional scourges to which they are prey. Indeed it leaves one amazed that fine singing exists at all.

The Human Condition. Around those formidable shoals that comprise the demands of a singer's career must run his personal life, the ordinary ingredients of existence—love, sex, meaningful relationships, raising a family, which most of us consider difficult enough to manage without all the extra strains and complexities that a professional singer has to endure. It won't come as any surprise to the reader then that many singers at least resolve (though life being what life is that resolution can be undermined) never to marry nor attempt to mix a family life with their careers. For obvious reasons this is more true of women singers than men. One who kept firmly to this vow was the glamorous Mary Garden.

The defenses of another beautiful singer in that era proved less redoubtable and Geraldine Farrar succumbed to her cost to the attractions of an actor, Lou Tellegen. Two fine vocal artists at the turn of the century and afterwards, Ernestine Schumann-Heink and Louise Homer, managed to be both mothers and mezzos as well, but they were exceptions. The beauteous Emma Eames tried marriage twice, first with the attractive painter Julian Story and later with the baritone Emilio de Gogorza. Neither was a success. Handsome Lillian Nordica, who was evidently naïve and too trusting of men, chalked up a score of three unsuccessful marriages. She is generally considered to be the original for the prima donna Willa Cather called Cressida Garnett, the much-worked heroine of the short story "The Diamond Mine." In all such marriages a great female star obviously cannot make the compromises expected of matrimony. Equally, the husband, unless he is an out-and-out gold-digger happy to live off his wife's large earnings, finds himself in the somewhat humiliating position of being Mr. Emma Eames or Mr. Lillian Nordica. But if he shares his wife's career in some way, either as another singer, or an authoritative musician such as conductor or coach, or acts on her behalf as agent or manager, the marriage would appear to have a better chance of survival.

MARRIAGES BETWEEN SINGERS

Not surprisingly, marriages sometimes occur between singers, enabling them to share the peculiar problems of the life that they lead. They may also share the operatic stage and concert platform, as currently do Evelyn Lear and Thomas Stewart. However, the tensions and jealousies inherent in a singing career can also contribute to the failure of these unions. In the following list an asterisk indicates some which did not survive.

Wives	*Husbands*
Wanda Achsel (soprano)	Hans Clemens (tenor)
Ada Adini (soprano)	Antonio Aramburo (tenor)*
Pierrette Alarie (soprano)	Leopold Simoneau (tenor)
Aurora d'Alessio (contralto)	Roberto d'Alessio (tenor)
Sari Barabas (soprano)	Franz Klarwein (tenor)
Jane Bathori (soprano)	Emile Engel (tenor)
Gemma Bellincioni (soprano and first Santuzza)	Roberto Stagno (tenor and first Turiddu)
Sophie Bischoff-David (soprano)	Johannes Bischoff (baritone)
Joyce Blackham (mezzo)	Peter Glossop (baritone)
Inge Borkh (soprano)	Alexander Welitsch (baritone)
Gemma Bosini (soprano)	Mariano Stabile (baritone)
Geori Boué (soprano)	Roger Bourdin (baritone)
Helena Braun (soprano)	Ferdinand Franz (baritone)
Clara Butt (contralto)	Kennerley Rumford (baritone)
Monserrat Caballé (soprano)	Bernarbé Marti (tenor)
Lina Cavalieri (soprano)	Lucien Muratore (tenor)*
Augusta Concato (soprano)	Nino Piccaluga (tenor)*
Fiorenza Cossotto (mezzo)	Ivo Vinco (bass)
Toti Dal Monte (soprano)	Enzo de Muro Lomanto (tenor)*
Pauline Donalda (soprano)	Paul Seveilhac (baritone)
Elen Dosia (soprano)	André Burdino (tenor)
Maria Duchêne (mezzo)	Léon Rothier (bass)*
Emma Eames (soprano)	Emilio de Gogorza (baritone)*
Florence Easton (soprano)	Francis Maclennan (tenor)*
Marta Eggerth (soprano)	Jan Kiepura (tenor)
Lucia Evangelista (soprano)	Jerome Hines (bass)

Wives	Husbands
Malfada Favero (soprano)	Alessandro Ziliani (tenor)*
Lily Foley (soprano)	John McCormack (tenor)
Malvina Garrigus (soprano and first Isolde)	Ludwig Schnorr von Carolsfield (tenor and first Tristan)
Maria Gay (contralto)	Giovanni Zenatello (tenor)
Ada Giacchetti (soprano)	Enrico Caruso (tenor)[1]
Christine Görner (soprano)	Benno Kusche (baritone)
Marie de Goulsin (contralto)	Jean de Reszke (tenor)
Mathilde Graumann (mezzo)	Salvatore Marchesi (bass)
Giulia Grisi (soprano)	Giovanni Mario (tenor)
Winifred Heidt (mezzo)	Eugene Conley (tenor)
Dagmar Hermann (contralto)	Hans Braun (baritone)*
Maria Ivogün (soprano)	Karl Erb (tenor)*
Mathilde Jonas (soprano)	Harry de Garmo (baritone)
Sena Jurinac (soprano)	Sesto Bruscantini (baritone)
Hermine Kittel (contralto)	Alexander Haydter (baritone)
Adrienne von Kraus-Osborne (contralto)	Felix von Kraus (bass)
Evelyn Lear (soprano)	Thomas Stewart (baritone)
Lilli Lehmann (soprano)	Paul Kalisch (tenor)*
Adele Leigh (soprano)	James Pease (baritone)
Gabrielle Lejeune (soprano)	Charles Gilibert (baritone)
Loretta di Lelio (soprano)	Franco Corelli (tenor)
Mary Lewis (soprano)	Michael Bohnen (bass)*
Ilva Ligabue (soprano)	Paolo Pesani (bass)
Lydia Lipkowska (soprano)	George Baklanoff (baritone)
Liselotte Losch (soprano)	Josef Metternich (baritone)
Christa Ludwig (mezzo)	Walter Berry (baritone)*
Marguerite Matzenauer (mezzo)	Edoardo Ferrari-Fontana (tenor)*
Mariette Mazarin (soprano)	Léon Rothier (bass)*
Tatiana Menotti (soprano)	Juan Oncina (tenor)
Ruth Miller (soprano)	Mario Chamlee (tenor)
Patricia Moore (soprano)	Dino Borgioli (tenor)
Lillian Nordica (soprano)	Zoltan Döme (tenor)*
Maria Olszewska (mezzo)	Emil Schipper (baritone)*
Marta Ornelas (soprano)	Placido Domingo (tenor)

[1]Caruso and Giacchetti were not legally married but she was the mother of his two sons. When she ran away from him he was heartbroken.

Wives	*Husbands*
Lina Pagliughi (soprano)	Primo Montanari (tenor)
Adelina Patti (soprano)	Ernesto Nicolini (tenor)
Luisa Perrick (soprano)	Miguel Fleta (tenor)*
Roberta Peters (soprano)	Robert Merrill (baritone)*
Clara Perry (soprano)	Ben Davies (tenor)
Leontyne Price (soprano)	William Warfield (baritone)*
Rosa Raisa (soprano)	Giacomo Rimini (baritone)
Marie Rappold (soprano)	Rudolf Berger (tenor)
Hilde Reggiani (soprano)	Bruno Landi (tenor)
Delia Reinhardt (soprano)	Gustav Schützendorf (baritone)*
Caroline Raitt (mezzo)	Hans Kaart (tenor)
Elisabeth Rethberg (soprano)	George Cehanovsky (baritone)
Bidu Sayão (soprano)	Giuseppe Danise (baritone)
Maureen Springer-Dickie (soprano)	Murray Dickie (tenor)
Adelina Stehle (soprano and first Nanetta in *Falstaff*)	Edoardo Garbini (tenor and first Fenton in *Falstaff*)
Grete Stückgold (soprano)	Gustav Schützendorf (baritone)
Gladys Swarthout (mezzo)	Frank Chapman (baritone)
Pia Tassinari (soprano)	Ferrucio Tagliavini (tenor)*
Carlotta Vanconti (soprano)	Richard Tauber (tenor)*
Sandra Warfield (mezzo)	James McCracken (tenor)
Claire Watson (soprano)	David Thaw (tenor)
Lore Wissman (soprano)	Wolfgang Windgassen (tenor)
Virginia Zeani (soprano)	Nicola Rossi-Lemeni (bass)

A male singer married to a non-professional wife has an easier time achieving the condition of a normal head of a family. His hours are a bit peculiar and irregular and he may be away from home for periods at a time, but probably no more than any hard-working salesman or ambitious junior executive. As I have already remarked, singers on the whole seem to be more than usually highly sexed and so the wife who kisses her husband goodbye and sends him off with a cheery wave to the intrigues and passions of the backstage world in which she does not mingle may be possibly exchanging peace of mind for a false illusion of fidelity. Singing as they do of heightened passions it is not surprising that male singers seek, sometimes tirelessly, to give expression to these emotions in a fundamental way. Marjorie Lawrence tells in her autobiography of her amazement following a joint recital with Ezio Pinza, when the magnetic *basso* declared his love for her: she was, she gathered, one more to be added to his list, like that of the Don whom he sang so marvelously. Handsome and energetic Giovanni Martinelli is another whose activities were said to be unfailing till the end of his days in his eighties. And of course the Sinatra legends top them all. His biographer declares that Sinatra's friends say when he arrived on the MGM lot to make the musical *Anchors Aweigh*, the singer tacked up a list of "desirable females on his dressing room door. As the shooting proceeded, pencil lines were drawn through various names."

Since sex and the singing voice seem to have such a close connection, this raises the question whether sexual over-indulgence will not put a strain on the vocal apparatus. Some teachers warn against the perils of sexual excess to which, according to Madame Ida Franca anyway, sopranos and tenors are most prone. In his autobiography *The Blue Bird of Happiness* Jan Peerce writes warily, "Singers can't afford to overdo sex . . . sex is risky for a baritone and very dangerous for a tenor who needs his high notes that evening." The tenor speculates that the longevity of his career may be due to what he calls his "conservativeness" saying that his rule has been "no sex for three or four days before a performance." Hastily he adds, however, and in italics at that: *"Denying sex does not make you sing well."*

The prima donna heroine of Marcia Davenport's enormously enjoyable novel *Of Lena Geyer* sings an "off" performance of Donna Anna after having spent the night with her lover Louis, Duc de Chartres, at whom she bursts out bitterly after the performance: " 'You and your love. I never want to see you again. I never want you to touch me. I ought to have known better than to make a mess of my life because of you.' "

Later when the nobleman succeeds in calming down the tall, wide-shouldered diva, she warms to the subject.

" 'Other women may be able to combine love and their art, if they have one,' " she continued, 'I cannot. We've talked of this before. In holiday time, perhaps, I could make love and not suffer from it. But not when I'm working.

". . . 'When I practice on a day after you have stayed with me, do you think I don't feel the difference, the let-down, the lack of resilience? Of course I do and I have been worrying about it . . . Do you know where I think the voice comes from?'

"I knew indeed and nodded.

"'Exactly. I once heard a teacher give a girl a terrible scolding for having a love affair, and I'll never forget what he said to her . . . It is not pretty . . . He said it could not come out in two places at once. It comes out either in bed or on the stage and she could take her choice.' "

Whether this would be true of all singers is a fact defiant of proof,* but it is nevertheless something they have to consider in their personal relationships, another extra imposition, to which we ordinary mortals need pay no mind.

The consequences of sex, a family, is also something that singers must consider carefully. During the period of training when the financial drain is so enormous, it would be most unwise for a student singer to take on the additional burden of raising children, apart from the physical strain and sleeplessness that the tyrannical infant imposes upon his parents. Once enough funds are coming in to support full-time help, the rearing of a family becomes more feasible, though a female singer ought to be prepared to take at least six months from her career for the birth of a baby. (Marilyn Horne says it took her at least a year to recover from the birth of her daughter.)

Female singers with child can and do sing up until almost the last minute before birth. (The extraordinary Ernestine Schumann-Heink was one.) But after the fifth month the pregnant singer may find that her breathing capacity becomes inhibited by the size of the child that has grown within her. Conversely she may notice that her voice never sounded more lovely. For this reason record companies sometimes engage a singer-mother-to-be knowing that her voice will have this bloom.

All the world realizes that bringing up children is difficult. But for singers who are parents, the separations imposed by a career make child-rearing particularly complex. Also, stating it bluntly, singers must put themselves first, a condition that does not lend

---

*There are stories of singers having sex in the dressing room just prior to a performance as a stimulus.

Mother of eight, mezzo-soprano Ernestine Schumann-Heink as the earth mother, Erda.

itself well to parenthood. Nevertheless great stars such as Kirsten Flagstad, Joan Sutherland and Marilyn Horne have derived great joy from being the mother of a single child. Risë Stevens also reared a son who turned into a fine professional actor and appears regularly on Broadway. The son of Jan Peerce became a successful movie director. Miss Stevens's predecessor in mezzo roles at the Metropolitan, Louise Homer, was the mother of six children (one of whom, Louise "Jr." made a limited career as a soprano).

The palm for the all-time singing mother, however, must go to another mezzo-soprano, Ernestine Schumann-Heink, who bore eight offspring and brought up a ninth, the child of her second husband, as well. Desperately poor at the outset of her career and deserted by her first husband, Herr Heink, the great singer's struggles to feed and care for her first four children make pitiable reading as described in her biography. Later during World War I, the much loved artist saw one son go into the German army and three others, including her last born called George Washington Schumann, enter the American service, while she sang for troops all over the United States.

Both these fabled mezzo-sopranos hatched out their broods at a time when household help was plentiful. Even so, it seems astonishing that they could find the physical and psychological resources to bring up such large families and make their careers at the same time.

The Force of Destiny. And so pass the arduous, exacting years of appearing before the public with its daily diet of tension, its nightly dose of applause. How long and how brilliant that career depends on many of the factors already mentioned—plus one other that turns up in the lives of even those who don't sing: luck. The course of history, for example, can have a great effect on a singing career. When the United States declared war on Germany in April 1917, the German wing of the Metropolitan, including the celebrated soprano Johanna Gadski, was forced to leave the country or be interned. German opera was banned at the New York house and the opportunity for Wagnerian singers of any nationality to perform their roles eliminated.

With the rise of the Nazis Jewish singers or those who could not abide Hitler's regime such as Lotte Lehmann, were forced to flee Germany and eventually Europe. After 1938 the career of one of the most marvellous sopranos of her time, Tiana Lemnitz, was limited to Germany because of her political views. She never sang in America.

The outbreak of World War II caused singing careers to be

Tenor Fritz Wunderlich, whose career was cut short tragically.

interrupted, disrupted, stopped altogether—or sometimes made. There was no greater martyr to that war than Kirsten Flagstad, unjustly reviled and demonstrated against in the United States, the country that had been the first outside her own to give full recognition to her peerless vocal and artistic qualities.

Singers as human being are also subject to the same accidents and illnesses that afflict the rest of us. The beloved Kathleen Ferrier's career was terminated in a tragically short time by cancer. Fritz Wunderlich, a truly named tenor with a wondrous voice, was killed by a fall down a flight of steps. Singers travel a great deal. The noted English concert singer Gervase Elwes, who only began his career at the unusual age of thirty-seven, fell under a moving train at Boston's Back Bay Station. The popular soprano Grace Moore was killed in an airplane crash in Denmark. Miraculously, Luciano Pavarotti escaped death when his plane broke in two landing in the fog at the Milan airport in 1975.

Finally there is the dark side of existence itself, the devils that haunt many human beings, which can cast a shadow on the career of a singer that should otherwise have been a source of unalloyed satisfaction. Thus great artists such as Lillian Nordica seemed to invite an unhappy love life. Jussi Bjoerling was an alcoholic and his colleague Robert Merrill describes how in company with Bjoerling's wife he would go out to various bars in New York searching for this incomparable artist. Miraculously, drink did not affect the quality of his voice. Presumably, however, the heart condition that destroyed him at a comparatively early age was a result of it. Nor was Billie Holiday able to lick the drugs that became her downfall. But then these are the imponderables of living and singers are no less vulnerable to them—indeed perhaps more so—than other people.

THE FORCE OF DESTINY

Ater the long and difficult struggle to develop a beautiful voice and reach the top, the careers of a number of singers abruptly were terminated for a variety of reasons.

Ettore Bastianini, died of throat cancer aged 44.

Gertrude Bindernage, a highly successful German soprano was shot to death by her husband, jealous of her lover, as she was leaving the Berlin Opera House following a performance.

Giuseppe Borgatti, a tenor, suddenly became blind on the stage of La Scala during a rehearsal of *Tristan und Isolde*.

Armando Borgioli, baritone, was killed in an air raid traveling from Milan to Bologna in 1945.

Luca Botta, who it was believed would be a successor to Caruso, died of a brain tumor aged 35.

Lina Bruna-Rasa, a noted Italian soprano, developed schizophrenic symptoms after the death of her mother. In 1937 at the age of 30 she threw herself into the orchestra pit during a performance. Three years later she was confined to an institution, though occasionally thereafter she was able to give concerts.

Madeleine Bugg, a French soprano who made a successful European career during the 1920's, disappeared after 1927 when she was 31. In 1936 a pathologist dissecting a body sent from a charity hospital recognized it as hers.

Maria Cebotari, a much-admired soprano, died of cancer aged 39.

Thomas Chalmers, an American baritone, was forced to end his singing career at the age of 38 because of a throat operation.

Buddy Clark, the pop baritone singer, was killed in an air crash.

Gervase Elwes, English tenor, died aged 55 from falling under a moving train in the Boston railroad station.

Saramae Endich, soprano, took her own life.

Kathleen Ferrier was struck down at the height of her career by cancer.

Amelita Galli-Curci developed a goiter which finally ended her career.

Judy Garland was another suicide.

John Garris, Metropolitan Opera tenor, was murdered while the company was on tour in Atlanta, Georgia.

Jeanne Gordon, a Canadian mezzo-soprano who sang at the Metropolitan for ten years, disappeared from the public at the age of 36, a victim of mental illness.

Trajan Grosavescu, a Roumanian tenor, was shot to death by his jealous wife at the age of 33.

Melitta Heim, Austrian coloratura, was the victim of a nervous disorder aged 34. Later, because she was Jewish, she had to flee to England where she earned a living scrubbing floors.

Helen Jepson, the American soprano, developed a "throat ailment" that shortened her career to eight seasons at the Metropolitan.

Zinaida Jurjewskaya, a Russian soprano, fled the 1917 Revolution to make a highly successful career with the Berlin State Opera. In a fit of melancholy while on holiday in Switzerland she took poison and threw herself into a mountain stream at the age of 31.

Mario Lanza's death remains a mystery. He died while hospitalized, either from natural causes resulting from excessive eating and drinking or he was murdered.

Aroldo Lindi, a Swedish-born tenor, died of a heart attack onstage in San Francisco during a performance of I Pagliacci just after finishing "Vesti la Giubba."

Joseph Mann, an Austrian tenor, dropped dead on the stage of the Berlin State Opera in 1921 during a performance of Aida. He was 42.

Cléontine de Meo, a 26-year-old dramatic soprano well launched on her career at the Paris Opéra, shot herself in a fit of depression.

Grace Moore, the popular American soprano, died in a plane crash.

Augusto Scampini, an Italian tenor born in 1880, lost his leg in the First World War, ending his career.

Aksel Schiøtz, originally a tenor, developed a brain tumor at the age of 54. The resultant surgery forced him to re-educate his voice as a baritone but it was never the same.

Meta Seinemeyer, a German soprano, died at the age of 34 of tuberculosis. On her deathbed she married the conductor, Frieder Weissmann.

Brian Sullivan, American tenor, drowned himself.

Conchita Supervia, the fascinating Spanish mezzo-soprano, died aged 41 of complications following childbirth.

Anna Sutter, a soprano who sang mainly in Germany, came to an untimely end aged 39—shot by a conductor, Alois Obrist, who then committed suicide.

Milka Ternina, the celebrated Croatian soprano, was forced to give up her career because of a facial paralysis.

Genevieve Warner, a promising young American soprano, was beaten and raped in an Edinburgh alley. She never resumed her career.

Leonard Warren, baritone, dropped dead on the stage of the Metropolitan Opera House during a performance of La Forza del Destino.

Walter Widdop, the English tenor, suffered a fatal heart attack while the audience was still applauding following a London concert.

Fritz Wunderlich, the superb German tenor, died aged 36 as the result of a fall.

The Hourglass. So it is that when the top has been reached, the position must be zealously guarded and maintained. A moment's relaxation and it can be threatened by a newcomer. Each time a star at the top performs he wonders, "Did I sound as good? Am I *still* at the top?" It is now that fans, lavish with their praise, unstinting in their admiration become a bulwark, even a necessity for a great singer. For the truth is that supremacy in the world of the singing voice is inexorably and continuously threatened by something over which the singer has no more control than a piece of wood bobbing on a current—the passage of time.

Indeed the singer has been fighting time throughout the making and maintenance of his career. As the years pass, though the voice may thicken, darken and grow larger, in doing so it will probably give up some of the bloom of youth that all the world worships. As the years pass too, the singer's art may become more refined and subtle together with a more perfect mastery of vocal technique that he did not possess when he was young. But now perhaps the high notes become more of an effort or are totally lacking, and he can no longer sustain long phrases, having to fall back on the device of "catch breaths" which he uses with great cunning. In the novel *Evensong*, with its merciless though otherwise foolish portrayal of Melba thinly disguised as "Irela," Beverley Nichols gives some harrowing descriptions of the soprano, whose secretary she was, fighting to maintain her career against the erosions of time.

" 'Do you realize why the orchestra plays *fortissimo* during the whole of the love scene in the first act of *Bohéme*, whereas Puccini only marked *forte* in the score?' " he has a one-time admirer of Irela's voice say to her niece. " 'Because she can no longer take the high notes without using every ounce of her strength. Do you realize why she cut out nearly a quarter of an hour from the second act of *Faust*? Because she can't last the course. Have you ever listened to her singing the very first phrase in *Faust*? . . . People used to come over from Paris in the height of the season merely to hear her sing that phrase. It was the loveliest thing in the world. It is still lovely . . . still, in some ways, incomparable, but it's no longer the same. She has to take four breaths where formerly she only took two. And the end of the phrase, with the low notes, it's no longer like a 'cello . . . it's harsh . . . strained . . . she gets away with it . . . of course . . . with nearly everybody. But not with me.' "

Sometimes during the course of a career, illness or over-singing may force an artist to retire from public appearances for a time with the immediate rumors that the voice has been lost and the career finished, which loyal fans indignantly deny. Nothing, not even the debut, is more dramatic than the return of a much loved singer. Will he be the same? Is the old magic still there? Here are excerpts from a description by Clara Leiser of Jean de Reszke's return to the Metropolitan in *Lohengrin* on 31 December, 1900, after he had missed a season and his career was feared for.

". . . as Lohengrin stepped from his bark a hush fell upon the audience. Out into the silence floated

Nur sei bedankt, mein lieber Schwan!

tender, beautiful, sweet as of old. The multiple sigh of relief was almost audible. Strangers smiled at each other. One enthusiast nudged another and whispered: 'Good as ever, old man! Good as ever!'

". . . That night Jean seemed to require less warming up than usual and when he uttered his soul's desire in the words, 'Elsa, ich liebe dich!' his voice rang with such splendid power that the impression he had made on his entrance was intensified tenfold. 'Good as ever?' retorted the second enthusiast to the first. 'Better than ever!'"

After the performance "the audience was hysterical. Men shouted themselves hoarse and mopped their brows, and women wept. More than thirty years later a rather stolid businessman said to me: 'I remember every detail of that performance as though it had been last night. I don't know how I ever lived through it. I remember being afraid that I should take cold on the way home, because I was so excited; I perspired so that at the end of the opera my shirt, and even my collar and tie, were wringing wet.'"

Another such occasion at which this author was present was the return of Kirsten Flagstad to the Metropolitan, the opera house that had made her internationally famous, but from which she had then been excluded by one of the intolerant groups that America is so adept at hatching out. The opera was *Tristan und Isolde* and when the curtain went up at the end of the Prelude revealing the familiar figure, her hair in a braid, reclining on a couch with her head sunk down on the back of her hand, the whole audience seemed to strain forward. The tension increased and became unbearable. As the Prelude died away to a buzzing of the strings it could no longer be endured. A single clap of hands like a shot sounded somewhere in the auditorium and a moment later had triggered the entire audience into an uncontrollable roar of applause that carried on through the Steersman's song. Irreverent of Wagner it may have been, but that ovation was essential to the feelings of everyone in the opera house. When at last the clapping died away a voice out of the darkness called, "Welcome back!"

And Madame Flagstad? What must she have felt at such a moment? Indeed one wonders how artists when the atmosphere trembles on the brink of tears can manage to keep control of themselves in order to sing at all.

These are reports of triumphant returns. Less is written about the much loved artist who lingers on. Melba's last appearances were not always unalloyed pleasure except to those whose loyalty stopped their ears to the aged sound of this once silvery, flawlessly produced voice. The singer who continues to cope with a vocal instrument from which time has rubbed its former lustrous beauty and effortlessness is a sad if plucky creature. In recent times it was regrettable that Giovanni Martinelli did not retire sooner, leaving audiences with more mellifluous memories of the voice of this great artist.

How long can a career be expected to last? The average one made in the opera house would seem to span about twenty to twenty-five years. Thereafter the wear and strain of singing takes its toll and a performance becomes too effortful for either artist or audience. The lighter voices usually make the career earlier and thus end it earlier. The dramatic soprano, as both Flagstad and Traubel illustrated, does not seem to attain full power and majesty till its possessor is close to forty. Thereafter it can be expected to stay in full vocal prime for perhaps ten years. (A few years of regularly singing Wagner noticeably took away the total effortlessness of Flagstad's high C's, which she had possessed when she first burst on the American scene.) As with individuals, some singers seem to age more successfully than others, holding on to their voices with surprising tenacity when others will lose theirs completely.

Opera Singer Longevity Chart

Name	Born	Opera Debut	Retired from Operatic Stage	Years Active	Died
Giovanni Battista Rubini	1794	1807	1844	37	1854
Luigi Lablache	1794	1812	1856	44	1858
Guiditta Pasta	1798	1816	1850	34	1865
Henrietta Sontag	1806	1820	1854	34	1854
Adolphe Nourrit	1802	1821	1839	18	1839†
Wilhelmine Schröder-Devrient	1804	1821	1847	26	1860
Maria Malibran	1808	1825	1836	11	1836†
Giulia Grisi	1811	1829	1861	32	1869
Rosine Stoltz	1815	1832	1849	17	1903
Joseph Tichatschek	1807	1837	1870	33	1886
Pauline Viardot-Garcia	1821	1837	1863	26	1910

Opera Singer Longevity Chart

Name	Born	Opera Debut	Retired from Operatic Stage	Years Active	Died	
Jenny Lind	1820	1838	1870	32	1887	
Enrico Tamberlik	1820	1841	1877	36	1889	
Julius Stockhausen	1826	1848	1870	22	1906	
Albert Niemann	1831	1849	1882	33	1917	
Jean-Baptise Faure	1830	1852	1876*	24	1914	
Adelina Patti	1843	1859	1888	29	1919	*Patti's first*
			1914	55		*New York*
Christine Nilsson	1843	1864	1888*	24	1921	*farewell*
Lilli Lehmann	1848	1868	1910*	42	1929	*was in 1888*
Victor Maurel	1848	1868	1904	36	1923	
Minnie Hauk	1851	1866	1891	25	1929	
Emma (Marie) Albani	1847	1870	1896*	26	1930	
Italo Campanini	1845	1869	1890	21	1896	*The longest*
Lucien Fugère	1848	1871	1932	61	1935	*known operatic*
Jean de Reszke	1850	1874§	1903	29	1925	*career*
Edouard de Reszke	1853	1876	1906	30	1917	
Etelka Gerster	1855	1876	1890	14	1920	
Marcella Sembrich	1858	1877	1909	32	1935	
Pol Plançon	1851	1877	1906	31	1914	
Ernestine Schumann-Heink	1861	1878	1932	54	1936	
Mattia Battistini	1856	1878	1924	46	1928	
Lillian Nordica	1857	1879	1914	35	1914	
Emma Calvé	1858	1882	1910*	28	1942	
Nellie Melba	1861	1887	1926	39	1931	
Milka Ternina	1863	1882	1906	24	1941	
Emma Eames	1865	1889	1909	20	1952	
Antonio Scotti	1866	1889	1933	44	1936	
Feodor Chaliapin	1873	1894	1937	43	1938	
Enrico Caruso	1873	1894	1920	26	1921†	
Leo Slezak	1873	1896	1934*	38	1946	
Giuseppe de Luca	1876	1897	1946	49	1950	
Titta Ruffo	1877	1898	1936	38	1953	
Emmy Destinn	1878	1898	1921	23	1930	
Geraldine Farrar	1882	1901	1922*	21	1967	
Lucrezia Bori	1887	1908	1936	28	1960	
Amelita Galli-Curci	1882	1909	1930*	29	1963	
Maria Jeritza	1887	1910	1935*	25	1982	
Lotte Lehmann	1888	1910	1945*	35	1976	
Giovanni Martinelli	1885	1911	1946*	35	1969	
Friedrich Schorr	1888	1911	1943*	32	1953	
Claudia Muzio	1889	1912	1936	24	1936†	
Tito Schipa	1889	1911	1957	46	1965	
Edward Johnson	1878	1912‡	1935	23	1959	

Opera Singer Longevity Chart *(cont.)*

Name	Born	Opera Debut	Retired from Operatic Stage	Years Active	Died
Lauritz Melchior	1890	1913§	1950*	37	1962
Kirsten Flagstad	1895	1913	1955	42	1962
Beniamino Gigli	1890	1914	1946*	32	1957
Elisabeth Rethberg	1894	1915	1942	27	1976
Rosa Ponselle	1897	1918	1936	18	1981
Lawrence Tibbett	1896	1923	1949	26	1960
Lily Pons	1904	1928	1962	34	1976
Zinka Milanov	1906	1927	1966	39	
Thelma Votipka	1906	1928	1962	34	

*Continued concertizing after retiring from the operatic stage
†Died at a young age
‡Sang previously in operetta
§A baritone to begin with

The singers of today, as with the lives of human beings, seem to last longer. Here is a sampling of statistics from artists who are still appearing before the public.

Contemporary Opera Singer Longevity Chart

Name	Born	Opera Debut	Years Active (As of 1984)
Italo Tajo	1915	1935	49
Jan Peerce	1904	1938	46
Jerome Hines	1918	1941	43
Regina Resnik	1923	1942	42
Birgit Nilsson	1918	1944	40
Robert Merrill	1919	1945	39
Christa Ludwig	1928	1946	38
Sesto Bruscantini	1919	1949	35
Renato Capecchi	1923	1949	35
Leonie Rysanek	1926	1949	35
Elisabeth Söderstrom	1926	1950	34
Lucine Amara	1927	1950	34
Roberta Peters	1930	1950	34
Nicolai Gedda	1925	1951	33
Leontyne Price	1929	1951	33
Joan Sutherland	1926	1952	32

Many opera singers have ended their careers in the opera house but prolonged them for a number of years by turning to the recital

hall where there is no orchestra over which the voice must be
projected, and music can be chosen to avoid the vocal deficiencies
that come with age. Certain careers, however, have lasted an
incredible length of time and in this matter baritones seem to
endure particularly well. Lucien Fugère, the French artist, with an
unforced, light voice sang before the public for sixty-one years.
The Italians Mattia Battistini and Giuseppe de Luca were still
performing while in their seventies. An energetic if not exactly
youthful-sounding record exists of Sir Charles Santley singing
"Non più andrai" when he was sixty-nine, and one, less vital, but
still authoritative made when he was seventy-nine. Robert
Merrill, the American baritone, sang the same aria with a
youthful fullness of tone though slight shortness of breath over
the radio at the age of sixty-five in the winter of 1984.

A legend in our own time is Jan Peerce, who at the age of
seventy-six recorded arias of Verdi, Puccini, Cilèa and Tchaikov-
sky at the Jerusalem Music Center with full orchestra in a richness
of tone and plenitude of breath that would make a tenor half his
age envious. Peerce attributes the longevity of his career to a
careful choice of repertory—and sexual temperance.

Popular entertainers have of course made fantastically long
careers because, thanks to the microphone, they do not subject
their voices to the tremendous strain of singing in large halls with
equally large orchestras and without amplification. While well
into her eighties the late Mabel Mercer held fans in thrall as does
Alberta Hunter who is somewhere in her nineties.

The decision to retire is obviously an agonizing one to make. A
few singers seem to lay away their careers with almost a feeling of
relief, as if to say, "There! I'm free of you at last. Now I can live."
The only trouble is the definition of the word "live" to a
professional singer in his late forties or early fifties, after years of
fame and adulation, who has frequently sacrificed the ordinary
accretion of personal relationships to make his career. Where now
goes all that formidable energy—that zest which has carried the
singer to the top of his profession?

VI

. . . . *The sixth age shifts*
Into the lean and slipper'd pantaloon
With spectacles on nose and pouch on side

His youthful hose well sav'd, a world too wide
For his shrunk shank; and his big manly voice
Turning again toward childish treble, pipes
And whistles in his sound.

Finally, inexorable time forces the decision to retire. "Not even in the theater, which is the only comparable world, is the inevitable tragedy of years so remorselessly imposed on the artist," writes Marcia Davenport, daughter of the lovely soprano, Alma Gluck. "In every other creative and interpretative avenue of life, age only richens and widens the artist's function and scope. In singing she must lose her means of expression when she is in the full flower of intelligence and experience with which to use it best. This is the reason for tears and sorrow at the thought of a singer's retirement; every sensitive person knows that the artist is condemned henceforward to prison."

Farewells of great singers have been variously made. Geraldine Farrar, who was beloved of the stage hands and corps de ballet at the Metropolitan as well as by her fans (called "gerry-flappers"*), made a huge, emotional goodbye as Zazà in Leoncavallo's opera. Thousands crowded around the stage door afterwards begging her not to leave them. The great prima donnas Emma Eames and Olive Fremstad, both retiring relatively early, made a simple speech before the curtain. Other artists have simply stolen away.

The St. Sulpice scene from Massenet's *Manon* that the greatly loved Lucrezia Bori sang in March 1936 for her farewell together with her spoken words of adieu can be heard on a recording. So can Lotte Lehmann's last recital at Town Hall in 1951 in which while singing the second stanza of Schubert's "An die Musik" when the soprano reached the second repeated

Du holde Kunst . . .

she broke down so that all the listener hears is, symbolically, silence.

How best to fill up these silent years which Marcia Davenport calls a prison? The most obvious way for a singing artist to extend his creative talent is by teaching and coaching. In this manner,

---

*So named because they left the clasps on their galoshes unfastened. Today Michael Jackson's fans leave the laces of their sneakers undone.

like parents, they live on through their offspring pupils.* And yet many great singers never teach, never impart the secrets of their art and technique to succeeding generations, some because they feel that they lack the ability to do so, others because they have no desire. Occasionally one hears of retired singers sponsoring a "protégé" whom they do not teach so much as help with psychological (and sometimes financial) encouragement, thus extending their own careers vicariously.

SOME VARIED WAYS IN WHICH SINGERS SPENT THEIR RETIREMENT YEARS

Lina Abarbanell, the first Hänsel at the Metropolitan, soprano born in Berlin, became a Broadway producer of such musicals as the original *On Your Toes* and *By Jupiter.* She also claimed to have discovered Leontyne Price, William Warfield, Dorothy Kirsten and others.

Aino Ackté, Finnish soprano, directed the Helsinki Opera 1938–39.

Suzanne Adams, the American soprano, operated a laundry in London.

André D'Arkor, a Belgian tenor, became director of the opera house at Liège.

Joel Berglund, Swedish baritone, became artistic director of the Stockholm Opera.

David Bispham, a pioneer American baritone, managed a New York City chamber opera from 1916–1919.

Michael Bohnen, the dynamic German bass-baritone, directed the Berlin Opera.

Dino Borgioli, Italian tenor, founded the New London Opera Company just before World War II.

Vina Bovy, Belgian soprano, directed the Ghent Opera from 1947–1956.

Carl Braun, a German bass, became a concert agent.

John Brownlee, the Australian baritone, became head of the Manhattan School of Music in New York City.

Victor Capoul, a French tenor, lost all his money through speculation and finished his years living in a peasant hut in southern France.

Emma Carelli, soprano from Naples, directed Rome's Teatro Costanzi, from 1910–1926.

Florencio Constantino, Mexican tenor, lived in total poverty in Mexico City and died in a charity hospital.

---

*Two of the most gifted and beautiful singers in the past two decades, Renata Tebaldi and Carlo Bergonzi, are now teaching in Italy.

Marie Delna, a much admired French contralto, ended her life in a poorhouse.

Andreas Dippel, German tenor, was co-director of the Metropolitan Opera during the first years of Gatti-Casazza's regime.

Louise Edvina, Canadian soprano, ran an antique shop on the Riviera.

Maria Galvany, Spanish coloratura, finished her days in total poverty.

Mary Garden, soprano, was the extravagant director of the Chicago Opera, 1922–23.

Emilio de Gogorza, baritone born in Brooklyn of Spanish parents, was artistic director of the Victor Company. He also taught Deanna Durbin.

Osie Hawkins, American bass, as stage manager for the Metropolitan Opera Company, never missed a performance.

Alfred Jerger, Austrian bass-baritone, directed the Vienna Staatsoper briefly after World War II.

Emma Juch, American soprano, ran her own itinerant opera company from 1888–1891.

Clara Louise Kellogg, a soprano and one of the first American prima donnas, was impresario of an opera troupe that gave performances in English.

Ottokar Mařák, for many years first tenor at the Prague Opera, was reduced to selling newspapers on the streets of Chicago in his retirement. A fund was raised in Czechoslovakia to enable him to return home.

Vanni Marcoux, a bass-baritone of French parents, managed the Opéra at Bordeaux.

Dorothy Maynor, the celebrated American soprano, ran the Harlem School of the Performing Arts.

José Mojica, Mexican tenor, in 1943 made a vow on his mother's deathbed to become a priest, which he did, entering a mission in Peru.

Jean Nadalovitch, the Roumanian tenor, trained as a doctor as well as a singer and retired in 1912 to open an Institute for the Physiology of the Voice in Vienna. In 1935 it was closed by the Nazis and he was thrown into a concentration camp at Theresienstadt in which he managed to survive through World War II.

Joseph Rogatschewsky, a Russian-born tenor who sang mainly in France and Belgium, directed the Brussels opera from 1953–59 after his retirement.

Thomas Salignac, French tenor, founded and edited a music magazine, *Lyrica*.

Antonio Scotti, Italian baritone, directed his own travelling opera company.

Susan Strong was another American soprano who went into the laundry business in London.

Erich Witte, German tenor, became chief stage director of the Frankfurt Opera.

Alessandro Ziliani, tenor, born in the same town as Giuseppe Verdi, became a concert agent and had an important influence on the career of Luciano Pavarotti.

Many retired singers have involved themselves in the problems of managing an opera house. Herbert Witherspoon, a former Metropolitan bass, became "Artistic director" of the Chicago Opera in the season of 1931–32. In 1935 he was appointed general manager of the Metropolitan. When, a few weeks later, he died suddenly, another retired singer, the tenor Edward Johnson, took his place in a tenure that lasted until the coming of Rudolf Bing in 1950. Kirsten Flagstad was appointed general manager of the Norwegian Opera, but filled the post for only a short time because of the onset of the cancer that eventually took her life. The charming Lucrezia Bori continued to mingle in operatic affairs after her retirement through her work with the Metropolitan Opera Guild, and more recently Risë Stevens attempted to fill up the days of her retirement by co-managing the Metropolitan Opera National Company, which however went down to a lamentable financial defeat. She continues to serve as adviser on Young Artists Development to the Metropolitan Opera and is on the board of the Metropolitan Opera Guild.

A number of divas continued their connection with opera after retirement by virtue of having married the boss, so to speak. Marie Roze, the French soprano, was married to the impresario James Henry Mapleson, while Emma Albani, the Canadian born prima donna was wed to the manager of Covent Garden, Ernest Gye.

A few singers have appeared before the public in a different guise after their singing days were over. Geraldine Farrar, in the early years of the Metropolitan Opera broadcasts, was an intermission commentator. Basil Ruysdael, a former Metropolitan singer, became a radio announcer. Kathleen Howard, who sang mainly character roles for twelve seasons at the Metropolitan, continued in her retirement to play character parts in Hollywood films, usually taking the part of a grumbling, comic domestic.

Adelina Patti, to whom singing came perhaps more naturally

than sleeping or breathing, managed not to forsake the stage by building a tiny theater in her castle in Wales. On it she performed excerpts from various operas for her house guests, and when her voice no longer served her, assigned the guests parts in various tableaux and pantomimes, thus enabling her still to face the footlights.

The French baritone, Victor Maurel, is remembered as the first Iago and Falstaff in Verdi's last two operas (also the first Tonio in *I Pagliacci*.) He not only filled up his retirement years as a teacher in New York City, but since he had been an artist before he began to sing, he designed the sets for the Metropolitan's first and only production of Gounod's *Mireille* in 1919.

At this point in his life the singer's existence is made up of memory. Many are persuaded to put down their remembrances in print, some by their own hand, but often "as told to" others. Gossipy, inaccurate and frequently totally self-absorbed, a few of these memoirs give absorbing accounts of the struggles involved in a singer's career, combined with amusing glimpses of the social life at the time when the star was in the heavens.

For those singers who lack the resources or the spirit that would involve them with a new generation of musicians, these can be gray, empty years. They may paint and garden and travel in order to while away the hours. Some are fortunate enough to have husbands and children to fill in the vacuity of these years, though in many cases the exactions of the career have blighted the chances of making normal family relationships. Retired singers instead sometimes have the consolation of a connection with a well-loved coach or accompanist. A maid, who once served loyally in the opera house, will perhaps continue with equal loyalty at home. And there are always dogs.

Living in the past this kind of retired singer finds little to admire in the present world of the singing voice. When asked to attend a performance of *Don Giovanni* at Glyndebourne after World War II, Emma Eames, who lived on for forty years after her retirement, divorced, neither teaching nor interesting herself in any activity, is said to have replied that in a *Don Giovanni* conducted by Gustav Mahler at the Metropolitan in January 1907, Gadski was the Donna Elvira, Sembrich the Zerlina, Scotti the Don, Bonci the Ottavio, Chaliapin the Leporello and she herself, Donna Anna. What need had she to go to Glyndebourne? Her opposite in

Caricature of the versatile French baritone Victor Maurel by Enrico Caruso.

retirement, always to be seen alert, smiling, interested, in the corridors of the Metropolitan Opera House, was Giovanni Martinelli right up until the time of his death. The same is true of the retired mezzo-soprano Risë Stevens, who devotes her time to the cause of opera and helping young singers.

For those artists existing in the shroud of their remembered careers, there can be an occasional moment when life seems real again, all the more poignant because at the same time it is actually *not* real. This can be when they hear their own records. For singers of the era when the recording process was crude, this was not so true as for today's retired artists. Not long ago I sat with one of the Metropolitan Opera Company's most renowned singers, now retired, listening to the records of some of her radio broadcasts. At times it seemed impossible to look at her face.

VII

> ....*Last scene of all,*
> *That ends this strange eventful history,*
> *In second childishness and mere oblivion,*
> *Sans teeth, sans eyes, sans taste, sans every-*
> *thing.*

As Emma Eames lay dying at the age of eighty-seven, the glories of the singing voice no longer had any meaning for her. When a member of the cloth called to give comfort she bade him strip back the bed clothes to reveal her feet. Once she had sung a part which required her to dance in her bare feet and they had been much admired. She asked the church father if he did not think they were lovely.

The beauteous American diva Lillian Nordica said for a singer there are three deaths: 1) the looks 2) the voice 3) the body.

As the daughter of opera singers, the sister of the famous Maria Malibran and of the singing teacher Manuel Garcia, the celebrated prima donna Pauline Viardot lived and breathed opera for her entire existence. Even on her deathbed she remained constant. Her last word, pronounced in a voice loud and clear, was of a role that she had always felt eluded her: "Norma!" she called out—and expired.

Reference Notes

NOTE: Figures in parentheses refer to the bibliography, which is numbered.

P. 3, l. 4. Cather (311): pp 59–60

P. 3, l. 16–22. Rex Warner from *The Stories of the Greeks*

P. 3, l. 37; P. 4, l. 1–4. Alexander Murray: *Manual of Mythology*, Phila. 1898: p. 268

P. 4, l. 38–40; P. 5, l. 1–7. Heriot (192): p. 51

P. 8, l. 1–3, l. 5–8. Wagenknecht (185): p. 11

P. 8, l. 17–20. Ponder (166): p. 131

P. 8, l. 31–32. Melba (152): p. 111

P. 9, l. 22–25. Quoted by Stassinopoulos (178): p. 152

P. 10, l. 3–5. Garden (106): p. 186

P. 10, l. 31–40; P. 12, l. 24–27. Cook (212): p. 14; p. 103

P. 15, l. 30–32. Quoted by Kay (32): p. 66

P. 16, l. 39–40; P. 17, l. 1–2. Lamb: *Essays of Elia*, London, Macmillan, 1898

P. 17, l. 9–15. Quoted by Traubel (182): p. 199

P. 21, l. 29; P. 22, l. 1–9. Bowra (252): p. 1

P. 22, Both poems quoted from Bowra (252): p. 213, p. 267

P. 24, l. 37–40; P. 25, l. 1–5. Lang (258): p. 2

P. 27, l. 16–18. Ibid., pp. 33–34

P. 28, l. 32–34, 39–40. Henderson (255): p. 22

P. 31, Poem in Henry Adams, *Mont-Saint-Michel and Chartres*, Houghton Mifflin, Boston, 1913: p. 222

P. 33, l. 25–31. Pahlen (198): p. 11

P. 35, l. 1–15. Letter in *Stereo Review* (244): November, 1966

P. 37, l. 35–37. Steane (238): p. 522n

P. 40, l. 1–6. Tosi (67): p. 108

P. 41, l. 1–5, Mancini (39): p. 58

P. 42, l. 7–15, Quoted by Newman (340): V.I, p. 112

P. 43, l. 35–40; P. 44, l. 1–5. Mancini (39): p. 58

P. 44, l. 10–12, Kay (32): p. 22

P. 45, l. 30–36. Meneghini (153): p. 61

P. 51, l. 20–23. Verdi (343): p. 59

P. 60, l. 6–11. B. Marchesi (41a): p. 223

P. 63, l. 31–32. Henderson (27): p. 297

P. 75, l. 35–40; P. 76, l. 1–3. Quoted by Seltsam (283): p. 184

P. 76, l. 5–6. Thompson (205): p. 234

P. 77, l. 26–27. Fitzlyon (101): p. 275

P. 78, l. 12–16. Schwarzkopf (235): p. 77

P. 81, l. 3–11. Ferrier (100): p. 235

P. 83, l. 15–18. Brown (5)

P. 85, l. 1–7, l. 14–21. Hardwick(s) (114): p. 79; p. 77

P. 92, l. 39–40. Caruso (88): Foreword, no page number

P. 94, l. 2–6. Kolodin (272): p. 281

P. 95, l. 2–5. Caruso (88): p. 76

P. 94, l. 8–9. Quoted by Newton (233): p. 199

P. 95, l. 14–22. Haggin (245): pp. 184–185

P. 106, l. 2–3. Schwarzkopf (235): p. 132

P. 106, l. 32–34. Schwarzkopf (235): p. 77

P. 122, l. f. Puritz (52): pp. 88–89

P. 123, l. 10–13. Poem by Elizabeth Jennings from Plotz (334): p. 48

P. 123, l. 22–25. B. Marchesi (41): p. 121

P. 123, l. 27–29. Tosi (67): p. 83

P. 124, l. 8–10. Steane (238): p. 264

P. 124, l. f. Ffrangcon-Davies (17): p. 119

P. 129, l. 11–16. Taubman (287): p. 14

P. 131, l. 20–25. Franca (20): Introduction, p. xviii

P. 140, l. 8–9. Crutchfield, *Ovation* (303)

P. 141, l. 18–20. Steane (238): p. 144

P. 141, l. 25–28. Schwarzkopf (235): p. 88

P. 145, l. 22–24. Pleasants (199): p. 174

P. 146, l. 31–32. Ibid., pp. 53–54

P. 148, l. 32–36. Ibid., p. 113

P. 149, l. 1–2. *High Fidelity* (295) Feb. 1969

P. 149, l. 5–7. *Stereo Review* (306) Dec. 1971

P. 150, l. 28–29. Quoted by Pleasants (199): p. 82

P. 152, l. 29–31. A. Shaw (174): p. 57

P. 152, l. 33–36. Pleasants (199): p. 121

P. 153, l. 27–31. Ibid., p. 123
P. 154, l. 7–10. Balliett (189): p. 52
P. 156, l. 3–5. Quoted by Pleasants (199): 172
P. 156, l. 18–21. Friedman (104): 130–131
P. 156, l. 34–35. Marsh (148): 230
P. 156, l. 40; P. 40, l. 1. Ibid., p. 156
P. 158, l. 10–14. Quoted by Schauffler (341): p. 157
P. 161, l. 24–34 Quoted by Newman (340): V.II, p. 594
P. 162, l. 1–2. Quoted by Fitzlyon (101): p. 358
P. 162, l. 17–27. De Bovet (336): p. 20
P. 162, l. 31–35. Quoted by B. Marchesi (41a): p. 287
P. 163, l. 2–5. Quoted by Curtiss (335): p. 110
P. 164, l. 3–4. Balliett (189): p. 30
P. 168, l. 3–14, de Hegermann-Lindencrone (115): p 70; pp. 162–163
P. 168, l. 19–22, l. 25–26. de Hegermann-Lindencrone (116): p. 160
P. 168, l. 34–37. Joyce (320): p. 423
P. 169, l. 15–16. Quoted by Ellmann: *James Joyce*, Oxford Press, N.Y., 1959, p. 612
P. 169, l. 17–18. Joyce, *Ulysses*, Random House, N.Y., 1934, p. 272
P. 170, l. 25–30. Alda (75): p. 292
P. 179, l. 16–22. Kay (32): p. 83
P. 179, 38–40. Greene (23): p. 40
P. 181, l. 27–28, l. 31–34. Franca (20): p. 11
P. 183, l. 19–20. Klein (33): p. 22
P. 183, l. 36–40, Horne (124): p. 30
P. 185, l. 12–14. Puritz (52): p. 15
P. 185, l. 14–17. Reid (53): p. 148
P. 187, l. 35–40. Henderson (27): p. 39
P. 188, l. f. Garcia (22): p. 13 f.
P. 189, l. 33–40; P. 190, l. 1–3. Moore (325): p. 409
P. 190, l. 15–20. Mozart (339): V.II, p. 552
P. 190, l. 31–32, l. 35–40. Curtis (9): p. 161
P. 191, l. 8–13. Seashore (59): p. 46
P. 191, l. 25–30. Ibid., p. 43
P. 192, l. 29–40; P. 193, l. 1–2. de Hegermann-Lindencrone (115): p. 87
P. 194, l. 5–8. Reid (53): p. 135
P. 196, l. 3–5. Mancini (39): p. 20
P. 196, l. f. Fuchs (21): p. 90
P. 196, l. 18–20. Garcia (22): p. 8
P. 198, l. 3–4. Rose (56): p. 150
P. 198, l. 5–6. Marafioti (40): p. 51
P. 198, l. 7–10. Reid (53): p. 71
P. 198, l. 11–13. Fuchs (21): p. 64
P. 198, l. 14–15. Quoted by Field-Hyde (18): p. 72
P. 198, l. 16. Browne, Behnke (7): p. 115
P. 198, l. 17–20. Lehmann (34): p. 112

P. 198, l. 21–22. Litante (36): p. 39
P. 198, l. 25–28. Punt (51): p. 57
P. 198, l. 33–34. Roma (55): p. 122
P. 199, l. 1–11. Shaw (250): pp. 39–40
P. 202, l. 25–30. Calvé (87): p. 64
P. 202, l. 32–35. Martens (43): p. 40
P. 203, l. 7–10. Pavarotti (161): p. 131
P. 203, l. 19. Fuchs (21): p. 64
P. 203, l. 20–22. Mancini (39): p. 20
P. 205, l. 40. Cather (312): p. 420
P. 207, l. 20–22. Moses (50): p. 16
P. 209, l. 9–10. Sills (175): p. 14
P. 210, l. 38–40; P. 211, l. 1–9. Arditi (207): p. 81
P. 211, l. 17–19. Kellogg (131): p. 129
P. 214, l. 16–17. Quoted by Greene (23): p. 78
P. 215, l. 1–2. Voorhees (69): p. 8
P. 215, l. 18–25. Quoted from Blom (332): p. 522
P. 217, l. 10–12, l. 14–19. Ponselle (167): p. 46
P. 221, l. 1–2, l. 9–23. Merlin (155): p. 9; pp. 3–4
P. 221, l. 35–38. Delacroix, *Journal*. Cornell U. Press, 1980: p. 60
P. 222, l. 33–36. Merlin (155): p. 9
P. 224, l. 4; P. 225, l. 1–3. Sand (265): p. 37
P. 225, l. 7–9. Quoted by Fitzlyon (101): p. 52
P. 226, l. 24–26. Schwarzkopf (235): p. 198
P. 227, l. f. Lawton (135): p. 213
PP. 228–229, Material drawn from J. Kaplan, *Mr. Clemens and Mark Twain*, Simon and Schuster, N.Y., 1966
P. 230, l. 17–23. Litante (36): p. 20
P. 230, l. 40; P. 231, l. 1–7. Quoted from Glackens (110): p. 340
P. 233, l. 14–16. Meneghini (153): p. 225
P. 233, l. 19–21. Haggin (246): p. 184
P. 239, l. 10–16. NATS Bulletin (298) October, 1968, Editorial
P. 240, l. 26–29. Horne (124): p. 65
P. 241, l. 11–26. Hines (193): p. 307
P. 241, l. 32–35. Pavarotti (161): p. 39
P. 242, l. 29. de Hegermann-Lindencrone (115): p. 15
P. 243, l. 10–11. Marchesi (41): p. 142
P. 243, l. 24–27. Eames (96): p. 52
P. 243, l. 28–30. Garden (106): p. 15
P. 243, l. 39–40. Alda (75): p. 45
P. 246, l. 10–21. Gipson (109): pp. 162–163
P. 249, l. 32–33; P. 250, l. 24–30. Homer (123): p. 60
P. 250, l. 37–40; P. 251, l. 1–9. de Hegermann-Lindencrone (115): p. 77
P. 251, l. 20–30. Du Maurier (315): pp. 437–439
P. 253, l. 37. Holland (121): V.I. p. 110

P. 255, l. 36–40; P. 256, l. 1–7. Brodnitz (4): p. 240

P. 256, l. 11–14. Caruso (88): p. 140

P. 256, l. f. Ferrier (100): p. 237

P. 257, l. 16–26. Henderson (27): p. 63

P. 258, l. 6–7; P. 259, l. 1–3, l. 4–9. Witherspoon (72): p. 52

P. 259, l. 12–18. Puritz (52): p. 50

P. 259, l. 34–40; P. 260, l. 1–2. Curtis (9): p. 160

P. 260, l. 21–22. Franca (20): p. 22

P. 261, l. 4–7. Caruso (88): p. 145

P. 261, l. 19–27. Lehmann (34): pp. 67–68

P. 261, l. 33–38. Kay (32): pp. 85–86

P. 263, l. 11–41. Rogers (170): pp. 250–251

P. 264, l. 12–15. Lehmann (34): pp. 65–66

P. 264, l. 16–20. Rose (56). p. 89

P. 264, l. 21–25. Herbert-Caesari (29): p. 165

P. 265, l. 29–33. Lawton (135): p. 118

P. 266, l. f. Verdi (343): p. 175

P. 275, l. 33–36. *Career Guide* (73): p. vii

P. 277, l. 1–12. NATS Bulletin (298), Feb.–March, 1970: p. 1

p. 284, l. 13–14. Bing, *A Knight at the Opera*, Putnam, N.Y. 1981: p. 65

P. 286, l. 15–18. Waters (187): p. 92

P. 289, l. 14–20. Henderson (27): pp. 386–387

P. 294, l. 27–28. Garden (106): p. 32

P. 294, l. 31–32. Caruso (88): p. 76

P. 295, l. 14–22. Punt (51): p. 4

P. 296, l. 5–11. Lehmann (139): p. 214

P. 296, l. 21–26. Caruso (88): p. 75

P. 296, l. 34–36. Leider (140): pp. 118–119

P. 297, l. 36–40; P. 298, l. 1–5; P. 299, l. 1–7. Caruso (88): p. 78

P. 299, l. 23–29. Marek (275): p. 296

P. 301, l. 15–24. Marchesi (41): p. 111

P. 303, l. 4–7, l. 18–20, Cushing (92): p. 244

P. 305, l. 6–20, Lehmann (34): pp. 287–288

P. 307, l. 9–12. Slezak (177): p. 15

P. 309, l. 29–30. Horne (124): p. 116

P. 310, l. 9; P. 311, l. 1–2. Marchesi (41): p. 14

P. 315, l. 12–14. A. Shaw (174): p. 79

P. 315, l. 21–23, l. 26–28. Levy (143): pp. 152–153

P. 315, l. 32–34, l. 37–40. Davenport (314): pp. 148–151

P. 316, l. 1–10. Ibid., p. 151

P. 323, l. 12–27. Nichols (326): p. 93

P. 323, l. 37–40; P. 324, l. 1–8. Leiser (141) p. 228

P. 324, l. 9–17. Ibid., p. 230

P. 329, l. 5–8. Davenport (314): p. 446

P. 335, l. 22. Quoted by Fitzlyon (101): p. 464

Bibliography

The following is a list of books that I have looked into in connection with writing *The Singing Voice*. I have divided it roughly into categories with recommendations of books that I think most interesting, sensible or authoritative concerning the singer and his song.

How to Sing

The literature is vast. The idea that somehow one can learn a vocal technique from a manual seems to have captured the imaginations of publishers and public alike. Of the hundreds and hundreds of books written on "how to sing" I have listed what amounts to a mere handful.

To this reader's mind, most comprehensive and sensible—though not always easy to follow—is William Vennard's *Singing, The Mechanism and the Technic*, Mr. Vennard can also lay claim to being not merely a theorist: he is the teacher of one of the most remarkable singers of perhaps any epoch—Marilyn Horne. *Keep Your Voice Healthy* by Friedrich Brodnitz gives helpful and valuable information to the singer or layman and I also found *The Art of Singing and Voice Technique* by Viktor Fuchs interesting and instructive. From a totally physiological point of view Margaret C. L. Greene's *The Voice and its Disorders* belongs on the reference shelf of anyone interested in the singing voice as does *The Singer's and Actor's Throat* by Norman Punt. Finally, Blanche Marchesi's *The Singer's Catechism and Creed* strikes me as much more considered and less manic than many of the other volumes on this list. Victor A. Fields' *Training the Singing Voice* will give the reader an idea of the size and contrariness of this literature.

1 Aikin, W. A. *The Voice*. London: Longmans, Green & Company, 1920.
2 Bach, Alberto B. *On Musical Education and Vocal Culture*. London: William Blackwood and Sons, 1881.
3 Bowlly, Al. *Modern Style Singing ("Crooning")*. London: Henri Selmer & Company.
4 Brodnitz, Friedrich S. *Keep Your Voice Healthy*. New York: Harper & Row, 1953.
5 Brown, R. M. *The Singing Voice*. New York: The Macmillan Company. 1946.
6 Browne, Lennox. *Voice Use and Stimulants*. London: Sampson, Low, Marston, Searle & Rivington, 1885.
7 Browne, Lennox; Behnke, Emil. *Voice Song and Speech*. London: Sampson, Low Marston & Company.

8 Croker, Norris. *Handbook for Singers.* London: Augener Ltd.

9 Curtis, H. Holbrook. *Voice Building and Tone Placing.* London: D. Appleton and Company, 1909.

10 Davis, Clara Novello. *You Can Sing.* London: Selwyn & Blount, 1928.

11 Drew, W. S. *Singing, The Art and the Craft.* London: Oxford University Press, 1937.

12 Duval, J. H. *Svengali's Secrets and Memoirs of the Golden Age.* New York: Robert Speller & Sons, 1958.

13 Elkin, Robert. *A Career in Music.* London: Novello and Company, 1960.

14 Ellis, Alexander J. *Pronunciation for Singers.* London: J. Curwen & Sons, 1877.

15 Emil-Behnke, Kate. *The Technique of Singing.* London: Williams and Norgate, 1945.

16 Evetts, Edgar T.; Worthington, Robert A. *The Mechanics of Singing.* London: J. M. Dent and Sons, 1928.

17 Ffrangcon-Davies, David. *The Singing of the Future.* Champaign, Illinois: Pro Musica Press, 1968.

18 Field-Hyde, F. C. *The Art and Science of Voice Training.* London: Oxford University Press, 1950.

19 Fields, Victor Alexander. *Training the Singing Voice* (An Analysis of the Working Concepts Contained in Recent Contributions to Vocal Pedagogy). New York: King's Crown Press, 1947.

20 Franca, Ida. *Manual of Bel Canto.* New York: Coward McCann, 1953.

21 Fuchs, Viktor. *The Art of Singing and Voice Technique.* London: John Calder, 1963.

22 Garcia, Manuel. *Hints on Singing.* London: Ascherberg, Hopwood and Crew, 1894.

23 Greene, Margaret C. L. *The Voice and its Disorders.* London: Pitman Medical Publishing Company Ltd., 1957.

24 Guilbert, Yvette. *How to Sing a Song.* New York: The Macmillan Company, 1918.

25 Hahn, Reynaldo. *Du Chant.* Paris: P. LaFitte, 1920.

26 Hast, Harry Gregory. *The Singer's Art.* London: Methuen & Company, 1925.

27 Henderson, W. J. *The Art of Singing.* New York: The Dial Press, 1938.

28 Herbert-Caesari, E. *Tradition and Gigli.* London: Robert Hale & Company, 1958.

29 ———*The Voice of the Mind.* London: Robert Hale & Company, 1951.

30 Jackson, C. and C. L. *Diseases and Injuries of the Larynx.* Temple U. Press, 1942.

31 Kagen, Sergius. *On Studying Singing.* New York: Dover Publications, 1950.

32 Kay, Elster. *Bel Canto and the Sixth Sense.* London: Dennis Dobson, 1963.

33 Klein, Hermann. *The Bel Canto.* London: Oxford University Press, 1923.

34 Lehmann, Lilli. *How to Sing.* New York: The Macmillan Company, 1960.

35 Levien, John Mewburn. *Some Notes for Singers.* London: Novello and Company, 1940.

36 Litante, Judith. *A Natural Approach to Singing.* London: Oxford University Press, 1962.

37 Mackenzie, Morell. *The Hygiene of the Vocal Organs.* London: Macmillan and Company, 1886.

38 MacKinlay, Sterling. *The Singing Voice and its Training.* London: G. Routledge & Sons, 1910.

39 Mancini, Giambattista (ed. Edward Foreman). *Practical Reflections on Figured Singing.* Champaign, Illinois: Pro Musica Press, 1967.

40 Marafioti, P. Mario. *Caruso's Method of Voice Production.* New York: D. Appleton and Company, 1922.

41 Marchesi, Blanche. *The Singer's Catechism and Creed.* London: J. M. Dent & Sons, 1932.

41a ———*Singer's Pilgrimage.* London: G. Richards, 1923.

42 Marchesi, Mathilde. *Ten Singing Lessons.* New York: The Macmillan Company, 1901.

43 Martens, Frederick H. *The Art of the Prima Donna and Concert Singer.* New York: D. Appleton and Company, 1923.

44 Martino, Alfredo. *Today's Singing.* New York: Executive Press.

45 Mayer, Frederick D.; Sacher, Jack. *The Chainging Voice*. Minneapolis: Augsburg Publishing House.
46 McClosky, David Blair. *Your Voice at its Best*. Boston: Little Brown and Company, 1967.
47 McKenzie, Duncan. *Training the Boy's Changing Voice*. London: Faber and Faber, 1956.
48 Metzger, Zerline Mühlman. *Individual Voice Patterns*. New York: Carlton Press, 1966.
49 Miller, Frank E. *Vocal Art-Science and its Application*. New York: G. Schirmer, 1917.
50 Moses, Paul J. *The Voice of Neurosis*. New York: Grune & Stratton, 1954.
51 Punt, Norman A. *The Singer's and Actor's Throat*. London: William Heinemann Medical Books, 1952.
52 Puritz, Elizabeth. *The Teaching of Elisabeth Schumann*. London: Methuen & Company, 1956.
53 Reid, Cornelius. *Bel Canto*. New York: Coleman-Ross Company, 1950.
54 Rizzo, Raymond. *The Voice as an Instrument*. New York: Odyssey Press, 1969.
55 Roma, Lisa. *The Science and Art of Singing*. New York: G. Schirmer, 1956.
56 Rose, Arnold. *The Singer and the Voice*. London: Faber and Faber, 1962.
57 Russell, Louis Arthur. *The Commonplaces of Vocal Art*. Boston: Oliver Ditson Company, 1907.
58 Santley, Charles. *The Art of Singing and Vocal Declamation*. London: Macmillan and Company, 1908.
59 Seashore, Harold. *Psychology of Music*. New York: McGraw Hill Book Co., 1938.
60 Schiøtz, Aksel. *The Singer and his Art*. New York: Harper & Row, 1970.
61 Scott, Charles Kennedy. *The Fundamentals of Singing*. New York: Pitman, 1954.
62 Shakespeare, William. *The Art of Singing*. Boston: Oliver Ditson Company, 1898.
63 Sutro, Emil. *Duality of Voice and Speech*. London: Dryden House, 1904.
64 Taylor, David C. *The Psychology of Singing*. New York: The Macmillan Co. 1908.
65 Tetrazzini, Luisa. *How to Sing*. London: C. Arthur Peason, Ltd., 1923.
66 Thorpe, Clarence R. *Teach Yourself to Sing*. London: The English Universities Press, 1954. In paperback as *A Short Course in Singing*. New York: Funk and Wagnalls, 1968.
67 Tosi, Pier Francesco. *Observations on the Florid Song*. London: J. Wilcox, 1942.
68 Vennard, William. *Singing, The Mechanism and the Technic*. New York: Carl Fischer, Inc., 1967.
69 Voorhees, Irving Wilson. *Hygiene of the Voice*. New York: The Macmillan Company, 1923.
70 White, Ernest G. *Science and Singing*. London: J. M. Dent and Sons, 1909.
71 Whitlock, Weldon. *Bel Canto for the Twentieth Century*. Champaign, Illinois: Pro Musica Press, 1968.
72 Witherspoon, Herbert. *Singing*. New York: G. Schirmer, 1925.

As was pointed out in the text an absolutely invaluable bulletin for the young singer is

73 *Career Guide for the Young American Singer.* Central Opera Service, N.Y. Updated to 1983.

The Central Opera Service sponsored by the Metropolitan Opera National Council puts out other publications listing opera producing companies in the U.S. and Canada, a directory of American contemporary operas, etc.

Instructive not only to would-be accompanists but singers as well is the authoritative:

74 Moore, Gerald. *The Unashamed Accompanist*. New York: The Macmillan Company, 1946.

Books by or About singers

Here again the selection is large and checkered. Many great singers have, or caused to have had written their memoirs. These follow the usual pattern of struggle, debut, success, glamorous life at the top hob-nobbing with royalty et al until the final performance is sung. Of the books listed below, Mrs. Caruso's recollection of her husband including some of his comical, deeply moving letters to her is a must for anyone interested in the singing voice and the human spirit. Mary Watkins Cushing's *The Rainbow Bridge* is a vivid, absorbing account of a great artist, Olive Fremstad. The first book about a singer I ever bought (when I was ten) was Clara Leiser's *Jean de Reszke*. It seems as enjoyable now as it did then. Clara Louise Kellogg, one of America's first prima donnas gives an effective picture of the era in which she sang. The struggles of Ethel Waters and Billie Holiday in their careers are incredible and appalling.

75 Alda, Frances. *Men Women and Tenors*. Boston: Houghton Mifflin, 1937.
76 Anderson, Marian. *My Lord, What a Morning*. New York: The Viking Press, 1956.
77 Ardoin, John; Fitzgerald, Gerald. *Callas. The Art and the Life*. New York: Holt, Rinehart & Company, 1974.
78 Ardoin, John. *The Callas Legacy*. New York: Charles Scribner's Sons, 1977.
79 Baez, Joan. *Daybreak*. New York: The Dial Press, 1968.
80 Bailey, Pearl. *The Raw Pearl*. New York; Harcourt, Brace & World, 1968.
81 Berteault, Simone. *Piaf*. New York: Harper & Row, 1972.
82 Biancolli, Louis. *The Flagstad Manuscript*. New York: G. P. Putnam's Sons, 1952.
83 Bispham, David. *A Quaker Singer's Recollections*. New York: The Macmillan Co., 1921.
84 Brotman, Ruth C. *Pauline Donalda*. Montreal: The Eagle Publishing Co., 1975.
85 Bulman, Joan. *Jenny Lind*. London: James Barrie, 1956.
86 Bushnell, Howard. *Maria Malibran*. University Park, Penn: Pennsylvania State University Press, 1979.
87 Calvé, Emma. *My Life*. New York: D. Appleton & Company, 1922.
88 Caruso, Dorothy. *Enrico Caruso, His Life and Death*. London: T. Werner Laurie, 1946.
89 Castle, Charles with Diana Napier Tauber. *This Was Richard Tauber*. London: W. H. Allen, 1971.
90 Chaliapin, Fedor. *Man and Mask*. New York: Alfred A. Knopf, 1932.
91 Charles, Ray; Ritz, David. *Brother Ray*. New York: Warner Books, 1979.
92 Cushing, Mary Watkins. *The Rainbow Bridge* (Olive Fremstad). New York: Putnam, 1954.
93 D'Alvarez, Marguerite. *Forsaken Altars*. London: Rupert Hart-Davis Ltd., 1954.
94 Domingo, Placido: *My First Forty Years*. New York: Alfred A. Knopf, 1983.
95 Dragonette, Jessica. *Faith is a Song*. New York: David McKay Company, 1951.
96 Eames, Emma. *Some Memories and Reflections*. New York: D. Appleton and Company, 1927.
97 Elwes, W.; Elwes, R.: *Gervase Elwes*. London: Grayson & Grayson, 1935.
98 Farrar, Geraldine. *The Story of an American Singer*. Boston: Houghton Mifflin, 1916.
99 ———*Such Sweet Compulsion*. New York: The Greystone Press, 1938.
100 Ferrier, Winifred; Cardus, Neville. *Kathleen Ferrier*. London: Penguin Books, 1959.
101 Fitzlyon, April. *The Price of Genius. A Life of Pauline Viardot*. London: John Calder, 1964.
102 Flint, Mary H. *Impressions of Caruso and his Art*. New York: Privately printed, 1917.
103 Franklin, David. *Basso Cantante*. London: Gerald Duckworth, 1969.
104 Friedman, Myra. *Buried Alive* (Janis Joplin). New York: William Morrow Co., 1973.
105 Galatopoulos, Stelios. *Callas La Divina*. London: Cunningingham Bass, 1963.
106 Garden, Mary, Biancolli, Louis. *Mary Garden's Story*. New York: Simon and Schuster, 1951.

107 Gerhardt, Elena. *Recital.* London: Methuen & Company, 1953.
108 Gigli, Beniamino. *The Memoirs of Beniamino Gigli.* London: Cassell and Company Ltd., 1957.
109 Gipson, Richard McCandless. *The Life of Emma Thursby.* New York: The New York Historical Society, 1940.
110 Glackens, Ira. *Yankee Diva. Lillian Nordica and the Golden Days of Opera.* New York: Coleridge Press, 1963.
111 Gobbi, Tito. *My Life.* London: Macdonald and Jane's, 1979.
112 Hammond, Joan. *A Voice, A Life.* London: Victor Gollancz Ltd., 1970.
113 Harris, Kenn: *Renata Tebaldi.* New York: Drake Publishers, 1974.
114 Hardwick, Michael and Mollie. *A Singularity of Voice.* London: Cassell and Company, Ltd., 1968.
115 De Hegermann-Lindencrone, L. *In the Courts of Memory.* New York: Harper & Brothers, 1912.
116 ———*The Sunny Side of Diplomatic Life.* New York: Harper & Brothers, 1914.
117 Helm, MacKinley. *Angel Mo' and her Son, Roland Hayes.* Boston: Atlantic, Little, Brown, 1942.
118 Hetherington, John. *Melba.* London: Faber and Faber, 1967.
119 Hines, Jerome. *This is My Story. This is My Song.* Westwood, New Jersey: Fleming H. Revell Company, 1968.
120 Holiday, Billie Smith (with William Dufty). *Lady Sings the Blues.* New York: Doubleday, 1956.
121 Holland, Henry Scott; Rockstro, W. S. *Memoir of Jenny Lind-Goldschmidt.* London: John Murray Ltd., 1891.
122 Homer, Anne. *Louise Homer and the Golden Age of Opera.* New York: William Morrow Co., 1974.
123 Homer, Sidney. *My Wife and I.* New York: The Macmillan Company, 1939.
124 Horne, Marilyn with Jane Scovell: *My Life.* New York: Atheneum, 1984.
125 Howard, Kathleen. *Confessions of an Opera Singer.* New York: Alfred A. Knopf, 1918.
126 Hoyt, Edwin P., *Paul Robeson.* London: Cassell and Company, Ltd., 1967.
127 Jackson, Stanley. *Caruso.* New York: Stein & Day, 1972.
128 Jeritza, Maria. *Sunlight and Song.* New York: D. Appleton and Company, 1924.
129 Jordan, René. *The Greatest Star* (Barbra Streisand). New York: G. P. Putnam's Sons, 1975.
130 Kahn, E. J. Jr. *The Voice* (Frank Sinatra). New York: Harper & Brothers, 1946.
131 Kellogg, Clara Louise. *Memoirs of an American Prima Donna.* New York. G. P. Putnam's Sons, 1913.
132 Key, Pierre V. R. *John McCormack: His Own Life Story.* New York: Vienna House, 1973.
133 Knapp, B. and Chipman M. *That Was Yvette* (Guilbert). London: Frederick Muller, 1966.
134 Lawrence, Marjorie. *Interrupted Melody.* New York: Appleton-Century-Crotfs, Inc., 1949.
135 Lawton, Mary. *Schumann-Heink, The Last of the Titans.* New York: The Macmillan Co., 1928.
136 Leblanc, Georgette. *Souvenirs.* New York: E. P. Dutton & Company, 1932.
137 Ledbetter, Gordon T.: *The Great Irish Tenor* (John McCormack). New York: Scribner's Sons, 1977.
138 Lehmann, Lotte. *Singing with Richard Strauss.* London: Hamish Hamilton Ltd., 1964.
139 ———*Wings of Song.* London: Kegan Paul, Trench, Trubner & Company, 1938.
140 Leider, Frida. *Playing My Part.* London: Calder and Boyars, 1966.
141 Leiser, Clara. *Jean de Reszke.* New York: Minton, Balch & Company, 1931.
142 Lethbridge, Peter. *Kathleen Ferrier.* London: Cassell and Company, Ltd., 1959.

143 Levy, Alan. *The Bluebird of Happiness* (Jan Peerce). New York: Harper & Row, 1976.
144 Linakis, Steven. *The Life and Death of Maria Callas*. New Jersey: Prentice Hall, 1980.
145 Mackenzie-Grieve, Averil. *Clara Novello*. London: Geoffrey Bles Ltd., 1955.
146 Mackinlay, M. Sterling. *Antoinette Sterling and Other Celebrities*. Hutchinson & Company Ltd., 1906.
147 Marchesi, Mathilde. *Marchesi and Music*. New York: Da Capo Press, 1978.
148 Marsh, Dave. *The Bruce Springsteen Story*. New York: Dell Publishing Co., 1981.
149 Martin, Mary. *My Heart Belongs*. New York: William Morrow Co., 1976.
150 Martin, Sadie E. *The Life and Professional Career of Emma Abbott*. Minneapolis: L. Kimball Printing Company, 1891.
151 McArthur, Edwin. *Flagstad, A Personal Memoir*. New York: Alfred A. Knopf, 1965.
152 Melba, Nellie. *Melodies and Memoirs*. London: Thornton Butterworth, 1925.
153 Meneghini, G. B. *My Wife Maria Callas*. New York: Farrar Straus & Giroux, 1982.
154 Mercer, Ruby. *The Tenor of His Time: Edward Johnson*. Toronto: Charles Irwin, 1976.
155 deMerlin, Countess. *Memoirs of Madame Malibran*. London: Henry Colburn, 1840.
156 Merrill, Robert (with R. Saffron). *Between Acts*. New York: McGraw Hill, 1976.
157 ———(with Sanford Dody). *Once More from the Beginning*. New York: The Macmillan Company, 1965.
158 Moore, Grace. *You're Only Human Once*. New York: Doubleday & Company, 1944.
159 O'Connor, Garry. *The Pursuit of Perfection*. (Maggie Teyte.) New York: Atheneum, 1979.
160 Paris, James R. *The Jeanette MacDonald Story*. New York: Mason, Charter, 1976.
161 Pavarotti, Luciano (with William Wright). *My Own Story*. New York: Doubleday & Company, 1981.
162 Pearce, Charles E. *Madame Vestris and her Times*. New York: Brentano's, 1923.
163 ———*Sims Reeves, Fifty Years of Music in England*. London: Stanley Paul & Company, 1924.
164 Peters, Roberta (with Louis Biancolli). *A Debut at the Met*. New York: Meredith Press, 1967.
165 Piaf, Edith. *The Wheel of Fortune*. London: Peter Owen Ltd., 1965.
166 Ponder, Winifred. *Clara Butt, Her Life-Story*. London: George G. Harrap & Co. Ltd., 1928.
167 Ponselle, Rosa (with James Drake). *A Singer's Life*. New York: Doubleday & Company, 1983.
168 Rasponi, Lanfranco. *The Last Prima Donnas*. New York: Alfred A. Knopf, 1982.
169 Robinson, Francis. *Caruso, His Life in Pictures*. New York: Bramhall House, 1957.
170 Rogers, Clara Kathleen. *Memories of a Musical Career*. Boston: Little, Brown, 1919.
171 Russell, Frank. *Queen of Song, the Life of Henrietta Sontag*. New York: Exposition Press, 1964.
172 Santley, Charles. *Reminiscences of my Life*. London: Isaac Pitman & Sons, Ltd., 1909.
173 ———*Student and Singer*. London: Edward Arnold, 1892.
174 Shaw, Arnold. *Sinatra*. London: W. H. Allen & Company, 1968.
175 Sills, Beverly. *Bubbles, A Self-Portrait*. New York: Bobbs-Merrill Company, 1976.
176 Slezak, Leo. *Song of Motley*. London: William Hodge and Company, 1938.
177 Slezak, Walter. *What Time's The Next Swan?* Doubleday & Co., 1962.
178 Stassinopoulos, Ariana. *Callas Beyond the Legend*. London: Weidenfeld, 1980.
179 Strait, Raymond and Robinson, Terry. *Lanza His tragic Life*. Prentice-Hall, 1980.
180 Tetrazzini, Luisa. *My Life of Song*. London: Cassell and Company, Ltd., 1921.
181 Teyte, Maggie. *Star on the Door*. London: Putnam & Company, Ltd., 1958.
182 Traubel Helen (with Richard G. Hubler). *St. Louis Woman*. New York: Duell, Sloan and Pearce, 1959.
183 Truman, Margaret (with Margaret Cousins). *Souvenir*. New York: McGraw-Hill Book Company, 1965.

184 Tucker, Sophie. *Some of These Days*. New York: Doubleday Doran, 1945.
185 Wagenknecht, Edward. *Jenny Lind*. New York: Houghton Mifflin, 1931.
186 Walska, Ganna. *Always Room at the Top*. New York: Richard Smith, 1943.
187 Waters, Ethel. *His Eye is on the Sparrow*. New York: Doubleday & Company, 1951.
188 Waterston, R. C. *Adelaide Phillips, a Record*. Boston: A. Williams & Company, 1883.

Collected Singers

189 Balliett, Whitney: *American Singers*. New York: Oxford University Press, 1979.
190 Breslin, Herbert (ed.). *The Tenors*. New York: The Macmillan Company, 1974.
191 Eby, Gordon M. *From the Beauty of Embers*. New York: Robert Speller & Sons, 1981.
192 Heriot, Angus. *The Castrati in Opera*. London, Secker & Warburg Ltd., 1956.
193 Hines, Jerome. *Great Singers on Great Singing*. New York: Doubleday & Company, 1982.
194 Klein, Hermann. *Great Women Singers of my Time*. New York: E. P. Dutton & Company, 1931.
195 Mackenzie, Barbara and Findlay. *Singers of Australia*. London: Newnes Books, 1968.
196 Marks, Edward B. (with Abbot J. Liebling). *They All Sang*. New York: The Viking Press, 1934.
197 Matz, Mary Jane. *Opera Stars in the Sun*. New York: Farrar, Straus and Company, 1955.
198 Pahlen, Kurt. *Great Singers*. New York: Stein And Day, 1974.
199 Pleasants, Henry. *The Great American Popular Singers*. New York, Simon and Schuster, 1974.
200 ———*The Great Singers*. New York. Simon and Schuster, 1966.
201 Sanchez, Tony. *Up and Down with the Rolling Stones*. New York: New American Library, 1979.
202 Sargeant, Winthrop. *Divas*. New York: Coward McCann, 1973.
203 ———*Geniuses, Goddesses and People*. New York: E. P. Dutton & Company, 1949.
204 Strang, Lewis C. *Famous Prima Donnas*. Boston: L. C. Page & Company, 1900.
205 Thompson, Oscar. *The American Singer*. New York: The Dial Press, 1937.
206 Thurner, A. *Les Reines du Chant*. Paris: A. Hennuyer, 1883.

Reminiscences and Criticisms of Singers by Non-Singers

G. B. Shaw, whose mother was a singer and teacher of singing, is wonderfully funny and astute about matters to do with the voice. Chorley, Cox, Hogarth and Mount-Edgcumbe all give detailed and carefully considered descriptions of singers before the days of recordings.

207 Arditi, Luigi (ed. Baroness von Zedlitz). *My Reminiscences*. London: Skiffington and Son Ltd., 1896.
208 Beecham, Sir Thomas. *A Mingled Chime*. London: Hutchinson & Company, Ltd., 1944.
209 Berlioz, Hector (ed. David Cairns). *Memoirs*. London: Victor Gollancz, Ltd., 1969.
210 Burney, Charles. *The Present State of Music in France and Italy*. London: T. Becket and Company, 1773.
211 Chorley, Henry F. *Thirty Years Musical Recollections*. London: Hurst and Blackett, 1862.
212 Cook, Ida and Louise. *We Followed Our Stars*. New York: William Morrow Co., 1950.
213 Cox, E. C. *Musical Recollections of the Last Half Century*. London: Tinsley Brothers, 1872.
214 Damrosch, Walter. *My Musical Life*. New York: Scribner's Sons, 1923.
215 Davenport, Marcia. *Too Strong for Fantasy*. New York: Scribner's Sons, 1967.
216 Davison, J. W. *From Mendelssohn to Wagner*. London: William Reeves, 1912.
217 Diehl, Alice Mangold. *Musical Memories*. London: Richard Bentley and Son, 1897.
218 Finletter, Gretchen. *From the Top of the Stairs*. Boston: Atlantic Little Brown, 1946.

219 Gaisberg, F. W. *The Music Goes Round.* New York: The Macmillan Company, 1942.
220 Gollancz, Victor. *Journey Towards Music.* London: Victor Gollancz, Ltd., 1964.
221 Hanslick, Eduard (ed. Henry Pleasants). *Vienna's Golden Years of Music.* New York: Simon and Schuster, 1950.
222 Hogarth, George. *Memoirs of the Opera in Italy, France, Germany and England.* London: Richard Bentley, 1851.
223 Hughes, Spike. *Opening Bars.* London: Pilot Press, 1946.
224 Huneker, James Gibbons. *Letters.* New York: Charles Scribner's Sons, 1922.
225 Kelly, Michael. *Reminiscences.* London: Henry Colburn, 1826.
226 Klein, Herman. *Thirty Years of Musical Life in London.* London: William Heinemann Ltd., 1903.
227 Kuhe, Wilhelm. *My Musical Recollections.* London: Richard Bentley and Son, 1896.
228 Mapleson, J. H. (ed. Harold Rosenthal). *Memoirs.* London: Putnam & Company, Ltd., 1966.
229 Maretzek, Max. *Crochets and Quavers.* New York: Da Capo Press, 1966.
230 Moore, Gerald. *Am I Too Loud?* London: Hamish Hamilton, Ltd., 1962.
231 Moscheles, Ignatz. *Recent Music and Musicians.* New York: Henry Holt and Company, 1873.
232 Mount-Edgcumbe, Richard. *Musical Reminiscences of an Old Amateur.* London: W. Clarke, 1823.
233 Newton, Ivor. *At the Piano.* London: Hamish Hamilton, Ltd., 1966.
234 O'Connell, Charles. *The Other Side of the Record.* New York: Alfred A. Knopf, 1947.
235 Schwarzkopf, Elisabeth. *Off the Record. A Memoir of Walter Legge.* New York: Scribner's Sons, 1982.
236 Sheean, Vincent. *First and Last Love.* New York: Random House, 1956.
237 Simpson, Harold. *Singers to Remember.* Surrey: Oakland Press n.d.
238 Steane, G. B. *The Grand Tradition.* London: Duckworth, 1974.
239 Walker, Francis. *Letters of a Baritone.* London: William Heinemann Ltd., 1895.
240 Walter, Bruno. *Theme and Variations.* New York: Alfred A. Knopf, 1946.

Other Critical Writing

241 Arundell, Dennis. *The Critic at the Opera.* London: Ernest Benn, 1957.
242 Finck, Henry T. *Chopin and Other Musical Essays.* New York: Charles Scribner's Sons, 1904.
243 ———*Musical Progress.* Philadelphia: Theodore Presser Company, 1923.
244 Gardiner, William. *The Music of Nature.* London: Longman, Rees, Ormz, Brown, Green and Longman, 1832.
245 Haggin, B. H. *The Listener's Musical Companion.* New Brunswick, New Jersey: Rutgers University Press, 1956.
246 ———*35 Years of Music.* New York: Horizon Press, 1974.
247 Porter, Andrew. *Music of Three Seasons.* New York: Farrar Straus & Giroux, 1978.
248 ———*Music of Three More Seasons.* New York: Alfred A. Knopf, 1981.
249 Shaw, G. B. (ed. Dan H. Laurence). *How to Become a Music Critic.* New York: Hill and Wang, 1961.
250 ———*London Music in 1888–89 as Heard by Corno di Bassetto.* New York: Vienna House, 1973.
251 ———*Music in London 1890–94.* (Three volumes.) New York: Vienna House, 1973.

History

252 Bowra, C. M. *Primitive Song.* London: Weidenfeld & Nicholson, 1962.
253 Drinker, Sophie. *Music and Women.* New York: Coward McCann, 1948.

254 Grout, Donald Jay. *A History of Western Music.* New York: W. W. Norton & Company, 1960.
255 Henderson, W. J. *Early History of Singing.* New York: Longmans Green & Company, 1921.
256 Hurst, P. G. *The Age of Jean de Reszke.* London: Christoper Johnson, 1958.
257 ——*The Golden Age Recorded.* London: The Oakwood Press, 1963.
258 Lang, Paul H. *Music in Western Civilization.* London: J. M. Dent & Sons, Ltd., 1942.
259 Sendry, Alfred; Norton, Mildred. *David's Harp.* New York: New American Library, 1964.
260 Stevens, Dennis (ed.). *A History of Song.* London: Hutchinson & Company, Ltd., 1960.
261 Suetonius. *The Twelve Caesars.* London: Penguin Books, 1957.
262 Wallaschek, Richard. *Primitive Music.* London: Longmans Green, 1893.
263 Wellesz, Egon (ed.). *The New Oxford History of Music: Ancient and Oriental Music.* London: Oxford University Press, 1957.
264 Wibberley, Brian. *Music and Religion.* London: The Epworth Press, 1931.
267 Anonymous. *Twenty Years of New York Singing Teachers' Association, Inc.* Philadelphia: Theodore Presser Company, 1928.

Operatic History and Lore

265 Briggs, John. *Requiem for a Yellow Brick Brewery. A History of the Metropolitan Opera.* Boston: Little, Brown and Company, 1969.
266 Cone, John Frederick. *Oscar Hammerstein's Manhattan Opera Company.* Norman, Oklahoma: University of Oklahoma Press, 1966.
267 Culshaw, John. *Ring Resounding.* New York: The Viking Press, 1967.
268 Davis, Ronald L. *Opera in Chicago.* New York: Appleton-Century, 1966.
269 Eaton, Quaintance. *The Boston Opera Company.* New York: Appleton-Century, 1965.
260 Goldovsky, Boris; Peltz, Mary Ellis. *Accents on Opera.* New York: Farrar, Straus and Young, 1953.
271 Kolodin, Irving. *The Opera Omnibus.* New York: E. P. Dutton & Company, 1976.
272 ——*The Story of the Metropolitan Opera.* New York: Oxford University Press, 1953.
273 Lahee, Henry C. *Grand Opera in America.* Boston: L. C. Page & Company, 1902.
274 Lawrence, Robert. *A Rage for Opera.* Dodd, Mead & Company, 1971.
275 Marek, George R. *A Front Seat at the Opera.* New York: Allen, Towne & Heath, 1948.
276 Mordden, Ethan R. *The Splendid Art of Opera.* New York: Methuen Company, 1980.
277 Noble, Helen. *Life with the Met.* New York: G. P. Putnam's Sons, 1951.
278 Peltz, Mary Ellis (ed.). *Opera Lover's Companion.* New York: Ziff-Davis Publishing Company, 1948.
279 Phillips, Harvey E. *The Carmen Chronicle.* New York: Stein and Day, 1973.
280 Rosenthal, Harold. *Two Centuries of Opera at Covent Garden.* London: Putnam & Company Ltd., 1958.
281 ——(ed.) *The Opera Bedside Book.* London: Victor Gollancz, Ltd., 1965.
282 Rubin, Stephen E. *The New Met In Profile.* New York: The Macmillan Company, 1974.
283 Seltsam, William H. *Metropolitan Opera Annals.* New York: The H. W. Wilson Company, 1947.
284 ——*First Supplement, 1947–1957.* New York: The H. W. Wilson Company, 1957.
285 ——*Second Supplement, 1957–1966.* New York: The H. W. Wilson Company, 1968.
286 Smith, Patrick J. *A Year at the Met.* New York: Alfred A. Knopf, 1983.
287 Taubman, H. Howard. *Opera Front and Back.* New York: Charles Scribner's Sons, 1938.
288 White, Eric Walter. *The Rise of English Opera.* London: John Lehmann, 1951.

Other References

289 Davies, J. H. *Musicalia.* London: Pergamon Press, 1966.

290 Jacobs, Arthur. *A New Dictionary of Music*. London: Penguin Books, 1958.
291 Kutsch, K. J.; Riemens, Leo. *A Concise Biographical Dictionary of Singers*. Philadelphia: Chilton Book Company, 1969.
292 Newman, Ernest. *Stories of the Great Operas*. New York: Alfred A. Knopf, 1928.
293 ———*More Stories of Famous Operas*. New York: Alfred A. Knopf, 1943.

Periodicals

294 *About the House.*
295 *High Fidelity.*
296 *London Times.*
297 *Metropolitan Opera Program.*
298 *NATS* (National Association of Teachers of Singing) *Bulletin.*
299 *The New York Times.*
300 *The New Yorker.*
301 *Opera.*
302 *Opera News.*
303 *Ovation.*
304 *Records and Recordings.*
305 *Saturday Review of Literature.*
306 *Stereo Review.*
307 *Time.*

Fiction

Of the numbers of writers who have woven the singing voice into their fiction, outstanding is the incomparable Willa Cather. In his recent study, *Music in Willa Cather's Fiction* Richard Giannone points out how "singers and musical performances held a special fascination for her, though she herself was musically an amateur with no technical knowledge of the art." *The Song of the Lark* is Miss Cather's only full length novel dealing with the development of a successful opera singer, in which she relates the artistry of her heroine, Thea Kronborg, to the land from which she came. "It wasn't like that," said Olive Fremstad, the soprano on whom the author is supposed to have based her story. Nonetheless it is a very beautiful book about a great singer, Lillian Nordica, who made several unfortunate marriages, is supposed to have sat for *her* portrait in "The Diamond Mine," one of a number of stories about singers contained in *Youth and the Bright Medusa. My Mortal Enemy* and *Lucy Gayheart* also contain references to singing which capture exquisitely the spell of great vocal art.

James Joyce was another who had the power to evoke in words the effect of the singing voice. This is particularly true of "The Dead" in *Dubliners. Ulysses*, of course, is flooded with references to singing.

Of some of the others novels listed, the singing voice has called forth fantasies that seem mad or merely preposterous from their authors. Marcia Davenport's *Of Lena Geyer*, however, is a colorful and thoroughly enjoyable story of a prima donna's life. James M. Cain's *Serenade* graphically details some of the physical sensations of singing, while Martin Mayer's *A Voice that Fills the House* (with a plot that would have awed the librettist of *Trovatore*) contains authentic atmosphere of the opera house with shrewd comments on singing.

I have listed the Tolstoy for the lovely description of Natásha's singing, and the Thomas Mann for the chapter in which Hans Castorp listens to phonograph records of great singers.

308 Atherton, Gertrude. *Tower of Ivory.* New York: The Macmillan Company, 1910.

309 Cain, James M. *Serenade.* New York: Alfred A. Knopf, 1937.

310 Cather, Willa. *Lucy Gayheart.* New York: Alfred A. Knopf, 1935.

311 ———*My Mortal Enemy.* New York: Alfred A. Knopf, 1926.

312 ———*The Song of the Lark.* Boston: Houghton Mifflin, 1915.

313 ———*Youth and the Bright Medusa.* New York: Alfred A. Knopf, 1920.

314 Davenport, Marcia. *Of Lena Geyer.* New York: Charles Scribner's Sons, 1936.

315 DuMaurier, George. *Trilby.* London: Osgood, McIlvaine & Company, 1896.

316 Eliot, George. *Daniel Deronda.* New York: Harper & Brothers, 1877.

317 Henderson, W. J. *The Soul of a Tenor.* New York: Henry Holt, 1912.

318 Huneker, James. *Painted Veils.* New York: Horace Liveright, 1928.

319 Joyce, James. *Dubliners.* London: Penguin Books, 1956.

320 ———*A Portrait of the Artist as a Young Man.* NY, Viking, 1947.

321 Mann, Thomas. *The Magic Mountain* (tr. H. T. Lowe-Porter). New York: Alfred A. Knopf, 1944. Chapter VII, pp. 635–653.

322 Mansfield, Katharine. *The Short Stories.* New York: Alfred A. Knopf, 1937. pp. 384–393.

323 Mayer, Martin. *A Voice that Fills the House.* New York: Simon and Schuster, 1959.

324 Merrill, Robert with Fred Jarvis. *The Divas.* New York: Simon and Schuster, 1978.

325 Moore, George. *Evelyn Innes.* New York: D. Appleton and Company, 1914.

326 Nichols, Beverly. *Evensong.* New York: Doubleday Doran and Co., 1932.

327 O'Brien, Kate. *As Music and Splendour.* London: Heinemann, 1958.

328 Sanborn, Pitts. *Prima Donna.* New York: Longmans Green and Company, 1929.

329 Sand, Georges. *Consuelo.* New York: A. L. Burt, 189?.

330 Tolstoy, Leo. *War and Peace* (tr. L. and A. Maude). New York: Simon and Schuster, 1942. Section 14, Book Four, Part One, pp. 367–370.

Anthologies

331 Bishop, John (ed.). *Music and Sweet Poetry.* London: John Baker, 1968.

332 Blom, Eric (ed.). *The Music Lover's Miscellany.* London: Victor Gollancz, Ltd., 1935.

333 Cole, William. *The Fireside Book of Humorous Poetry.* New York: Simon and Schuster, 1959.

334 Poltz, Helen (ed.). *Untune the Sky.* New York: Thomas Y. Crowell Company, 1957.

Biographies

335 Curtiss, Minna. *Bizet and his World.* London: Secker and Warburg, 1959.

336 De Bovet, Marie-Anne. *Charles Gounod.* London: Sampson, Low, Marston, Searl and Rivington, 1891.

337 Harding, James. *Gounod.* New York: Stein and Day, 1973.

338 Martin, George. *Verdi: His Music, Life and Times.* New York: Dodd, Mead & Co., 1963.

339 Mozart (ed. Emily Anderson). *Letters.* (Two Volumes.) London: The Macmillan Company Ltd., 1976.

340 Newman, Ernest. *The Life of Richard Wagner.* (Four Volumes.) New York: Alfred A. Knopf, 1961.

341 Schauffler, Robert Haven. *Beethoven, the Man Who Freed Music.* Garden City, N.Y.: Doubleday & Company, 1925.

342 Stendhal. *Life of Rossini.* New York: Orion Press, 1970.

343 Verdi, Giuseppe (ed. Charles Osborne). *Letters.* London: Victor Gollancz Ltd., 1971.

Index

NOTE: Vocalists appear in small capital letters. Every effort has been made to date them correctly but singers *lie*. When reference sources give varying birth dates both (or more) have been included, but the reader would do well to assume the earlier one.

2/85